THE COAST LINES
OF THE
CAMBRIAN RAILWAYS

Double heading at Towyn on 3rd August 1955. *H. F. Wheeller*

THE COAST LINES
OF THE
CAMBRIAN RAILWAYS

VOLUME TWO

DOVEY JUNCTION TO DOLGELLEY
including a general history
from 1865 to 1996

BY

C. C. GREEN M.B.E.

WILD SWAN PUBLICATIONS LTD.

SYMBOLS USED ON PLANS

ELP	Electric light post
GDS	Goods
HSE	House
OFF	Office
PW	Permanent way
REFR	Refreshment
RM	Room
SP	Signal post
SMR	Station master
TP	Telegraph post
TT	Turntable
WTG	Waiting
WHSE	Warehouse
WM	Weighing machine

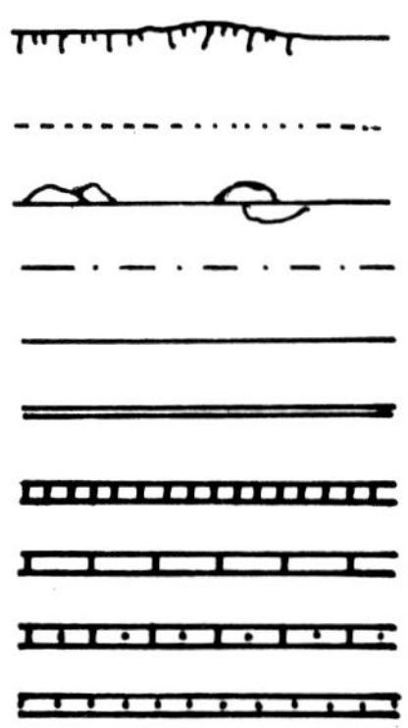

Embankment
Edge or change of surface
Hedge
Wire fence
Fence
Wall
Running lines
Shunting roads
Loco service roads
Standage

PLANS

There was no official policy for holding reference plans for the entire line. Engineer George Owen did not need them because he knew exactly where he had put everything since the earliest days.

His successor A. J. Collin reported this lack of plans to his Board and announced his intention of remedying it, but possibly never succeeded. Some of his 1 chain to 1 inch plans have survived and the author has adopted this scale for his drawings. A similar state of affairs would then have been inherited by his successor G. C. McDonald. However, all three seem to have been able to produce reasonable drawings when they had to convince the Board that some envisaged expenditure was necessary. Usually these plans are to the scale of 40ft to 1 inch, and crosschecking two plans can throw up inexplicable differences in distance between immovable buildings. For some places the 1 in 2,500 land plans are all that has been discovered so far.

So that there should be no confusion among railwaymen as to train direction, the conventions 'down' and 'up' were adopted on all railways. For the Cambrian, 'down' was from Whitchurch to Aberystwyth and to Pwllheli, and the reverse direction was 'up'. These terms applied right across the adjoining railways, and 'up' extended onwards to Manchester, Euston and Paddington.

Distances are given in miles and chains as all old railway records showed them, e.g. 82 III is 82¾ and also 82m 60c.

STATION PLANS

Most Cambrian station plans (where they exist) and all land plans were drawn with 'up' to the right and 'down' to the left, and this convention has been applied throughout as it is the one most nearly compatible with geographical maps which all have the north point upwards.

STATION SIGNALLING DIAGRAMS

These have been presented as the installation was seen by the signalman standing at his frame.

DEDICATION

To the memory of Eric Hannan, indefatigable researcher of railways and good friend.

CYFLWYNIAD

Er cof am Eric Hannan, ymchwiliwr dyfal o'r rheilffyrdd a ffrind da.

COSTS

For those interested in relating costs mentioned in the text to present-day money, a table of very approximate multipliers is attached. This has been compiled from the proper tables kindly provided by the Economics Division of the Bank of England, and to which a little guesswork has been added, hopefully, to bring them up to the 1990s. It was considered that to give a present-day equivalent after each cost in the book would both disjoint the flow and date the text unduly.

1855-1857	30	1902-1914	40	1920 & 1921	15
1858-1878	35	1915	30	1922-1926	20
1879-1885	40	1916	25	1927-1939	25
1886-1901	45	1918 & 1919	20	1940-1948	18

ACKNOWLEDGEMENTS

My thanks and appreciation of much kind help are due to the following: Denis Bates, James I. C. Boyd, Phil Burke (CAN Ltd), H. W. Burman, John Burman, Cambrian Coast Line Action Group, W. A. Camwell, Roger Carpenter, the Rev. D. Ridley Chesterton, George Clifford, J. M. Cummings, Pat Dalton, Jack Davies, John J. Davis, John Dawson, Tony Donovan, George Dow, Andrew Dow, John Edgington, the Rev Bernard Edmonds, Edward E. Evans, G. Evans, Tom & Margaret Evans, Richard Foster, Patrick Garland, L. T. George, Norman Greenwood, J. S. Griffiths, W. E. Hayward, Arthur Humphries, Frank Hemming, Selwyn Higgins, Evan Howells, Anne and Susie Howells, Gwilym Hughes, Frank Jones, Hugh Jones, K. Jones, Richard Kidner, Hugh M. Lewis, Aneurin Lloyd, Chris Magner, Bob Miller, Duncan Morris, Joe Moss, Tom O'Marah, Steffan ab Owain, Denis Owen, G. B. Pearson, Percy Pike, Chris Preston, J. P. Richards, Frank Roberts, John D. Rogers, R. C. Stallard, R. E. Thomas, Thomas Wynne Thomas, L. J. Vaughton, Oliver Veltom, Hubert Wheeller, Patrick Whitehouse, A. Williams.

I am particularly indebted to Mike Christensen not only for his expertise on Cambrian Railways signalling but also for casting an astute eye over the manuscript. Similar help with the manuscript has come from Larry Bridges. Especial thanks are also due to three friends of very long standing, Eric Hannan, Ifor Higgon and Mike Morton Lloyd (Cambrian Steward of the Historical Model Railway Society). For overseeing my halting effors to put English equivalents to the Welsh place names, and for the dedication and postcript, I would like to thank Mr. Tom Evans, the well-known presenter for BBC Wales.

I am most grateful for unfailing kindnesses and help received at Birmingham City Council Reference Library; the offices of British Rail; Ceredigion Museum at Aberystwyth; Gwynedd Archives at Caernarfon and Dolgellau; the House of Lords Record Office; the National Library of Wales at Aberystwyth; the Public Record Office at Kew; the Royal Commission on Ancient Monuments in Wales at Aberystwyth; the Welsh Industrial and Maritime Museum at Cardiff; the Institution of Civil Engineers and the Coastguard Service.

The following periodicals have also been consulted: *The Cambrian News; The Times and Express Gazette; The Welsh Gazette; The Great Western Railway Magazine; The Locomotive Magazine; The Railway Magazine; The Engineer* and *Engineering.*

ISBN 1 874103 29 1

Designed by Paul Karau
Printed by Amadeus Press Ltd., Huddersfield

Published by
WILD SWAN PUBLICATIONS LTD.
1-3 Hagbourne Road, Didcot, Oxon, OX11 8DP

CONTENTS

FOREWORD

The great beauty of this land of Wales needs no wordy descriptions from the author; all has been told already and we will let the photographs and historical extracts speak for themselves as we go. 'Go' really is the active word as each item of interest is presented in the order in which it would be seen when going on holiday by train.

Place names were frequently given an Anglicised form in timetables, handbills, advertisements, and on the station nameboards to attract and assist the visitors. As a courtesy, both forms are given in all the place histories. Nearly all the Welsh place names are impressive or charming descriptions of the place, or its character or where to find it, and the nearest English equivalent is given where attainable.

I hope to cover the remainder of the coast lines and the rest of the Cambrian Railways system in a series of volumes, and perhaps in the future a special volume may have to be considered on operation with details of services, timetables and tickets, and another on Oswestry where the Cambrian Railways Society is still keeping traditions alive with its restorative work on engines and with its extremely interesting museum.

ROUTE MAPS

The route plans have been drawn for reading from the bottom upwards as features and landmarks would come into view from a train travelling towards the sea, and in the 'down' direction along the Coast (as the author walked and worked when making his own surveys).

They are based on the first edition of the 2½in Ordnance Survey with much kind help from the Bodleian Library at Oxford. The station distances are cited from R. A. Cooke's invaluable *Atlas of the Great Western Railway*, and the bridge distances came from official records. The milepost positions were inserted from observation and measurement.

GRADIENT PROFILES

George Owen drew his first publishable gradient profiles c.1866 to fit the largest standard drawing board of his day which took the 29in x 46in paper known as 'Double Elephant', and he made others as required for passing working instructions on to his foremen.

In 1889 he produced his real showpiece for the edification of his Board and for use in publicity articles in the various papers and magazines. To exaggerate the vertical scale, he chose 100ft to 1in while making it all fit onto 'Double Elephant' paper by squashing the linear scale down to 3 miles to 1inch. The result was extremely spiky and quite unreadable in detail but totally late Victorian in dramatic effect. It was considered that something more readable should be contrived for this book.

To fit alongside the 2½in to 1 mile route maps, the new gradient profiles have been drawn at 2in to 1 mile, with a vertical scale of 100ft to 1 inch from mean sea level. 'Up' is to the right and 'down' is to the left to conform with all the other plans and maps, and this matches the more recent British Rail gradient profiles.

THE ABERYSTWITH & WELSH COAST RAILWAY
1865 TO 1922
ONE OF THE CAMBRIAN RAILWAYS

AFTER the passing of the Amalgamation Act on 5th July 1865, the directors of the Cambrian Railways, Montgomeryshire-oriented as they were, might well have been congratulating themselves on having won the partially-built Coast line. After all, the route would soon be completed and earning revenue from an extensive tourist traffic; this would offset the disappointing returns from the inland lines, which had been caused by the receipts from mineral traffic. They should have known better.

Firstly, they should have read the 'Coast' company's minutes, which would have enlightened them about the sort of industrial sharks they were inviting to join them. Then they should have studied the Amalgamation Act itself a bit more thoroughly; it read like a perfect recipe for factions and divisions of interest. But the Montgomeryshire directors could at least take comfort from having avoided an invasion of alien interest all along the Coast line in the form of takeover bids from the Great Western and the London & North Western companies. No doubt those two concerns had expected the Cambrian to bankrupt itself in trying to complete the Coast section, and were just waiting for the pieces to drop into their hands at knockdown prices.

Later the 'inlanders' might even have wished that such a takeover had occurred, had they been able to foresee just how many times the 'Coast' company's creditors and stockholders were going to put them into Chancery, even if the Receivers appointed were most frequently their own officers.

The history of events prior to the amalgamation on 5th July 1865 is set out on pages 10–12 of Volume 1, but are summarised here.

The Cambrian Railways Act of 25th July 1864 had created The Cambrian Railways Company, from four constituent companies. These were the Llanidloes & Newtown (the first tiny line, which was to act as the flux for soldering together the system as it was eventually established), the Oswestry & Newtown, the Oswestry, Ellesmere & Whitchurch and the Newtown & Machynlleth. Under the Act, the Cambrian, so formed, was empowered to accept into the fold the 'missing' Aberystwyth & Welsh Coast Railway, but only after they had complied with clauses inserted in all railway acts which stated that no railway company might be amalgamated with any other before it had completed the construction of half of its railway, and had expended half of its capital. The only part of the 'Coast' company's line which had by then been opened for traffic was the 20½ miles from Machynlleth to Aberystwyth, and the isolated section from Aberdovey to Llwyngwril (10¼ miles).

After July 1864, the Cambrian left the 'Coast' company (with its contractor, Thomas Savin) to get on with the compliance of the requirement of half completion, with a little guidance from their own engineer, Mr George Owen.

Meanwhile, the Cambrian's newly-constituted General Purposes and Parliamentary Committee had busied themselves with the promotion of the three additional Acts needed before amalgamation could be contemplated. On 26th October 1864 they resolved to seek powers to 'Construct the Aberdovey Extension' and 'To amalgamate with the Coast Company', and on 10th November 1864 they resolved 'to proceed with the getting of powers to complete the gaps at the northern end of the Coast line and to proceed with the amalgamation'.

The Cambrian Board of Directors were also busy, and on 14th September 1864 approved the draft of an agreement by which the Cambrian would work the Coast line. This accord was subsequently finalized, and on 13th October 1864 the Board had agreed that the company should operate the line for 45% of the gross receipts. In addition, they had approved the extension of the electric telegraph system to Aberystwyth. On 27th January 1864, they had authorised the payment of £100,000 to the 'Coast' company to keep the work going; of this, half had been paid straightaway, and another quarter followed in March 1865.

On 3rd July 1865, the 'Coast' company opened the sections from Llwyngwril to Barmouth Junction, and from Barmouth Junction to Penmaenpool, for all traffic. This added just 9 miles to the 36¾ miles already opened, out of a total scheduled mileage of 80½. This was a meagre qualification, but sufficient (despite the foreshortening of the service along the Dolgelley Branch to a point nearly 2¼ miles short of the intended destination) for the company to qualify for having opened 50% of its line. So, on 5th July 1865, the two companies were granted the three Acts of Parliament they so badly needed.

The Aberystwith & Welsh Coast Railway Act, 1865, conferred all deviation and variation powers needed for the completion of the Coast line (these have been given in some detail on page 11 of Volume I). Naturally, all these powers devolved immediately to the Cambrian.

The Cambrian Railways (Additional Powers) Act, 1865, empowered the company to:

1. Abandon the Wem branch and sell the land.
2. Transfer the company's agreement to work the Aberystwith & Welsh Coast Railway to Thomas Savin.
3. Grant a lease of the company's undertaking to Thomas Savin, after the approval had been obtained of three-fifths of shareholders present at a General Meeting.
4. Create various legal provisions as to the lease and tolls (but without giving any specific rates).

The Cambrian and Coast Railways (Amalgamation) Act, 1865, provided that:

1. 'Coast Railways' would mean all railways and works of whatever description, whether finished or unfinished.
2. All preference shares and stock of the 'Coast' company would retain all their priorities, and become stock of the Cambrian.
3. All unraised 'Coast' capital would, when raised, be applied to debts of the 'Coast' company and completion of the Coast railways.
4. All income from the Coast railways would be accounted for separately.
5. All such income would be applied as forty-five per centum to the general revenues of the Cambrian company and fifty-five per centum to 'Coast' charges. Any residue would be applied as dividends to the 'Coast' shareholders.
6. For the purpose of estimating tolls or charges for traffic conveyed partly over the Coast railway, the railway would be treated as one railway.
7. The Great Western would have their traffic facilities over the Cambrian extended to the Coast, and the same would apply to the London & North Western's powers and facilities.

For so powerful a troublemaker, this Act was comparatively short, only nineteen clauses on six pages.

A number of events centred around Afon Wen, Portmadoc and Pwllheli. The construction of a Carnarvonshire Railway had been forecast in a cynical account published by the *Railway Times* of 1858, into which the reporter had inserted references to the unseen arranging and backhanded dealing in which most railway promoters were supposedly (and in which many actually were) indulging. The Aberystwith & Welsh Coast Railway had intended to build a Carnarvon branch, but this was withdrawn from its 1861 Bill by agreement with the (then horse-worked) Nantlle Railway. The Nantlle (probably with some unidentified backing) then commenced the promotion of its own Bill to block the West Midlands' Shrewsbury to Portmadoc scheme, but withdrew after the failure of the West Midlands. In order to block the next scheme for a Carnarvonshire Railway, the Nantlle tried to persuade the 'Coast' company to construct a branch northwards from Afon Wen to join with their own route. In this they failed, and both the Coast Act and the Carnarvonshire Railway Act became law on 29th July, 1862.

The Board of the Carnarvonshire Railway consisted of Chairman David Williams, MP, of Castell Deudraeth, Portmadoc, and three London-oriented gentlemen, including that 'Coast' troublemaker, Captain Jasper Wilson Johns (see Volume I, page 8). The field work on which the Bill had been based had been carried out by the Piercy brothers and Thomas Savin. After Savin's quarrel with Benjamin Piercy (Volume I, page 5), C.E. Spooner had been appointed engineer, and the construction work was completed by John Savin.

There was some indecisive chaffering between the two Boards, each of which had acquired the right to construct a railway between Portmadoc and Afon Wen. By 1864, John Savin was in the position of being able to construct the Portmadoc to Pwllheli section for the 'Coast' company with the help of the steam paddle tug *James Conley*. He also undertook to make the Carnarvonshire line, starting from Afon Wen, the Cambrian assenting to this arrangement in 1865. Also in that year, two fresh proposals for lines to be called the Carnarvon, Beddgelert & Portmadoc, and the Carnarvon, Penygroes and Pwllheli Direct were thrown out in the Bill stages. The Great Western's bid for the Coast traffic at Barmouth by means of their nominees' promotion of a line from Ruabon to Barmouth had been opened as far as Corwen.

So, from 5th July 1865, the Cambrian Railways was fully constituted, and able to get on with the business of working the five little railways as one, though their principal feeders and rivals were quite prepared to take advantage of them whenever possible.

The Coast Board, which had a month to run before it was dissolved, recommended their secretary, W. Roberts, for a senior post in the Cambrian hierarchy, but the Cambrian Board informed him on 29th August 1865 that there was no vacancy for him. On 5th January 1866, the Cambrian Board received from the four active Coast directors their report on the condition of the Coast railway, and passed a resolution of thanks to Messrs Pryce, Williams, Gartside and Tootal 'for the trouble they have taken'.

They then went on to instruct the solicitor, Mr Howell, 'to prepare a Draft Contract with Mr Savin for the construction and completion of the Welsh Coast Railway', and to authorise Captain Johns 'to deface the company seal of the late Company'. The last minute on that day relating to the 'Coast' company took notice of financial settlements arising from the takeover of the Coast company's assets, with an observation that an unrecorded sum of £82 5s 0d had been discovered, deposited with the North & South Wales Bank at Oswestry. At the end of that Board meeting, matters seemed to be under control, and the prospects for a reasonably straightforward completion of the Coast line looked good. Assets were known, liabilities had been forecast, and the contractor Thomas Savin was at work, both on constructing the Coast line and as the company's legally authorised appointee for the running of all the Cambrian's passenger and goods services. There was even a thought that the name might be changed to The Great Cambrian Railway. Alas! the transition from elation to depression was to take only four months.

Thomas Savin (whom a faction of the Coast directors had supported against Piercy and the others) suspended payments on 5th February 1866, and his affairs became the business of his Inspectors in Bankruptcy (who were the specialists we know today as Receivers). He had accepted too many shares in the companies whose railways he had been building, instead of cash, and he had borrowed to finance his private ventures (such as his projected chain of Coast hotels). His creditors had become uneasy about his ability to repay, and had pressed him for the impossible. At least he had from the outset placed the Cambrian's traffic receipts in the company's own bank. From the date of his bankruptcy he withdrew from acting as the contractor for constructing the Coast line. Fortunately, his younger brother John (by arrangement with the Inspectors and the Cambrian) was able to salvage as much as possible for the benefit of his creditors by completing the Coast, the Carnarvonshire and other railways. The Cambrian might well have recovered from this first setback without too much difficulty.

Henry Conybeare was still active as the engineer albeit from time to time in consultation with the Cambrian's own engineer, George Owen, and by February 1866 one of the Manning Wardle saddle tanks had been driven up a roughly-laid Carnarvonshire Railway as far as Penygroes.

The Cambrian management's first task was to discuss with Savin's Inspectors how the construction was to be completed. On 21st March 1866 the Board heard that this was in hand, and they approved on 5th April that payments for land should be deferred until agreement had been reached with the Inspectors. The following day, they gave an instruction that none of the Coast workers or other personnel were to have free passes over the rest of the Cambrian system.

There had been a confrontation between Earl Vane and Savin on 5th April 1866, wherein the latter had been obstructive about his situation, and he was instructed not to attend future meetings except by prior arrangement; this ruling had the effect of terminating his ready access to and his influence over the affairs of the Board.

So far, the Board's entrepreneurial enthusiasm continued quite unrestrained and on 26th April the shareholders were told of plans involving the continuation of the Porthdinllaen Harbour scheme, amalgamation with the Carnarvonshire and the Nantlle Railways, and of mergers proposed with the Beddgelert and Corris narrow gauge railways.

Discussions continued during May about financing the continuation of the work on the Coast line, with some considerations as to deferring and reducing claims for professional work. They needed to borrow further monies to pay for the construction work, and to satisfy the immediate need to pay dividends due on preference shares, and interest on debentures; and the North & South Wales Bank was delaying the reply to their request for a loan of £30,000.

These problems were nothing as compared with those the Cambrian faced after 10th May 1866, known afterwards as 'Black Friday'. It has been stated that this crisis was precipitated by the London, Chatham & Dover Railway; that company had felt cut off from the City of London on the north side of the Thames, and had embarked on an ambitious scheme to construct an extension past the north side of its London Bridge terminus, round Southwark Cathedral by means of an unsightly and over-costly high viaduct, and across the Thames into a cramped site off Cannon Street. It was too much for the company to fund and in their failure to raise the excess between estimate and final cost, and to service what it had already borrowed, the company brought down Overend & Gurney (the world's largest share discounting house, which specialised in making advances to holders of railway shares such as those issued to contractors in lieu of cash). Of itself this was trouble enough, but the main effect on the future of the Cambrian and its Coast line was the loss of public faith in railways as a safe form of investment, and an almost complete refusal to take up any more shares. Some would not even pay further calls on their holdings, and their forfeited shares were almost worthless to the company which had repossessed them.

Later dealings between the Cambrian and Savin's Inspectors were mainly concerned with general claims made by the company, including the complex resolution of which locomotives and rolling stock belonged to which of the companies he had been involved with. There were also the counterclaims for work already allegedly completed; on 18th May, a claim was made on behalf of Savin for £103,263, of which £46,000 was stated to be for work on the Coast line already completed. The final settlement of this was for £54,000 in Lloyds' Bonds, and the withdrawal of all Savin's suits against the Cambrian. The people of Aberdyfi were quite convinced that the final stroke that had caused Savin's bankruptcy was his undertaking that the cost of the Deviation would not exceed the cost of the abandoned bridge.

To reduce expenditure as much as possible, the Cambrian Board discussed ways and means for reducing payments for professional work.

On 25th May a shareholder, who had applied by letter for his expected dividend, was informed: 'Now that Traffic returns are divided between the Cambrian and the Aberystwith & Welsh Coast there is no balance in the Coast account from which Dividends may be paid.' This brought about a great deal of trouble as landowners with unsatisfied claims, disappointed shareholders, and the holders of debentures and preference shares all banded together in litigatious groups. In this they were led mainly by lawyers whose principal expertise lay in the embarrassment of the many struggling little railways of the mid-Victorian period; some lawyers even obtained a shareholding that would entitle them to all circulars, and to attend all general meetings. To provide a little ready money with which to stave off a few of these problems, the Board managed to borrow £23,000 from Lloyds Bank as a part substitution for the £30,000 they had failed to obtain from the North & South Wales Bank.

The Cambrian's Engineer reported on 20th June that there had been no planting of the necessary quickthorn hedging, and the solicitor was instructed to approach the Inspectors to ascertain whether they had funds to pay for it. On 5th July 1866 the Board was told of a claim from a solicitor for £98 19s 2d relating to work in promoting the Welsh Coast Steamboats Bill (which failed), and of four Bills in Chancery served by landowners.

Meanwhile, work had continued on the new line, and on 28th June 1866 the Board were informed that the Coast new works (with the exception of Barmouth viaduct) were ready for inspection by the Board of Trade. The contractors had been running a number of trip trains, including one in July when they took Sir Watkyn and Lady Williams-Wynn from Barmouth to Carnarvon. This was done without consulting the Cambrian officers, who had no powers in such matters until the line had been handed over to them, having been passed by the Board of Trade Inspector. In August, John Savin, with a train consisting of two coaches and a van, conducted the Earl and Countess Vane on a trip 'to see the country' from Machynlleth to Portmadoc.

Arising from four Bills in Chancery, bailiffs could seize trains out on the line (where the staff could not defend them). C.P.Gasquoine has written of runs carrying livestock and goods to Portmadoc, halting at farms to make deliveries, whilst occasionally there might be a passenger or two in the vans. However, the bailiffs could be bribed with pleasant evenings in hostelries while the short trains made their dashes after dark over rusting rails and already-decaying sleepers.

At committee level, attempts were being made to persuade landowners to defer their capital claims in return for a short-term rent for the land over which the rails were laid. In addition, on 26th July 1866, the Board resolved to defer payment on a certificate for £18,000 issued by Henry Conybeare 'until Savins's Inspectors have paid amounts owed by them'.

The Cambrian Railways (New Works) Act 1866 took effect on 6th August 1866, and empowered the company to:

1. Make a deviation at Pwllheli, and construct wharves, shipping and landing places there.
2. Divert or build anew two miles, four furlongs, and two-and-a-half chains of public road next to the line across the Traeth Mawr at Portmadoc.
3. Purchase land in order to divert Afon Glaslyn, convert the Traeth Mawr between the line and The Cob into a larger harbour, and 'construct and maintain upon the said Sands and Lands Quays, Wharves and other Work and Conveniences'.
4. Improve construction and facilities at Oswestry, Welshpool and Newtown.
5. Issue £142,000 in new Inland shares or stock and £300,000 in new Coast shares and stock, and borrow by mortgage £47,000 for Inland purposes and £100,000 for Coast purposes after half of the new capital had been issued and half had been paid up, and at least one fifth had been paid up in respect of each separate share.

At thirty clauses on eight pages the 1866 Act was a little longer than that of 1865, but the mortgage clauses occupied a full page and were so restrictive as to render the Act virtually useless. Under the circumstances it was a rash promotion, and (probably) only the works at Oswestry Welshpool and Newtown were even started.

Left out of the works authorised, but to which the deposited plans still bear mute witness, was an item headed 'Aberdovey Harbour', which was actually a proposal for the construction of 'A Floating Dock' at Ynyslas (page 308). The term 'Floating Dock' in those days meant a dock in which there was a constant water level, so that vessels were always afloat whatever the state of the tide. In this proposal, the level was to be maintained by a single lock upstream and a double-lock entrance channel leading from the estuary.

The deviated line was to be laid as single track with power to double later, and so preserve the Cambrian dream of double lines all the way from Whitchurch to Pwllheli.

In August the line was physically complete for some way beyond Afon Wen, and could soon be completed to Pwllheli (contractor's rails were probably there already).

On 6th September 1866, before the granting of the Board of Trade certificate, John Savin ran an excursion train from Portmadoc to Carnarvon. It was derailed at Brynkir through someone interfering with the points, and six passengers were killed. At the inquest, Savin and the company were exonerated. The Savin brothers had taken up shares in the Nantlle Railway, and had masterminded the regauging of the portion from Penygroes to Nantlle for standard gauge locomotive use. The Carnarvonshire line was passed for traffic in October 1866 and was operated by members of the Savin family who, by some internal jugglery, had contrived to retain the family interests and to keep John Savin's name clear of the bankruptcy proceedings.

On 24th September 1866, the Cambrian Board authorised the sale of unused materials lying along the Coast line, and the sale by auction of any plant and machinery to be found there. An attempt was also made to obtain further cash with which to appease the landowners. This was another stormy meeting, and the secretary wrote and crossed out whole passages of minutes before arriving at something he could expect the chairman to sign at the next meeting. One clear item was the dismissal of Henry Conybeare from his post as engineer leaving the completion of the Coast line to the Cambrian's own engineer, George Owen. On 4th December, the committee heard that Henry Conybeare had obtained 'an Order of Attachment over the Funds of the Company' and the solicitor was instructed to arrange bail so that trains could continue to run.

In January 1867, George Owen reported that, while the track was stated to be ready for inspection, there was not one goods shed or siding anywhere along the new line, and that a further expenditure of £10 per mile would still be required to complete the Coast railway. Later, he had also to report that he was still trying to obtain the customary set of plans from Henry Conybeare. The minutes of the Board meeting on 26th January 1867 show that Owen was by then signing all the certificates for work completed for payment, and they renewed the instruction 'to dispose of all Coast materials'. Furthermore, Savin's solicitors, Quilter, Ball & Company (who were also acting for a London-based group of shareholders) were pressing for the release of £28,040 in Coast stock to those parties. On 12th February 1867, they agreed to 'the transfer of £75,000 of Coast Stock into the names of Henry Gartside and Robert Davies Pryce as Securities to themselves and the North & South Wales Bank' who were requiring more security to cover present and future advances.

During March 1867, the Board considered correspondence with Savin's Inspectors covering the 'Non-completion of the Coast', which commented on 'the great sacrifice of the interests not only of the Company (Savin & Co) but of the Estates of Mr Savin'; completion in this context implied all stations, sidings, signal boxes, warehouses etc., whereas as yet there was only the bare track on a scanty formation. The Coast secretary was instructed 'to ask Mr Taylor for his Copy Agreement with Mr Savin re. the accommodation works' to find out what Savin & Co's obligations were. The financial restrictions contained in the 1865 and 1866 Acts had crippled the Cambrian's ability to raise fresh capital, and a further Bill would have to be promoted to relieve the position.

It was reported to the Board on 22nd March 1867 that 'Conybeare's Action had been compromised at £1,125'. At the same meeting, a special committee was appointed to confer with Savin's Inspectors over the uncompleted Coast works. The Board also decided that, in future, no more pre-preference shares (which were accorded prior rights of receiving dividends out of any funds available) should be issued.

On 3rd June 1867 the new section between Barmouth Junction and Barmouth was opened for passenger services.

This was the only bit of good news, for on 5th July the committee was treated to a lengthy rundown on how matters then stood: 'There were still roughly only forty miles opened and forty miles not opened'. Thomas Savin had suspended payments in February 1866, and 'after his suspension works had been proceeded with by money raised by his Inspectors'. 'Several liabilities had to be discharged before the forty miles of unopened line can be made available or yield any revenue' (mainly land to be paid for and in respect of which injunctions had been taken out) whilst 'extra work had been required by the Government Inspector on Barmouth Viaduct'. Other accommodation works were required to develop the traffic. '£80,000 was still required to complete the Coast Works and because of Savin's failure to complete, the Company have no funds available for that purpose but by Acts already passed the Company can raise £50,000 from Coast Debentures and £50,000 re Rent Charges. The £80,000 must be raised before any further income can be expected'. An appeal for £410,312 of additional capital was recommended 'from those already interested in the Railway but who cannot realise any return on their Interests until this additional money can be made available'.

In pursuance of this policy there were a number of proposals for a general restructuring of the company's loan and share capital. It was suggested that the Coast debentures should remain at a total of £850,462, that the Lloyds bonds should be halved to £101,231 and, most unpopular of all, that the Coast preference shares should be halved in their nominal value, or that the unissued ones should be subtracted from the nominal capital as stated.

As a result, the Cambrian Railways Finance Act, 1867, came into force on 15th August 1867. The preamble included the phrase 'And whereas the Affairs of the Company require that they should be enabled immediately to borrow the several Sums by the Act of 1866 authorised to be borrowed on Mortgage or Part thereof they are unable to do so'. The act authorised:

1. The deletion of the requirement that at least one fifth of the share capital authorised had been received on each separate share before borrowing, on mortgage, the £47,300 Inland loan capital and on £50,000 of the Coast £100,000 mortgage capital.
2. A year's extension of the time required for the completion of the Dolgelley branch.
3. The purchase by agreement (instead of by compulsory order) of part of an area near Dolgelley known as Marian Mawr.

None of the money so borrowed could be used to finance the pursuance of future Bills, and if by 1st November 1867 no contract had been made for the completion of the Dolgelley branch, or no arrangement had been made with the Bala & Dolgelley Railway, the Cambrian was to be precluded 'from opposing any Bill for the Powers to make so much of the said Railway as shall not have been completed by the Company'. This last item had, of course, been inserted by the influence of the Great Western. In general, the invaluable five-and-a-half pages of the Act staved off the worst of the company's troubles for a further year.

On 14th August 1867, the 'Deviation' line between Glandovey Junction and Aberdovey was opened for traffic. Apart from the prohibition on the conveyance of goods across Barmouth bridge, the Cambrian system was now connected from Inland up to Barmouth. The remainder was laid, but still to be declared fit to use.

Meanwhile, the affairs of the Carnarvonshire Railway had been advanced with few of the problems which had so badly delayed the opening of the Coast line. It was opened for traffic on 2nd September 1867.

The Cambrian hired out two engines to the Carnarvonshire, 0-4-2 Sharp Stewart No.7 *Llanerchydol* and 2-4-0 Sharp Stewart Tank No. 59 *Seaham,* under an agreement dated 14th September 1867. Their own rolling stock had been arranged under a hire-purchase agreement, financed (like so many other small-company rescue packages) by two debenture holders.

The Carnarvonshire Railway Act, 1867, had come into force on 25th July of that year, authorising reciprocal running rights with the Cambrian between Portmadoc, Afon Wen and Pwllheli. Precisely what services were actually run is not known.

On 14th September 1867, the Cambrian Board approved the appointment of a special committee. This body was to include Mr W. Griffith, a solicitor acting with the Earl of Powys to represent the Welsh shareholders, and also for some of the Coast landowners; he reported to the Board that he had arranged satisfactory terms with twenty-one of the Coast landowners. They also heard that arrangements for selling surplus Coast materials on site were in hand, and that the money so obtained would be applied to payments required to open the Coast line. On this matter, Counsel's advice had been sought, and he had advised against opening at that time because:

- 'Not all the the land had been acquired'.
- 'Works, especially along the Friog, were defective, also Aberdovey Tunnel and the extension viaducts generally'.
- 'Securities already given to the Contractor and his Inspectors had been largely in excess of the Work done.'
- 'In the opinion of the Board the Aberystwith & Welsh Coast under their Act of Parliament should discharge these liabilities'.

The Board weighed up the situation with regard to the expected Act of Parliament, and the special committee's progress behind the scenes. They decided that if they did not press on with the opening of the line, it was likely to remain moribund for a long and indefinite period. So they agreed to take a risk in extending the goods service northwards into Barmouth, and opening the Coast Extension right through to Pwllheli on 10th October 1867. On 25th October 1867, the Board decided that notices should be given for the acquisition of the land between Penmaenpool and Dolgelley, in order to complete that line.

At their meeting on 15th January 1868, the Board examined the details of a proposed scheme for the reduction of capital and for a fresh division of the net income. This would be allocated Coast 35% and Inland 65% for three years, followed by Coast 37½% and Inland 62½% for the following four years. At the end of the seven years, an arbitrator would be appointed to settle these two rates permanently for the future. Copies of the scheme were to be circulated to each member of committee appointed to consult with other Boards.

The revealing of 'The Scheme' had no effect whatever on the creditors (including the mortgage and shareholders), and the company found itself in Chancery on 15th February with its deputy chairman, Captain R.D. Pryce as Receiver. In March 1868 it was decided to insert 'The Scheme' into the Act of Parliament then being prepared in Bill form. The appointment of the special committee (to whom all might have access) seemed to have worked, and on 28th April the Board approved the lodging of the finalised Bill, with the addition of the right of Coast shareholders to appoint their own directors. The four-year period for the division of the net profit had been adjusted to Coast 37% and Inland 63%.

In June 1868 the Board were informed that the Carnarvonshire Railway had returned 0-4-2 Sharp Stewart No.7 *Llanerchydol* at the end of the hire period.

On 1st July 1868, the old stalwart, contractor and director, David Davies, was persuaded to accept election to directorship once again, and to apply his professional expertise to bringing still-dissenting parties and factions round to the acceptance of the provisions of the Bill, soon to become law. When he came to examine all the figures he saw at once that, with a revenue of around only £55,000 for the current year, the Coast was in hopeless debt, and was being carried by the Inland section. Later he would described the Cambrian's agreement for working the Coast for 45% as completely disastrous, as it produced receipts of only £28,080 per annum against actual working costs of around £48,300.

The Cambrian Railways Finance Act, 1868, received royal assent on 31st July 1868 as:

'An Act for fusing all the Revenues of the Cambrian Railways Company and settling the Application thereof; and to confer the Rights of voting on all Preference Shareholders of that Company; and for other Purposes'.

There were three pages of preamble which recognised and presented the following facts (given here in greatly summarised form.):

- 'Receipts from Inland Railways are not sufficient to pay Five Pounds per Centum on their Capital.'
- 'Forty-five Pounds per Centum per Annum of the Receipts from the Coast Railways is not sufficient to cover their working expenses.'
- 'Failure of the said Thomas Savin has caused the embarrassment of the Company and they are unable to raise the sums authorised by Parliament.'
- 'Coast landowners have instituted Proceedings in Chancery and obtained injunctions to restrain the Company from working the Coast line but these are suspended in anticipation of the passing of this Act.'
- 'The immediate raising of £100,000 of Coast capital and of £47,300 of Inland capital is necessary to meet the claims of Landowners and other creditors who have it in their power to seize the rolling stock and other property of the Company; and thereby stopping the working of the railway and its income from which their claims might be met.'
- 'In order to extricate the Company from its difficulties a stay of all proceedings is necessary except for those brought against it as a common carrier.'
- 'Inland mortgage and preference stockholders have objected to the Company's continuing to work the Coast as so far opened and to the opening and working of the unopened Coast lines as all losses so incurred must be borne by the Coast subscribers' (i.e. not by the Inland subscribers).
- 'Many fixed-term mortgages have expired and their subscribers and some preference shareholders have all commenced Actions and Suits (including holders of Llanidloes and of Machynlleth preference stocks) because their dividends have not been paid.'
- 'Disputes have arisen between the various claimants.'

Having thus identified the problems, the Act proceeded to recognise the situation as a continuous lawyers' birthday party:

'And whereas in order to prevent the further Waste of the Revenues and the Resources of the Company in Litigation, and the Seizure and Sale of their Rolling Stock and Plant under Judgements, Decrees and Executions and the Stoppage of the working of the opened Inland and Coast lines and opening of the unopened portion of the Coast line etc, etc.'

The Act then proceeded to make its stipulations:

- 'All revenues to be placed in one common fund and only the net surplus is to be divided between Coast and Inland.'
- 'Arrangements are Provisional from 1st July 1868 to 31st December 1868.'
- 'Separate fund accounts between Coast and Inland are to be kept.'
- 'Four Coast Directors and Six Inland Directors.' (Of these, two were the hereditary directors, the Earls Vane and Powys, or their appointed representatives.)
- 'Net surpluses to be credited to the Coast and Inland fund accounts in the agreed proportions.'
- 'Unexpended capital from Coast sources to be applied to the completion of the Coast sources to be applied to the completion of the Coast lines.'
- 'Net surplus from the common fund to be apportioned between Coast and Inland according to the net intrinsic Value or Merits present and prospective for the time being of their Traffic.'
- 'Through trains to be apportioned on a basis of mileage.'
- 'The Company to retain 45% of the Coast gross receipts.'
- 'Inland further to be debited and Coast credited with half the 1866 amount i.e. 22½% as to net receipts.'
- 'Rebate collected by the Inland section in respect of traffic arising from or going onto the Coast lines was to be apportioned between the two.'
- 'Disputes to be settled by arbitration and two such arbiters to be appointed, at the first Extraordinary Meeting.'
- 'Arbitrators may appoint an umpire.'
- 'Their awards (apportionments) may be revised up to three times during the provisional period.'
- 'Three revisions won by the Coast shall terminate the provisional period.'
- 'Provisions as to common fund and apportionments to be approved by at least three-fourths of Coast Mortgagees, Inland Mortgagees, Coast Shareholders and Inland Shareholders.'
- 'The additional £47,300 of Inland Capital and £50,000 of Coast Capital to be raised after written consent of three-fourths by value of all existing mortgages has been received.'
- 'The £50,000 of new Coast Capital and the £50,000 still subject to the restrictions of the 1866 Act to be applied in order to:
    1. Landowners and including works to be executed for them.
    2. Other creditors than those already in existence.
    3. Costs re. Actions and Suits.
    4. Recouping income for capital items paid out.'
- 'The same stipulations as to the Inland £47,300.'
- 'Receiver for Robinson against The Cambrian Railways Company dismissed and the suit transferred to the Court of Chancery.'
- 'New Actions, Suits and Proceedings except as Common Carrier suspended for five years.'
- 'Disputes between Mortgagees to be settled by the Master of the Rolls or a Vice Chancellor and earlier ones against the Company to be stayed.'
- 'Costs of the Act to be divided equally between Coast and Inland and to be paid out of the capital so authorised.'
- 'All arbitration costs to be paid by the Company.'
- 'Jasper Wilson Johns and David Williams to be Coast Directors.'
- 'James Bancroft, David Davies, Robert Davies Pryce and Henry Gartside to be Inland Directors.'

It should be noted that the guileful Henry Gartside, lawyer and Clerk to Altrincham Town Council, had opted to retain his position as an Inland director in pursuit of his Manchester-based interests, wherefrom he would die 'possessed of a great estate'.

The inference to be drawn is that the official opening of Barmouth bridge for goods traffic and the remainder of the Coast line for all traffic was a token ceremony to test the strength of the opposition. The bailiffs' 'passive' activities recorded by C.P. Gasquoine evidently took place between 10th October 1867 and December 1867, after which time the creditors voluntarily stayed their proceedings in expectation of the passing of this Act.

Engineer's and traffic manager's reports suggest that refreshment rooms at Harlech, Portmadoc and Afon Wen were not in business much before the end of December 1868. The first reports of minor accidents affecting trains moving at the upper end of the Coast line do not appear before February 1868, which suggests that few trains were run.

With all its attention to detail, the 1868 Act should have settled matters for some time but, because of the endemic shortage of money, the comparative peace was to last for only sixteen months.

The Corwen & Bala opened for traffic to Lake Halt on 1st April 1868, and on 4th August the ill-equipped Bala & Dolgelley (with its qualified certificate from the Board of Trade) was opened too. The Great Western lobby at the Board of Trade had perhaps been hard at work ensuring that its protégé was first into Dolgelley, despite Lt.Col. Hutchinson's reservations at the number of stations which consisted only of wooden huts. Within those companies, the hope was that the Cambrian would fail to comply with the 1867 Act and not complete the connection in time.

On 10th December 1868, the committee was told of a considerable amount of trespassing on the Coast line, with farmers driving their herds across it to their pastures. The solicitor was instructed to press only the minor charge of trespass, not the major one of endangering the safety of passengers.

In December 1968, 2-4-0 Sharp Stewart Tank No. 59 *Seaham* was returned to the Cambrian at the end of her hire by the Carnarvonshire Railway. The rates charged had been 10d per mile plus 2% for shunting for *Llanerchydol* as the passenger engine, while the charge for *Seaham* as the goods locomotive had been 1/- per mile plus 10% for shunting.

On 11th June 1869, the Board of Trade Inspector passed for traffic the two sections of line (one Cambrian and one GWR) linking Penmaenpool with Dolgelley. Their end-on junction between the two was locatated at a point known as Frondirion (just to the west of the Great Western goods warehouse), where the Cambrian erected a wooden platform and a hut which served as a temporary terminus for the Cambrian passenger service from 21st June. The engineer reported on 23rd June that he had settled an account for £5,314 17s 1d submitted by 'Ward the Contractor' for completion work on the Coast, and on 1st July the traffic manager reported he was 'getting advice from the London & North Western Railway on the installation of the Electric Telegraph from Aberdovey to Pwllheli and Dolgelley' (at £20 per mile for 42 miles).

The first Cambrian train steamed into Dolgelley Station on 1st August 1869, the deadline date for construction having been met by a bare six weeks (although 0-6-0 Manning Wardle saddle tank No. 18 *Cardigan* had already managed to deliver a wagon of coal for Mr Jones's Ship Inn at Dolgelley on 25th February).

On 17th September 1869, the Board approved that 'Accommodation Works were to be carried out on the land of D. Williams Esq MP under the circumstances of the state of his health' (no doubt his position as a Coast director had some influence as well). On 11th November they heard that 'The Coast and Inland Arbitrators have completed their report which the Arbitrators will deliver on receipt of their costs of £328 6s 6d' — even the appointed arbitrators would not trust their report to the Cambrian before their money was on the table! The Board approved the payment, and the report was found to have adjusted the division of the net surplus from the common fund to become 34.57% to the Coast and Inland 65.43%.

A shareholders' pressure group formed a 'Committee of Reconstruction, on 27th October, and in the following month even asked Captain Pryce to resign and make room for their nominee. He refused. This shareholder group had not been the only faction plotting behind the scenes though, and after having been advised by their own solicitor 'to apply to the Court for authority to complete Coast and Inland Land Purchases out of Revenue' (on 25th November), they had, on 12th December, to face up to the decision of both the Master of Rolls and the Vice Chancellor to give leave to the landowners to sell Coast land and close the railway unless they had been paid before the beginning of Michaelmas Term (Sept 29th). Counsel advised that these payments could be paid out of revenue unless the privileged classes of shareholder objected. The Board immediately approved the drawing of these cheques, including one for £3,627 3s 10d to Sir Pryse Pryse, and another for £3,162 12s 9d as agreed with his solicitor. A few of the landowners did stay their proceedings on receipt of shares as securities, with the interest to be paid promptly out of income.

On 24th November 1869, the engineer reported that all the Coast telegraph posts and wires had been erected, and on 5th January 1870 he indicated that all was complete and working; the traffic manager immediately suggested that 'one line [i.e. telegraph wire] should be sold to the Government'. There had also been a suggestion that a rolling stock rent fund should be raised to pay interest to creditors stayed under the 1868 Act. On 19th January 1870, the engineer reported that he had received a threat of legal proceedings in respect of 'Public Roads and Footpaths stopped by the Company'.

In February 1870, the Manchester faction of shareholders demanded the resignation of the whole Board except for the chairman and his deputy, and on 4th March there was a general shareholders vote of 'No confidence in the Board'.

During March 1870, the committee had to approve the expenditure of £36 for a culvert on Mr. Kirkby's land 'if he will not accept a cheaper alternative'. On 30th March, Elijah Elias advised them that he wanted to take the refreshment rooms on the Coast line into Cambrian hands and 'let them as the Inland refreshment rooms are let' (i.e. let by tender to the highest bidder).

The Board had another really rough time of it on 31st March when two of their own number tabled special letters. F.A. Fynney's letter was one of protest that 'the Solicitor Morris was also solicitor to both Savin and the Coast and should never have been appointed to conduct the Parliamentary proceedings as he would be favouring Savin and Coast interest as against those of Inland'. After this one they had to consider two letters from Henry Gartside. In the first, he criticised 'Mr Boult's motives as representing the Coast' with the comment 'and at the proper time I shall be prepared to exposed them', whilst in the second letter he offered to resign and refused re-election 'if all the Inland Directors and the two Old Coast Directors so do'. It appears that Mr Boult was a member of Ashurst & Morris, the company's outside solicitors. On 5th May 1870, the solicitor was instructed to inform Ashurst & Co 'that they represented the interests of the Coast only in Chancery proceedings' (Re. James v Cambrian).

At the meeting of 9th June 1870, the engineer reported that Mr John Casson had refused to sell enough of his land at Llanfihangell-y-traethaû to enable track to be doubled as originally fenced, but indicated that he would accept if paid in cash. (Casson was the owner of the Festiniog slate quarry known as Diphwys Casson).

In September 1870, Henry Cattle, the newly-appointed traffic manager, put in a plea for mackintoshes to be supplied to station masters, particularly those at the Coast stations; on the following day, the committee approved a scheme whereby the company would pay half the cost and the balance would be recovered from the station masters by instalments deducted from their wages. They also approved that 'Messrs Williams & Williams should attend and regulate the Coast clocks for £6 per annum and a free Pass while engaged on the work'.

On 14th October, the committee approved the expenditure on twenty-three miles and twenty-one chains of quick fencing to fill in the many gaps at 6/- per chain (£558 in all). The engineer was instructed to examine and report on 'maintaining a nursery of Quicks' (blackthorn or hawthorn). In the following month, the committee approved that the quicking should be planted by Salisbury & Son.

On the application of the former Coast secretary, Mr. William Roberts, for compensation for loss of office, the Board announced that he had already been dismissed by the Coast company.

In 1870, the Carnarvonshire Railway was taken over by the L&NWR, and the reciprocal running arrangements between Pant, Portmadoc and Pwllheli were put into abeyance. This situation would mean that, in trying to obtain the arrears of rebate on the through transition of passengers and goods via Afon Wen and Carnarvon, the Cambrian administration would henceforth have to deal with a more tricky and devisive railway management.

On 8th May 1871, George Owen produced his first estimate of what it might cost to put the Coast into proper order as an operating railway:

1. Aberystwyth Section: Doubling the line between Machynlleth to Glandovey Junction £8,000; Glandovey Junction Station £2,000; Glandovey £800; Ynyslas £500.
2. Coast to Pwllheli: Aberdovey £2640; Towyn £455; Llwyngwril £800; Barmouth Junction £1,800; Barmouth Town £3,400; Dyffryn £1,800; Pensarn £800; Harlech £800; Talsarnau £800; Penrhyndeudraeth £1,600; Portmadoc £1,800; Criccieth £800.
3. Dolgelley Branch: Arthog £800; Penmaenpool £800; Dolgelley £700.
4. Other Items: Merionethshire Railway Junction £700; Croesaû Extension to Harbour (Portmadoc) £737.

All in all, the cost of replacing Savin's legacy of timber sheds for booking offices and various other shacks came to £32,532. The new proposals were far from extravagant, and highlighted many of the shortcomings of the existing structures. There were no damp courses and frequently no proper fire hearths; during one tour of inspection one station master was asked how his house was, and he replied that 'he had the devil in his kitchen', for he had borrowed an iron-basket 'firedevil' (provided for the comfort of platelayers during frosty weather) to keep his own family warm. Nevertheless, Owen was sent back to think up ways of reducing the amounts needed.

On 14th May 1871, the committee noted that a further 21 miles and 6½ chains of quicking had been planted for £546 5s 9d. During September 1871, the Board received another report on the 'Coast Scheme' (as it was being called), and on 20th October the engineer presented another account on the proposed expenditure needed for the Coast section: Plan 1 was for a standard level crossing house, to cost £110; Plan 2 was for a road needed at Aberdovey, costing £140; Plan 3 was for the larger stations, at £1,200 each (Barmouth and Aberdovey), while Plan 4 was for a smaller standard station for Dyffryn, Harlech, Pensarn and others (subject to modifications where necessary).

The Merionethshire Railway Company received its powers to construct a gravity railway with locomotive propulsion for the return journey back from Llandecwyn (on the Cambrian) to the Festiniog and Blaenau Railway at Festiniog, on 29th June 1871. The Act did not specify any gauge, and the deposited plans showed direct connections to both the two-foot and the standard gauge; the unstated intention was to have transfer sidings at the lower end. Its principal promoters were Samuel Holland, and the Cassons, supported by other quarry owners, but they were persuaded to drop this rival scheme and to be content with the services of the nearby Festiniog Railway.

On 22nd December 1871, the Board approved that 'the half year's income from the Coast plus £7,000 from Coast Revenue A/c be applied to Debenture Interest', and that 'The Balance of Coast Capital and Revenue A/cs including the unissued Capital less the £7,000 be applied to completions of Works, Stations etc. on the Coast and £37,000 Land acquisitions.' The engineer thus had to tailor the completion works around what might be left over after the land acquisitions had been finalized, and he would need to design and obtain fresh approval, which would be given or withheld according to the circumstances. On 11th January 1872, the Board approved in principle a 'Coast Scheme' as arranged by the arbitrators.

Further accidents were reported on the line, including one to footplate staff: 'Fireman David Lewis advanced to the front of the engine on Good Friday to perform some duty when unfortunately he fell off and was run over by the train'. Exactly where on the Coast this tragedy occurred was not stated.

On 25th January 1872, George Owen came back with a completely new estimate for work on the Coast stations, which was to cost only £17,601 12s 2d. The Board duly considered this.

The arbitrator's awards of interest in 1872 pleased very few, and on 19th April the Board saw copies of a letter circulated to all debenture holders by Mr Earp, a stockbroker, in which he objected to the reduction of interest to 4% and 'to the placing of Capitalised Arrears before Capitalised Interest on Debentures'. The Board noted that the effects of the company's 1868 Act had come into effect and that the company had been able to make second, third and fourth calls of £2 per share on 'Coast Ordinary Capital'. In addition, the fifth and final call to pay would be made in November 1872. Not all shareholders actually paid up however, and there were some forfeitures.

The general manager's reports show that he was having a lot of arguments with Mr Moon of the London & North Western Railway over the 'Coast Rebate'. R.D. Pryce was acting for the Coast shareholders, to ensure that a fair share of the Coast rebate went to them, as well as being the Receiver for the company in 'Robinson & Jones versus the Company'. On 21st August 1872, the Board heard that the latest 'Coast Scheme' had received all the necessary approval, and further debenture stocks were to be issued.

On 1st February 1873, the Great Western took over responsibility for maintenance on the Bala & Dolgelley Company's line.

During April 1873, the traffic manager advised of the introduction of a fourth class in the passenger carriages. This was the 'Intermediate' class, between 'Government' and 'Second class', which later became 'Third class'; this extra class was not to run in the first up and down trains of each day. In committee discussion, it was mentioned that, under the 'Coast Scheme', Third class fares could be increased to 1½d per mile, though on 26th June the traffic manager reported that it would not be worthwhile to make this increase as 'it would mainly be consumed by Government Duty'. The anomaly here was that trains were already shown as '1, 2 and 3' in the timetables, '3' being a euphemism for 'Parliamentary'.

After discussion at the meeting of 27th June the committee approved that additional signals should be ordered. On 25th July, they dismissed Mr. Poole, District Superintendent, Coast Section, for not heeding a warning about defalcations. On the same day, the Board received a protest from the four Coast directors, Captain Johns and Messrs Mann, McAndrews and Lovedale, against 'Rent of Rolling Stock being charged as working expenses'. A fracas followed, because the Coast faction wanted Coast rebate credited separately, but on an amendment the Coast lost two votes against four.

During October 1873, the engineer reported 'all new works completed except Dolgelley pitching'.

On 19th December 1973, the Board received a warning that 'the Coast Directors might find it in their duty to claim a revision of the Award from the Arbitrators.' Subsequently, the Coast directors once more brought up their objections to the common fund, and yet again were overruled by the Board; and on 20th March 1874 they objected to 'the appointment of a private individual as Arbitrator re. the Rebates at Afon Wen because the Railway Commissioners were the proper Arbitrators'. On 19th June, the Board heard that 'Mr. Justice Speed has pronounced for Hire of Rolling Stock to be paid for out of Working Expenses', so, once again the Coast faction having support in Manchester and London wasted officers' time and company money in an action which came to nothing. Then on 3rd July 1874, they objected to the re-election of Mr J.E. Bolden of Rugby as deputy chairman after his resignation as deputy chairman and managing director, (a move to save the company the salary of a managing director), but he was duly re-elected.

For some time, the Great Western had been trying to bully the Cambrian into allowing them running rights through to Barmouth, and on 31st July 1874, two directors were appointed to treat with the GWR; however, the Great Western took the dispute to the Railway Commissioners, who found for them. Most of the Great Western engines proved to be too heavy to cross the Barmouth bridge (as it was then), so the ploy was a waste of time and Cambrian money. Once it became known that a change of engine was unavoidable, the Great Western largely kept their engines back at Dolgelley as before, although one or two may have worked down to Barmouth Junction on trial or for turning.

Because of the poor quality of the timber that the contractors had been using, much renewal of bridges was becoming necessary, and there were further problems caused by rising sea levels; extra-high tides had been scouring offshore protective banks of shingle. On 17th July, the Committee therefore gave the engineer general approval to proceed with the remedial work as needed, including the Inland bridges as well. On the same day, the traffic manager was instructed to arrange for a special train to be run from 18th to 20th July for a 'Directors' Inspection of the Coast Section'. There was the usual background of protest from the Coast directors, who considered that the ordinary service trains could be utilised.

On 28th July 1874, the Board were notified of yet another instance of dissenting litigation overthrowing the decisions of the arbitrators: 'The Lords Justices had issued a Correction of Accounts Order transferring £4,908 14s 11d to Coast Net Revenue Account and that £5,924 3s 6d be charged to the debit of the same account'. The Coast faction then tried to mount an objection to the Board's acceptance of the Justices' order, but they lost by five votes to three on a show of hands.

The meeting on 21st August ran true to form, and after the re-election of S.E. Bolden as managing director by a narrow margin, there followed seven angry clashes over seven different items. On the subject of the presentation of the accounts, the Inland faction defeated the Coast element, but only by the chairman's casting vote. The succeeding meeting was even worse. The shareholders had voted to replace J.A.Mann (a retiring Coast director, but eligible for re-election) by Frederick Adolphus Fynney of Manchester (Coast). Mann declared that he would not leave the chair unless removed by force which, under the protocol of the day, would have required the secretary to lay his hand on Mr Mann's shoulder and conduct him out of the meeting. Chairman Bolden declined to give this order. Instead the remaining directors were ushered into another room from which Mann was excluded. Captain Johns still tried unsuccessfully to get Mann re-elected.

At their meeting on 11th December 1874, the Board heard that 'Ashurst & Morris, Solicitors for the Coast Directors, were applying for a Coast Bill to overthrow the Scheme (as prescribed in the 1868 Act) and to overthrow also the decision of the Arbitrators'. On 19th February 1875, the Parliamentary Committee (specially reconstituted) approved the mounting of an objection by the company to this proposed Coast Bill, and agreed that a special circular should be sent round 'to all Ordinary and Preference Shareholders except the Petitioners'. In April, the Board resolved 'To make endeavors towards a pacific settlement of present differences', and arranged for a special meeting at Londonderry House with representatives from both sides present. On 30th April, the Parliamentary Committee reviewed the results of two such special meetings between the disaffected parties. Finally, on 7th May, the Board assented to a grouping of the points as finally assented to by the majority of the protagonists at both meetings, and approved them as 'Heads of Arrangement' for the officially-proposed Bill (Mr. Fynney objecting, and requiring his objection to be placed on record).

The resulting Cambrian Railways Act, 1875, became law on 11th August of that year and amended the 1868 Act, so that the two Acts were to be construed as one. The preamble showed that the purpose was 'An Act for making better provision for settlement of differences between the Coast Section and the Inland Section of the Cambrian Railways Company; and for other purposes'. In the preamble (here very much summarised) the award of 5th November 1869 was restated as Coast 34.57% and Inland 65.43% of the net from the common fund. Next, the accounts of the half-year ended 31st December 1873 were identified as the main reason for dissent and for the arbitration then pending.

The Cambrian Railways Act, 1875, provided that:

1. The provisional period was to end on 30th June 1875, but the provisions as to the appointment of Coast and Inland directors should remain in force until 31st December 1878.
2. The pending arbitration which would have adjusted the award of 1869 was determined, and proceedings were stayed. Accumulated costs arising were to be settled by the three arbitrators to be appointed under this Act.

3. The 1868 Act arbitrators and umpire to be retermed 'The Three Arbitrators'. They should sit together, and the award of any two shall be the award of all three. A vacancy should be filled by an appointee of the remaining two arbitrators or, if they could not agree, by the Board of Trade.
4. An award which altered the proportion of net from the common fund should be back-dated three-and-a-half years.
5. Disputes which, under the 1868 Act, might be taken before the Court of Chancery were now to be settled by the three arbitrators.
6. All disputes between Coast and Inland or their directors were to be settled by the three arbitrators.
7. No matter might be referred anywhere at all after the arbitrators had made their final award, unless the arbitrators allowed a time for so doing, and such time extension might not be granted beyond 31st December 1878.
8. All new or additional capital created or raised after 1st July 1875 would be the liability of the company as a whole, i.e. no more separate Coast Stock.
9 Costs of obtaining the Act were to be divided between Coast and Inland as the arbitrators might decide.

This time the Cambrian had a financial and political regulating Act which was fairly straightforward, contained few loopholes, and placed a terminal date on the Coast versus Inland internal struggles. The troublemakers' only recourse henceforth would be to go directly to the Court of Chancery, which they had already planned to do if the 1875 Act was not wholly to their liking.

On 27th August 1875, the Board voted Mann the sum of £500 as his arrears of director's fees plus his expenses, and appointed two arbitrators, David Davies to represent the Inland interests and Captain Jasper Wilson Johns to represent the Coast. On 24th September, they assented to 'details of certain special items in the Accounts being supplied to Johns and Mann'. In December it was decided that 'Ashurst, Morris & Co's Account for £2,514 3s 11d was to have attention early in the New Year'. The company's solicitor, Mr. Corfield, was instructed to look it over and to report, which he did on 28th January 1876. Ashurst & Morris had agreed to accept £500 on account, £500 on 1st March, and the balance after all queries had been settled.

The year 1876 was to prove to be a period of comparative peace for both directors and officers. As the effects of the 1875 Act took effect, the hoped-for capital came in, although not perhaps quite in the amounts expected. There were not too many overseas investors,but one notable entry was for Herr Brandeis Weikersheim, Vienna, Empire of Austria. Of the 1876 hay crop, worth £1,030, the Coast had contributed to the value of £502.

On 8th March 1877, the hatchets came out again (in advance of the passing of yet another Parliamentary Bill promoted by the company) with an anonymous letter from 'a proprietor of preference stocks' sent to all other debenture and shareholders (see Appendix III).

At the meeting held on 22nd March 1877, the engineer reported on some unidentified Coast work, that £2,000 had already been expended, and that it would cost £3,136 13s 4d when completed; this may possibly relate to renewal of the rotting timber viaducts.

Despite the circular put about by the 'proprietor of preference stocks', the Cambrian Railways Act, 1877, became law on 14th August of that year; but because of his protest, the Porthdinllaen Extension was not revived, and a proposed extension beyond Pwllheli to a harbour some seven miles south-west of the town was also dropped. The only item of Coast interest was the acquisition of land at Criccieth for the extension of station facilities. This survived in clause 4, along with land acquisition on the Inland section for the abandonment of the old Llanfyllin branch and its replacement by the Llanymynech Curve, to save the back shunting of branch trains out of Llanymynech. Powers were given to raise £50,000 (by issue of shares, or by issue of preferential mortgage) to finance these station improvements, to pay off the costs of the impending final arbitration award, and for the purchase of new rolling stock; this was the first act for some years to bear no reference to the raising of separate Coast stock or mortgages.

On 16th November 1877, the arbitrators made known their final and permanent award under the 1875 Act, having settled that (for accountancy purposes) the future division of the income was to be Coast 38% and Inland 62%. Also in 1877, the Bala & Dolgelley Railway ceased its independent existence, being absorbed into the Great Western.

At a meeting on 22nd February 1878, the Board approved 'The Issue of £30,000 in No 5 Debenture Stock under the Coast Scheme of Arrangement 1872' — this was the last reference found to the issue of separate Coast capital.

During two meetings in March the Board's attention was given mainly to the scurrilous 'Manchester Circular' issued by Messrs Fynney, Hilditch and McEwan. The motion was tabled: 'Is it necessary for the Board, in defence of its own honour, to take any steps?' The voting was 'noes four' and 'ayes three', and the Board then rose. After this, a Mr. Bancroft made a derogatory speech, but the Board again decided that no action should be taken.

On 24th May 1878, the Board considered 'The Coast and Inland Final Arbitration', minuting that 'Subsidiary points in difference are now agreed'. The officers were instructed to give a statement to the arbitrator, to obtain his opinion and direction to avoid further costs. Subsequently, on 25th January 1879, the Board accepted the information that the arbitrator had made his second award relating to the fusion of Coast ordinary stock with that of the

Inland's ordinary shareholders, so that when a major restructuring of capital came up in the future, there would be only one class of ordinary shareholder to be left out in the cold. On 19th February, the Board approved the final settlement of 'The Final Costs of Arbitration':

Ashurst, Morris & Co. — Solicitors	£1,000 0s 0d
Abraham Howell — Solicitor	£1,000 0s 0d
Price, Waterhouse — Settling Claims	£1,500 0s 0d
Cawley, Newton & Smith	£171 7s 6d
Deloitte & Holliday	£381 8s 8d
Total	£4,052 16s 2d

This could well represent a considerable sum thrown away by obstinate, greedy people, unwilling to concede to commonsense for the common good.

During the meeting of 7th December 1879, the engineer commented that he had nothing to report as 'owing to a severe and almost unparalleled frost on the Coast all works have been suspended'.

In May 1880, the general manager reported that the L&NW was trying to capture the Coast traffic via Afon Wen. Later in that year, the Board heard that a Mr. Gibson, holder of £8,000 in Coast stock, was pressing for the Coast line to be sold. Shortly afterwards, violent October gales brought down signals all along the Coast line, and another storm on 26th and 27th November washed away whole sections of the ballast.

During a meeting on 24th June 1882, the solicitor was instructed 'To ascertain the cost of making an inventory of the Aberystwith & Welsh Coast papers', but nothing seems to have come of this and, so far, none of the papers have come to light. On 10th October, the Board approved 'that the £150,000 of forfeited Coast Stock (i.e. ordinary shares) be sold to Mr.W.Emmens or to the Chairman for the time being of the National Bank at £12 per cent should he take same at any time during the next three years from this date'. It was a sad reflection on the losses sustained by the ordinary shareholders that shares costing £100 could sell for £12.

The Cambrian Railways Act, 1883, which took effect on 29th June, gave powers to construct an enlarged Aberdovey harbour, and to make another harbour next to Pwllheli old station, with powers for the raising of the necessary money.

Traffic manager Edwin Liller's report of 5th February 1884 contained information about stranded vessels which could be seen from the Coast trains. On 24th January, *Moab* (Liverpool to Valparaiso, with 1,300 tons of coal) was ashore near Harlech, and on 29th January, *Endurance* (Calcutta to Liverpool, with 1,400 tons of wheat as well as a quantity of jute) was lying on Sarn Badrig; he gave his comments on storm damage to the line as well.

On 6th February, Liller was instructed 'To ascertain what pecuniary assistance will be given by other Companies in advertising the Coast District', and on 26th March the committee approved 'Arrangements for advertising the Coast District provided that other Companies contribute and half cost is provided by Local Bodies'. During April, instructions were given as to 'The Keeping of a separate Cost of Advertising Account which may be inspected by Local subscribers', and the committee resolved also that they 'will look favourably on making subscriptions to Regattas, Bands of Music etc. at the Watering Places'.

At the meeting of 16th August, Liller reported on the possibility of through traffic via the Brecon & Merthyr, the Mid-Wales and the Cambrian onto the Coast line, stating that there was 'A remarkable absence of provision in any of the relevant Acts, particularly as to the Aberystwyth & Welsh Coast', but he urged 'careful consideration as any arrangement between the three companies is bound to result in reprisals from the Great Companies'.

Mr Justice Chitty's award in the Court of Chancery rising from secretary Conacher's great work on the restructuring of the whole of the Cambrian's capital, was duly enrolled on 14th July 1885. While this was a general measure (which will be dealt with in a later volume), it was still the direct result of what may now be termed 'The Coast Shenanigans'. The committee were extremely happy to note that all had been now settled and filed.

On 24th August 1887, the traffic manager (now George Lewis, doubling with his regular appointment as general manager) reported that Barmouth and other Coast resorts were asking for cheap 'Tourist' rates for fares booked from those stations He had pointed out to the applicants 'that these were to get Visitors and Tourists to visit and holiday on the Coast which is already to the benefit of the residents'; the concession was refused.

In the course of a meeting on the 7th November 1887, the engineer reported that the timber bridges on the Coast were a constant source of trouble, and that the only remedy would be to replace them with girders, as on the inland sections The report was accepted in principle, but the engineer would still have to get individual sanctions when required. The Traffic Manager reported in October that action was being contemplated under the Railway and Canal Act, 1888, to obtain relief from the Coast Act of 1865 as to charging for only six miles between Ynyslas and Aberdovey, whereas all passengers and goods had to be conveyed the twelve miles via Dovey Junction. The Cambrian's invocation of this Act brought objections from the Great Western in respect of a claim of running powers which they never exercised. By this outrageous claim, which was not substantiated, the Cambrian would have lost the right to charge for the 8m 61c (12m 15c via Dovey Junction, less the 3m 34c of the abandoned direct line).

On 9th July 1889, the Cambrian Railways (Steamboats) Act was passed (see the section on Aberdovey, page 96).

A fall in tourist traffic was noted in 1892 when, on 8th August, the general manager ascribed the decrease in the holiday bookings to 'Lassitude with the public in consequence of the Elections and it is thought that a large number of these will have no holidays this Summer or defer them until the Autumn'. In January 1893, he announced: 'Day Excursion Rates open to all members of the public in September and October, even if they have arrived by coach (e.g. ex-Aberglaslyn), where they wish to extend to other places in Wales'. He reported further, on 7th November, that 'Weekend Bookings and Tourist Bookings all the year round had finally been agreed to by the London & North Western from Birmingham, Liverpool and Manchester and other principal towns in Northern and Midland counties to Aberystwyth, Borth, Towyn, Dolgelley and Barmouth'. Might the indefatigable Victorian railway traveller have preferred the more scenic route via Chester, Caernarvon, Afon Wen and Barmouth Junction to Dolgelley, instead of via Crewe, Dovey Junction and Barmouth Junction? Both routes appear to be tortuous by comparison with what the Great Western could provide via Ruabon, but the offer was there.

The Board approved on 14th October 1894 the proposal that all Coast stations could display collecting boxes for the Royal National Lifeboat Institution, whilst in January 1895, the committee deferred erection of further crossing keepers' houses until the annual inspection. On 2nd April, the general manager reported that he proposed to follow the Isle of Wight Railway by introducing 'Cheap Weekly Tourist Tickets', and this was agreed by the committee for the summer months.

Later that year, the engineer reported on the 'furious gales and high tides on the night of 7th October . . . the effects of the storm were most disastrous . . . damage estimated at £4,000 to £5,000 . . . All the Rockmen and relaying gangs have been discharged and these will have to be re-engaged but many of the best men have obtained employment at the Birmingham Water Works . . . Miles of fencing

A Sharp Stewart 0–4–2 on a Dolgelley local train at Barmouth Junction c.1882. At this time there was a branch loop, but only the one platform. The Coast line to Dovey Junction diverges to the right. *Cty. George Dow*

As soon as Corbett had built his promenade at Towyn, its abrupt thrust seawards was destroyed before he had time to erect any houses.
Author's collection

have been blown down and carried away.' On 27th October, the Board and the general manager recorded their thanks to the weary engineer and his exhausted staff:

> 'I deem it my duty to call your special attention to the skilful organisation and manipulation by Mr. George Owen of the whole of the Engineering staff, which was largely augmented, enabling the traffic working to be resumed in the shortest possible time. Considering the extent of the damage at different places, and especially that between Towyn and Tonfanau, it is remarkable that the engineer was able so promptly to accomplish this'.

In 1896, the Great Western formally absorbed the Vale of Llangollen, the Llangollen & Corwen and the Corwen & Bala companies, and its ownership of 'The Barmouth Road' was complete.

The Cambrian Railway Act of 1896, passed on 2nd July, conferred the following powers affecting the Coast:

1. Afon Wen, extension of the ballast quarry.
2. Barmouth Junction, acquisition of land to construct an access road.
3. Llangelynin, extension of the ballast quarry.
4. Glandovey, acquisition of land to construct an access road.
5. Pwllheli, revival of 1883 Act powers to make a harbour near the site of the old station.
6. Extension of period for acquiring or constructing hotels.
7. Authorisation for the establishment of coach services with or in extension of the railway system.

On 29th June 1898, the committee agreed to the new general manager, C.S.Denniss, extending his campaign against trespassers to include the Coast line. He had reported 'Difficulty in stopping trespassing along the line owing to the extent to which it has been permitted in the past and the convenience which the line affords residents and others', and his subsequent actions produced 'a flood of applications for permission to walk the line by those ordered off'.

The engineer reported that on 11th August 'The Coast Ballast Gang consisting of Contractors' men struck and went home for paltry reasons [mainly delayed meal breaks to finish off jobs]. All were dismissed and a new Gang of our own experienced local men will be put together and so saving lodging allowance'. The year 1898 ended with severe storms and flooding on 27th December, with another severe storm and flooding in the new year, especially (again) around Towyn; exceptionally high tides between 10th and 14th February completed the story.

The Cambrian Railways Act, 1901, received royal assent on 2nd July, and conferred powers to:

1. Construct the Pwllheli Extension from the old station to the site of existing one.
2. Use steam vessels for tourist traffic. (It is unclear what vessels might have been used.)

On 16th October 1901, the general manager reported on an extraordinary proposal from a firm of electrical engineers to electrify the whole length of the Coast line from Machynlleth to Pwllheli, with Llyn Gwynant as a reservoir for generating the power. The route would be operated by the Northern Counties Electric Traction Company, with Gantz locomotives and systems served by 3,000 volts direct current with three-wire polyphase distribution. According to these engineers, Messrs. Bennett and Ward-Thomas, they could offer to work the Coast trains for 7d per mile. However, the Cambrian's engineer and locomotive superintendent were extremely doubtful about this claim and the overall practicability of the scheme. They also considered that the heavy axle weights of the locomotives were likely to create problems in track maintenance (at that time, jack-shaft drives to electric locomotives were in their infancy, and a very heavy motor sat squarely on an axle without any springing in between. The scheme was shelved at the beginning of 1902, and was finally rejected by the Board on 11th October 1916 (see Appendix IV).

This picture of Penmaenpool c.1885 features a boating party from the George Hotel. Beyond lay the river bridge, with the railway station at its southern end. Prominent is the 'station signal' – two arms on one post, with two spectacles served by one lamp. If the signal was at danger, the driver had to stop at the correct place. He was simply expected to know where this was! *George Hayward*

Heavy weather on the Coast section continued to take its toll, and on 1st December 1902 a ganger was knocked down and injured by the sea breaking across the line. In February 1903, tests were made along the Coast line with 'the heaviest tank engine' (0-6-0 Sharp Stewart tank No. 13 *Talerddig*, and on 21st April 1903 the committee were told that, after reinforcing certain cattle creeps, the company's heaviest engines could be permitted along the Coast. More bad weather was experienced on 2nd February 1905, when a storm took out a considerable length of telegraph wires; this resulted in pilot working between Towyn and Harlech for two days.

At the meeting of 30th October 1910, the engineer reported on the weak character of the signal indications received along the Coast telegraph system 'Due to damp and salt atmosphere owing to the proximity of the sea'. He suggested that the insulators should be changed 'to modern porcelain insulators instead of the old brown earthenware sort' (what would now be known as salt-glazed stoneware). He wished to try out the new insulators initially between Machynlleth and Barmouth at a cost of £25 2s 6d, and added that Saunders (the Cambrian's contractor responsible for maintaining signal and telegraphs) wanted £112 to change the insulators over the whole length to Pwllheli; the committee referred the £25 2s 6d cost to the Board for its approval. Because of the considerable improvement obtained in the use of the porcelain units, the remainder were changed over shortly afterwards.

Between 4th and 11th May 1911, the new secretary and general manager, Samuel Williamson, organised a special tour of all stations between Dolgelley and Criccieth for a party of press representatives, arranged by The Cambrian Resorts Association. Trips were run to Pwllheli, Llanbedrog, Nevin and Beddgelert. Only a few of the newspapers and magazines which sent their reporters all those years ago have survived to the present day; they included *The Queen, Madam, Town and Country, The Bradford Observer, The Nottingham Daily Guardian, The Irish Times* and *The Belfast Northern Whig*, to name a few.

During August and September 1911, the senior officers had to devote much of their time to the assessment of a proposal to construct and work a light mineral railway from Pwllheli to the Carreg Estate (beyond Aberdaran), but their deliberations brought them to an unfavourable conclusion.

Severe gales between 12th and 15th February 1914 earned the engineering gangs another commendation from the chairman, who authorised an award of two days extra pay to each of the men who had worked so well in repairing the damage; this cost the

Penmaenpool Yard, looking from the road entrance c.1910. The sign beckoning to Barmouth and beyond, was intended to encourage road traffic to use the toll bridge. *Cty. Owen Williams*

A period scene at Penmaenpool c.1895 featuring a local baker who appears to have been selling a roll of bread to a guard. The engine in the background was No. 23, one of the Nasmyth Wilson 0–4–4 tanks. *Cty. R. E. Thomas*

H. W. Burman

An unidentified 0–6–0 Dean Goods on an up passenger ascending Y Friog.

No. 36, the ex-Metropolitan tank converted to a 4–4–0 tender engine, was a regular sighting from the golf links, on the local trains between Machynlleth, Barmouth and Pwllheli. It is seen here leaving Aberdovey for the north c,1920.
H. W. Burman

Cambrian about £30 between the eighty-nine men involved.

On 27th February, the committee approved in principle that the sea defences should be strengthened, whilst on 8th May they approved the application of steam heating to the Coast line carriage stock. More severe storms over 22nd September 1918 made extra works immediately necessary, and the Board had to approve the expenditure after they had been put in hand.

After this, much of the officers' and directors' time was given over to keeping things running against the general background of postwar shortage of money. This situation had been caused largely by the Government's policy of helping industry at the expense of the railways, by restricting freight charges. The Government's solution to the overall problem was the creation of the 'Big Four', in which the lesser fry were mostly gobbled up by the larger companies, or by combinations of them. Some of the constituents had, in earlier days, been their combatants in the many petty traffic wars which were such a feature of the 19th century. The Cambrian had hoped that they would be lucky enough to be included in the same group as the London & North Western, and lived in fear of an unhappy liaison with the generally-hostile Great Western. Their worst fears were realised when they were forcibly absorbed into the Great Western group on the word of an unsympathetic cabal of civil servants headed by Sir Eric Geddes, who became notorious later for his 'pay cuts for all' policy (nicknamed 'the Geddes Axe'). The date set for the absorption was 1st January 1922, after which the Coast line was truly integrated with the Great Western.

The new owners began a substantial programme of track and signalling reconstruction designed to overcome the wartime neglect and to bring all up to the mainline standards of the GWR. The post-1922 history of the Cambrian Line was still distinctive because of its relative isolation from the rest of the Great Western system, and will be given in full detail in Volume III.

Meanwhile, and for the sake of continuity when referring to the individual station histories in this volume, a brief summary of the recent history is not out of place.

In 1948 came the Labour government's panacea for all evils, nationalisation, and the Cambrian area went with the rest of the Great Western into Western Region; this change did not have much effect by way of disturbance at local operational level.

The main changes came after the Beeching report, which had been calculated to show the government how the British railways could be run at a profit by closing most of them. From 1st January 1963 the Cambrian system was swept, along with the rest of the Great Western lines in North Wales, into London Midland Region. The Coast line survived but its good yards, loops and surplus sidings were lifted or simplified in accordance with a plan which received approval in 1967. The process of closure to goods traffic was hastened by the miners' strike of 1983 which drove many more people to change to oil or liquid gas heating rather than depending on coal, and subsequently by the closure of Barmouth viaduct to locomotive-hauled trains (and to all trains for a short time) because of severe damage to the timber piles by the teredo worm.

A proposal to close the entire Coast line in 1971 was fought successfully by the Cambrian Coast Line Action Group convened originally by John Rogers, and this has given it the title 'The Line that Refused to Die'. With modern Sprinter stock and the Radio Electronic Token Block signalling system (installed over the weekend of 1st/2nd October 1988), the Coast line lived on to celebrate its 125th anniversary marked by British Rail's highly-successful exhibition at Barmouth on 10th October 1992.

Together with the inland stem, commencing at Sutton Bridge Junction outside Shrewsbury and ending at Machynlleth, the Coast line became a part of Central Region of Regional Railways, and was directed by a Line Manager whose office was at Machynlleth. The little system was accorded the historic title of Cambrian Lines.

This simple and effective way of running the railway was disrupted on 1st April 1994 by the Government's application of powers conferred by the Railways Act 1993. It imposed a two-year implementation period, at the end of which it expected to have franchised off more than half of the British Rail network to private enterprise. In pursuit of this objective, the former single organisations, as assisted by the expertise of the major technical departments, have been separated into a sort of indigestible layer cake with flavouring designed to appeal (or so it was hoped) to the profit seekers.

The various levels consist of operators who have to go to owners and leasers for their trains, stations and track; maintenance is carried out by bits of the old technical departments recast into the roles of subcontractors. The old 'all for one and one for all' spirit has gone for good and 'Commercial Confidentiality' and 'Contractual Obligation' have taken its place.

Now the passenger service over Cambrian Lines is run by the Director of the Central Train Operating Unit (retitled Central Trains Ltd) who rent offices in Stanier House, Birmingham. They have a group station manager at Shrewsbury to implement their responsibility for arranging the train services and for marketing and issue of tickets. They have an assistant station manager at Machynlleth who looks after the station staff, the ticket sales and 'customer interface situations'. The drivers based at Machynlleth and Pwllheli are supervised by a traction inspector who comes under a driver manager at Worcester, and the conductors are taken care of by trains leaders at Shrewsbury, who come under the trains manager in Birmingham. The carriage cleaners at Machynlleth and Pwllheli come under the fleet manager in Birmingham. The Cambrian Lines operating staff come generally under a movements manager who is employed by Railtrack Midlands Zone in Birmingham.

Central Trains Ltd have to lease their 153 and 156 Sprinters from Porterbrook Leasing Company Ltd (one of the three rolling stock and leasing organisations set up by British Rail). Of the other two, Eversholt hold and lease out the electric stock, and the remainder is held by Angel Train Contracts. Porterbrook maintain the trains at the level required and withdraw and replace as heavy repairs become necessary.

Having thus put together their staff and leased their trains, Central Trains Ltd have only to pay Railtrack's 'Access Charge' for the stations, line and signalling, and they are in business.

Railtrack own and maintain the 'Infrastructure', i.e. the land, bridges, stations, track and signalling. They employ signalmen, crossing keepers, a crossing inspector, and movement inspectors, and are generally responsible for train safety and the working timetable. Railtrack obtain their technical services from BRIS (British Rail Infrastructure Services), into which all the former civil engineering sections have been grouped as IMUs (Infrastructure Maintenance Units). The IMUs are contracted to maintain bridges, formation and permanent way, and the IMU responsible for the Coast has its offices in Birmingham after having been moved from Crewe. From September 1995, Railtrack is to be permitted to invite tenders for maintenance etc. from private contractors in competition with the IMUs. BRT (British Rail Telecommunications) maintain the main radio masts and stations where the few signalmen are to be found, the repeater masts and the cab equipment.

The skilled men required for running repairs to the trains at Machynlleth are employed by Central Trains Ltd who hold a contract from Porterbrook for the day-to-day maintenance of the multiple units.

Under this many-tiered management, the Coast line was relaunched with its own identity as 'Cambrian Coaster' in 1994 in an effort to build up public awareness of the line and stimulate business, particularly off-peak.

DOVEY JUNCTION to ABERDOVEY

– 79m 09c to 84m 74c

2–4–0 'Barnum' No. 3225 on a Pwllheli train, with all doors open as passengers change trains, at Dovey Junction on 21st July 1934. Note that GWR platform widening by 10ft left a gap between the edge of the awning and the edge of the platform. *Lens of Sutton*

Leaving Dovey Junction, the line curves due west on a rising embankment, made up of rock from the cliff behind Machynlleth station. It then crosses Afon Dyfi by means of a 21-span bridge built mainly of timber trestles but with three steel girder spans in the centre.

After a mile-and-a-quarter of straight, the route curves in a south-westerly direction to follow the north shore of the Dyfi, barely managing to squeeze itself between the turnpike road of 1827 (now the A493) and the estuary shore. It curves round some of the headlands, cuts through the smaller ones, and tunnels through another three; it is a truly fascinating and lovely run.

After No. 1 (Frongoch) tunnel, comes the site of Frongoch quarry, with its little stone jetty, now a thriving marina and boat repair yard. No. 2 (Morfa Bach) tunnel gives onto a stone embankment with a bridge crossing the Tafol inlet, for some years the site of Abertafol Halt and the ganger's house. The rest of the run is marked by the cuttings and overbridges of Trefri (a house on a headland) and Picnic Island.

No. 3 (Penhelig) tunnel disgorges the line across a road bridge into Penhelig Halt, with its views of rooftops and chimneys; the road recurves under the line again before the railway enters the short cutting at the entrance to No. 4 (Craig-y-Don) tunnel. Beyond are yet more rooftops and Copper Hill Street bridge, after which the line curves round to negotiate Craig-y-Don bridge, with magnificent views of the sea and the harbour, before entering Aberdovey station.

Initially, the tunnels had been numbered from the Aberdovey end, but the Cambrian altered this immediately to numbering from the east end, as they are known today. George Owen, the Cambrian engineer, informed his Board in 1866 that the road bridges had not been constructed in accordance with the plans but, rather surprisingly, did not also report on the inadequate finishing of the tunnels (which were then mostly bare rock). He was formally made responsible for overseeing the deviation from 22nd March 1867 after the expiration of the contractor's maintenance period. His first concern inside the tunnels seemed to have been the side walls, and later he gave more attention to the provision of brick arching. In 1884 he vigorously drew his Board's attention to the substandard clearance of thirteen feet from the top of the

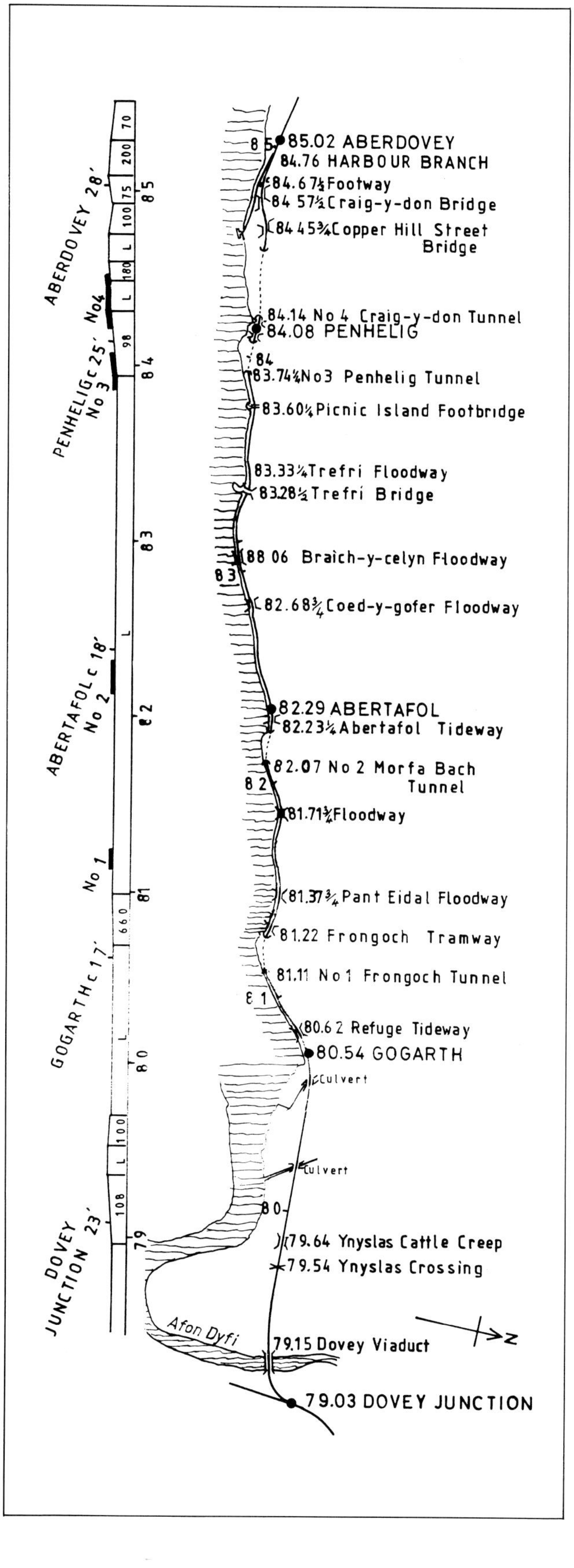

rails, and it took until 1895 before he pronounced that all necessary remedial works had been completed. It had been the inadequate width inside the tunnels which had caused Inspector Tyler to refuse to sanction the opening of the deviation to traffic in 1866.

On Saturday, 27th June 1936, a Manchester to Aberystwyth extra train via Ruabon and Barmouth Junction had to be diverted en route because it contained LMS stock, which was too wide to run through the tunnels; the unfortunate trippers had to be content with Barmouth instead. In the following year, 'Dean Goods' 0–6–0 No. 2490 took the Oswestry template truck and a set of GWR and LMS 68 ft × 9 ft coaches through the tunnels and all the way to Afon Wen to make sure that a royal train, scheduled for July, could get through.

From time to time, the Cambrian assisted the Towyn Urban District Council by free surrender of strips of land for road widening and buttressing against collapse; indeed, the strata supporting the road did collapse onto the line several times. In 1884, a slip thirty yards to the east of No. 3 tunnel fetched a locomotive and two carriages off the line, and two hundred tons of rock came down nearby; the sum of £280 was expended in building a retaining wall at the site. In 1888, another serious fall had to be remedied immediately, before the road itself collapsed. In the 1920s, the Great Western spent £1,000 under a contract let to Hugh Lewis (of Aberdovey) for rebuilding sections of the boundary wall. Between 1935 and 1941, another £1,160 was spent, all on walling.

The sea wall protecting the line was giving cause for concern by 1882, and a mile-and-a-quarter was rebuilt at a cost of £2,886 1s 7d; the work was damaged and delayed by high tides on 2nd, 28th and 29th September, and again on 2nd and 3rd October 1883. Although the Great Western seemed to have covered much of the repairs arising under the heading of ongoing minor works, it fell to the Western Region to carry out a major overhaul, involving the placing of block stones on the beaches to break the force of the waves. This work was seen to be more than justified when the high tides and floods of 1990 set the waves lapping at the top of the walling for most of its length.

As to the bridges, the Trefri was found to be deflecting in 1892, and 'Stronger Plate Girders' were installed for £150, with the stipulation that the old girders should be used to replace a timber bridge with a span of less than twenty feet on the square. The Great Western replaced the road bridge between Penhelig Halt and No. 4 tunnel in 1926, at a cost of £855.

In 1899, the Cleveland Bridge and Engineering Co. replaced the old timber-decked elliptical girder bridge beyond the west end of No. 4 tunnel. The new steel-floored girder bridge cost £693 10s 0d, less 2½%. A cigarette thrown from a train in 1919 set the sleepers smouldering, and Miss Atkin of Craig-y-don walked to the station and told the staff, who ran and put the fire out.

The Post Office was allowed to instal a wall letter box in the abutment of one of the bridges.

On 24th May 1910, the 5.15 a.m. down goods came round the curve upon Pant Eidal bridge (at 81m 71c), which was on fire from cinders dropped the night before, and the driver got his train safely across. The Bishop of Bangor put one of his men on watch, and motored to Machynlleth to give the alarm. Services were maintained by halting trains short of the bridge, and passing passengers and their baggage round by the road to other waiting trains, all worked by propelling the trains in one direction. The timber bridge was replaced by iron girders for £30. On 1st June, the committee passed a resolution recording that 'The Thanks of the Directors be offered to the Bishop of Bangor for the action taken by His Lordship on the occasion of the fire on 24th May last.' The bridge was replaced again in 1923.

There was one accident in the open between tunnels Nos. 2 and 3 on 25th September 1877, when Catherine Anne Jones (aged six), who was travelling to Liverpool with her mother, managed to open the carriage door and fall out. Luckily, 'She received only several contusions on head, legs and hands but nothing serious', and 'she was taken back to Aberdovey and was left with her grandfather'.

Because the travellers on two services timed to meet at Dovey Junction could often see the other train as a plume of flying steam and smoke in the distance on the other side of the Dovey estuary, bets would be made as to which of the trains would be the first to halt at the platform. Bribes to the train crews to persuade them to work their engines harder were not unknown, and when an inspector happened to be on the 'losing' train, the winners could be in a spot of bother (or so it used to be told).

It is ironic that, in 1922, the Great Western had acquired this highly-scenic and troublesome route, having previously opposed its construction, because of the threat it posed to the Ruabon & Barmouth Junction traffic. The GWR withdrew its objection only after being given the power to build the first-proposed Dovey bridge within ten years if they wished, and after the insertion of a clause setting the rates for carriage of goods between Aberdovey and Ynyslas (and points north and south) as if the mileage between those places was as it would have been had the Dovey bridge been built, rather than the actual mileage via Dovey Junction.

DOVEY JUNCTION

78m 72c to 79m 8c (Coast Loop to 79m 9c)
formerly Glandovey (Doveybank) Junction,
now CYFFORDD DYFI.

Dovey Junction was the only former Cambrian station where steam-hauled trains were served from buildings of the post-war construction.

There had always been problems with levels at Dovey Junction because the old building remained firm on sixty foot deep piles while the platforms and track, which were not so well supported, kept on sinking.

The running lines and sidings at the Machynlleth end of the station sank more than the rest, and a water level indicator was sited opposite the Coast platform. When this was submerged, any train which had managed to get to this point had to remain there until the high tide had receded, which might take from forty minutes to two hours. Usually the front of the train would be against the Coast platform and transfers to Aberystwyth trains could still be made.

In the end it was the decay of the old buildings that hastened their replacement rather than the failure of the piling. The old station was surveyed and a drawing of it was made dated 19th November 1951. Three years went by and a plan of a luxurious replacement, which included a bar, was drawn up dated 13th September 1954. Economic forces intervened and three smaller but quite adequate buildings were erected on three-foot deep concrete cellular rafts, with a signal box further up the platform. The rafts in effect floated on the boggy ground, supporting buildings and platform surfaces alike. The 'modular' buildings, being light structures, were particularly suitable for the task, if austere in appearance and with no awnings. The reconstruction was finally completed and the signal box was opened on 21st February 1959.

The signal box was closed on 21st October 1988 and the signalling and operation of the junction points (which had been resited at the Machynlleth end of the up sidings to reduce the risk of the electric point motor being disabled by flood water) came

4–4–0 'Dukedog' No. 9027 on an up local ex-Pwllheli in 1955. A few passengers only left the train to go and wait for the next down train to Aberystwyth. *Author*

Dovey Junction on 13th August 1959, with No. 5556 alongside the platform. *Collection R. S. Carpenter*

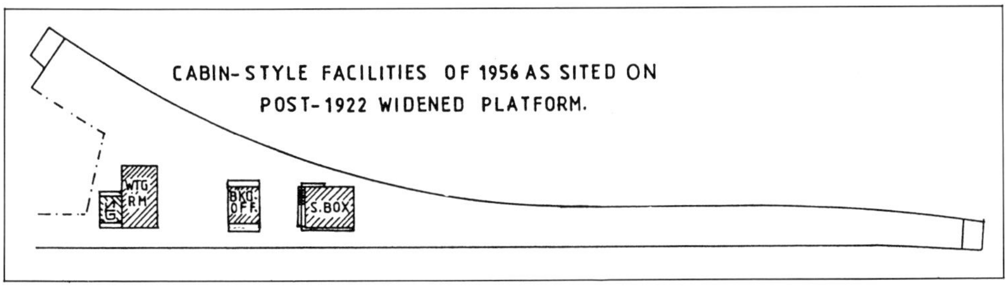

Top left: Coast side signal box, booking office and rear of waiting room. *Top right:* A closer view of the booking office and rear of waiting room, with detail of south window. *Above left:* Main side toilet block, waiting room, booking office and signal box. *Above right:* A closer view of the signal box. The man with collar up and hands in pockets shows that a typical Dovey Junction breeze was blowing. These pictures were taken in 1960 and 1961. *K. G. Draper and J. J. Davis*

under the control of Machynlleth. Machynlleth also became the preferred centre for the exchange and transfer of passengers between Aberystwyth and Pwllheli lines.

Fewer trains stopped at Cyffordd Dyfi (as it was renamed) and the three deserted buildings grew shabbier each year as they stood next to the pit in which the locking frame of the signal box had been fixed. In 1993 they were demolished, the floorings of the rafts were knocked in and they were filled up with ballast stone and fenced off for safety. The signal box frame pit was concreted over as a site for a bus shelter without a seat and a seat without any shelter.

This picture, taken from the Pwllheli portion of the up Cambrian Coast Express as it coasted gently over the Dovey bridge, shows the portion from Aberystwyth in the distance, entering Dovey Junction. 27th September 1963. *J. H. Moss*

2–6–0 No. 5399 entering Dovey Junction on an up Coast train on 11th August 1961. The rise at 1 in 108 from the platform on to the Dovey bridge is evident. *Collection R. K. Blencowe*

DOVEY BRIDGE 79m 15c

A wonderful setting! Dovey Viaduct from the Aberystwyth branch, with the bridgekeeper's house on the northern bank of the river. August 1958. *Author*

If railway bridges could be listed for preservation like historical buildings, this unique specimen would be a strong candidate. Its basis is a Victorian cast-iron pile frame system of 1866, absolutely intact. Above are cast-iron pedestals adapting it to carry a wrought-steel three-span girder bridge of 1914. It was an extremely rare pattern of underdraw bridge with a clear opening of thirty-six feet for ships to pass through. It was designed to satisfy the local opposition to the scheme which had called for an opening of thirty-five feet. The original plan for the Morben Railway had been for a wider fixed bridge with a footway, but the footway was not incorporated in the underdraw bridge, probably on the grounds of the extra cost. The first trial train crossed on 30th July 1866.

On 14th January 1867, a vessel collided with one of the piers and repairs were needed. Then on 9th August 1870, Richard Edwards failed to replace the cotters, and the opening span dropped $5\frac{1}{2}$ inches under the weight of the 8.10 ex-Barmouth Junction. The teeth sheared off the winding cogs, and the movable section had to be jacked up and secured for some time. As a consequence, the sloop *Mary Jane,* laden with pitwood, was detained upstream from Wednesday until Friday at a demurrage charge of £4, paid by the company. Richard Edwards was dismissed 'for his great neglect'.

Shortly afterwards, Saunders & Co. were brought in to repair the electric telegraph, reported to be 'in dangerous state'. At that time, the traffic manager asked for instructions on the subject of passengers walking across the bridge in order to take the train; seemingly this habit was to be stopped, but it would crop up again and again, the inhabitants of the Pennal district being nothing if not extremely persistent.

Towards the end of 1872, the engineer's submission that a bridgeman's house was needed because of increasing traffic was approved. The building was completed by 23rd October 1973, for £250.

In September 1884 the Pennal vet, Mr John Lloyd, offered to pay an acknowledgement and to sign an indemnity for permission to walk across the bridge; however, 'consideration was deferred'.

The bridge was opened for a boat for the last time in 1890.

At the end of 1898 (in the wake of C. S. Denniss's campaign against trespassers) there came a petition for a footbridge. The engineer recommended that powers be obtained to annul the requirement of opening the bridge, as a movable footbridge would cost £350, but only £170 if the bridge were fixed. Power for closure of the channel was approved for insertion in the General Powers Bill of 1901, but had to be withdrawn because of 'strenuous opposition on the part of the Machynlleth and district residents and others who had not needed to send a boat through for the past eight (sic) years but still wanted the footbridge'.

South elevation, looking upstream. The location of the former opening span, towards the right-hand end of the bridge, can be seen in this silhouette view. 5th June 1963. *Author*

The north elevation, showing the different height of the three piers which formerly bore the carriage rails by which the opening span was drawn down to create the opening in the bridge. 5th June 1963. *Author*

Detail of the pile frames on the north elevation and showing the widening at the site of the former drawbridge. 5th June 1963. *Author*

However, on 16th June 1901, Mr W. H. Bayliss, his housekeeper and visitors were given permission to walk across the bridge on their way to the station. Then, on 1st August, Mrs. M. Davies and Mrs. Perkins of Pennal tried to cross the bridge with three children while the afternoon 'Coast' was leaving. Mrs. Davies tried to get across to the children and fell between the rails, and the engine and two carriages passed over her before the train could be stopped; 'Mercifully she had only a bruised forehead and nose'. This incident was seen to justify Denniss's ruling that walking permits were for men only, and brought about the proposal that Dovey Junction station should be closed; the booking office was closed as from 1st January 1902.

On 21st April 1903, the committee had to approve expenditure on the fitting of more packing to the

The north elevation of the bridgekeeper's house. 5th June 1963. *Author*

Looking towards the station and showing the difference in width between the former drawbridge section and the timber viaduct. 5th June 1963. *Author*

The west end of the bridgekeeper's house, looking across the 'hump' of the viaduct to Dovey Junction station. 5th June 1963. *Author*

The rear (south elevation) of the bridgekeeper's house. 5th June 1963. *Author*

bearers, so that heavier engines could be used. On 1st July 1904, a fire damaged timbers to the value of £21, which was covered by the insurers (The Guardian).

By 1912 the structure was failing; piling had therefore to be inserted under the sagging centre, and opening became impossible. As it would have cost between £4,000 and £5,000 to restore as an opening bridge, and only £600 to rebuild as a fixed bridge, the committee elected to obtain closure powers by the Bill of 1913, and the new fixed steel girder centre had been completed by the end of 1914. It was proposed to re-use the old lattice girders on the new Tanat bridge on the Tanat Valley Light Railway.

At the end of 1918, Captain Morgan of Aberdovey – a regular agitator of railway officials – sought to prove that there was an established public right of way across the bridge, and that an underbridge should be built for the use of landowners, but not by fishermen.

In 1932, the Great Western made extensive reconstruction to the timber portions at a cost of £5,200.

On Bank Holiday Monday, 26th August 1991, No. 37421, hauling a trainload of day trippers bound for Pwllheli, derailed at the end of the trestle portion at the Dovey Junction end of the bridge. No damage was done, but the trippers had to be content with Aberystwyth instead. The Motive Power Department blamed the track, which was overhauled, but later it was discovered that No. 37421 was the rogue engine of her class and had derailed the same bogie twice before.

YNYS CROSSING – 79m 54c

In 1870 the Pennal folk asked for a siding, but it was thought that the traffic would not justify the cost of stopping trains. By 1874, the formation was sinking, but restrictions in the landowners' agreements prevented diversion or widening, so more ballast was piled on, and the engineer was instructed to 'keep an eye on matters there'. Twelve years later, the embankment was firm, but a depressed sluice at 80m 10c was flooding Penmaen-isaf land; a temporary bridge had to be constructed while the sluice was rebuilt, and the whole job cost £200.

In 1897, the pile bridge cattle creep needed re-timbering (at a cost of £69 1s 3d) after damage arising from a westerly gale in October 1896, which drove water right across the line but did not wash away the formation. The Great Western renewed the timber cattle creep as a girder bridge in 1915.

A cattle loading ramp was constructed in 1934, and trains were stopped there by arrangement; this practice seems to have been discontinued after the end of the war.

In 1947, the culvert to the west of the crossing had to be renewed for £350.

Opened: 1934
Closed: c 1950

Working Instructions, 1943

Livestock Accommodation at Ynys Crossing between Dovey Junction and Aberdovey—79m. 54ch.

Accommodation for the purpose of dealing with livestock is provided on the Up side of the line at Ynys Crossing, situate 50 chains on the Aberdovey side of Dovey Junction.

When there is a sufficient margin the traffic can be loaded into or unloaded from Up and Down Coast Freight Trains at the site, and when such a course is practicable the trainmen must be informed by the stations at which the empty wagons for loading or loaded wagons for unloading are attached.

If it is not possible to deal with the traffic by the Freight Trains the empty or loaded wagons must be taken to and detached at Dovey Junction, from which point the vehicles may be propelled to the site, provided there is a brake van or suitable brake vehicle leading, in which the Guard must ride, keep a sharp lookout, be prepared to warn anyone on the line of the approach of the train and to hand signal the Driver. The engine must remain attached to the vehicles and after the work at the site has been completed, the train must return to Dovey Junction from which point the traffic will be worked forward.

The accommodation is under the control of the Dovey Junction Station Master, who will make all arrangements for dealing with the traffic, and also arrange with the Locomotive Department for the provision of engine power when necessary.

Stations forwarding traffic for unloading at the site must immediately wire Dovey Junction particulars of the traffic and time of despatch.

Left: Ynys Crossing. The cattle and sheep were driven 'on the hoof' to be penned in at the end of the lane on the left, and the vans were halted between the cattle grids for loading by portable ramp. 17th June 1992. *Right:* Culvert near Ynys. September 1967. *Author*

The straight run between Dovey Junction and Gogarth, looking in the up direction to Dovey Junction. To the left of the line (on the right seen by an approaching driver) was an illuminated sign acting as a reminder of the severe speed restriction commencing here. 14th June 1964. *Author*

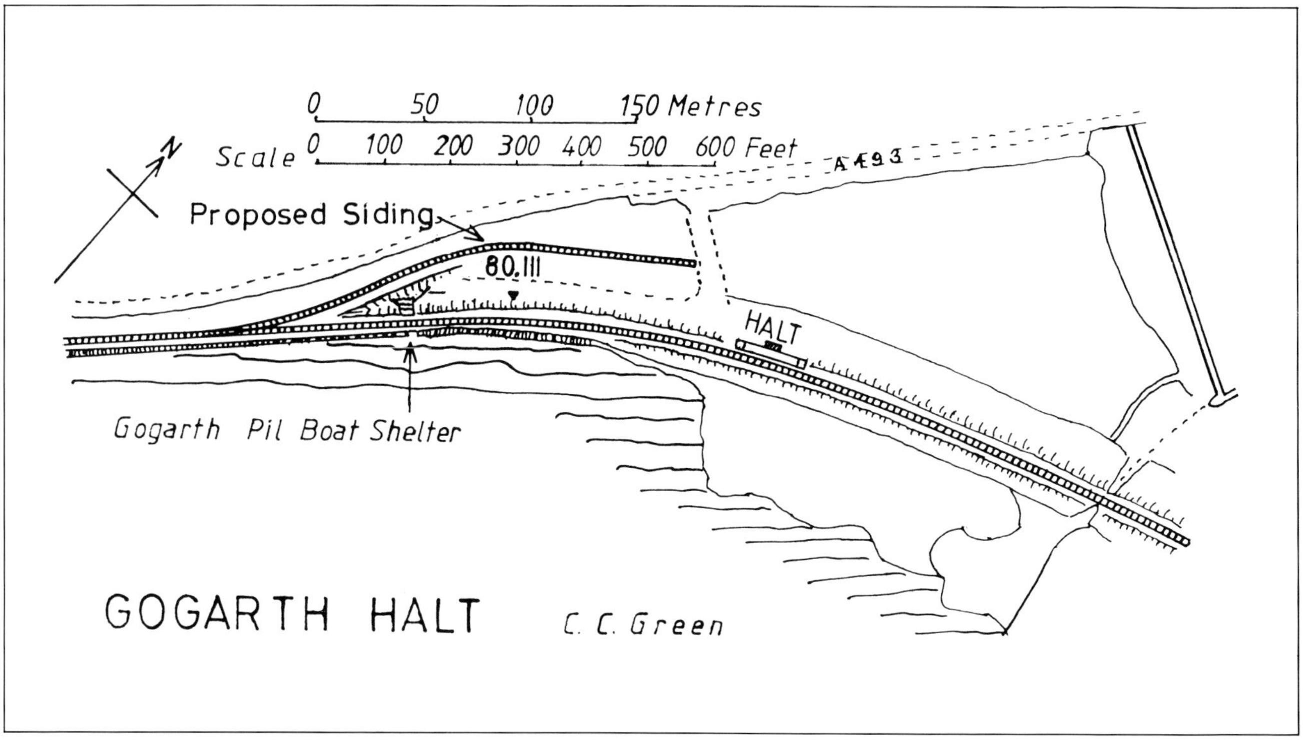

GOGARTH HALT – 80m 54c

Gogarth Halt, looking down, towards Aberdovey. 14th June 1964. *Author*

There was a sad and horrific accident here on 26th June 1893, long before there was a halt: 'John Owen of Tynycelyn was seen walking ahead of the Down coast goods 1.50 p.m. and the Engineman blew his whistle. Owen looked round and stepped clear of the train but afterwards walked right in front of the train when it was about twenty yards from him. He was knocked down and run over, his head being completely severed from his body'. The verdict was 'Accidentally killed by a Goods Train' and that 'the Company's servants had taken every care to avoid the Accident'.

In January 1900, a proposal for a station with a house and siding was costed at £370 for the works, plus £200 for the house, making £570 in all; the project was to be proceeded with if the inhabitants contributed £300, and if the land was given free. In 1901, they asked for the facility, but without making an offer.

The Towyn Council asked for a siding at Pil Gogarth in 1913, with promises of local contributions towards the cost. The following year, it was proposed that a siding for timber traffic (using the 1900 plan), with a 111 ft (three-carriage) platform and a waiting shed, costing £400 in all, should be provided, but this time the locals decided that they wanted the facility at Quay Ward instead.

In 1917 the council came back again, asking the company to put in the siding and the halt (which by then would have cost £788) with a generous offer of a £50 local contribution; the general manager commented: 'I do not think that the local authorities should expect us to put the work in hand until after the War'. However, in December he recommended laying just the siding using spare track (lifted from Bow Street) for loading an expected felling of timber.

A firm proposal to construct the facility by filling in the inlet known as Gogarth Pil Boat Shelter brought trouble from yet another direction. Letters of protest were received, claiming that:

> 'Before the railway had been built vessels and lighters used to lay on this beach to load Bark and Timber etc. A small Lime Kiln used to be, and still remains, above the beach and small vessels brought cargoes of Lime Stones to be discharged on this well-sheltered beach... We therefore beg the Railway Company to reconsider their decision and make the proposal without depriving the public of access to and from the River Dovey to the Main Road... Also the only available shelter for Fishermen and all using the river to run for in stormy weather to save their Lives, Boats and Gear from destruction. Therefore we appeal to you to protect our right.'

This quote was included in a letter addressed to the Harbour Department of the Board of Trade, dated 10th August 1918. It was then discovered that this letter had never been sent to the BOT, and Captain Morgan of Aberdovey (who had claimed to have sent it) refused to produce his copy signed by all the protesters,

Gogarth Halt. 14th June 1964. *Author*

Rear of Gogarth Halt, 14th June 1964. It was a remote and windswept place. Strangers were often surprised by the number of school-children who joined the train here, even in the 1960s and 1970s. *Author*

Gogarth Halt, down end. 14th June 1964. *Author*

claiming that it was immaterial whether it had been signed by fifty persons (as alleged) or by ten. The last word came from Mr. Haydn Jones, who wrote: 'It is monstrous that a man like Morgan should be able, by trumping up a trivial case like this, to block a great public convenience'. So, in December the Board voted for obtaining the necessary powers, but nothing came of it.

It was the Great Western who, in 1923, actually built a 99 ft platform with a waiting shed, costing £386.

During the gales and floods of 28th and 29th October 1927, which did so much damage along both sides of the Dovey, a motor boat weighing about ten tons was deposited across the line, and an engine and crane had to be sent to lift it clear.

The reason given for British Rail's closure of Gogarth and Abertafol was that both were in a dangerous condition, and that it would have cost £8,000 to repair each.

Gogarth Halt, looking up. 14th June 1964.
Author

The waterway left for Captain Morgan's Gogarth Pil boat shelter. 14th June 1964.
Author

No. 1 (FRONGOCH) TUNNEL – 81m 11c
Length: 199$\frac{3}{4}$ yards
A report of a slip discovered here in 1876 comments that of the 1,150 yards of tunnels, only 600 yards were then partly lined. It was the least troublesome of the four tunnels, and the facings and linings were upgraded as accidents in the others focused attention on the advisability of carrying out preventative work.

FRONGOCH QUARRY – 81m 22c
This started as a slate quarry belonging to the Ynys-y-maengwyn Estate, whose spoil tips were later quarried for road works. This location was the starting point of Hen Ffordd Corbet (Corbet's Old Road), the remains of which can be seen hacked out of the rock around the promontories all the way to Aberdovey. It was constructed about 1808, and was also used by the pannier ponies to carry copper ore from Pant Eidal. It was used by the horsemen of the Royal Mail, too. The road was rather near to the water's edge, and the track surfacing was always being washed away. Victorian guide book writers added it to their long list of spurious 'Roman Roads'.

The east or up portal of No. 1 (Frongoch) tunnel. 14th June 1964. *Author*

Detail of the east portal of No. 1 (Frongoch) tunnel. 14th June 1964. *Author*

The west portal of No. 1 (Frongoch) tunnel, looking along the bridge which carried the line above the Frongoch Quarry tramway. 14th June 1964. *Author*

Frongoch Quarry tramway bridge, which also serves as a floodway. 14th June 1964. *Author*

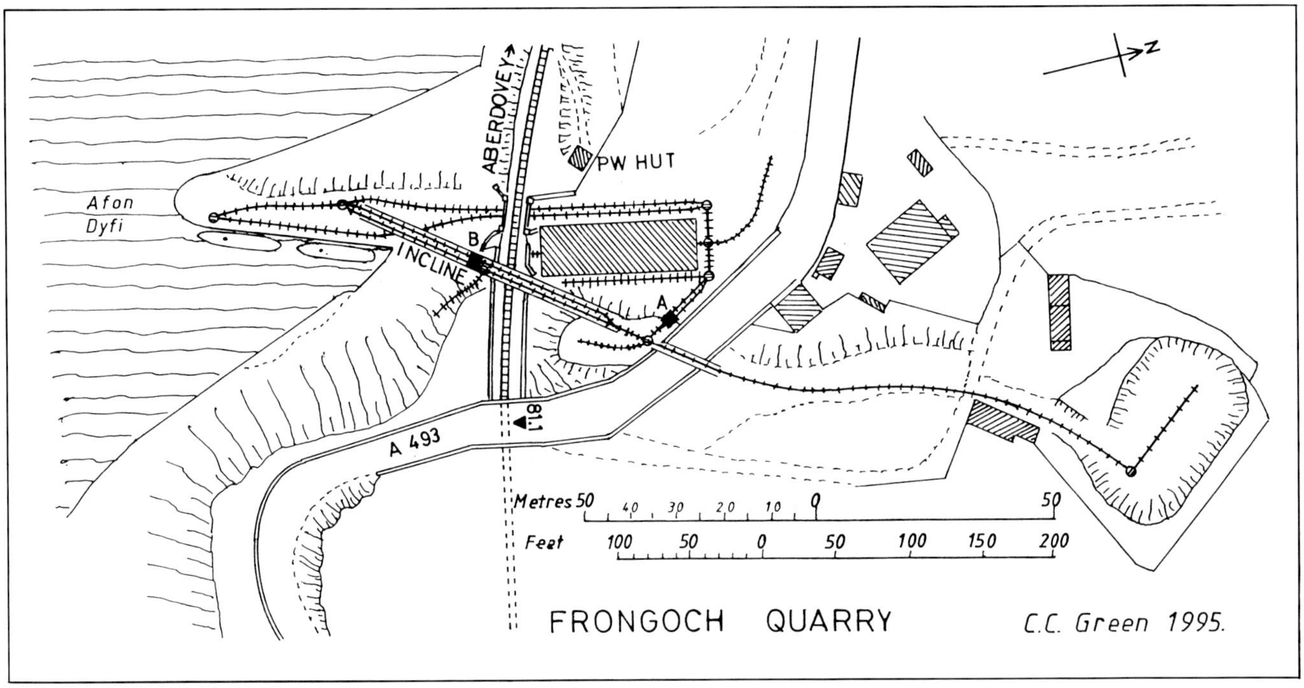

Conjectural plan showing (at A) the winding drum and trestle incline probably used for a short time, and (at B) the drum and incline needed if the bridge required under the 1865 Act had been built.

Frongoch Quarry tramway bridge and the outlook westwards to Aberdovey. 14th June 1964. *Author*

Frongoch Quarry PW hut and run-off for the ganger's motor trolley. 14th June 1964. *Author*

A clause in the Aberystwith and Welsh Coast Railway Act, 1865, required the construction of a bridge across a double line of tramway tracks leading from the lead mine to the jetty, and for sixteen feet of headroom under a bridge carrying another double line of tramway leading to the jetty. When, in 1873, Mr Brett asked for a siding to the quarry, the traffic manager reported that 'it would be a great danger because of its nearness to the tunnel', and 'the quarry not to be as remuneratively opened as he thinks'.

4–4–0 small Sharp Stewart on an up train approaching Frongoch Quarry on 7th July 1914. *H. W. Burman*

The dressing shed features in the background of this photo of Mr. H. W. Burman with his 1914 Perry two-seater at Frongoch in 1919. *E. Burman*

Approaching No. 1 (Frongoch) tunnel, taken from an up train in June 1956. *Author*

Frongoch Quarry – the remains of the former jetty, shown on the plan on page 38. September 1967. *Author*

Pant Eidal tideway embankment, near the 81.33 milepost, looking towards Dovey Junction with the road bridge across Nant Eidal on the left. 14th June 1964. *Author*

Pant Eidal tideway, looking west and showing the area behind the embankment which regularly floods. September 1967. *Author*

Nant Eidal in September 1967. Formerly the bridge was simply two pairs of beams bolted together with a timber deck, easy to construct and easy to set on fire, as observed by the Bishop of Bangor. *Author*

The bridge over the route of the erstwhile low-level tramway was replaced in 1985.

No. 2 (MORFA BACH) TUNNEL – 82m 7c
Length: 219 yards
On 10th July 1876, a block of stone weighing about two tons fell out of the roof, and was hit by the No. 1 up goods due at Machynlleth at 11.30 a.m. The engine and tender were thrown off the line, and eight loaded slate trucks mounted them, completely blocking the tunnel up to the roof. The crew were, luckily, only slightly injured. Three wagons were totally destroyed, and four required repairs, whilst damage to the track was costed at £2 16s 4d.

Another pretty section of the line, looking up from the 82 milepost. The gap in the wall is yet another floodway, seen in detail below. 14th June 1964. *Author*

Floodway bridge at 81.37¾ miles. 14th June 1964. *Author*

The east (up) portal of No. 2 (Morfa Bach) tunnel. 14th June 1964. *Author*

Abertafol tideway, looking towards the west end of No. 2 (Morfa Bach) tunnel. 14th June 1964. *Author*

Abertafol tideway. 14th June 1964. *Author*

ABERTAFOL – 82m 79c

Abertafol, looking down from the top of No. 2 (Morfa Bach) tunnel. 14th June 1964. *Author*

Abertafol, the ganger's house built from timber salvaged from Barmouth Viaduct. 14th June 1964. *Author*

Another view of the ganger's house and halt, looking towards Aberdovey. 14th June 1964. ***Author***

In 1875 a Mr. Holroyd Smith, who was building a new house (destined to be opened as a young ladies' school) requested that a 'flag station' should be opened here. The general manager favoured setting up nearer to Pennal at Gogarth, but if Mr. Holroyd would reimburse all expenses including a (telegraph) wire between both stations, he might have his 'flag station' at Abertafol. Of course, Mr. Holroyd declined.

It was decided in 1887 that the old cottage near Penhelig should be replaced by a more centrally-sited ganger's house which could be made from old timbers from Barmouth viaduct for only £50, and for which the ganger would pay a rent of 2/- per week.

In 1923, the Great Western rebuilt the bridge leading into the inlet behind the line for £429.

Finally, in 1935, the halt was built, comprising a platform (only 75 feet long) and a waiting shelter, for the sum of £135. Here, Frank and Evelyn Hemming once decided that walking back to Aberdovey would make them even more tired, so they waited for the train, and took two tenpenny single tickets. The guard commented: 'That's tenpence the company is out of pocket; it costs half a crown in brake shoes and coal to stop and start the train'.

Opened: 18th March 1935
Closed: 14th May 1984

The ganger's house and halt, seen from the public stairs leading down from the roadway above. 14th June 1964. ***Author***

Abertafol Halt, looking in the down direction towards Aberdovey. 14th June 1964. *Author*

At the head of the public footpath a finger post beckoned passengers from the public roadway. 14th June 1964. *Author*

An up train from Pwllheli headed by a 45XX 2–6–2 tank, piloted by a GW rebuild of a Jones 0–6–0, passing Abertafol and about to enter No. 2 tunnel c.1935. The first vehicle was a Cambrian milk van, the third a Cambrian bogie third. *G. H. W. Clifford*

Abertafol Halt and inlet could be seen from the road above (by hanging over a bit!). 14th June 1964. *Author*

Coed-y-gofer floodway, looking up the estuary towards Dovey Junction. *Author*

Trefri, the private road bridge to the house, looking in the up direction. 14th June 1964. *Author*

Trefri floodway bridge, looking up towards Dovey Junction. 14th June 1964. *Author*

Trefri floodway. 14th June 1964. *Author*

Looking up towards Trefri, showing traces of Hen Ffordd Corbet (incorrectly captioned 'Roman Road' by the romantic, but historically inaccurate, manufacturer of the card). *Courtesy E. W. Hannan*

GWR 'Barnum' 2–4–0 on a train of clerestory coaches, approaching Penhelig, with Trefri in the distance, c.1924. *H. W. Burman*

Section of old and renewed embankment walling, looking east to Trefri on 29th July 1912. *H. W. Burman*

An up train headed by 'Barnum' 2–4–0 No. 3217 going away towards Trefri on 12th August 1935, and giving a sense of scale of the embankment required along the Deviation route beside the Dovey Estuary. *H. F. Wheeller*

Picnic Island, looking west towards Aberdovey, with Hen Ffordd Corbet cut round above sea level and No. 3 (Penhelig) tunnel beyond, c.1930. *Courtesy E. W. Hannan*

Picnic Island bridge, looking west on 14th June 1964. *Author*

Looking east towards Trefri House from Picnic Island bridge. 14th June 1964. *Author*

Looking towards Aberdovey from Picnic Island bridge on 14th June 1964. The ledge of Corbet's Old Road is visible at the foot of the railway embankment. *Author*

Sharp Stewart 2–4–0 No. 43 returning light engine to Machynlleth, east of Penhelig on 4th July 1913. *H. W. Burman*

GWR 0–6–0 Collett goods No. 2256 on an up train approaching Picnic Island on 4th August 1955. *G. H. W. Clifford*

No. 3 (PENHELIG) TUNNEL – 83m 73c
Length: 191 yards
This was the first tunnel to give trouble, and was found to be 'crushing for several yards' in January 1867. On 20th December 1867, L&NWR Wagon No. 10918 (loaded with stone) broke an axle while in the tunnel causing 'an accident to one of our trains'.

On 29th July 1884, Ganger Woosnam was found lying dead between the rails inside the tunnel; it was presumed that he had been run down by the last goods from Barmouth, which had passed through at about 10.40 p.m. He had been walking home, as it was recorded that a dilapidated house between Nos. 2 and 3 tunnels had been repaired in 1870 for about £10 'so that a platelayer could live there and have a more careful supervision of the works of this particular [No. 3] tunnel'.

Despite having received attention during the additional lining work carried out in all the tunnels during 1889, No. 3 required further repair in 1904, at which time a section collapsed as the restoration work was starting, on Monday 11th January. The old, unstable brick arching had fallen in with a quantity of rock; nevertheless, a 'goods-only' service was maintained by propelling trains (made up with empties to more than the tunnel's length) in at one end, and pulling them out by means of a second engine waiting at the other end. Passenger arrangements were suspended from the Wednesday to the Friday. The engineer's report ran quaintly thus:

> 'The pulling down of the brick arch on Wednesday night exposed some timbers which must have been put in when the tunnel was first constructed some thirty five years ago to strut rock that was likely to fall, and I was very much afraid that these would give way and cause a serious fall, but I was agreeably disappointed in this.'

No. 3 (Penhelig) tunnel, east portal, on 14th June 1964. *Author*

No. 3 (Penhelig) tunnel, west (or down end) portal on 14th June 1955. This view was taken from the end of the platform at Penhelig Halt (hence the handrail on the left) and gives an appreciation of the closeness of the platform, road underbridge (No. 16) and the tunnel mouth. *Author*

Penhelig Road (No. 16) bridge, south elevation, on 14th June 1964. *Author*

Penhelig harbour and the newly-cut railway c.1868. The Dovey viaduct would have curved in across the vacant ground adjacent to Bridge No. 16 in the foreground – land later used to build Penhelig Terrace (see plan on page 311). The railway embankment here cut across the inlet and reduced the size of Penhelig harbour. Aberdovey harbour lies around the headland. The larger ship was the schooner *Dovey Packet*, built at Aberdovey by Roger Lewis in 1845. The sloop was the *Anna Maria*, built at Derwenlas in 1816, lengthened in 1855 and lost with all hands on Margate Sands in November 1881.

Cty. Mrs. C. F. Ellis

PENHELIG HALT

– 84m 08c

Penhelig, viewed from above Deviation No. 3 tunnel across (in order) No. 16 bridge, Penhelig Halt, No. 17 bridge to the mouth of No. 4 tunnel. The rear of Penhelig Terrace now closely bounds the railway on the seaward side. (c.1938?) ***Pope/Parkhouse Archive***

Opened: 8th May 1933

Miss Buddug Pughe, a talented writer and artist, has left a poignant account of what it was like to live in a small, quiet location, across which a contractor was making a railway:

> 'The next event I remember is the coming of the Railway. People were much disturbed by this. We children listened to the talk of our elders, mostly servants, and grew more terrified every day. The operations going on preparatory to its arrival were tremendous and upheaving. The solid rock was blasted with shattering noises; fragments of rock were then hurled into our dear little cove, completely blocking it up until our house grew darker each week as the hideous embankment grew higher and higher. The terrific monster for whom all this was done – what was he like? A great black iron animal with one monstrous nostril which belched out smoke and breath, whose mouth was behind its head, which ate coal and had no legs but claws that tore the ground. I did not know that he had to keep to his rails and so I was afraid that he would dash into our house and crush it, banging down trees and frightening the fairies and the birds. When one saw him come snorting out of one black hole one felt as though he must be going to the devil in hell with his train of boxes in which people sat. I do not remember going into the station or into the train until years afterwards: the twelfth child cannot go many jaunts'.

There was always an undercurrent of feeling that the main station at Aberdovey had been built too far to the west, and that some facility ought to be built nearer to the houses. The site of the station was linked to its history – it was sited where the harbour line joined the Deviation. The first call for an additional station was made in 1870, when Mr. C. A. Thruston asked for a flag station by Copper Hill Street; the committee magnanimously assented, provided that the gentleman gave the land free, and erected a house for the platelayer in charge of the siding and signals.

In 1899, the Reverend John Williams wanted to reclaim more of the foreshore in order to build salt

GWR 0–6–0 Collett Goods No. 2289 bringing the down Cambrian Coast Express out of No. 3 tunnel and into Penhelig Halt in June 1956. *Author*

Penhelig Halt, looking towards Aberdovey, on 14th June 1965. *Author*

Penhelig Halt, showing the ticket office with waiting room beyond, on 14th June 1965. *Author*

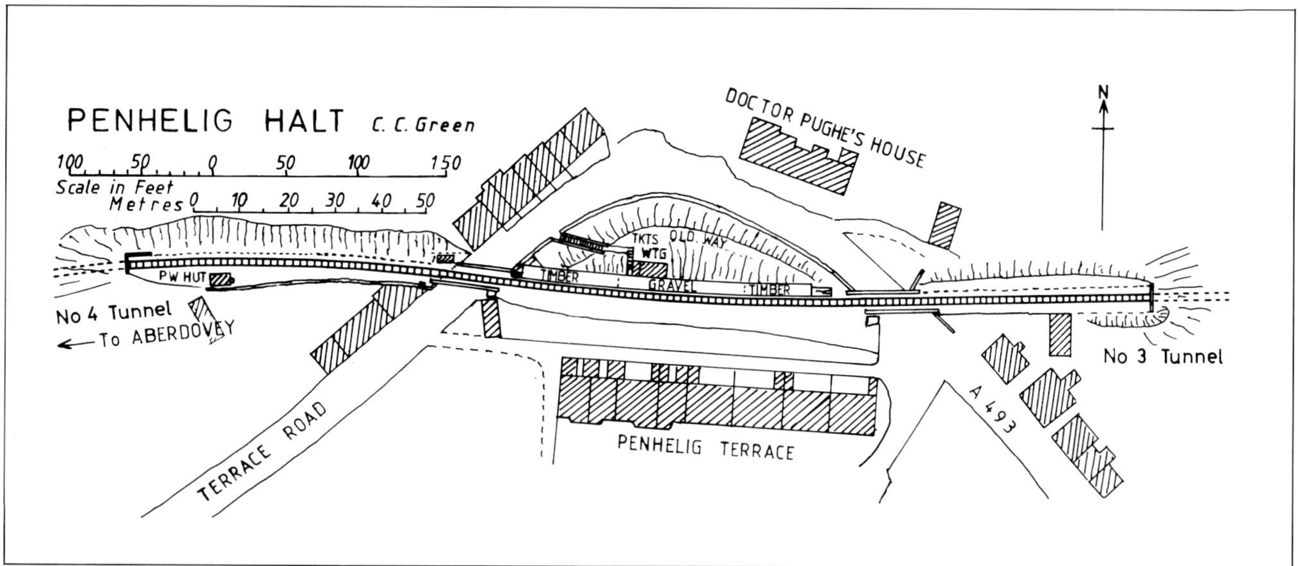

water baths, and he asked for the services of the Cambrian engineer, Mr. A. J. Collin. He had recommended that an engineer accustomed to river work should advise his company, as he himself was not able. Between 1902 and 1906, it was evident that there had been some bungling over land acquisition, both behind the Penhelig Arms and in the matter of what the Vicar was claiming to be old Glebe land. The company allowed the Ecclesiastical Commissioners to buy back most of it for £25, and retained only the strip that was necessary for the railway.

During 1905, the company gave a donation to Captain Enoch Lewis's scheme for creating a 'Harbour of Refuge' for fishing boats near Penhelig.

In 1909 the Cambrian gave a necessary strip of land (measuring 117 sq. yds) so that the road could be widened, whilst the local council took over the drainage, and built a new retaining wall.

When, in 1932, the Great Western assented to the proposal for a second station, the site once proposed, by Copper Hill Street, was chosen. However, an outcry from the inhabitants led to a rethink, and the present halt east of No. 4 tunnel was opened on 8th May 1933, comprising a 200 ft-long platform, and a waiting shed with a ticket office. The cost was around £300. The ticket office was closed during the Second World War, and Penhelig survives today as an unstaffed halt. There may have been a siding on the down (seaward) side for the first few years, but no documentary evidence has yet come to light.

In 1938, goods and parcels were collected and delivered free of charge within a one-mile radius by cartage service or by porter.

The south face of the original Piercy underdeck bridge (No. 17) spanning Terrace Road in Penhelig. *G. H. W. Clifford*

The south face of the rebuilt Terrace Road bridge on 14th June 1965. *Author*

Penhelig Halt, with passengers waiting for an up train on 28th July 1955.
H. F. Wheeller

Penhelig Halt, looking in the up direction from No. 4 tunnel across No. 17 bridge on 14th June 1965. *Author*

The north face of Penhelig Road (No. 17) bridge on 14th June 1965. Optimistically, the bridge abutment had been made wide enough for a double-track bridge, though the single-bore tunnels were built to a very tight loading gauge. *Author*

No. 4 (CRAIG-Y-DON, ABERDOVEY, OR COPPER HILL STREET) TUNNEL – 84m 14c
Length: 533 yds
This tunnel was originally to have been built as part of Railway No. 2, at the end of the acute curve leading the line off the Dovey viaduct. Piercy had later tried to avoid its construction by that impudent scheme, the Mindovey Railway, which would have carried the line straight out of No. 3 tunnel and directly along the sea front – he had, of course, surveyed the rock formation in great detail, and was aware of the problems. A good local quarry and rock man, Tom Ellis Maybank, was employed to oversee the work on all four tunnels which, to save expense, were ordered to be tight to width and to a height of only thirteen feet from rail table.

In December 1868, the first fall was reported at the east end. Later, the platelayers thought that there was some subsidence (October 1869), but this was brushed aside as being a false alarm; however, the engineer did learn that it had fallen in during construction 'by the little cottage at the bottom of Bryndovey's garden'.

No. 4 (Craig-y-don) tunnel, east portal, on 30th September 1991. The GWR would not have countenanced weed-infested track. *Author*

The east or up portal of No. 4 (Craig-y-don) tunnel, on 14th June 1964, showing the platelayers hut. The later-tipped material may be on the site of the tunnel maintenance siding. *Author*

On 26th January 1889 George Owen reported that, at the Aberdovey end, the tunnel had not been lined out, that it was insecure, and that he had ordered the work of stone-walling and brick-arching as a matter of urgency. He noticed further movement, and had a travelling gauge fitted onto a wagon. On the morning of Friday, 13th of September, he reported:

> 'I observed that the Arch had still further flattened and found several fissures in the land above, showing that mischief was going on below. At about 4 pm the funnel of the Engine of a Goods Train brought large stones down on the boiler. I therefore deemed it advisable after passing all trains through that evening to stop the Traffic. They started to remove the fifteen feet of old roof and exposed a construction shaft which had been timbered over and tons of shale and loose soil fell out into the tunnel and had to be got away and for some days it fell out as soon as it was being removed.
>
> 'The lining of this Tunnel is now completed partly with the old Arching of stone and partly with the new Arching of brick. The Rails through No. 4 Tunnel although of Steel and laid in the spring of 1878, have, owing to the continued humid state of the atmosphere, become so worn and thin on the web that the flanges of the wheels strike the chairs.'

He asked for half-a-mile of bullheaded rail, and stated that the old rails could be taken out, turned over (being therefore doubleheaded), and re-used in other portions of the line; Mr. Owen concluded: 'I am glad to be able to report that the work was carried out without the slightest injury to any of the men employed'. He was given authority to relay in 80 lb steel bullhead rail.

A further report indicated that, by January 1892, about twenty-seven feet of old arching in the centre of the tunnel needed replacement urgently, and that he had already put the work in hand. By 31st October of that year, the steel rails put down in 1889 were so badly rusted that they weighed only 61 lbs to the yard, and so worn and deeply grooved into the chairs that the latter were again being broken through, being struck by the wheel flanges; so, once more the track through No. 4 was totally replaced.

After that, there was no more trouble, and modern engineering skills keep it that way. The track bed was lowered in 1950 to allow modern stock to pass through without the necessity of reducing speed.

Working Instructions

Generally in Cambrian days, two locos coupled together were not permitted.

There was an overall speed limit of thirty m.p.h. (twenty-five by 1947), though speeds through Nos. 3 and 4 tunnels were restricted to five m.p.h. Across the Dovey bridge, speed was restricted to twenty m.p.h. (latterly fifteen).

Earlier passenger stock had bars screwed to all windows, and there were always provision for locking the carriage doors before entering the Deviation and for unlocking them on leaving it.

Working Instructions, 1943

Damage to Carriage Doors in Tunnels, Dovey Junction-Aberdovey Section:

> 'All doors on the off side of Down passenger trains must be locked before the train leaves Machynlleth or Dovey Junction. The Guard must satisfy himself that this is done and arrange for passengers for Gogarth, Abertafol or Penhelig Halts to travel in the vehicle nearest that in which the Guard rides. On arrival at the Halts the Guard must unlock all necessary doors to enable passengers to detrain or entrain and afterwards relock the doors.
>
> 'All doors on the offside must be unlocked by the Guard at Aberdovey or as and when convenient after passing Aberdovey'.
>
> 'The staff at stations should request passengers for the halts to travel in compartments near the Guard's compartment'.

Corresponding instructions applied in the opposite direction.

No. 4 (Craig-y-don) tunnel, west portal, on 14th June 1964. *Author*

ABERDOVEY

(now ABERDYFI) – 84m 74c to 85m 10c

The line behind the town, looking east and showing the down distant signal for Aberdovey and west portal of No. 4 (Craig-y-don) tunnel in 1925. The bridge over Copper Hill Street can be seen above the bushes in the foreground. *H. W. Burman*

Station at 85m 02c Signal Box at 85m 02c Opened: 24th October 1863 Connected: 14th August 1867

The name 'Aberdovey' can be translated as 'At the Mouth of the Dark River'; other opinions maintain that it is the 'Calm' or 'Pleasant River'.

When the section between Aberdovey harbour and Llwyngwril first opened in 1865, the station was merely a timber shed at the point where the line levelled out after climbing up from the beach; Savin's workshops, engine shed and yard lay between the line and the road, where sidings and buildings were later situated. There was a staff of five men.

In January 1867, Savin asked for a lease of the ground occupied by his workshops, and this may have been granted for a short term. By 14th August, the line had been connected through from Dovey Junction, and traffic from the Cambrian main line commenced on that day.

On 18th December 1868, the Board agreed to sell to Savin's inspector (in bankruptcy) the site for his proposed hotel.

Whilst a certain amount of initiative was required of the more senior staff, a line was drawn at the alteration of traffic arrangements without due reference to the appropriate bodies. The station master was admonished by the committee on 28th May 1869 for arranging for trains to stop at Clynin (about one mile south of Llwyngwril) and at other places for the convenience of favoured passengers.

On 24th November 1869, the engineer reported the need to spend £60 on extending the old engine shed as storage for superphosphate of manures (Peruvian dried guano), brought in by the Portmadoc schooners and other similar small sailing vessels.

By 1870, the water supply at Machynlleth was proving unreliable during the summer months, and expenditure of £54 8s 6d was authorised to enable engines to top up at Aberdovey. On 13th October, the new supply was reported to be 'of the greatest utility'.

A new, brick-built station was provided at Aberdovey in 1872 at a cost of £1,200, this being part of the general replacement of Savin's ramshackle provisions all along the coast. As an economy, the committee had withdrawn the provision of a gentlemen's waiting room, but had allowed an approach road for £140. A level crossing house was also provided at Trefeddian, for £140. The new station was to be lit by gas, as suggested by Mr. Collingwood (the owner of the new gas works).

The Liquidator of Savin's Aberdovey Hotel venture asked for the company's assistance, and the solicitor

GWR 0–6–0 Dean Goods on an up passenger train on the ascending curve leading off behind the town. c.1925. *H. W. Burman*

was instructed to examine the bank and hotel contracts, and to circulate the information to the company's larger shareholders.

Mr. Collingwood asked, in 1875, if the company would allow him to lay a gas main to the township alongside the line. This was granted 'on sufferance and under the supervision of the Company's Engineer'.

From 1877, the water supply for the tank was arranged to be taken from a stream on the estate of Mr. Edward Morgan (a solicitor, of Machynlleth) at an annual cost of £2 10s 0d.

The first request for better accommodation at the station was received in 1878, when the traffic manager asked for a 50% extension to the manure warehouse, and proposed to charge a storage rent of 6d per ton. The manure was then coming from Ireland, and there were 900 tons inside the existing warehouse and 300 tons stacked outside: 'The Manure is afterwards sold by agents and sent all over the Company's Line and Traffic has quite outgrown the capacity of the shed'.

In 1880, the Board instructed the engineer to have new workshops erected, and approved his estimate of £184 2s 10d, using materials lying at Ynyslas; the original estimate using new materials had been £558 18s 0d. On 22nd December, the shops were reported as 'working extremely well'. The objective was to save the running of rolling stock all the way to Oswestry for repairs and, with three men and one boy, the workshop could repair one carriage and three or four wagons at a time. There was also a small sleeper creosoting plant which might have been a relic from Savin's yard, but it was not adequate for all requirements.

Cutting and houses behind Aberdovey, west of Copper Hill Street bridge, looking towards Penhelig in 1961. The photo was taken from a location approximately beside the locomotive tender in the photo above. *Author*

The general manager reported that a hundred and twenty Jesuits were to occupy the closed hotel, 'and it is probable that the Traffic of this Town will be very much increased'.

A Mr. Tomlin of Warwick wished to erect a flour mill, and Mr. Humphreys-Owen and the solicitor were instructed to look into the company's right so to use the land. Their report was favourable, and Mr. Tomlin proceeded with his building work.

By 1882 it had been realised that a considerable amount of time in the workshop was being lost in the winter because work could not commence before daylight, and had to cease at dusk. The engineer therefore proposed to spend £6 5s 10d on gas lighting, 'which could be recouped by the additional time that

A 4–4–0 'Earl' class on an up passenger, leaving Aberdovey to pass behind the town on 28th July 1955. On the left are the houses of Bodfor Terrace, beyond which the harbour branch can be seen curving down parallel to the main line. *H. F. Wheeller*

would be kept'. He was also given authority to erect a shed at Llanfyllin for the cement that was being shipped round to Aberdovey.

In 1883, there was much debate about providing a 'Cover for Mr. Tomlin's Trucks'. At the end, it was suggested that the company would pay half the cost of £125 so long as Mr. Tomlin provided the labour for the erection of the structure, and undertook to send all his traffic along those routes most favourable to the company.

In 1884, Mr. Tomlin asked for a siding to be laid down out of the company's empty wagon storage siding to a new warehouse he proposed to erect at the end of his mill. He laid it in with his own labour to the engineer's satisfaction, and paid 20 shillings per annum for the use of the company's land, and a proportion of the cost of the interlocking apparatus in the signal box.

The manure shed had become 'quite dangerous' by this time, and needed £150 spending on it; however, the necessary repairs were deferred. By 1885, the cost of repairing the dilapidated shed had risen to £200, whilst a new one would have cost £268 – no positive decision was recorded on the matter.

In June 1885, a new siding for the discharge of petroleum casks (paraffin) was needed, at a cost of £99 14s 4d. The project was approved on 26th October, but at an outlay of £62 19s 8d, using old unsaleable flat-bottomed rail. The reason given for the necessity of this siding was to avoid delays in passenger services, so there must have been some unloading of this early product of Texas from wagons standing at the station platforms.

The secretary was instructed to arrange a contract for 10,000 'Creosoted Sleepers' at a suitable price in 1886, and he was also authorised to treat for the sale of a creosoting plant (the purchase of such by the company). On 24th January 1887, the engineer described the sleeper creosoting plant erected by the timber merchants R. & S. Williams:

'One New Wrot Iron Tank fifty feet long and six feet wide by five feet deep of $\frac{1}{4}$ inch Boiler Plate for containing Creosote.

'One second hand Cylinder fifty feet long by six feet in diameter of $\frac{1}{2}$ inch Boiler Plate with loose end and clamp for securing same complete – For putting sleepers in to be creosoted.

'One second hand spare piece of cylinder twelve feet long and two pieces of 5 inch Cast Iron Flange Pipe for lengthening the Cylinder if necessary.

'One engine complete on bedplate seven foot by seven foot. Vertical driving cylinder 16 inch with two fly wheels on 2 inch shaft with two sets of cog wheels to throw air pump or creosote pump out of gear. Makers John Tickle Providence Foundry, West Bromwich.

'One Vertical Boiler three feet in diameter six feet six inches high on frame and ash pan three feet four inches square by nine inches high with fire bars, pipes, guage (sic) glass, injector etc. complete and fixed ready for work.

'Maker Robey & Co Engineers, Lincoln, No. 6300.

'Sundry tools and spare pipes and ironwork for repairs in case of emergency.

'This machinery is covered by a wooden shed and is in working order. I estimate the value of same at £350.'

The Committee authorised an offer of £200 for the plant, and this was accepted.

Despite the fact that horses and carriages had to be ridden or driven the four miles to Towyn for loading onto trains, the committee refused to sanction £71 18s 8d for a loading dock at Aberdovey.

An incident involving the parting and subsequent collision of a train at Aberdovey in 1887 was reported thus:

'On 29th November 1887 as the 6.45 a.m. ex Machynlleth Down Mail drawn by Two Engines left No. 4 Tunnel a screw coupling failed on BRYNMALLY COAL wagon No. 45 and the train divided. As it pulled up in the loop the rest of the train, 21 wagons and a van arrived too. One wagon was thrown off the rails.'

The traffic manager reported:

'The drawbar couplings of the Brynmalley Company's Coal Wagons are of a very objectionable description and I have called the attention of the Great Western Company to the risks arising from their use.'

The engineer suggested on 27th January 1888 that savings could be made by making arrangements for the locomotive superintendent to have certain work carried out at Aberdovey.

Whilst the timber structures were cheaper to build than those of brick, they had certain disadvantages,

The Aberdovey station built in 1872, looking towards Dovey Junction c.1900.
Cty. M. E. M. Lloyd

2–4–0 No. 43 leaving Aberdovey with a local train consisting entirely of six-wheeled stock, on 14th July 1914. The line in the foreground was the Harbour branch.
H. W. Burman

most especially when it came to a fire. Many buildings were engulfed in flames at Aberdovey on Sunday, 3rd January 1889:

'Fire destroyed the entire range of timber buildings housing the Smithy, the Wagon Shops, the Creosote Works and the Manure Warehouse fanned by a violent gale. Fourteen old Deadbuffered Wagons and one Cattle Truck were also destroyed. The Manure Warehouse alone was not insured and was scheduled for reconstruction.'

On 21st October 1889, the construction of a down side waiting shed was authorised at the sum of £128 6s 10d. The high cost was explained by the necessity for piling to support it on the bad ground.

A tablet-locked siding to the Dysinni Gas Works was approved for installation in 1893 at their expense, and with special charges levied for services – terms which seemed to have put the gas company off the idea, as the siding was not put in.

In January 1895, a request was received that the company should build a more substantial station in a more convenient place, and that the coal wharf should be removed from the beach. Consideration was deferred until the directors' annual inspection, and the removal of the coal wharf was refused because there was no other suitable site.

Stephenson 'Big Belpaire' 4–4–0 No. 97 leaving Aberdovey with the 9.20 a.m. up train on 5th August 1916.
H. W. Burman

Driver G. Parry and fireman J. Caffrey with 0–6–0 Sharp Stewart rebuilt goods No. 45 shunting at Aberdovey c.1920. Note the end of the water tank wagon on the left.
H. W. Burman

0–6–0 Dean Goods on an up goods leaving Aberdovey c.1930.
H. W. Burman

Stephenson 4–4–0 No. 32, renumbered by the GWR as 1085, approaching Aberdovey down the gradient from Penhelig, with a down train c.1924.
H. W. Burman

A request for a donation towards the formation of the Dolgelley Nursing Association was refused, although £5 was voted by the committee to the prize fund of the Aberdovey Golf Club, which was increased in May by the Board to a figure not exceeding seven guineas (£7 7s 0d) for an inscribed Challenge Cup, to be renewed as necessary as the winner for two consecutive years was entitled to keep it.

Also in May 1895, the committee approved an arrangement whereby Mr. Chidlaw Roberts might transfer his timber yard from Towyn to a site on company land at Aberdovey. At the same time, they instructed the engineer to report on the cost of a new creosoting plant.

On 16th July 1895, Porter J. R. Jones was making his way in order to ascertain whether or not the driver of the 10.25 ex-Machynlleth goods had possession of the tablet. But, instead of walking along the platform as he had been instructed to do by the station master, he chose to step across the buffers of wagons standing at the up platform, and jumped down onto the track just as the engine was passing on the down line. He was run over, and killed instantly. The jury added the comment that, while they did not attribute the accident to the lack of a footbridge across the line, they considered that there should be one.

In January 1896, the engineer reported the likely cost of new creosoting plant consisting of a 60 ft × 6 ft cylinder with door and carriages, crab-winch, steam engine and boiler with double acting pump from Messrs Finch & Co of Chepstow to be £1,250 plus £250 for foundations and a shed; the committee deferred con-

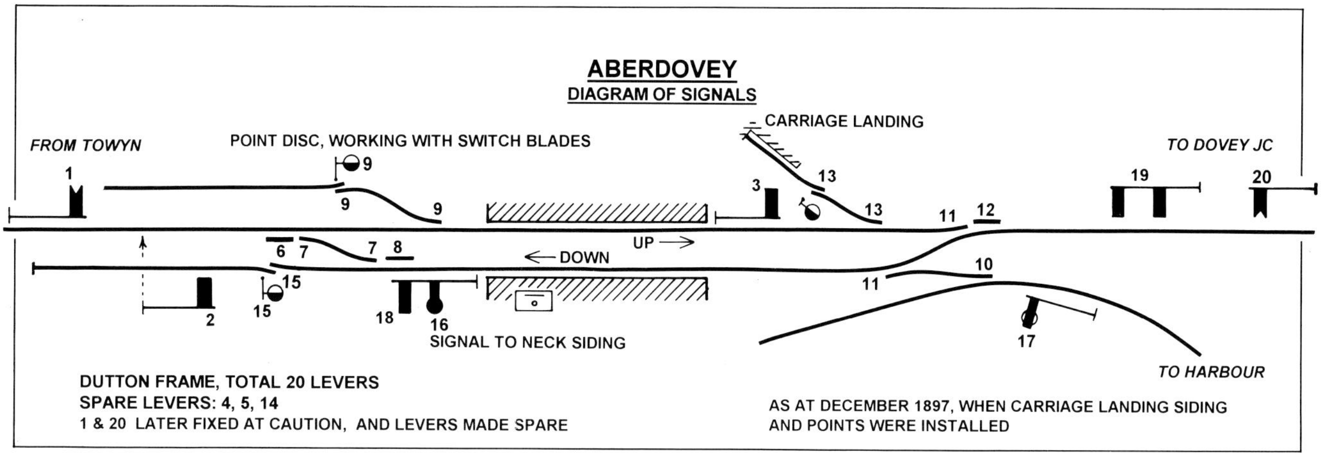

Approach to Aberdovey station, looking towards Towyn on 28th July 1935. The short carriage landing siding built in December 1897, with its own loading gauge, can be seen on the right. The disc signal working with 13 points can also be seen between the siding and the up loop line.
H. F. Wheeller

'Barnum' 2–4–0 No. 3213 on an up train waiting to leave Aberdovey c.1930.
Cty. R. S. Carpenter

sideration. It appears from this that the plant installed with the insurance money after the 1889 fire must have been a poor job.

On 26th February 1897 yet another memorial for a 'more commodious station' was considered, and this one reminded the directors of a promise they had given in 1893 which had included the removal of the coal wharves from the beach. The matter came up again on 21st September when 'The Golf Links etc being completed will lead to a large addition to the residents', but 'The Council feel that the position and present condition of the Railway Station must act prejudicially to the development of the place.' However, the thought of all those golfers coming to Aberdovey did cause the committee to approve the construction of the long-overdue horse and carriage dock for £71, plus £10 for fencing.

Mr. Abraham Williams had, under Savin's regime, been allowed to build himself Aberdovey House on a site beyond Tomlin's mill: 'There is no agreement, nor does he pay rent. He has rendered the Company considerable service from time to time'. An agreement was argued out by 27th October whereby he was permitted to acquire his site for £343 5s 0d on similar terms to those conceded to Mr. James Tomlin for the construction of his mill. It was also proposed: 'the old sheds now used as Signal Stores to be taken down and re-erected at Mr. Williams' cost on a site to be approved nearer the station.'

In December, a proposal for Messrs. Dempsey & Co (who were importers of large amounts of timber through Aberdovey) to take over the site occupied by Jones & Jones was considered. At the same time, the company discussed a scheme to put down its own creosoting plant, as the present machinery had become obsolete, and was incapable of creosoting the sleepers in a satisfactory manner (the new plant would cost between £1,800 and £2,000). Nevertheless, the idea was deferred, and the staff was left to carry on with the messy old manual equipment.

By the end of 1897, Tomlin had become insolvent. He had spent around £8,000 during the first few years of his venture but, despite having a local monopoly with

The waiting shed on the down platform. The boy doing his 'birdie' act for the camera is John Edginton.
Cty. John Edgington

the finest milling machinery of its day, the depression of 1893 had defeated him. At one time, he owed £10,000 to Ross T, Smith & Co. of Liverpool. He managed to make a composition with his creditors for 7s 6d in the pound during September 1895, and carried on working during the following year with little success and no credit. His impatient creditors then forced the sale of the mill for a miserable £1,600, although it had been valued at £7,885.

In 1899, yet another proposal for a new station was deferred.

Two bus drivers, Tomkins and Edwards, had annoyed passengers by quarrelling over who should take them and their luggage, and the general manager had reprimanded them both in 1899. Tomkins alleged that Edwards (who was the station master's brother) was being given undue preference. To ensure fairness, they were then allotted the first position in the yard on alternate weeks, but this move had failed, and both were banned from the station. Tomkins sued the company for loss of business, but lost his case, and the solicitor secured an injunction against his trespassing on company property.

In January 1903, the secretary brought up the case of Miss Evans and her ailing sister who, because of an alleged illness, had not been paying their rent. They were living in 'The Old House beyond the Station'.

Looking eastwards from Aberdovey platforms, with the carriage landing on the left. The boarded foot crossing at the end of the platforms was the only means for passengers to reach the down platform (on the right). Penrhos crossing beyond, was an occupation crossing. The carriage landing point was originally in tandem with the facing crossover; the GWR installed the non-overlapping layout shown here. The Harbour branch and wagon weighbridge house can be seen on the right. c.1950. *P. J. Garland*

'Small Prairie' No. 4560 about to leave with an up passenger on 26th July 1955. The illuminated indicator in front of the up starting signal acted as a reminder of the 25 mph speed restriction on the curves beyond. *H. F. Wheeller*

Aberdovey station, looking towards Dovey Junction, on 2nd August 1958. *J. J. Davis*

Their doctor would not issue a certificate and it was approved that an ejectment order should be obtained.

On 28th October 1903, the new station proposal was deferred yet again.

On 5th April 1906, the subject of a siding for the Dysinni Gas Company was brought up again, this time at a cost of £130; like its predecessor, the proposal came to nothing.

Trouble was being experienced at Aberdovey with the inadequate water supply, which came from a stream that dried up during the summer. Engines were having to run to Llwyngwril to fill up, and to take empty casks to bring back water for the steam crane at the harbour. It was reported:

> 'We endeavoured to come to terms with the [Towyn] Urban District Council but their demands were so exhorbitant, viz. 2s 6d per 1,000 gallons for the use of the Locomotives at Aberdovey and 7s 6d per 1,000 gallons for the use of the Steam Crane at the Wharf that we recommend that the present supply be continued.'

In 1907, there was an invitation for tenders for the supply of 20,000 creosoted sleepers, which suggests that the old works was inadequate, and incapable of fulfilling all the demands.

On 28th June 1910, the directors halted at Aberdovey on their annual inspection to admire the newly con-

BR Class 2 2–6–0 No. 78000 about to leave with a short up goods in 1961. *Author*

Left: The east end of the station building and porch, viewed from the yard, in April 1957. *Right:* The disused main entrance. April 1957. *Author*

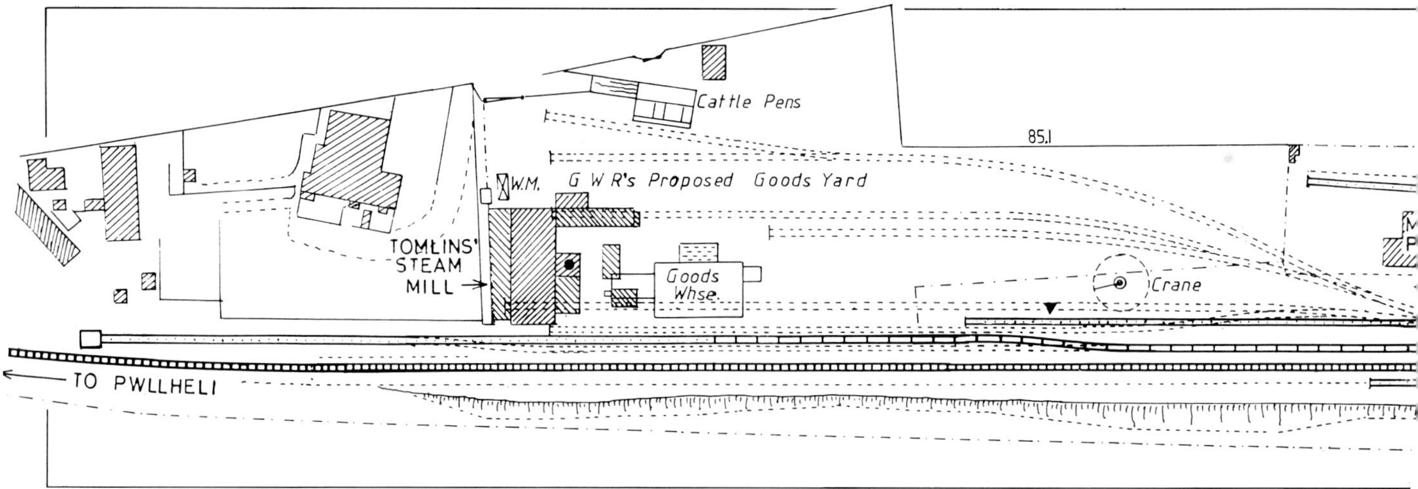

Aberdovey station on a very wet day in April 1957. *Author*

Under-canopy detail shown up by reflection off the wet platform. April 1957.

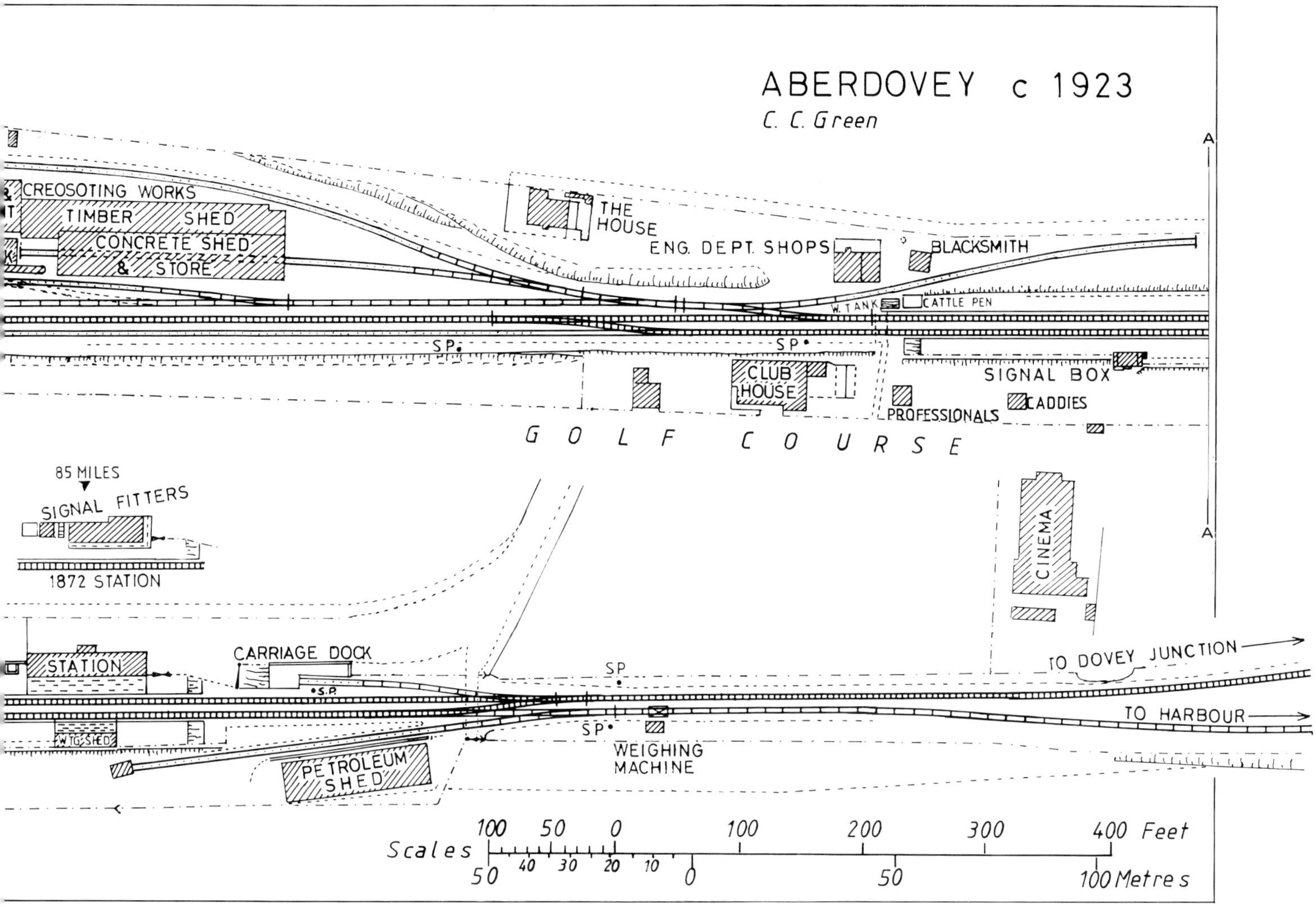
ABERDOVEY c 1923
C. C. Green
CREOSOTING WORKS
TIMBER SHED
CONCRETE SHED & STORE
THE HOUSE
ENG. DEPT. SHOPS
BLACKSMITH
W. TANK
CATTLE PEN
SP
SIGNAL BOX
CLUB HOUSE
PROFESSIONALS
CADDIES
GOLF COURSE
85 MILES
SIGNAL FITTERS
1872 STATION
CINEMA
STATION
CARRIAGE DOCK
S.P.
TO DOVEY JUNCTION
TO HARBOUR
WTG. SHED
PETROLEUM SHED
WEIGHING MACHINE
A
Scales
100 50 0 100 200 300 400 Feet
50 40 30 20 10 0 50 100 Metres

Author

The waiting shelter on the down platform was simple but substantial as it needed to be, for the wind sweeping off the sea across the dunes behind can be fierce indeed. April 1957.
Author

Looking north-west through the station, with the signal box on the left and the water tank at the far end of the up platform. Beyond lay the sidings serving the 'concrete store' shed. The down loop line extended as a shunting neck parallel to the single line for some distance – in practice this allowed a long down train to draw fully clear of the single line from Dovey Junction and an up train to pass. 1955/60. *J. H. Moss*

Right up to closure on 24th April 1968, the signal box at Aberdovey retained its Cambrian name-board, not replaced by the standard GWR product. Only a handful of signal boxes had this distinctive feature by the 1960s. 1955/60. *J. H. Moss*

structed station buildings, which had been brought from Pwllheli and re-erected brick by brick. The building time had been only eleven months from the approval date at a cost of £600. That year, the company had also sold its rights over Aberdovey Common to Towyn Urban District Council.

It was discovered that the value of sleepers held outside the works in 1914 was in excess of the quantity insured, and cover was increased from £1,000 to £2,300.

On 12th February 1915, Foreman Evans was travelling backwards on the step of the shunting engine, and was crushed between the engine and a wagon left so close to the points on the adjoining line as to be only seven inches away from the moving engine. He died the next day.

In 1920, Mr. E. L. Rowlands wished to form a syndicate for building twelve houses on the site of Tomlin's disused flour mill, and there was another proposal for the storage along the mill siding of Festiniog slate for the Ministry of Health's post-war housing schemes.

The signal box in 1961. It carried the bargeboards and finial which betrayed that it was supplied by Dutton and Co (opened 6th July 1891) and contained a 20-lever frame made by the same firm. *Author*

Water tank and cattle dock c.1950. The water tank was at the 'wrong' end of the up platform because it was intended to serve shunting engines, not the engines of through trains. The location of the small cattle pen was a reflection of the fact that the existence of the Harbour branch effectively split the provision of freight facilities at Aberdovey. Coal, bricks and the like were dealt with on the sea front. That would not do for cattle brought from local farms, nor would it have been proper to drive them up the station approach road (which is how the vehicles to load at the carriage dock arrived). So cattle were brought along a pathway at the west end of the station (now the path to the golf club) and then driven up the platform ramp into the pens (hence the anti-slip treads on the platform ramp). It was a very narrow slope on which to have to handle cattle. Maintenance of the fire at this tank was the responsibility of the Traffic Department. *P. J. Garland*

On 1st December 1920, a public telephone for the station was approved. The rental was £5 per annum, and, because it was half-a-mile to the town, five hundred calls each year were expected.

It was noted in 1922 that the tablet instruments were in the office, and that there was room for them in the box. The signalmen were part-time, i.e. the cabin was not manned at night.

The wooden water tank was 14ft × 5ft 6 in × 4ft 4 in and was rated at 2,077 gallons, with a gravity water supply from Hillside (payable to E. Morgan, at £5).

The permanent way inspector's depot was demolished in 1923, and a new one set up at Barmouth. In 1925, another of Aberdovey's timber buildings was removed to Machynlleth; it has not been easy to establish just what was built between the station and the

The north-west end of the station, with the golf club house to the left and the 'concrete store' on the right. The very slender arm on the down starting signal characterised the Cambrian line. The 'to shunting neck' arm below was unique to the Cambrian. The circular end had two cut-out segments, which helped to reduce the resistance to the wind. 4th July 1955. *M. E. M. Lloyd*

The former concrete shed and store, latterly used for the overhaul and repainting of camp coaches. 18th July 1965. *Author*

site of the mill, but there does seem to have been a fair collection of sheds and shacks of every description.

On 25th July 1929, the serving of a Notice to Treat was authorised for the acquisition of one acre, three roods and thirty-two perches of land to allow the creation of more space around the station. This was the final development, and from this date the station remained largely unaltered.

On 5th August 1931, a 'Jones Goods' at the head of the 6.0 p.m. (approx.) ex-Dovey Junction derailed at the east end facing points (No. 11), which were part of a three-way point, and slewed across into the carriage dock. The points were repaired, but it was not until after the end of the Second World War that they were replaced by two separate switches.

There were two loading gauges over the running lines at the east end of the platforms (see photo on page 66). The one over the eastbound (up direction) line was set for the Deviation tunnels 1–4, whilst that over the down side was set for Great Western clearances for the Barmouth Junction to Ruabon section.

In 1938, goods were collected and delivered free by cartage service, as were the more distant parcels. Local parcels were delivered by a porter.

The Great Western had introduced camping coaches at various beauty spots around the system in 1934, including six on the Cambrian coast. By 1939, an eight-berth camp coach was resident at Aberdovey.

The cast iron columns carrying the verandah bore, in raised letters, 'J. MORRIS IRONFOUNDER

Detail of down starting and shunt signal and the standard Cambrian warning notice to trespassers (showing 'Cambrian Railways' blacked over). This photograph shows nicely the detail of how the shunt arm was constructed. The circular end was a metal pressing, with a stiffening ridge around the edge, fixed to a short wooden arm. 1956. *Author*

A 2–4–0 Sharp Stewart with timber-sided cab making the first delivery into Tomlins flour mill c.1881. The mill dominated the west end of Aberdovey village in its day, and provided plenty of work for the Cambrian's shunting engines.
Cty. O. Tomlins

WELSHPOOL.' The verandah (by then called the awning) was removed for re-erection at Towyn in 1982.

Working Instructions. 1903
Drivers of down trains were to run cautiously through the (tandem three-way) facing points.

The whistle codes for Aberdovey in 1903 were:

Up and Down Main Line	1
To Harbour from Main Line	2 Short
From Harbour to Main Line	2 Long
From Harbour to Oil Siding	3 Short
From Main Line to Up Siding ..	1 Crow
To or from Shunting Neck	1 and 1 Crow
To Harbour Wharf	1 Long
To Harbour Pier	1 Short

The whistle codes in 1943 were:

Harbour from Main Line and vice versa	1 crow
From Main Line to Up Siding	1 short, 1 crow
To or from Shunting Neck	4 short
To Carriage Dock	2 short

1912
Tickets were to be examined on all Up trains.

1943
The down platform was classed as low, and portable steps were to be kept there for the assistance of passengers.

The 'Mill Road' siding was rated as a refuge siding for fifty wagons plus van and engine (up trains).

Re-railing ramps were kept at Aberdovey.

Loose vehicles, light engines or engines and vehicles must not be allowed to stand on the Down Spur Siding which must be kept clear and only used to enable a long Down Train to draw clear on the Down Loop in connection with the crossing of trains.

No shunting must be allowed outside the Down Home Signal whilst a Freight Train is running in the section towards Dovey Junction until a period of five minutes has elapsed after the train has left Aberdovey.

Down Freight Trains putting off traffic on Harbour Line.

When it is necessary for Down Freight Trains to stop outside the Down Home Signal for the purpose of detaching vehicles on to the Harbour Line; before the engine is detached, the portion of the train to be left on the Main Line must be secured by the Van Brake being tightly applied also a sufficient number of wagon brakes on the leading vehicles and, if necessary, making use of sprags, in accordance with Rule 151 to prevent the train, or any portion of it, moving.

All vehicles placed on the Harbour Line must be secured inside the catch point by the hand brake being tightly applied.

Harbour Line.

The connection with the Harbour Line is from the Down Loop. Vehicles may be propelled from the station to the harbour, provided there is a Brake Van or suitable Brake vehicle leading in which the Guard must ride, keep a sharp lookout and be prepared to warn anyone on the line of the approach of the train, and handsignal to the Driver. If a suitable vehicle is not available, the Guard or Porter must walk in front to warn anyone on the line. Before leaving the station sufficient brakes must be applied on the leading vehicles to control the train down the incline.

The gates across the Harbour Line, near the entrance to the Harbour Sidings, must be kept locked across the line by means of a padlock and the key kept in the Signal Box.

The Guard or Porter will be responsible for obtaining the key from the Signal Box, unlocking and opening the gates, closing and locking the gates after the passage of a train or engine and returning the key to the Signalman on completion of the work.

All engines and trains to and from the harbour must come to a stand clear of the gates until handsignalled by the Guard to proceed.

ABERDOVEY HARBOUR BRANCH – 84m 78c

Looking towards the station from the Harbour branch c.1920. *G. H. W. Clifford*

Laid down as Contractor's line: 1861
Opened for passenger trains meeting the Steam Ferry *Elizabeth*: 24th October 1863
Goods only: from 14th August 1867, together with junction on Deviation line.
Closed: 4th May 1964.

Savin established his yard and workshops for the construction of Railway No. 2 (Aberdovey to Towyn section) during 1861, after the passing of the Coast Act on 22nd July. The 'main line' from Aberdovey station to Llwyngwril was connected to the port of Aberdovey by what was to become the Harbour Branch. Its original course into the yard past the future site of the station remained as the beginning of the 'Long Siding'.

After the opening of the Deviation line to Dovey Junction, the Harbour Branch diverged from the east end of the down loop line and descended through a shallow cutting in the sand dunes, which frequently needed digging out again after high winds. Eventually the flanking dunes were cleared away, first as loco sand (in the days before continuous brakes, and even afterwards, engines carried buckets of it to improve adhesion to the rails), and latterly as bunkers on golf courses, including the course on the top of Constitution Hill at Aberystwyth (the contents of whose bunkers

Wagon weighbridge house and Harbour branch exit signal c.1920. *G. H. W. Clifford*

were always being blown away entirely). The going rate around 1900 was 7s 6d a truckload, at the nearest point.

At $8\frac{3}{4}$ chains, a brick-arched tunnel gave public access to the beach; there was also a gate across the rails, which was kept padlocked until the guard opened it to allow his train onto the public part of the beach past Sands Sidings, and so onto the wharf. The length of the branch from the station points up to the viaduct leading onto the pier was $32\frac{1}{2}$ chains.

Aston 0–6–0 Goods on a down goods train approaching Aberdovey station c.1925, with the Harbour branch in the foreground. Note the simple arrangement of the telegraph wire run with only two cross arms required. During Cambrian days, the telegraphs were maintained by J. B. Saunders & Co., and each pole bore a number plate. *H. W. Burman*

ABERDOVEY HARBOUR

Contractor's Yard:
Savin's materials shipped in 1861–2, ferried in from September 1862
Steamer ferry landing: from 24th October 1863
Connected to the through route: 14th August 1867
Designated as a goods station: 1st April 1885
Closed as a railway terminus: 4th May 1964
Rebuilt: 1969–70, with official re-opening as a leisure facility on 28th September 1972.

No account of the early facilities has yet been found, but one period print shows a small timber jetty halfway along towards St Peter's Church, and the Cambrian Railways' single pier with one rake of wagons. An axle from an early 2ft-gauge line using double-flanged wheels has been discovered by Aberdyfi's chemist, Mr. Geraint Evans, while digging a garden behind the Medical Hall. There had been mining activities here and, from a little quarry behind the shop, Abraham Williams once supplied ballast for ships departing without cargo.

Having been appointed contractor to the 'Coast' company, Savin quickly commenced operations, probably with a bit of pushing from Piercy, though also driven by his own ambition to establish a position away from the shadow of David Davies. Some materials for the construction of Railway No. 2 must have been shipped in direct by sea during 1861.

Another yard had been established at the end of the line under construction (Ynyslas) by September 1862, and materials were then ferried across by both the Fferri Fawr and the *James Conley's* barges. By then, it seems that Savin had erected a short single-line timber jetty, which was later to form the nucleus of the Cambrian pier, though large or heavy items, such as rolling stock, would be ramped out of the barges grounded on the beach using mariners' tackle. It would also have been possible to send materials downriver from Derwenlas.

The steamship *Elizabeth* commenced her service on 24th October 1863, by which time the pier must have been available as a landing stage for the passengers.

On 26th October 1864, the Cambrian General Purposes Committee resolved to seek powers to construct a wharf, and to purchase the toll of the ferry. Further, on 11th November, they also proposed to establish powers to operate steamboats between Aberdovey and Waterford.

In 1865, the 0–6–0 Manning Wardle saddle tank *Merion* was despatched from Aberdovey on a barge towed by the *James Conley*, being rerailed just to the north of Barmouth Junction on 27th June to assist in the completion of the line to Penmaenpool.

A siding was laid on the beach in 1866 to carry the traffic of the Aberdovey Slate Company. The line on Savin's pier was most likely to have been exclusively for wagons, and accessible only by a turntable. It would then follow that the coal stacks would be placed at the end of the running line, where they would be readily approachable from the road; and, because there were few houses in the vicinity, the facilities would have been regarded as conveniently placed, rather than as the nuisance they became when the town began to expand. *Elizabeth's* passengers would have walked off the pier to the train, waiting on the beach.

The *James Conley* started to make tourist trips to Bardsey Island, with a connection by rail from Towyn as well. In July 1866, sixty passengers sailed on the first voyage, and of the last trip of the season it was announced: 'This trip has been prepared with more care than the previous one'. The schedule was:

Towyn	depart 7.40 a.m. (Train)
Aberdovey Harbour	arrive 7.55 a.m.
" "	depart 8.0 a.m. (Steamer)
Bardsey Island	arrive 12 noon
" "	depart 4.0 p.m.

and returning at similar timings. The trips were still being advertised in 1870 (though taking three hours each way) with a harpist playing to the passengers.

On 9th January 1867, Savin asked if he could lease the sands for his own enterprises, and was refused. On 6th April, the traffic manager asked for an extension of the wharf, and the provision of another siding for the slate traffic. The staff of the harbour was recorded as 'an Outdoor Superintendent and four Flatmen' (small-boat sailors).

On 2nd June 1868, the solicitor was instructed to give notice terminating the tenancy of the ferry.

The Engineer reported on 7th January 1869 that complaints had been received from the slate quarries regarding the inadequate wharfage, and that a proposal for its extension was supported by Griffiths & Jones, the principal merchants. At the same time, the traffic manager complained that the wharf was so silted that only one vessel could be brought alongside at a time, and that he was expecting three vessels daily from London with guano.

On 25th November 1869 it was approved that the parcel of land newly-purchased from the trustees of the Ynys-y-maengwyn Estate be let to Jones & Griffiths at 5% per annum of the purchase price, and that they were to extend the frontage of the wharf. It was also decided that the company would not purchase the foreshore.

In an item on 23rd April 1870, the *Cambrian News* referred optimistically to increasing trade in Aberdovey: 'large quantities of superphosphates' were being

The Sands Sidings as seen from the upper bedroom of No. 5 Bodfor Terrace, with a large Sharp Stewart 4–4–0 on the 8.22 a.m. up passenger at upper right, on 26th September 1912. The five-plank wagon (No. 681) is loaded with slates and the two-plank with sand. The sidings beside the road here was always the main place for freight handling at Aberdovey, the GWR's proposal to construct a 'proper' goods yard to the west of the station never being implemented. The presence of a railway yard on the prime beach was an annoyance to those who sought to develop Aberdovey as a seaside resort. *H. W. Burman*

shipped in, 'Great quantities of slate and slab which are shipped from Aberllefenni, Corris and Bryneglwys', and 'the reopening of old mines as well as the Alltgoch Slate Quarry which has turned out one of the best on the coast'. A further report indicated: 'Engine Houses and wharves to be built by Mr. G. G. Fremlett of London'. In fact, the slate boom was to last only seven more years, and the ventures mentioned all failed.

On 15th September, the traffic manager reported: 'We provide wagons to convey slates from Towyn to Aberdovey and pay 2s 6d per day for a Horse to draw the wagons to the side of the Ship.' The rate was 8d a ton, and he recommended that, to avoid a loss, this be increased to 1 Shilling.

It was reported that, in 1871, goods were being left in open wagons because there was no adequate

The harbour gates, with 'Cambrian Railways' blacked over on the trespass warning sign. The difference in height between the running line, which climbed away from Aberdovey station, and the Harbour branch, which was on a falling gradient, is clearly seen in this view of a double-headed down train approaching the station. Date unknown. *G. W. Allen*

Harbour branch gate, looking towards Bodfor Terrace and the site of Sands Siding (now a car park). The 'bandstand' situated on Penrhyn Hill behind was a viewing platform. This hill provides a good view over the harbour and estuary. In times past, the fishermen's wives gathered here to watch for the boats and gossip – hence the local name of the 'Hill of Liars'. 1961. *Author*

A small 'Prairie' tank on an up passenger about to cross the road just west of Bodfor Terrace, on 26th July 1955. The Harbour branch gate and upper points to Sands Sidings feature in the foreground. The GWR telegraph pole route carried a lot more wires than its Cambrian predecessor (see page 82). *G. H. W. Clifford*

An up train disappearing behind Bodfor Terrace, on the short climb of 1 in 100 up towards No. 4 tunnel. Date unknown. *G. W. Allen*

warehousing. However, the cost of £400 for a suitable facility caused a deferral.

On 26th January 1872, it was approved that cattle pens, carriage dock sidings and a goods shed be provided at Aberdovey harbour at a cost of £330.

At this time, the trustees of the Ynysmaengwyn Estate were asking £60 per annum as rent for the site of the siding down to the ferry, a figure which was considered excessive; it was to be abandoned unless more satisfactory terms could be agreed.

Some idea of the accommodation provided at Aberdovey for manure traffic can be gauged from the statement from the traffic manager in 1875, when pleading for the provision of manure sheds for the trade to Welshpool and Montgomery: 'I only ask for a long wooden shed similar to the place we have at Aberdovey'.

He was protesting again on 24th October 1877 as, in the previous August, the captain of a timber ship had positioned his vessel against the company's jetty and

By the 1960s, the Harbour branch saw little traffic, so the chances to photograph a shunting movement from the windows of Bodfor Terrace were few. The train crew had brought the brake van down the branch rather than leaving it blocking the running lines. Date unknown.
G. W. Allen

had refused to remove it; this action had delayed outward shipments of lead ore from the Van mines:

> 'The Aberdovey authorities have no rules and regulations nor do they seem to have any power over the Ships' Captains and I am afraid we have no such power. I have thought of drawing up regulations but I am afraid we have no power to enforce them if the occasion should arise. I should be glad of advice or instruction as to what would be-the best to be done in this matter.'

On 25th January 1878, a further shed for the manure traffic was ordered for a sum 'not exceeding £80'.

The General Manager reported on 22nd January 1880 with regard to the unsatisfactory state of affairs relating to foreshore rights. Savin had failed in both 1866 and 1868 to safeguard the company's rights, and the Cambrian was having to rent six acres, one rood and four perches for £40 per annum, and three acres, two roods and thirty-six perches for £18 per annum. In August 1879, an agent had bid (and secured for the company the area outlined for £900) at the auction of Mr Corbett's estate. This was inclusive of the ferry rights, formerly rented by the company for £25 per annum, though the whole action had been forced up in price by brisk competition from parties antagonistic to the Cambrian. At first, the Crown had demurred, but 'after resorting to every conceivable excuse they ultimately agreed'. The assignment of the lease was effected on 29th September 1879. No dues had ever been collected by the Ynysmaengwyn Estate, but for 1878 the income (at rates current in Aberystwyth) would have been £129 8s 4d for the 180 vessels. Rates per ton were:

Cargo Outwards – 3d
Cargo Inwards – 4d
'In Ballast' Inwards – 3d
'In Ballast' Outwards – (unknown)

This was certainly enough to set the Board thinking hard about the future of their only maritime venture.

The General Manager also reported that the first of a consignment of 3,000 tons of new rail was expected shortly, and that an additional pier was urgently needed; this was authorised on 21st February 1880 at a cost of £487 10s 0d.

On 20th August 1881, it was approved that the sum of two hundred pounds should be spent on a warehouse extension, to house four pairs of kibbling (grinding) stones for the Aberdovey Import & Export Co Ltd (Messrs. Dugdale and Kempster). The secretary of that concern, Mr. John Conacher, was about to become secretary to the Cambrian Railways.

Strong feelings were reported against the coming introduction of pier dues, and it was agreed that 'strong measures will have to be resorted to before they can be enforced'. The tariff was:

Pier, Landing Stage or Wharf.

All Unloading from Foreign Parts	3d per ton.
All Unloading from Coasting and other Vessels:.	
not from Foreign Parts	3d per ton.
If in Ballast or loaded with Lime Stone	2d per ton.
All Loading	3d per ton.
All Steam Vessels exclusively employed in carrying Passengers and their Luggage	1d per person.
All Boats and Vessels exclusively employed in Fishing	Exempt.

Any part of the Foreshore

Foreign Unloading	2d per ton.
All Unloading from Coasting and Other Vessels not from Foreign Ports	2d per ton.
All Loading	2d per ton.
If in Ballast or loaded with Lime Stone	2d per ton.
For all Vessels beached, such sum as may be agreed upon.	

There is no mention of the ¾d for ringage, which was actually levied and collected (ringage is the charge for the mooring of a vessel). Mooring rings can be on a jetty, pier or wharf, attached to buoys in midstream, or attached to blocks of stone or concrete buried in a beach (known as deadman moorings).

On 1st October 1881 the station agent, Richard Clayton, was appointed 'Collector of Rates and Charges'. At about that time, a proposal for the installation of a crane on the pier was deferred.

It was noted that coal was coming by rail from the South Wales collieries, and from the Broughton & Plas Power colliery near Wrexham.

In 1882, an extension to the pier and sidings was constructed for the sum of £294 2s 10d; afterwards, the SS *Marion*, carrying 15,000 sleepers (including 10,000 for the Cambrian) 'came in and the Cargo was discharged and she left with amost as much ease as if she had put out of Liverpool.'

A proposition was put to Messrs. Truman, Hanbury, Buxton & Co that they should run a vessel into Aberdovey for the distribution of their stout traffic to North Wales.

Following a proposal from Savin, in which he was to construct a dock costing between £30,000 and £40,000, another plan for an improved Aberdovey pier and embankment was submitted to the Board of Trade. A trial invitation was floated to the shareholders to see what financial support might be forthcoming for the proposed pier stock issue of 1883. There were heated disputes over the harbour dues, 'as never before had there been any serious attempt at proper regulation of the affairs of the port and the sailors had always been used to doing just as they pleased.' A request for a siding for the Import & Export Company was also considered, and deferred.

On 10th February 1882, a meeting was held to hear the views of the people of Aberdovey, arising from the rumours of what the Cambrian might be proposing to do. They agreed in the end not to oppose the scheme for rebuilding the pier and wharf, if:

1. The distance over which the Cambrian was to have control was left to a ruling from the Board of Trade.
2. The new wharf was not to extend further eastwards than the old cannon opposite the windows of the east side of the Dovey Hotel.
3. The Cambrian would not take steps to acquire the foreshore rights eastwards of the old cannon.
4. The Cambrian would improve the beach east of the old cannon by removing the surface rocks.

It was a regular practice to place rows of disused ex-naval cannon (muzzle down, buried to a depth of around six feet) so that ships could be tied to them as mooring posts.

The local Board of Health proposed 'to erect a Urinal on Company Land at their own expense and on sufferance which is agreed to', whilst on 20th May, Ellis Jones was granted the use of a site on the beach for a sawmill, with permission to land timber on the beach.

On 7th July 1882, it was approved that a fence be erected at the seaward limit of the company's right to the foreshore, but it is doubtful whether such an obstructive affair was ever put up. Later that month, the Committee heard that the Liverpool Waterworks cement traffic was to be shipped in through Aberdovey, and that the Board of Trade had recommended that a provisional order legitimizing the maximum scale of dues should be applied for in the next ensuing session, although this was later supplanted by the decision to submit another Bill. The pier was added to the insurance policy with the Royal Insurance Office.

It was decided on 21st November not to purchase the reversion of the foreshore rights to the east of the

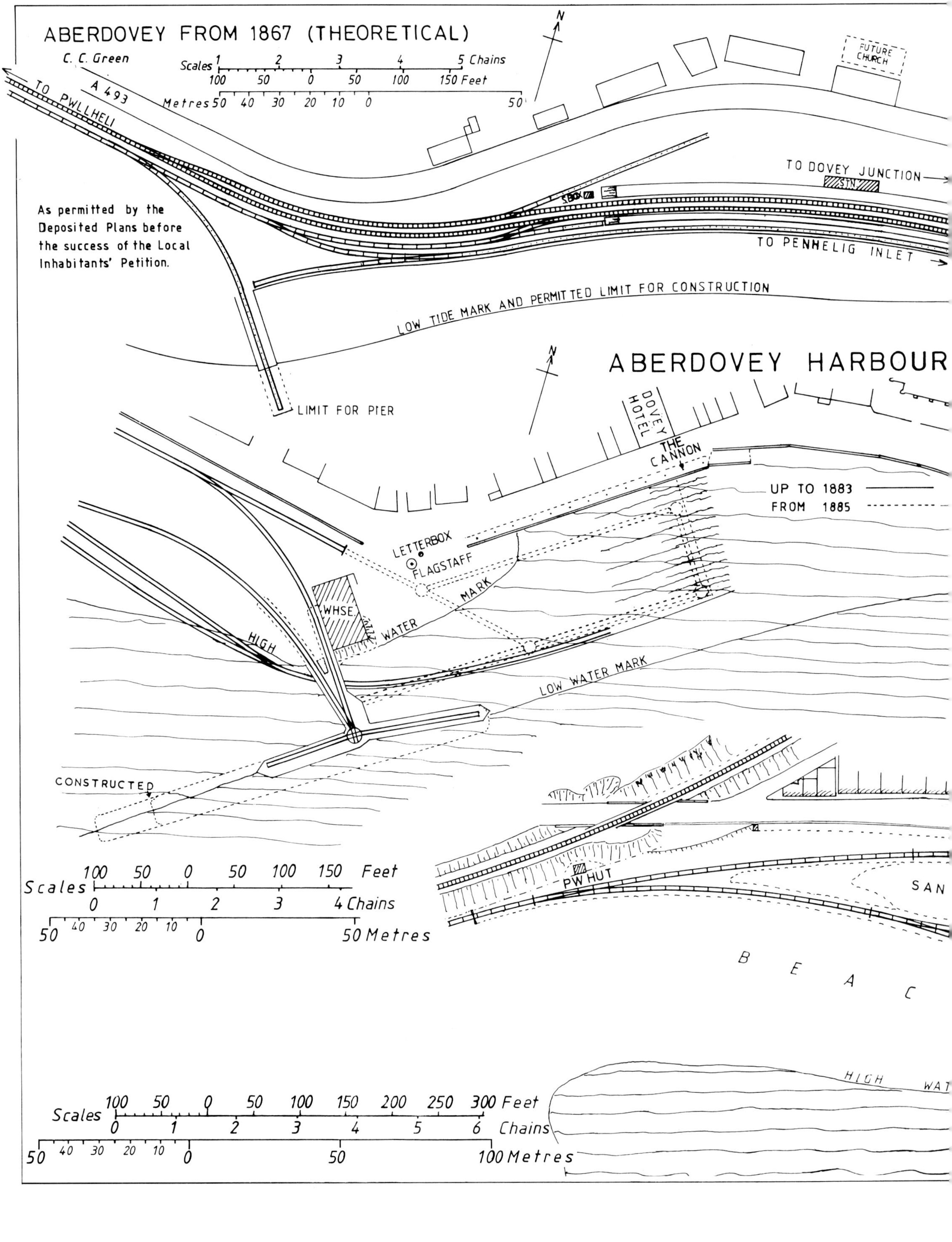
ABERDOVEY FROM 1867 (THEORETICAL)
C. C. Green
Scales 1 2 3 4 5 Chains
100 50 0 50 100 150 Feet
Metres 50 40 30 20 10 0 50
N
FUTURE CHURCH
A 493
TO PWLLHELI
TO DOVEY JUNCTION
STN
SBOX
TO PENHELIG INLET
As permitted by the Deposited Plans before the success of the Local Inhabitants' Petition.
LOW TIDE MARK AND PERMITTED LIMIT FOR CONSTRUCTION
LIMIT FOR PIER
ABERDOVEY HARBOUR
N
DOVEY HOTEL
THE CANNON
UP TO 1883
FROM 1885
LETTERBOX
FLAGSTAFF
WHSE
HIGH WATER MARK
LOW WATER MARK
CONSTRUCTED
PW HUT
SAN
BEAC
Scales 100 50 0 50 100 150 Feet
0 1 2 3 4 Chains
50 40 30 20 10 0 50 Metres
HIGH WAT
Scales 100 50 0 50 100 150 200 250 300 Feet
0 1 2 3 4 5 6 Chains
50 40 30 20 10 0 50 100 Metres

wharf, and notices already sent to the tenants thereof were to be withdrawn.

On 13th December 1882 a sailor named Humphrey Roberts (aged about fifteen) had been helping to push a wagon onto the pier from near to the Import & Export Company's warehouse, when he was crushed between buffers, 'from the effects of which he died'. The Coroner's Jury gave a rider, as follows: 'The Jury are of the opinion that had the arrangements of the Cambrian Company for the protection of human life during the time of shunting been more efficient the accident would not have occurred.'

A complaint was received from Mr. Ellis Roberts about rubbish being deposited on the foreshore in front of the site for his house. The company agreed to stop dumping refuse at this spot, and to have it removed to a site near the pier; Mr. Roberts was also invited to remove the rubbish arising from his site to the company's new dump.

On 14th February 1883, the committee agreed to accept the Crown's offer of a 99 year extension of the lease of foreshore rights, as from 10th October. Station master Davies, who was acting as pier master as well, asked for a full-time official to be appointed in the latter post, as he was too far away to be certain of collecting all the dues. In March, Foreman Lumley (from Machynlleth) was appointed at 22 shillings per week.

In May, the traffic manager reported that two cargoes of cement (600 tons) for Llanfyllin had sustained considerable damage from rain while in transit 'because of the torn and imperfect Waggon sheets in use'. His enquiries had discovered that, of the 1,062 sheets on the books, only 728 could be traced, and of those not more than 250 were sound; scarcely any were waterproof. The next month, he reported that better arrangements had been made for the next two cargoes, and that they would not have to be stored; he would therefore not be needing extra warehousing. It is not known whether he had been provided immediately with new sheets, or whether covered vans had been found (or 'borrowed' from the Cambrian's favourite source, the L & NW). So the warehousing extension was abandoned, but the installation of a 20-ton waggon weighbridge went ahead at a cost of £144.

On 23rd May 1883, the Board declined to pay any compensation to the mother of the late Humphrey Roberts, killed on the pier during the previous December, but they would subscribe to any fund being raised on her behalf.

At a meeting on 18th July, the Board approved the acceptance of 20 shillings per annum from John Bell, the old Ferrymaster, as an acknowledgement of the company's right to the ferry. They were told that there was a possibility of revenue from fish traffic, and that several cargoes of timber had been sent elsewhere

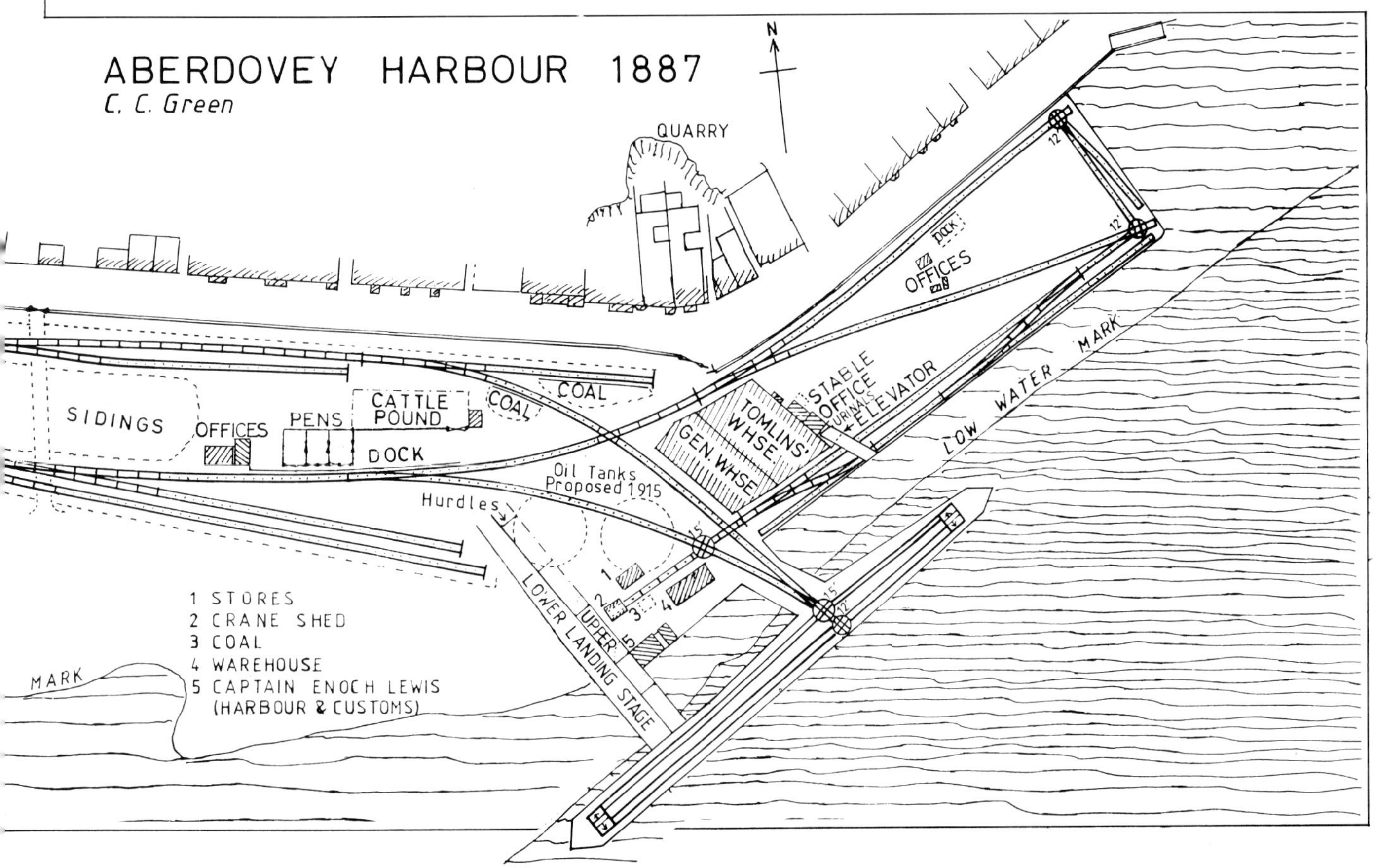

The Sands Sidings c.1910. The open storage of merchandise on the foreshore was acceptable then, but became a source of controversy with those who wished to develop the 'seaside resort' image for Aberdovey. The arrangement of the huts (it is really stretching the use of the word to call them offices) beside the landing stage can be seen in the background, alongside the short viaduct which led out to the upper level of the landing stage. *Cty. H. W. Burman*

because of lack of unloading facilities at Aberdovey. So, on 30th August, they approved the despatch of new plans to the Board of Trade, and the charging of pier dues as from 1st September (under the newly-obtained Cambrian Railways Act of 29th June 1883). Among other items, this Act gave the Cambrian full control of their harbour, the power to reconstruct it, and the power to raise £20,000 in pier stock, to be entitled to dividends only from the tolls, rates and charges so authorised.

During the 16th and 17th October, the highest tides known for some years were experienced, and the entire harbour area disappeared beneath a wind-driven sea. Piling against the wharf was washed askew, and the sidings were displaced and covered by shingle to a depth of several feet. The pier emerged undamaged, and the pier master was given specific authority to order shipmasters to unberth and moor out in the river when storms were threatened. Several wagons were derailed, and twenty more were blocked in.

In November 1883, the traffic manager estimated that between six and seven thousand tons of fish traffic might be expected each year.

On 19th February 1884, the Board approved that £15,000 of pier stock be offered to 'existing Proprietors of the Company', and later that the issue be advertised to the public.

The Board accepted Abraham Williams' tender of £1,870 on 29th April for the new pier and wharf, and on 29th May they approved new bylaws. They also passed an unusual resolution on 21st June: 'That on satisfactory completion of the Works Abraham Williams and his family will not be disturbed in the occupation of the House under the Company within a reasonable time.' The engineer reported that 'The New Wharf is well in hand as Contractor has received the greater part of the timber for the piles.' Then the Board extended the scope of the contract by ordering the provision of space for two vessels at the inner berth; on 30th July, the committee approved the despatch of amended plans to the Board of Trade.

On 18th August 1884, the engineer proposed a scheme for sidings, a warehouse, and steam cranes at a cost of £3,304 5s 11d; this figure made the committee blench, and they asked him to consider alternative plans. Six weeks later, they opted for a proposal costing £1,031 6s 8d. Finally, at a site meeting on 28th October, they assented to a further amended layout costing £1,654 12s 3d with an extra £809 15s 2d for piling.

Meanwhile, back at Oswestry, Edwin Liller (the traffic manager) was having difficulties too. In presenting his report on the company's failure to find the capital to improve the facilities for the fishermen, he judged this to be costing the company 'several thousands of pounds from the Mackerel and Herring Fishery', and went on: 'I would further allude briefly to the strenuous exertions which the Directors have enabled me to make in the cultivation of tourist traffic as well as the passenger traffic generally and which the Directors are aware have not been entirely unsuccessful.'

Of the obstruction caused by the reconstruction of the harbour, he reported having to hold four sailing ships and a steamer at anchor (these carrying mainly cement for the Liverpool Waterworks). Seven slate cargoes were being delayed, too.

On 17th February 1885, the engineer reported happily that Abraham Williams had finally completed the new wharf, originally estimated at £2,287 6s 4d, but finally costing £2,212 4s 8d. The committee, who had heard of complaints from shipmasters, then sent him away to report on the best method of deepening the water alongside. He was also to act in concert with the Officer of Customs to fix a site near the south end of the pier and above the high water mark of medium spring tides for depositing ballast, and to take measures for that location to be sanctioned by the Board of Trade instead of the place previously appointed. Also,

Sands Sidings c.1900, showing disused cattle pens (intended for the Irish cattle traffic) and driveway ramps, by this time used mainly for timber and a little slate. The tiny sloping arm sticking up out of the tall narrow shed on the left shows that the steam crane bought from Abraham Williams was 'at home'. Note in the distance the low-tide state of the Leri waterway and the original timber refuge tower. c.1900.

Cty. H. W. Burman

Detail of the cattle pens, lower level landing ramp and upper level cattle driveway, c.1900. Bodfor Terrace features in the left background and Glandovey Terrace to the right of the gap – soon to be filled by more houses.

Cty. Hugh M. Lewis

Schooner *Adventure* loading brick and tiling. Note the crude wooden trough slides and the high-level gangway used for wheeling craned-up loads of corn to the upper level of Tomlins' warehouse. Later it would be shovelled out, to be loaded into wagons for removal to his steam corn mill. These ships are tied up to the side of the wharf, which has always been dry at low tides. The jetty just features on the right, with access from the wharf across the bridge in the foreground. Penhelig can be seen in the far distance. The hills above the coastal road were almost devoid of housing at this time – compare with the 1898 view opposite.

J. Thomas, cty. John Parry

when the position had been fixed, the engineer was to pile it as cheaply as possible to form the foundation of a wharf.

On 25th March, the committee approved the designated name of 'Aberdovey Harbour Station' in connection with the use of the pier for goods, mineral, livestock and fish traffic. The business of the main Aberdovey station on the through line would in future be restricted to passenger and parcel traffic. The additional charge distances would be '34 chains for Inland Traffic and 44 chains for Traffic Northwards, giving the Company an additional mile in the division of receipts on Through Traffic via Afon Wen, Dolgelley and Llanidloes Junction.' The committee was also told that the new wharf, sidings and turntable were complete and working, and that the ballast ground had been selected with the agreement of the resident Officer of Customs so as to render the site suitable for further extensions at a piling and boarding cost of £529 9s 0d. Finally, they approved warehouse accommodation for the Aberdovey Import & Export Company at a cost of £600, to be charged against Pier Stock.

The Committee were informed on 6th May that the one farthing charge per ton for ringage made by the Ynysmaengwyn Estate was producing only £15 5s 8½d per annum. They authorised new charges of three-farthings per ton register ringage for vessels moored alongside the pier and wharf, and one farthing per ton register for vessels moored on the open foreshore.

On 19th June 1885, the engineer reported that £40 would have to be expended on the provision of mid-stream moorings to relieve the rough-weather strain against the wharf, as vessels often could not, in time, lay out their anchors. The company was learning that there was more to running a harbour than just building it and taking the revenue.

Next, the committee authorised the purchase of a steam crane, bought new by Abraham Williams for £255. Williams had offered it for £235, but the engineer thought it was worth only £220 and secured it for that figure. It was discharging cargoes for the company by 21st August.

About that time, the traffic manager was investigating the company's powers to charge for siding

Brig *Excelsior* of Portmadoc unloading timber into Cambrian wagons c.1898. The timber facing to the wall of the wharf inevitably decayed, and has now been replaced by sheet steel piles and concrete. *Cty. John Parry*

services on the beach and wharf, with marked objections from the Abergynolwyn Slate Company.

At the end of September, Mr. Tomlins wrote to the chairman about the necessity for increased accommodation at the pier where the larger vessels were berthed. In fact, it was now becoming evident that the committee and Board had wasted a lot of money by being too niggardly and penny-pinching, and by instructing the engineer to design and build a pier and wharf that were too small. So they now told him to submit plans and estimates for widening the existing pier, and for carrying it out to deeper water within the limits authorised by the company's Act of 1883.

On 6th October 1885, the Board authorised the solicitor to take steps to eject those masters still mooring without authority or payment on that part of

Looking east over the pre-1883 quay. This wharf had no face on the east side, it just tailed off into the foreshore of the estuary. The stone walling to protect the coast road from erosion had yet to be built. *Cty. Hugh M. Lewis*

A Cambrian water tank wagon, drawn by the steam crane, discharging its load into the tank of a schooner.
Cty. E. W. Hannan

the foreshore now leased to the company. They also approved rates for conveying slates from Towyn to the harbour, at one shilling per ton in owners' wagons, and one shilling and four pence in company wagons. They approved, too, the despatch to the Board of Trade of the proposals for the new and larger installation.

At the meeting on 30th January 1886, the engineer reported that 'Additional Moorings were needed in consequence of vessels of greater draught now playing to this Port, the strains on the moorings of the old pier have materially increased.' The additional moorings were to be provided by laying a deadman on the beach, in a northerly direction from the end of the pier, by sinking a stone of about five tons in weight into the sand, connected to a buoy by thirty fathoms (180 feet) of 'floating' chain at a cost of £25 per buoyed mooring. This they approved, in addition to the affixing of the company seal to 'A conveyance of the soil of the River Dovey required for the extension of Aberdovey Pier' from the Commissioners of Woods and Forests (also the grantors of the foreshore lease).

In March, the traffic manager reported to the Board on the tentative arrangements he had made with Captain J. Lewis & Co., steamship owners of Aberdovey, on rates for imported Spanish haematite ore; a charge of 6s 8d per ton (in company wagons) to Birmingham and the South Staffordshire district would be made. Steamers could be chartered to Aberdovey at the same rates as for the Bristol Channel ports, namely five shillings per ton. The Board also approved the tender of J. Hughes Jones for the extension of the pier, for £1,720. He was the main timber merchant, and probably had an arrangement with Abraham Williams for the extraction and redriving of some of the piles the latter had put in scarcely two years earlier. This time, the engineer was empowered to employ a clerk of works to supervise the contractors on behalf of the company.

During August 1886, the nearby residents sent in a plaintive letter about the dirt, dust and nuisance arising from coal and lime being unloaded in front of The Terrace. No response was noted.

On 21st September, the Board obviously felt unequal to dealing with the lighting of piers and channels, and deferred consideration while advice was sought; accordingly, they instructed the engineer to obtain details and estimates, and to include a costing for 'Coal Shoots'.

The engineer reported on 11th October that the extension to the pier had been completed, and that 'The Wagon Traversers I have designed prove to be all that could be desired and are much superior to working by turntables.' Under general matters, he made the first reference to a possible service to Waterford.

Two days later, the Board deferred once again a decision on pier and channel lighting. Then they instructed the secretary to write to the Trinity House Corporation to enquire if they would provide a light forty feet up on a mast above the Refuge (on Cerrig-y-Penrhyn), and another at mast height on a boat which was to be movable so as to indicate the shiftings of the Aberdovey bar.

The ketch *Suzanna* of Bideford down to her marks and ready for unloading, c.1895. Note the interesting angles of wagons on the east face of the quay, two on the diagonal road and others on both tracks along the south face, and how close the flat-bottomed rail was to the edge (this allowed the side of the wagon to be in line with the edge of the quay to facilitate loading and unloading). The masts of Dafydd Jones' *Volunteer*, lying against the east face, can just be made out. *Cty. Ozzie Lloyd*

On 23rd May 1887, the Board received a self-congratulatory report from the general manager. The pier and new works had been completed, and 'The Company now possesses a deep water Pier with high and low landing stages, cattle pens, and other accessories capable of carrying on a large traffic.' He also mentioned the idea of a new lighthouse on the hill beyond Aberdovey.

On 30th January 1888, the company executed a Deed of Surrender to the Crown of all foreshore leasings no longer specifically required.

A Sunday School outing on the beach c.1898. Note the long lines of wagons along the sidings, and the viaduct leading to the upper level of the landing stage. *Cty. T. I. Hughes*

A publicity leaflet appeared on 1st October, outlining all the facilities on offer and, apart from the opening paragraph, this remained in circulation until the end of the company in 1922.

The Cambrian Railways (Steamboats) Act became law on 9th July 1889, though the only provision affecting the harbour was the power to issue the balance of pier stock as ordinary debenture stock, amounting to £11,915 out of the £20,000 authorised in 1883. Power was also given to convert existing pier stock into ordinary debenture stock, and to apply both portions of the capital so raised to any purposes already authorised by any Act in force.

The interest during 1890 was centred on a general managers' report, given on 19th November. He stated: 'Some of the leading wholesale merchants in Liverpool have put a Steamer on. It has made two trips this month and is advertised to sail each alternate Wednesday.' This was the start of the Aberdovey & Barmouth Steamship Company's 'Grocery Boats'; he also reported that 'their Agent has taken for £50 per annum No. 2 warehouse at Aberdovey which has been vacant since the Aberdovey Import & Export Coy. ceased business.' Then there was 'some disagreement with Mr. Tomlins who wished to rent for £25 per annum if the Company would remove the Corn Bins to give him clear space over all the floor below. He claimed to be in the position of a tenant and refused to give up the key in his possession so the Company has changed the lock.'

In January 1895, there came a request that the coal wharf should be removed from in front of Glandovey and Sea View Terrace. To place it at the entrance of the first tunnel would cost £100, and the general manager 'could not recommend the removal just at present'; the committee agreed with him.

On 27th February, they considered a proposal from the Birmingham Corporation Water Works in conjunction with the Elan Valley reservoir project. If the tonnage rate for cement could be reduced from 6s 8d to 6s 3d, they would have all the cement shipped in through Aberdovey; this was approved.

At a meeting on 25th May, it was agreed that Mr. Tomlins should be permitted to build his own warehouse with an elevator on the wharf, at his own expense.

In November, the Board agreed to allow a wayleave to the council to lay a sewer under the company's installations, to discharge into the river near to the pier.

At the end of April 1986, the first shipload of cement was on the seas, bound for Aberdovey, and by August the Elan Valley traffic had exceeded the capacity of the fifty new goods wagons and twenty-five new vans provided, and another fifty were urgently needed.

By March 1897, trouble was being experienced with the berths, which were silting up; Mr Chidlaw Roberts, a timber merchant, was claiming compensation for the delay in getting his vessels alongside. The committee refused, with the lame excuse that the company was not responsible for the silting, and further refused the suggestion of free cranage as another form of compensation. The engineer set his men to work on 'loosening the sandbanks'.

As the provision of the regular ferry service during the winter had become onerous, unremunerative and unnecessary, John Bell sought to break the requirement to provide the service by giving notice as from 30th September, withdrawing himself and his boats. A fresh agreement was drawn up for the summer months only at ten shillings per annum – the Cambrian had not permitted him to halve the charge payable for the ferry rights, but only to halve his attendance.

A part of the Cambrian warehouse was partitioned off during 1898 at a cost of £29 10s 0d, to be let at £25 per annum, with a footnote to the committee that the letting of the warehouse (instead of charging for the storage of the flour) relieved the company of liability for damage by rats.

In August, Towyn Urban District Council were allowed, at a wayleave of £1 per annum, to lay a one-inch water pipe across the wharf for the servicing of ships. This should have caused the end of the Cambrian's arrangement involving a water tank on a wagon chassis, shunted alongside by horse (or by the crane, being used as a locomotive), but the Cambrian still provided their service for some time afterwards. Perhaps they were cheaper.

In the *Railway Magazine* for October 1898, C. S. Denniss gave an interview in which he claimed for Aberdovey:

> 'not only is the sea passage short but the currents are extremely favourable as compared with the passage to the Bristol Channel ports. We have also the additional advantage of the much shorter rail conveyance from the seaboard to the Midland counties thus giving the Aberdovey route special advantages for cattle traffic.'

This rather brash claim was put into proper context during the following year. A request (dated 24th April 1900) from the District Collector of Customs at Caernarvon 'that the Station Master should act also as Customs Agent at the Creek' reveals at once the true status of Aberdovey, and of its decline as a harbour, with only 'ten vessels arrived from foreign' in the previous twelve months. The duties (with the District Collector's comments in brackets) were to be:

> To wire such arrivals and departures to Carnarvon.
> To receive the transires of the Coasting vessels (of which there had been 102 in 1899) and to forward them to Aberystwyth.
> To collect Light Dues from such vessels as should pay them. (There will be hardly any work under this head).
> To take charge of wreckage washed ashore and to wire notification of vessels in distress to Aberystwyth.

The salary was to be £6 per annum, and the company gave their assent as a matter of policy.

On 6th November 1900, the committee resolved to seek powers to operate excursion steamers.

More modern youngsters could experience the joy of being photographed in front of a magnificent express engine, Large Sharp Stewart 4–4–0 No. 68. It was not just small engines which worked the Harbour branch. c.1914.
Cty. M. E. M. Lloyd

At their meeting on 21st April 1903, the committee once again deferred consideration of removing the coal wharves from the sea front. In 1905 they were still deferring considerations over buoying and lighting arrangements, and how such matters lay is not revealed. Part of the original jetty was now in a dangerous state, as a beam had fractured under the weight of the crane, and on 4th May the committee had to accept the engineer's ultimatum and authorise the expenditure of £490 in renewing defective piles and framing. On the same day, they assented to the council's proposal to set the wall back into company land in order to widen the road; the council was also allowed to erect a public lavatory.

During 1907, a large ship carrying a deckload of sleepers for the creosoting works took the old course through the bar after a northerly shift in the channel, of which the skipper was unaware, and the lookout failed to notice the change in position of the buoys. She grounded and broached (rolled broadside on), and some four thousand sleepers had to be thrown overboard on the rising tide to get her off. Most of these came ashore up the estuary, and became the property of the Maritime Insurance Company of Liverpool. The engineer arranged to buy them for 2s 10d each, thrown over the company's fence.

The blacksmith at Penhelig hastily made handspikes, and men and boys spiked, lashed, rafted and heaved them (for a sum paid by the insurance company), whilst a ballast train crawled along and collected them. The engineer reckoned that, after allowing 1¾d per sleeper for labour and carriage to the works on the 3,600 so saved (ordered originally at 3s 3¾d per sleeper), the company was £60 better off.

On 31st August 1908, the committee deferred repairs to the decking of the pier, despite the urgency conveyed in the general manager's report of the seriousness of the problem which had been caused by penny-pinching over the previous years. However, the solicitor pointed out that the company was under obligation to the Crown to maintain the pier, despite the general falling off of traffic. The engineer thought that by sawing out the better planking it could be used elsewhere, so that some expenditure could be saved. On 23rd October, the committee gave way and authorised repairs costing around £900, to be capitalised and written off over the next ten years.

After lengthy exchanges, the Aberdovey & Barmouth Steam Ship Company's lease of the warehouse was renewed in 1910 for another seven years. Tragically, their ship, the S.S. *Dora*, was sunk by a German U-boat on 1st May 1917 and they asked to be released from the payment of the five years rent then owing. On 6th June, the general manager commented 'The warehouse is a large one and I am afraid that the prospects of securing another tenant at the present time are not bright'; on 5th December, the committee was informed that the Steam Ship Company had gone into liquidation. By then, the annual income of the harbour had declined to £69 15s 11d while the foreshore lease for the land on which it had been built cost the company £100 per annum in rent.

The waiver of the warehouse rent was refused, and the solicitor was instructed to press for the value thereof in the bankruptcy. Since 1913, the Steam Ship Company had literally been paying the foreshore lease, and henceforth there was to be a regular annual loss on the harbour account. Its capital value at that time was represented by £9,702 in 4% debenture 'A' stock out of the £20,000 the stock had been expected to raise.

In August 1918, some mischievous boys burnt down the ancient Ferry Refuge on Cerrig-y-Penrhyn, and Towyn Urban District Council instructed their clerk to write to the Cambrian claiming that the railway company were liable for its replacement. The Cambrian asked the Council to produce documentary evidence of such a liability which, of course, the Council was unable to do.

The Counties of Montgomery, Merioneth and Cardigan had combined in 1919 to generate schemes for the provision of work for demobilised soldiers and, at a meeting held at Machynlleth on 12th February, the Dovey barrage was mooted. Three thousand acres of land would be reclaimed and, by controlling incoming tides, the flooding of another ten thousand acres would be eliminated. The dam from Cerrig-y-Penrhyn was to carry a road and a railway. However, the chief engineer to the Board of Agriculture and Fisheries reported that Aberdovey, as a resort, would be destroyed, and the Director of Land Reclamation, having ascertained that the recovery of land worth £100,000 was going to cost £700,000, was therefore of the opinion that he would not be justified in proceeding with the scheme.

The year 1920 passed in long consultations between the company and the Council, from which came a suggestion that the Council should lease the foreshore and ferry rights for £10 per annum if the Cambrian would rebuild the Refuge. This was subsequently reduced to £8 per annum, and the council would rebuild the Refuge. It emerged that, at the time, the income from the foreshore was £5 per annum (the ferry), and £1 15s 0d from bathing machines, and that the Cambrian would insist on a clause protecting the ferryman. That foundered, and the Refuge was eventually replaced in 1931, and then only by public subscription and fund-raising efforts led by Aberdovey's much-respected chemist, Mr. Thomas Wynn Thomas. The target was £200, and the plans were drawn by an architect free of charge. It was to have 'an artistic cabin and a platform outside for the purpose of signalling the shore', and 'All will stand four-square to all the tempests and winds that blow'. In the event, the 'artistic cabin' could not be afforded.

Griffiths, Davies and Son, corn and seed merchants who had been paying £35 per annum as sub-tenants of a portion of the warehouse, were given a five-year lease in 1921 for £60 per annum.

By 1923 the boiler of the steam crane was now too defective to continue in use without costly repairs or renewal. The crane was Cambrian No. 9 (Great Western No. 1417). The boiler was pressed at 60 lbs per sq in, and the jib was credited with a three-ton lifting capacity.

The Great Western's first act in 1923 was to replace all regulations and bylaws with their own standard versions. Administration came under the Docks and Steamboats Committee, and with so much of greater importance to be attended to, little was done about a harbour that was found to be so little used (except by pleasure boats). In March, there had been a public meeting in the Imperial Hall convened by the Towyn Urban District Council, which had passed a resolution urging the new owners to rebuild and refurbish the entire front. Accordingly, the Great Western produced a scheme, costing £9,350 which they were willing to carry out, but only at local expense; so that was the end of that!

All Cambrian engines had found their way onto the wharf except the '95' class, and the Great Western barred the passage of outside-cylindered types.

In 1932, £120 was spent on roofing. Repairs to the warehouse and partial renewal of wharf and jetty cost £350 in 1935, and a further £350 was expended on

The end of Sands Sidings and the jetty. The jib sticking out of the tall narrow shed shows that the steam crane was 'at home'. The coal stacks there were both for the use of and the annoyance of the landladies of Bodfor and Glandovey Terraces. Because of the tidal range in the estuary, the jetty had two levels, one serving boats when the tide was in, and a lower level which served boats when the tide was out. This was below water level when the tide was in, as it was when this view was taken.
H. W. Burman

Sharp Stewart 0–6–0 No. 14 as rebuilt, with four-wheeled tender, shunting on the Harbour branch. 16th July 1912. Wind-blown sand played havoc with the motion of the engine.
H. W. Burman

similar repairs in 1946. The local name for the piling on the coast was 'Abraham Williams' Teeth'; a local workman told the foreman that he would need the big crane from Swindon because the Aberdovey piles were Williams's eye teeth. He was right – they all had swivel pieces to stop them from lifting.

The British Transport Commission announced in 1959 that it wished to surrender the foreshore lease. Nevertheless, it took six years of negotiations, ending with an appeal to the Secretary of State for Wales, Mr. James Griffiths, before the Council could purchase the rights for £2,766, which was generously donated by the Aberdyfi Advertising and Improvements Committee.

After the completion of a new sewage system in 1968, the wharf was restructured for £49,367, with a 75% grant from the Welsh Office, and one of 9% from Merioneth County Council. The area of the sidings was made into a car park for £9,769.

The jetty provided a nasty shock in the form of the teredo (wood-boring) worm, and a brand-new and slightly smaller version was constructed for £28,242. The British Rail contribution for dilapidation had been calculated in 1962 at only £6,000, but the day was saved by a contribution of 47% by the Outward Bound Sea School, and another donation of £12,030 from the Aberdyfi Advertising and Improvements Committee.

Even after all this open-handed support, three hundred and forty-three people put their names to a petition of protest against the building of the Snowdonia National Park Information Centre on the new

A Sharp Stewart 0–6–0 shunting Sands Sidings. Most of the wagons were Cambrian but the one private owner wagon on the right displayed the Stafford Knot. The left-hand group of houses are Bodfor Terrace. Beyond is Glandovey Terrace.
Cty. T. I. Hughes

Shunting the Sands Sidings beside the road wall, Sharp Stewart rebuilt 0–6–0 Goods No. 46 with Morris Jones & Sons coal wagon (later Griffith Davies & Son, later sold to Towyn Co-op) on 11th July 1914. The driver was G. Caffrey.
H. W. Burman

wharf. In fact, Merioneth County Council and the National Parks Commission were paying for it. The Dyfi Sailing Club built its clubhouse next to the slipway, and the council provided shelters and gardens; and so was completed the showpiece which has received awards from The Prince of Wales Committee, and in the 'Best-Kept Village', 'Wales in Bloom' and 'Britain in Bloom' competitions. Thus are the old Cambrian wharf and pier commemorated by these excellent works, which have created a marina and holiday village in a place of great natural beauty, which is well worth a visit.

ABERDOVEY SHIPPING AND TRADE

A busy scene on the jetty (not the wharf quay) showing the clearing of a deck cargo of timber from the Baltic. The empty wagons on the inner road were waiting to be horse-shunted round via the traversers at either end. This view also shows a schooner and a brigantine side by side at the inner berths and a ketch at the east face. c.1910.
Cty. Hugh M. Lewis

By the time the railway reached Aberdovey, the town had already several centuries of maritime tradition behind it:

1188 Recorded as a ferry landing place.
1569 Mentioned in Queen Elizabeth's Survey of Ports, Creeks and Landing Places as 'Deveye', with only three houses and no boats.
1650 Established as a fishing village, landing mainly herring and mackerel, but also some salmon.
1750 A Controller & Port Watcher had been appointed. Some cargoes were discharged and loaded against the sea wall and some were transhipped at anchorages. Exports were ores of copper and lead, and imports included salt and wine from France. The Derwenlas fleet had begun to ply.
1860 Now established as a flourishing port, with loading and exchanging carried on from a little wooden pier as well as from anchorages and the sea wall. Beached, flat-bottomed ships could be served by horse and cart at low water. The Derwenlas fleet was at its height, and it was stated that eighty boats could go up on a single tide. Exports were still lead ores and a little copper, with some manganese, bark, timber, oak pit-props, woollen goods and a deal of slate. Imports were coal, limestone (often as ballast), malt, rye, wheat, flour, hides and wine.

A portion of the first Cambrian 'Rates, Dues and Charges Collected' book has survived, covering the period 1st December 1882 to 30th May 1888, providing a fascinating insight into the maritime trade.

At first, there was a variety of small coasting dandies, flats and smacks, with a few schooners and fewer steamers, and one or two interesting larger ocean-going vessels.

The dandies were ketch-rigged thirty to seventy-tonners with such names as *Pert, Fame, Cadwgan* and *Heather Bell*, whilst the smacks were generally smaller, only twenty-five to thirty tons, and included the *Sage, Brothers, Eliza, Lerry* and *Charming Nancy*.

Typical assignments brought in were:

Ship	*Cargo*
Schooner *Cambrian*	Cement, ex-London.
Schooner *Mary Jane*	Gunpowder, ex-Briton Ferry.
Smack *Lloyd*	Gunpowder, ex-Neath.
Schooner *Betsy*	Petroleum, ex-London.
Smack *Ruth*	Bricks & Pipes, ex-Aberayron.
Schooner *Little Willie*	Barley, ex-Saffir.
Barque *Bartholomes Simone*	Indian Corn, ex-Baltimore.
Barque *Kolumbus*	Deals & Lop, ex-Richmond.
Brig *Walhalla*	Deals & Mouldings, ex-Skutskar.
Barque *Favorit*	Petroleum $510\frac{1}{2}$ tons, ex-New York.
Schooner *Laura*	Cement, ex-Antwerp (returning with Lead Ore from the Van Mine).
SS *Bessemer*	Cement, ex-London.
SS *Cambrian*	Cement, ex-London.

This picture shows the grocery boat S.S. *Dora*, now empty, and having come stern-first out of her usual place at the inner berth, getting under way for Liverpool with the bilge pumps at full pressure. Penhelig can be seen behind with a trace of steam showing beyond the tunnel. c.1920. *E. Burman*

SS *Thracia*	Timber & Sleepers, ex-Riga.
SS *Benedict*	-do-
SS *Electra*	-do-
SS *N.S.Caine*	Grain, Bran, Oatmeal & Machinery for Mr. Tomlins.

A good deal of the cement brought in at this period was for the building of Liverpool's Vyrnwy Reservoir, sent up the Cambrian main line and then via the Llanfyllin branch, thence by horse and cart to the site of the dam in the hills beyond Llanfyllin.

Exports were mainly slate, slabs and blende ore, but many ships left in ballast.

Trippers were coming from Aberystwyth on the SS *Countess of Lisburne,* and from Portmadoc (via Bardsey) on the Portmadoc Harbour Tug *Snowdon,* being charged 1d each for landing at Aberdovey.

THE ABERDOVEY & WATERFORD STEAM SHIP COMPANY

On 10th November 1864, the Cambrian committee resolved to seek powers for the running of steamboats, but they were not granted.

At a meeting on 23rd December 1880, the Board were informed of a 'Proposed Line of Steamers from this place to America'.

The Board heard a proposal from Messrs. Jamieson & Co of Liverpool on 22nd July 1882 to put a suitable steamer on passage between Aberdovey and Wexford, if the Cambrian would give a rebate on the rail traffic arising. They resolved that this should not exceed 50%, and on 10th August the committee approved $33\frac{1}{3}$%, with a minimum of £100 per annum. However, on 12th December the Board were told: 'The Wexford negociations [sic] have come to an end.'

Mr. Jamieson came back to the Board in 1883 with a proposal for a Liverpool, Aberdovey and Wexford route, involving the purchase of a suitable steamer for £12,000, of which he asked the Cambrian to contribute half. Edwin Liller was instructed to contact the Dublin, Wicklow & Wexford Railway to see if they would join in, but they would not.

On 29th July 1884, Mr. Liller proposed an arrangement for a cross-channel trade, making reference to a Captain Drake, who had directed his attention to a small steamer which could be obtained on line charter at the very low price of £300 per month. She was the SS *Acacia,* given as about 260 tons net register, with a crew of twelve or thirteen hands all told. Her speed was 9 knots, burning between 5 and 6 tons of coal in 24 hours. The charterers were to be liable for all dock and port charges. The committee then produced a proposal that the Aberdovey Import & Export Company should be approached and asked for the terms on which that company would be willing to 'provide a Steamer for the Cross-Channel Trade'. However, they were unwilling to become involved in this business.

Looking east along the jetty on 14th July 1913. The steamer berthed against the quay was S.S. *Dora*. In the foreground can be seen one end of the traverser by which wagons were moved from one line to the other at the western end of the jetty. Unlike the quayside lines, the rails on the jetty were set back from the edge. *H. W. Burman*

Unloading groceries from S.S. *Telephone*, by emptying the skip into the Cambrian three-plank wagon and wheeling them along planks into the van. c.1923. *G. H. W. Clifford*

Top left: The 15ft turntable which formerly was used to turn wagons onto the south face of the quay. *Top right:* The 15ft junction turntable on the jetty. April 1957. *Author*

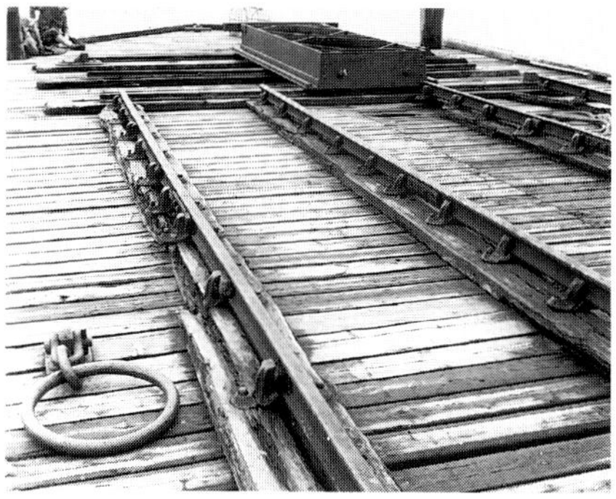

Right: West end of the jetty and wagon traverser. *Far right:* West wagon traverser. August 1958. *Author*

Above: The pier (on line of Savin's pier) looking through to the inner berths. *Left:* West end of the jetty. 14th June 1964. *Author*

S.S. *Telephone* berthed against the outer face of the jetty, which had been somewhat damaged by ramming. This picture shows the tide in, and the sandbanks of the estuary beyond covered by water. c.1923. *G. H. W. Clifford*

A year later, the steamer committee authorised the deputy chairman, Mr. Bailey-Hawkins, and Mr Humphrey-Owen to negotiate for a steamer to trade regularly with Aberdovey (and on 18th November 1985, the Board authorised the invitation of tenders for the proposed extension of the pier).

On 10th August 1885, the committee considered letters from Messrs. Flack and Hawkins concerning an Aberdovey to Wexford proposal, and Mr. Flack and Captain Lee visited Aberdovey later to advise on pier design. The L&NWR kindly provided the Cambrian with a list of shipping rates from Waterford, Wexford and Ballywilliam.

In September 1886, secretary John Conacher, with engineer George Owen, visited Rosslare, Waterford and Wexford, and reported on the catchment lengths of the various railways there; the most favourable seemed to be Waterford, with:

Waterford & Limerick Rly.	272 miles.
Waterford, Dungarvan & Lismore Rly.	43 miles.
Waterford & Central Ireland Rly.	31 miles.
Waterford & Tranore Rly.	7 miles.
Total	353 miles.

They also managed to get some data on the business of the Great Western's Waterford & Limerick Junction Rly, and sailings (not on record).

At the same time, Mr. Humphreys-Owen went to the nearest Irish port to Aberdovey – Arklow – but reported that it was not big enough to turn a large ship in the inner harbour.

On 22nd December 1886, the Board approved the institution of bi-weekly sailings between Aberdovey and Waterford.

Mr. Flack was reported to be willing to put on a steamer for six months, though the cost of working a powerful steamer capable of 12 knots (to save tides at Aberdovey) would be £524 per month. From this, the costing situation was mentioned as 'looking dubious'. The report is unclear, but mentions another owner (or charterer), Mr. Stuart, with whom were made the arrangements that did produce the service. He assented to sailings at £100 per month subsidy, paid by way of rebates on the freight charges by rail from Aberdovey to destination, which was about the only way a railway company with no powers to operate steamers could take any sort of hand in so doing. There was to be a trial period of six months, starting at Easter 1887, with an arrangement for five years if successful.

So the Waterford & Aberdovey Steamship Company was brought into being, and was admitted to the 'South of Ireland Conference' (a monopolistic cartel with a high-sounding name). The company was allowed to arrange through rates for the transit of livestock and merchandise; this had been prepared in response to a suggestion from Mr. Roberts of the Waterford & Limerick Rly. While they had been waiting for admission to the 'Conference', the Waterford & Aberdovey had constructed a cattle enclosure at Aberdovey, with lighting for livestock inspection during the hours of darkness, and had leased a yard at Waterford for 7 years at £12 12s 0d per annum. They spent £172 on fitting out the latter, which measured only 36 ft × 39 ft.

On 19th April 1887, after a fair passage, the 246-ton SS *Liverpool* docked at Aberdovey with a general cargo and 60 pigs. Only then did they begin to find out that there was little demand for Irish cattle in Wales, or indeed in many other places. The engineer noted that departures from Waterford had to be timed to suit the tides at Aberdovey.

The old folk at Aberdovey told a horrific tale about the voyage which finished the venture off, and one newspaper even accused the author of making it up.

This mid-1950s view was taken at the junction of the quay and quayside wharf lines, looking towards the station. The sand blown over the line was a common occurrence. *G. W. Allen*

The warehouses in 1961, with the branch to the station behind the photographer. *Author*

North gable of Tomlins' grain shed on 14th June 1964. *Author*

The story ran that the L&NWR agent at Waterford got the master and mate drunk, so that they mistook the buoys and missed a tide, and a lot of thirst-crazed cattle had to be beached at Trevena (Towyn) to be slaughtered. In fact, each part of it has some basis in truth, but it seemingly did not all happen on the same voyage.

As soon as the service commenced, the Great Western refused to give any assistance with arrangements for livestock traffic imported through Aberdovey, the London & North Western withdrew its half-promised support for any destination north of Crewe, and Irish agents formed a 'no traffic' ring.

On 4th May 1887, the captain was found to be too drunk to bring the steamer into harbour and the mate, Mr. Morgan, had to be put in command after the ship had missed a tide.

Six days later, a gale caused the *Liverpool* to run for shelter in St. Tudwals Roads; this diversion did cause a few cattle and pigs to generate a thirst.

Detail of warehouse ends, showing peculiar angling of the end of the general warehouse. 14th June 1964. *Author*

The last retreat of rail-borne coal, the east end of the quay, where the coal merchant can be seen shovelling the coal off the wagon into bags for weighing (on his legally required weighing machine) carried on his ex-army truck. 1961. *Author*

Left: The south gables of the warehouses. *Right:* Buildings added on to the east side of the grain warehouse. The addition on the left provides (very basic) public toilets – a sign of the transition of this place from a working harbour to a leisure site. Both photos were taken on 14th June 1964. *Author*

This picture, looking westwards with Glandovey Terrace on the right and the quay on the left, shows GWR 0–6–0 Collett Goods No. 2286. Having deposited a van at the far end of the diagonal road, the engine was returning to pick up the rest of the 8.40 a.m. Machynlleth–Towyn Goods left standing on the main line (see also page 112). 1961. *Author*

Looking westwards across Aberdovey Harbour, showing the quay and its east wall ending in a slipway in front of the Dovey Hotel. The arrangement of the bridges which connected the quay to the jetty (on the left) can be seen, with the two warehouses dominating the quaysite site. Only the rails and the coal stacks remain as evidence of railway activity on the quay and the warehousing was being converted to other uses. *Author's collection*

During June, much of the management's time was taken up with disputes with the GWR and the L&NWR over rebates – they just would not give any. It was noted that the returns were poor.

By 25th July, the *Liverpool*'s passages were getting slower, and Mr. Stuart promised to find a faster boat; but the Cambrian refused to increase the subsidy to the required figure of £250. Then Captain Morgan voiced his suspicions that the four stokers from Waterford had been bribed as part of a conspiracy against the venture, and they were replaced by four men from Liverpool. Stuart asked for better Tyldesley coal, and it was then found out that he was paying only £170 per month for the charter of the *Liverpool*. In August, he said that the SS *Glasgow* would be making the sailings in future; but the *Liverpool* still came wheezing in.

For the 28th September docking, the *Liverpool* made her offing after dark; the first (outer) buoy was missed, the second (inner) was mistaken for the first, and she ran aground on the bar. The steamer was thereafter to be provided with an electric light mounted in her bows.

The *Liverpool* arrived for the last time on 23rd October 1887, having lost the Cambrian a total of £439. The shipments were falling off because of the conspiracy at Waterford, and the ring were threatening Agent Fitzgerald with a complete boycott of all his business if he continued to send livestock to Aberdovey via the steamship company's boats.

On 24th October, everyone flocked to the sea front to watch the arrival of the SS *Magnetic*. Being of 290 tons net register, she was little bigger than the *Liverpool*, but she had been specially converted for carrying livestock, and had electric lighting on all decks. Also available was the SS *Electric*, but the port book covering the period from June 1888 to March 1895 is missing, and there is as yet no proof that she ever sailed on charter to the Waterford & Aberdovey Steamship Company.

The *Magnetic*'s second trip, on 26th October 1887, was a great disaster. She rolled abominably in severe gales, and the conversion had been done badly, with the stallage constructed at too low a level so that the beasts were thrown over the tops onto others in the next stalls. The ventilation was also quite inadequate. She had set sail with 149 head of cattle, and arrived with 31 of those dead, and a further 25 injured. A butcher from Towyn was sent for, and he slaughtered another three immediately, whilst the other 22 had to be sold off locally as being unfit for further travel. So, only 93 could be certified as fit to continue, and it was 16 hours before the *Magnetic* had been washed and scrubbed down sufficiently to allow the return trip to Waterford.

There was a considerable legal wrangle over insurance, primarily because no cover had been ordered! Both Stuart and the Cambrian each argued that the other was responsible for arranging cargo insurance; that single trip cost the Cambrian £719 2s 6d in compensation. The *Magnetic*'s ventilation was improved, but fewer and fewer people would send their cattle in her, and she became more and more a pig-carrying boat.

By Christmas 1887, the *Magnetic* had managed to make nine out of the seventeen advertised sailings, and had managed to lose the Cambrian a further £103. The captain reported that she was doing nicely on the South Wales coal that the Cambrian had arranged, but 'it is stiff and slow in starting to burn'. However, it was still quite impossible with only one ship to maintain three sailings each week, and the service was reduced to two only. The Cambrian then expressed its willingness to increase the subsidy to £200 per week to keep the service going for a while longer, and did so.

A report dated 1st May 1888 stressed that the *Magnetic* was 'too low between decks and only fit to convey pigs, sheep and small store cattle', and 'a better boat was needed as shippers were refusing to send cattle on her.'

On 1st June the owner, Mr. Gourlay, indicated that he wished to sell the *Magnetic*, but was unable to do so while she was engaged to the Cambrian; so he offered her to the company for £8,000, but the Board refused. Instead, they looked at a plan of a bigger steamer, built to carry 1,000 head of cattle and costing £20,500, and at hiring another on offer from Earle's Shipbuilding Company for delivery to the Clyde Shipping Company (which then backed out, claiming that the Aberdovey trade was too small for them). Then the Board offered Gourlay up to £4,000 for the *Magnetic*, but he in turn refused.

The August sailings had to be cancelled because of a damaged propeller; and it was found that the new one, of a different pitch, required 20% less coal to drive the ship along.

The steamer committee had still not learned from its experiences, and next propounded a scheme for changing the venue from Waterford to Rosslare. This was still under discussion when they decided to suspend the sailings after 30th November.

Secretary John Conacher informed his masters on 11th December 1888 that 'Since the *Magnetic* has been withdrawn the Waterford Steamship Company have put up the rates and the shippers are now wishing that they had given better support to the Waterford & Aberdovey Steamship Company'.

The final account for the first year's sailings revealed a net working loss of £415 18s 11d, with a footnote that if the *Magnetic* had been in service for the entire year, the loss would have been only £40 5s 0d.

Between 20th April and 23rd October 1887, the *Liverpool* made 48 voyages. As related, she had brought only 60 pigs and a little general cargo the first time, and no cattle at all until the fifteenth sailing. Two voyages were with a little general cargo only. Her total livestock imports were:

Cattle	1,361
Sheep	2,766
Pigs	2,805

Up to 30th May 1888, the *Magnetic* made 57 voyages, and carried:

Cattle	929
Sheep	261
Pigs	8,692
Horse	1

Cattle shipments had virtually ended by December 1887; either the boycott had become pretty effective, or there was little or no demand anyway.

On 9th July 1889, the Cambrian Railways (Steamboats) Act came onto the Statute Book with the following provisions:

> 'The Company may from time to time build or buy or hire and may use maintain work and or let or enter into arrangements for using working or maintaining steam vessels for the purpose of carrying on a convenient and efficient communication by means thereof between the ports and places in North Wales of Aberdovey Aberystwyth Portmadoc and Pwllheli and the ports and places in Ireland of Wexford Rosslare Waterford Wicklow and Arklow or any or either of them and may therein and thereby convey or carry between such places and ports aforesaid Passengers animals minerals Merchandise and goods and may do all acts that may be necessary to enable them to carry fully into effect the purposes aforesaid.'

The company was also given the power to demand and recover such reasonable tolls and charges as they thought fit.

The only effective part of the Act authorised the Cambrian to convert the £20,000 authorised pier stock into class 'A' debenture stock. The effect of this was to allow the holders of the only pier stock issued (£8,085) to receive dividends out of ordinary revenue instead of out of harbour profits only; and of course, takers might also now be found for the £11,915 of pier stock which remained unallocated.

It was discovered, however, that the legal advisers had blundered, and had omitted to use wordage which would allow the Cambrian to expend any capital in pursuit of the objectives of the Act. This came on top of threats from the GWR and the L&NWR of covert actions if the Cambrian did try to exercise all the powers contained in the Act.

The agency at Waterford lingered on with shipments of livestock to Aberdovey in general service vessels until the agent, Mr. John Downey, gave notice of resignation as from 31st December 1892. The company tried to sell the fitted yard there for £150, but ended up with salvaging only £20 from the Waterford & Limerick Railway for the box office; it had cost £90, but was not considered worth dismantling and shipping back to Aberdovey. Then the lease ran out.

On 4th April 1894, the committee authorised the chairman and the general manager to negotiate with the Dublin & Glasgow Steamship Company for a general service between Dublin and Aberdovey.

At their meeting of 29th April 1897, the committee instructed the new general manager, C. S. Denniss, to handle a proposal received for yet another steamer service between Aberdovey and Waterford. This involved the diversion of a regular Liverpool to Waterford steamer to run via Aberdovey once a week on the return passage, with rather complicated charge rates amounting to around £200 per month.

The 'Rates Dues and Charges Collected' book for the period from 1st June 1888 to 30th April 1907 has yet to be found. It would have included the first sailings of the Aberdovey & Barmouth Steamship Company Ltd., which was formed on 6th May 1892. The first ship to call was the SS *Telephone*, which plied until the arrival, in August 1900, of the newly-built SS *Dora*, which came to be known as 'The Grocery Boat'. She became a most regular visitor, leaving Liverpool with general goods and occasional trip passengers, going straight to Aberdovey so as to lighten her cargo before making the tricky entry into Barmouth harbour on the return. On 1st May 1917, she was stopped by a German submarine, and sunk by a charge detonated against her hull plates. This sad event finished the steamship company.

However, the Cambrian harbourmaster also had to keep a 'Register of Vessels', of which a fragment from this period has survived. By way of an illustration of the period, the following vessels and consignments were recorded in the document for 1895:

The schooner *Mervinia* of Aberystwyth (96 tons register) docked on 27th March with oats from Dublin, and sailed on 29th April with slates from Abergynolwyn for Sligo.

The schooner *Dreadnought*, also of Aberystwyth, docked on 31st March in ballast, and set sail on 20th April with slates from Braichgoch, also for Sligo.

The smack *Margaret Ellen*, of Cardigan, docked with gunpowder on 11th April, and sailed on 18th May to Neath with slates.

Another Aberystwyth (Aberdovey) schooner, Dafydd Jones' dandy-rigged *Volunteer* (of only 96 tons) came from Aberystwyth in ballast on 27th June, and got away on 24th July with Abergynolwyn slates, destination not entered.

NOTE

All the Aberdovey boats were registered from Aberystwyth.

The period covered by the last (and intact) 'Rates Dues and Charges Collected' book ran from 1st May 1907 to 31st October 1961, and contained the following interesting items:

1907

	Ship	Cargo
4th May	Schooner *Salvador*	$105\frac{3}{4}$ Standards of Floorboard.
15th May	SS *Arrival*	Ammunition from Woolwich Arsenal.
13th June	SS *Countess of Lisburne*	Loading Lead Ore.
28th June	Schooner *Vriendschap*	Cement.
8th July	SS *Telephone*	General (in place of *Dora*)
20th July	SS *Telephone*	Loading Lead Ore.
22nd July	SS *Telephone*	General (in place of *Dora*)
26th August	SS *Beaver*	Sleepers from Port Talbot.

When Aberdovey heard organ music from the other side of Snowdon. Marconi's yacht *Elettra* moored at the outer face of the jetty, probably the 1920 voyage when reception from Cefn-ddu was tested at several places down Cardigan Bay. *Cty. J. W. Burman*

The steamer *May* came regularly in the summer with trippers from Aberystwyth; but often, *Dora* was the only caller.

Apart from the regular deliveries of general goods by the *Dora*, sporadic arrivals with cement, manure, sleepers and timber continued, and there were the odd arrivals by the *Telephone* with such items as potatoes and grain. Another passenger tripper from Aberystwyth, the SS *Countess of Warwick*, appeared for the first time on 29th June 1908. Along with the coastal and ocean-going steamships, the dandies, schooners and smacks continued to ply their trade into Aberdovey.

By 1914, Aberystwyth's SS *May* had ceased to call, but the *Countess of Warwick* still came in, together with the SS *Kenilworth*, and the larger motor-engined *Mauretania*. Then, after 19th September, when the schooner *Voorwaarts* unloaded timber from Frederickstadt, there was only the *Dora*, once relieved by the *Telephone*. Her last docking was on 11th November 1916.

After the war, the Aberystwyth trippers started again, with the *County* and the *Wild Rose* added to the fleet. Occasionally, there was a cargo ship with potatoes, flour, grain, superphosphate or basic slag, whilst the Fishery Protection's police boat, the SS *James Fletcher*, became a regular visitor.

On 15th August 1921, an entry reads Yacht *Elettra*, with the merchant's name recorded as Marconi. A loudspeaker was set up and directed down across the pier, whilst a crowd gathered and waited in silence. On the northern slopes beyond Snowdon, at Cefdu, a time clock tripped a switch, and 56 valves (each the size of a football) glowed softly, driven by immense banks of wet accumulators. Then the clock tripped another switch, another clockwork mechanism started spinning the turntable of a gramophone, and the amazed assembly heard organ music from a vulcanite record turning fifty miles away. So it was demonstrated that wireless sound waves could go over mountains and across land and sea, and the Marconi-inspired network of broadcasting stations would be successful; by 1922 we were wearing headphones, and tuning the first crystal sets to hear 'Two Emma Tock Writtle calling'. Soon after came 2LO London, 5XX Daventry, and all the others.

A fair quantity of cement arrived during 1925, and a lot more in 1926; the shipments continued steadily until the last load (on 26th December 1939) was brought by the MV *Kixudiesel*. Nearly all of this was for Birmingham Corporation's great Claerwen dam.

No dues were collected after that date until August 1941, when the Army's *Prince Louis* moored, and stayed until May 1943. She had been joined by *Camroux III* in July 1942, which duly remained as the sole paying occupant until November 1945. Between that month and November 1947, the harbour was monopolised by the Royal Army Service Corps Amphibious Training Unit, based at Towyn. They had an old hulk moored out in midstream as a focal point, and on an occasion when a 'Buffalo' (an amphibious tank) hit the hulk, the armoured vehicle was so damaged that it only just made the shallow water near the beach before it sank. The hulk showed only the loss of a splinter or two.

The method of selecting suitable drivers was to order four prospectives to hang on, one at each inside corner of a DUKW, and take them across Aberdovey bar – those who were not seasick were in and were selected for further training! One 'Weasel' was recovered after going up the hill too smartly, and rolling over into the cemetery.

From 1947, the only residents were the Royal Army Service Corps boats *Grand Parade*, *Newman Noggs*, *Sikes*, *Chadband*, *St Julien* and *Blue Peter* (up to September 1947), although a few private and pleasure boats started to moor, and there was an occasional visitor from the Admiralty or Fisheries; but this was in the summer only, and the berths were empty during the winter.

From October 1959, there is a continuous (and almost unreadable) entry – 'Thomson Lines Hotel' – until August 1961, when the port book and the story both come to their respective ends.

Having left its diminutive goods train (the 8.40 a.m. Machynlleth to Towyn) on the main line, and with the guard on the footplate, 0–6–0 Collett Goods No. 2286 is shown here crossing over to the down loop line. From here the engine propelled the van all the way to the far end of the quayside line. The operation took a good few minutes, and the van would not have been left parked 'in section' unless there was a very ample margin before the next train was due. Otherwise the van (and the rest of the train) would also have to be propelled down the Harbour branch – there was nowhere else readily available to refuge it, short of running round and propelling into the down shunting neck. 1961. *Author*

ABERDOVEY to TOWYN
– 85m 10c to 88m 40c

THE line runs level over low-lying ground for the whole distance. When the railway was built, the terrain was much more marshy than it is today, and it was this that forced Soloman Andrews to abandon his proposal of 1899 to make a rival passenger tramway, running parallel to the Cambrian, from Towyn to Aberdovey. His worst problem was the Aberdovey Marsh, where the Cambrian had already squeezed in its trackbed as close to the firmer ground as was possible.

The route leaves Aberdovey along half-a-mile of straight, and then bends gently northwards. At the start of this bend comes Trefeddian Crossing and, just where the line straightens again, Aberdovey Gasworks lay inland. In 1903, a siding was to have been put in to Aberdovey Gasworks (at 85m 70c). The Cambrian asked for a contribution of £220 but the manager, another Mr. Dennis, stated that he would expect a refund if a coal wharf was put in near to the station. To the west are the golf links, and the way northwards deflects gently to keep to the firmer ground for about a mile-and-a-half, with Rifle Range bridge as the only feature. The views inland at this point are of the Happy Valley, flanked by outliers of the mountains. After

Trefeddian Crossing, looking round the curve towards Towyn on 18th July 1965. The path on the crossing led from the road (off to the right) across the golf course to the dunes and the heath beyond. *Author*

Trefeddian crossing-keeper's house on 18th July 1965. *Author*

curving to a north-westerly course over about another mile-and-a-half, a smart-looking four-storey building can be seen inland – this was once a mill and is now a hotel.

At 87m 38c was Bodtalog Mill siding, curving eastwards from the main line to serve a large water-powered mill. This was out-of-use and disconnected by 1875, but the rails were still down. Early in that year, Mr Evan Newell asked for it to be restored as he wished to reopen the flour mill, and to erect a brick kiln; it was approved that every facility should be given to him, but at his expense alone. If traffic exceeded £250 per annum, he would be reimbursed at 10% per annum. The new installation was passed for service in January 1877.

Later, the place became a slate enamelling works, and engines could take water here (when the Aberdovey source dried up) by running to a column fed from the launder which supplied the overshot water wheel. This facility, known as 'Mill Siding' was in use in 1896, though it may have been disconnected when road widening caused the demolition of the wooden trough which brought the water from the leet to the wheel. The exact date of demolition is not known, but to

The fixed distant signal for Aberdovey, looking in the up direction with Trefeddian Crossing in the background. 18th July 1965.
Author

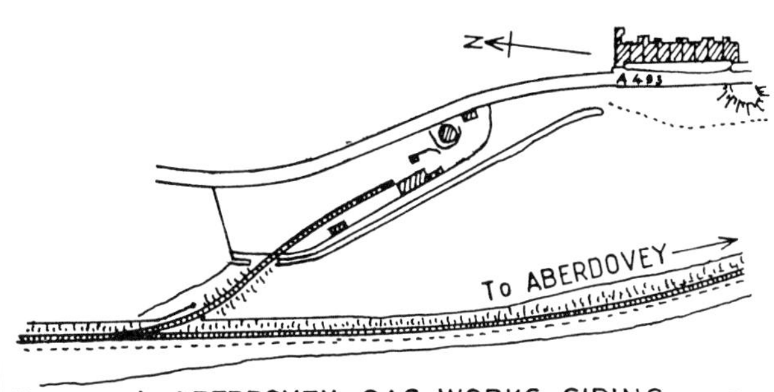

Proposed ABERDOVEY GAS WORKS SIDING *C. C. Green*

A Dean 0–6–0 on an up goods passing Aberdovey gas works and approaching the up distant signal for Aberdovey. Note the gas wagon at the front of the train. c.1920.
H. W. Burman

replace the emergency supply, a water tank was erected near to the Afon Dyffryn-gwyn culvert, at about 87m 75c.

On 15th July 1874, a little girl fell out of a moving carriage, landed lightly (as children can) and, despite a grazed cheek and a bruised arm, ran after the train, which had halted after the alarm cord had been pulled.

A severe snowstorm blocked-in a northbound train on 1st March 1886, a mile to the south of Towyn. This drift was cleared so that a local service could be run as far as Towyn, but the Towyn to Llwyngwril section remained blocked for several days.

A boisterous gale in 1908 brought an abandoned deck cargo of 37 pitchpine logs ashore along this section of line. After negotiating with the Receiver of Wrecks, the engineer secured them all for 10d a cubic foot, and arranged a contract with a local fisherman for them to be towed round to Aberdovey for five shillings each. The ultimate cost to the company was 1 shilling per cubic foot as compared with the ruling price of 1s 8d delivered.

There was an outcry in 1916 when, on 24th October, the stiles which had been erected near the gasworks in 1895 (so that the golfers could cross the line) were removed without warning. Following strong protests by the owners of the Trefeddian Hotel and other local people, they were restored during the following January on payment for a notice reading 'PRIVATE', the cost of the new stiles, and a wayleave.

In 1919, the Mid-Wales Basket Making Company inspected the lineside terrain owned by the company, and agreed to plant experimental osier beds.

Two years later there was a further dispute, over the removal of the ladder stiles at the Trefeddian Crossing.

In 1922, the defective Rhowniar timber pile bridge (at about 87m 10c) was replaced with concrete pipes for £208; it had already been rebuilt once, in 1897, at a cost of £73 5s 6d.

It was noted in 1923 that the Trefeddian public crossing was not signalled.

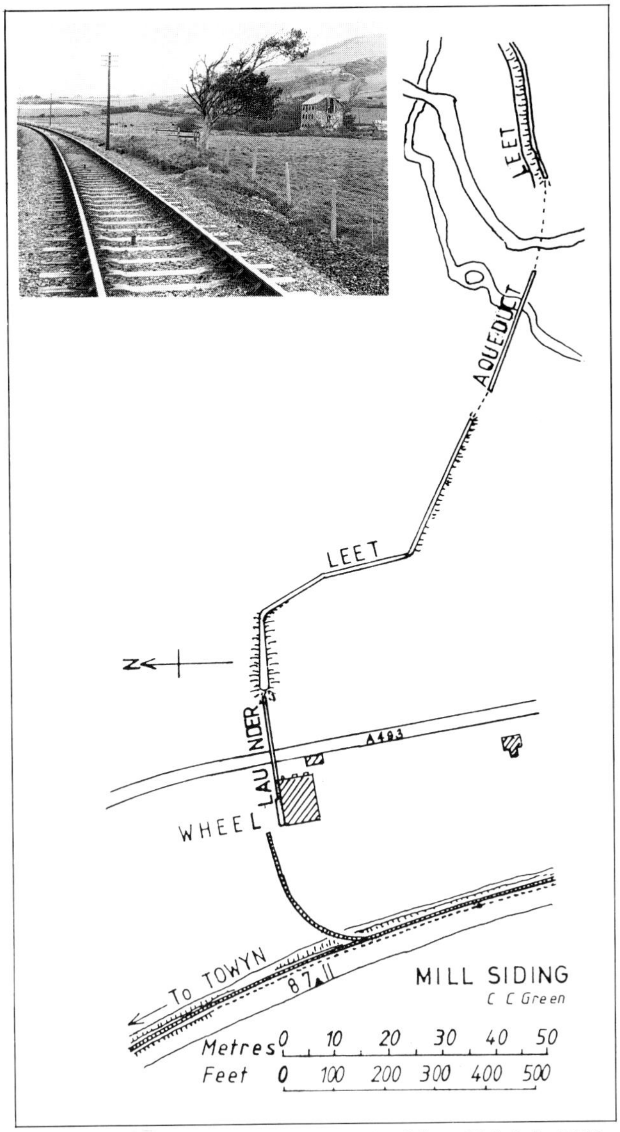

Inset picture: The site of Bodtalog Mill Siding, 25th July 1965. The siding diverged to the right through the gateway to serve Newell's Mill, seen in the right background (now converted to a restaurant and hotel). *Author*

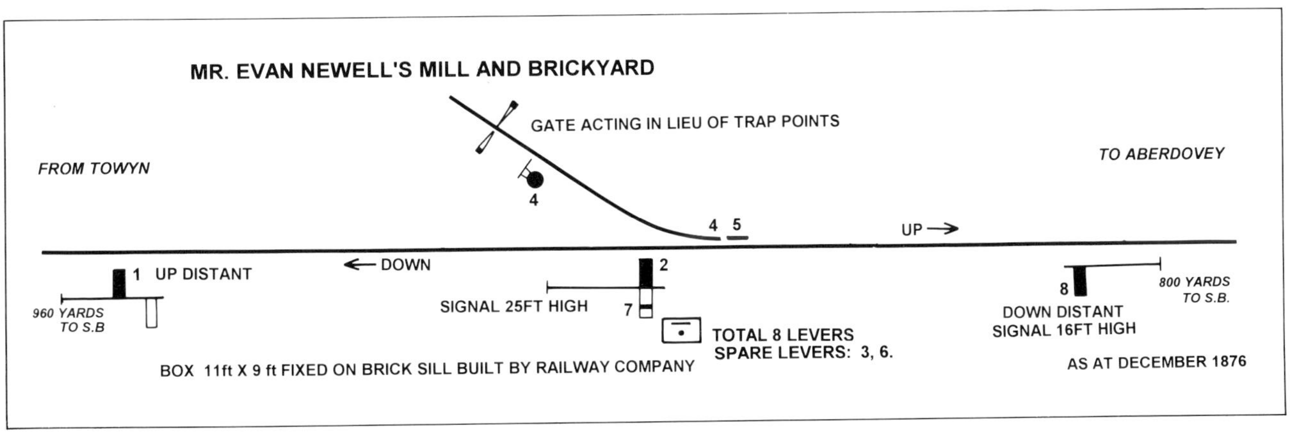

Rifle Range bridge, looking in the down direction towards Towyn, on 25th July 1965. The bridge was made for two tracks though the chance of the line ever being doubled was always remote indeed! *Author*

Rifle Range bridge roadway, looking seawards. Note poor, thin parapet coping. *Author*

TOWYN

(now TYWYN) – 88m 40c to 88m 66c, (to Sandilands, 89m 9c)

Station at 88m 57c
Signal Box at 88m 47c (GWR signal box)
Opened: 24th October 1863

In April 1862 there was an unofficial ceremony on The Green, near to the Corbett Arms Hotel, Towyn. Savin and Piercy attended, while Mrs. Foulkes of Aberdovey cut the first sod, 'and a few scores of persons cheered lustily'. Eighteen months later, the station opened for traffic, the line being opened from Aberdovey to Llwyngwril.

It was noted that Towyn had a staff of only three in 1866. In that year, the Board refused to sell land to the Talyllyn Railway; this was probably the site of the 'Old Ballast Hole' next to the wharf, though the committee did approve the sale to the Talyllyn of the wharf site (which was already in use) for £303 2s 6d.

A complaint was received in 1868 that the old public road to the beach had been destroyed during the construction; this may indicate the date of the lowering of the roadway to pass under the line at what came to be known as Platform Bridge. During the night of 7th/8th April, the 'temporary station with no residence' was 'burglariously entered', but the station master seems to have been in the habit of carrying the takings home for safety.

In February 1870, permission was given to a Mr. Holloway to enable him to open a refreshment room 'as this is the worst station on the Line in every respect.' In March, approval was given for the construction of a new station with refreshment rooms, not as 'Plan B' costing only £220 14s 0d, but as 'Plan A' (though without the verandah) costing £451 8s 0d; this had been completed by 9th June. A suggestion for the inclusion of a station master's house was deferred 'until the Company have more funds.' On 18th August, the newly-appointed traffic manager, Mr. Henry Cattle, reported that he had caught the station master and the booking clerk purloining thirty shillings and £5 18s $10\frac{1}{2}$d respectively.

Towyn station, looking in the down direction and showing the North signal box beyond the road underbridge c.1905. The smaller arm on the starting signal on to the single line to Llwyngwril applied to movements from the down platform to the shunting neck. This was not an arm with a circular end but was set on a small bracket, the other method commonly used on the Cambrian for signalling a move straight on into a shunting neck. This arm was added c.1907 (compare with the photo on page 119). *Cty. R. E. Thomas*

Mr. Holloway refused to pay the £52 for the new refreshment rooms, and a Mr. Projer took up the lease at £51 per annum, whilst the committee approved that Captain Pryce should call on 'some of the Merionethshire Magistrates' who would attend the licensing sessions to 'arrange' for the granting of a spirit licence.

It was noted that, in 1871, goods had to be left out in open wagons, but the provision of proper accommodation for £420 was deferred. However, a goods shed, carriage dock and sidings costing £310 were approved in January of that year. The company had provided an additional lamp on the station road by Christmas 1872.

In the summer of 1873, Sandilands Crossing was fitted out with signals for £66 5s 2d.

The cattle pens at Towyn were paved in March 1876 for the sum of £5 16s 2d. On 16th October, the traffic manager reported 'the traffic has quite outgrown the accommodation at this place', and of Carter William Williams, 'I spoke to the old man who is very infirm and physically unable to perform the work which is so badly done that we get into great disgrace.' He indicated that he had arranged with Mr. Seaton, proprietor of the Corbett Arms Hotel 'and who is a respectable man', to deposit £50 as personal security, and to continue the service at the same rate, two shillings per ton.

The statement about the derailment of a passenger train on 12th December 1876 reads:

> 'Towyn is a Station arranged for Trains to pass each other when travelling in opposite directions. Distant Signals are interlocked with the Facing Points leading into the Loop Line at both ends of the Station. When the Distant Signals are at Danger the points are unlocked and can be moved for shunting purposes. The Distants are kept at Danger and lowered for the oncoming train that whistles first where two trains are arranged to meet each other'.

A goods train ex-Pwllheli had arrived first, and was admitted into the loop. The 8.35 a.m. passenger ex-Machynlleth whistled, and the porter had tried to lower the distant, but could not do so because of an obstruction in the points. The passenger train had run on cautiously instead of stopping, and had been derailed at the points. Colonel Rich had happened to be on site shortly afterwards to inspect 'the new siding which has been constructed into the Brick Yard'. He read and accepted the evidence. Disciplinary action was not recorded.

On 16th December, 'as a person was passing over the Bridge near Towyn Station shortly after the Up Mail had passed he heard groans as from someone in distress'. Edward Evans, mining agent of Machynlleth, had 'wandered down the line in a state of intoxication'. He 'lingered on until Sunday morning'.

In January 1877, arising from the derailment on 12th December the previous year, Colonel Rich required 'Blockhouse Signalling and alterations to the Permanent Way', which cost £650.

The additional sidings so urgently needed could not be ordered, the 'Balance of Capital Accounts being so small'. By June 1877, the solicitor had completed the sale of 'The Old Ballast Hole' to Mr. John Jones Hughes as a site for his Jones & Griffiths timber yard. At first, he had wanted a layout which required a signal box and signalman, but later he reduced his ideas to a siding only.

Taken between July 1890 when the brake third No. 70 was built for £456 and June 1891 when No. 7 *Llanerchydol* lost her nameplate. This picture shows the end window lettered 'Second class waiting room'. The ballast on the 'six-foot' between the loop lines can be seen up to the height of the rails, and the sleepers, too, are covered, as was the practice of the time at stations.
Cty. Mrs. C. F. Ellis

At the end of November 1878, William Humphries, a coal and brick merchant, was given permission to erect his own wooden stable for a ground rent of £3 per annum.

A 15-ton weighbridge was installed for £132 15s 0d during 1883.

On 21st September of that year, the engine and two loaded wagons of the 9.50 p.m. up goods were derailed at the up 'indicator points' (i.e. the point at the north end of the station, facing an up goods proceeding to Machynlleth) at about 11.5 p.m. The driver of the earlier 8.25 p.m. ex-Machynlleth was at first dismissed, but later reinstated and admonished for running through the points, in a trailing direction, against the setting, and bursting the locking arrangements. Porter Owen Owen disappeared after the mishap, and 'turned up again. On enquiry and after much cross-swearing on the part of the men employed, it has been established that he failed in his duty to see that the points were correctly set.' He was dismissed, and sought reinstatement, but was refused.

The traffic manager reported on 21st August 1885, that he was having trouble with the Abergynolwyn

Slate Company, who were refusing to pay the company's charges for:

Use of sidings – 3d
Checking, Clerkage, Watching and Labelling – 2d
Total (Towyn) – 5d
Use of Sidings – 3d
Weighing – ¼d
Checking, Clerking and Watching – 1¾d
Horse Shunting – 2d
Total (Aberdovey harbour) – 7d

The reason given was that railways were common carriers. The solicitor sent notice that, notwithstanding the failure of the Aberystwyth and Welsh Coast Railway Act of 1861 to authorise the making of such charges, the situation had been altered in favour of the railways by the judgement given in the Queen's Bench Division in 'Hall versus The London, Brighton & South Coast Railway'. All the large railway companies had immediately given notice that they were not common carriers within the relative Acts, and the Cambrian now followed suit. The carriage rates from Towyn to Aberdovey were 1s 4d per ton in Cambrian wagons, and one shilling in other wagons.

On 10th October 1885, a rake of narrow gauge wagons broke loose from a Talyllyn train, ran through that company's Towyn station, overturned a Cambrian wagon, and spread themselves all over the Cambrian main line. Prompt action resulted in a delay of only nine minutes to one passenger train but the traffic manager indicated: 'I have asked the Talyllyn Company to state what means they propose to adopt to prevent the recurrence of an accident of this kind.'

The down waiting shed and North signal box c.1895, with 0–6–0 Sharp Stewart No. 40, formerly *Cyfronydd*, as rebuilt. As at Aberdovey, there was a substantial station building on the up side, but only a shelter without doors or awning on the down platform. The North box lacked the storm porch with which many others were equipped. *Cty. R. E. Thomas*

Towyn South signal box with Sharp Stewart 0–6–0 No. 27 *Cambria* c.1894. This was the principal signal box at Towyn and had a distinctive porch covered by an extension of the roof of the box. The wooden trunking covering the area in front of the box where the point rods led out and the ballast covering many of the sleepers all made it safer to walk about, but routine maintenance was much more difficult. *C. J. Young*

Newly-trained and equipped soldiers marching on and forming up on the down platform ready to join the L&NWR train which took them to Liverpool for shipping out to South Africa. 1900. *Cty. R. C. Riley*

During 1886, the traffic manager proposed the adaptation of old Cambrian wagons for carrying loaded Talyllyn wagons direct to Aberdovey harbour, but this seems to have failed because the Talyllyn did not possess enough wagons to permit a rake to be absent from their own system even for half a day, and a shipping delay could have halted output entirely.

In April, approval was given for the lengthening of the down platform by 104 ft, ostensibly to stop passengers crossing the line from the end ramp on the up side; however, the cost was found to be £160, and the idea remained just a proposal.

There was a lengthy argument in December 1886 over the rates for conveying slates to Aberdovey, which culminated in the withdrawal of the slate company secretary's cheap rate ticket, and of any relaxation of demurrage and siding rent charges at Aberdovey.

On 7th January 1887, a coal wagon was being shunted by means of a pole between the headstock and the tender of the engine (a common but prohibited practice). The pole fell away as the engine accelerated, and the tender was derailed when the engine caught up with the wagon at a crossing in the pointwork. 'I have called the attention of the staff to the danger which arises from using the pole for shunting purposes', reported Edwin Liller, the traffic manager.

The local health board served notice on the company in 1888, complaining of the smallness of the urinals, the inadequate ventilation, and of the general want of proper accommodation. However, facilities for the loading and offloading of both horses and carriages had been provided by that year.

Another of the sad little accidents, so common on Victorian railways, happened on 29th June 1889. A four-year-old boy, the son of Mr. Hugh Daniel, a painter, wandered onto the line near Sandilands crossing, and was knocked down by the 10.15 a.m. ex-Machynlleth goods train 'and received serious injuries to the head, little hope being entertained of his recovery'.

In March 1891, a new waiting shed was put up on the down platform, at a cost of £40 'to replace the old structure which had been part of the original station'. There were still two wire-locked facing points, the operating levers for which, adjacent to the points, had to be held down when trains passed in a facing direction.

On 29th June 1893, Hugh Davies (aged 7) was seen 'sitting on a tree' (a pile of trunks) around which work was taking place. He was ordered to leave, but he hid behind the pile, and while a log was being lifted, another rolled off the top, 'killing him on the spot.'

In September, it was agreed with Mr. Dennis of Ruabon, the proprietor of the Dysinni Gasworks, for the laying down of a siding with signalling (etc.) at his expense, and with special charges for services.

On 17th July 1894, the engineer warned the committee that the yard points were still not interlocked. Inevitably, there was another mishap, on 5th September. Porter David Owen omitted to hold down the lever working the wire-locked facing points, and the 8.23 a.m. ex-Glandovey Junction derailed completely – engine, tender and six carriages. Then, on the 14th 'Senior Porter Walters who also lowers the signals from the levers on the platform failed to put the Down Distant back to danger after a train had passed and the next up train had burst through the points'. (The train could normally have trailed through the points safely, since they were controlled only by a weighted lever, but with the down direction signal at clear, the wire-worked locking was engaged and would have been broken as the train forced its way through the points.) Everyone from the station master down was reprimanded, as was the signal fitter who had failed to report repairing the damaged gear, presumably in an attempt to save all his mates from getting into trouble.

The coal merchants complained in 1895 that the goods shed was too close to the passenger platform, and should be moved. The general repositioning needed

This picture of 0–6–0 Jones Goods No. 38, running as GWR No. 864, on an up passenger, also shows the timber footbridge.
Author's collection

Station and PW staff, and further detail of the timber footbridge, a view taken looking south towards Aberdovey, c.1920.
H. W. Burman

was to cost £3,702, and included moving the cattle pens, alterations to the permanent way, and extending the platforms. Mr. Chidlaw Roberts was reported to be vacating his site, and setting up at Aberdovey with a new sawmill.

During 1896, the Corbett Estate was planning an extensive development of the area to seaward of the line, and was generally raising levels about the station to bring their roads up to platform level. They were also given permission to lay a new sewer under the line. In April, a contract was let to Mr. Phoenix of Wrexham for making the new promenade, for the letting out of building sites, and for the building of houses. Stone was to be brought from Mr. Corbett's new quarries at Tonfanau, and 'it is proposed to lay down another tramway from the Station Yard if the Cambrian will provide a wharf and siding to meet the narrow gauge line at the fence'. This cost £20.

In an interview with the *Railway Magazine,* C. S. Denniss referred to Mr. John Corbett 'of Droitwich salt fame' expending between £60,000 and £70,000 'in developing a splendid promenade', and two years later, in *Wild Wales,* T. Booth wrote:

> 'We see the builder has been busy at work erecting new dwellings to cope with the growing reputation of the place as a holiday resort and to house comfortably the tourists whose numbers are annually augmented. The town too is full of antique lore and legend hath it that Owain Glyndwr in the hour of his adversity took refuge at this pretty village by the sea.'

At Whitsuntide 1896 there was an encampment of Volunteers (the equivalent of the Territorials of the

The Talyllyn Railway Company's wharf, 16th August 1935. *H. F. Wheeller*

4–6–0 'Manor' No. 7818 passing the Talyllyn wharf on the approach to Towyn station, with a nine-coach special train, in September 1953. The site of the former 'ballast hole' was behind the engine. The line on which the wagons were standing was the exchange siding whilst the line in front of that was the up shunting neck. *P. J. Garland*

The Talyllyn Railway's Wharf station in early preservation days, with *Dolgoch* sitting in the middle of an empty yard. The Talyllyn Railway entered its station at Towyn Wharf at nearly 90 degrees to the Cambrian's line, necessitating the use of turntables to reach the 2ft 3in gauge siding which ran along the top of the wharf at the Exchange siding. As the slate traffic from the TR ceased, the siding increasingly became used for storage of wagons not immediately required for traffic. 1955/60. *J. H. Moss*

A fine view looking south from the Neptune Road bridge in Towyn, towards Aberdovey, with the TR Exchange siding on the left. The adjacent shunt neck was relaid by the GWR using concrete blocks tied together at each fourth pair of blocks, a common feature on the Cambrian lines. The coaches left at the far end of the shunting neck were there for the next weekend. 1955/60.

J. H. Moss

Looking north, in the down direction, through the bridge which carries Neptune Road over the railway. The two spare coaches and various wagons in the distance were standing on the down refuge siding in the West siding. 1955/60. *J. H. Moss*

Looking northwards from Neptune Road bridge, with the down refuge siding (the West siding) on the left. Not many Cambrian stations had the advantage of a refuge siding, this one having been partly relaid using concrete blocks. The siding had been shortened when the new Central signal box was built in 1923 replacing the North and South signal boxes. The wall beside the refuge siding had formerly been a loading wharf. The up loop line on the right extended under the bridge as a shunt neck (headshunt) whilst the goods warehouse road on the right extended to form the Exchange siding with the TR. Shortage of space dictated that the up starting signal (levers 3/4) was on the right-hand side of the down loop. 1955/60. *J. H. Moss*

No. 9012 leaving Towyn station with an up local train for Machynlleth on 28th July 1955, with 'tail traffic'. By this date, up starting signal 3/4 had been replaced by a WR tubular steel version.
H. F. Wheeller

20th century) on land around the station. The Cambrian spent £38 19s 2d on the construction of a special baggage and equipment wharf, to avoid the dissatisfaction and inconvenience caused in earlier years by the inadequate facilities, which might have caused the removal of the camps to another venue (a suggestion heartily supported by the inhabitants and the council, as the unwelcome visitors numbered several thousands).

On the night of 7th October, there was a 'furious gale and high tide and the Corbett development was inundated.'

Eight days later, Porter Owen Williams took hold of the wheel (instead of the handle) of the crane, and had

A view from beside the signal box, showing the coal wharf, the cross-overs at the up end of the layout, and the West siding, on 25th July 1965. *Author*

Two views of 0–6–0 Jones Goods No. 101, renumbered 895 by the GWR, refuged and waiting in the West siding to be overtaken by a passenger train, in September 1953. *P. J. Garland*

The GWR replaced the North and South signal-boxes by one larger box (the new box had 38 levers) as from c.July 1923. The new box was this wooden structure, brought to Towyn in sections after being dismantled at its former location, Maidenhead East. 29th July 1966.

J. J. Davis

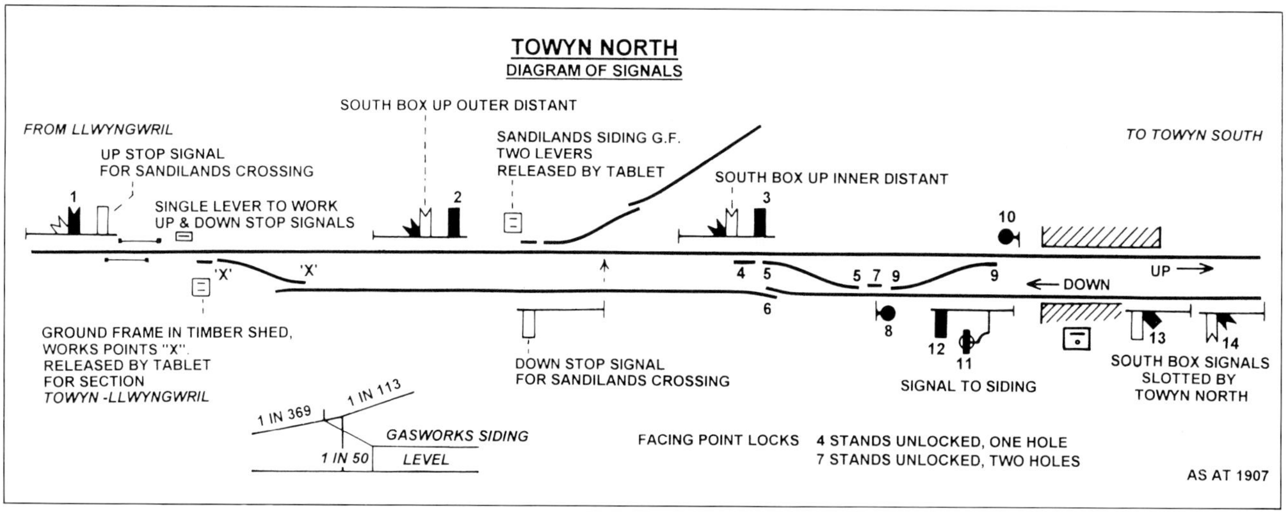

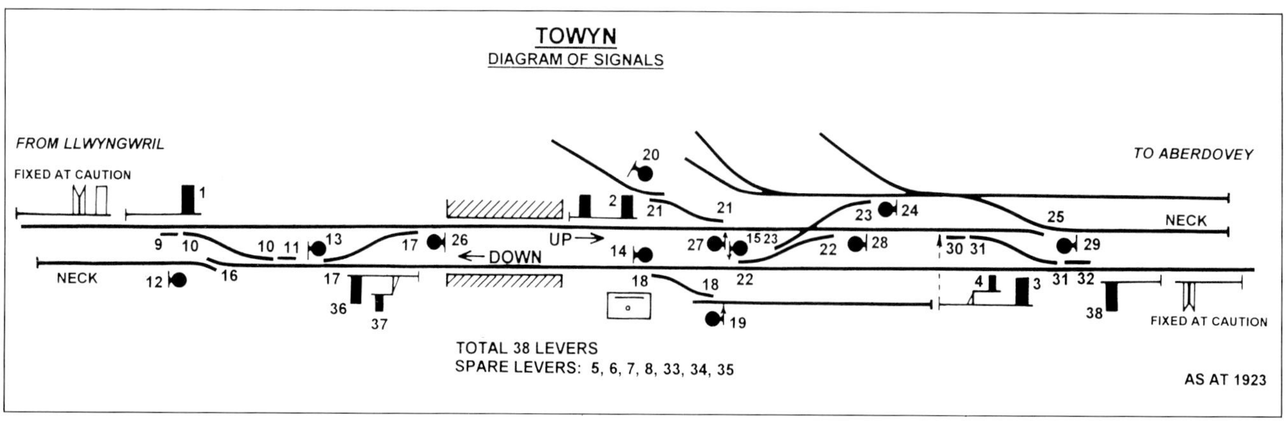

his hand crushed; this was the second accident of the kind in the same month.

On 29th April 1897, expenditure of £240 8s 1d was authorised for the 'enlargement of Spiers & Ponds inadequate Refreshment Rooms.' The general manager had reported the need with the recommendation that it should be decided at the next annual inspection, but the committee had decided that it was far too important a matter to be deferred in such a manner.

In October 1898, the Chief Constable of Montgomeryshire lodged the complaint, that:

> 'a great deal of drinking takes place in the Station Refreshment Rooms on Sundays by persons who are not bona fide travellers by train. Their mode of action is to take a ticket either to Aberdovey or to Tonfanau and it is transferred from one person to another for the purpose of obtaining a drink. The persons who do this are mostly of the lower working class and upon whom therefore there can be no call to travel on Sundays.'

This was refuted, as the Sunday takings did not average more than one shilling, and it was decided that in future Spiers & Ponds would apply for a six-day licence only. It seemed that the trouble was really being caused by the workmen engaged on the construction of Corbett

The rear of the signal box was well provided with windows, both at operating floor level and in the locking room below. 1968.
M. Christensen

Towyn signal box and 0–6–0 Collett Goods No. 2286 with ballast empties bound for Machynlleth (behind the photographer). At Towyn there were no token set-down and pick-up posts on the up line and only a setting-down post on the down line, so the signalman was provided with low platforms from which to do the exchange. The feeble oil lamp did not really provide enough light to make this operation safe at night. 1961.
Author

Signalman T. F. Owen exchanging tokens with the up Cambrian Coast Express headed by 2–6–0 No. 4377 in the mid-1950s. *Cty. Denis Owen*

The main goods warehouse, looking north in 1961. Note the large coal neatly stacked on the wharf, which by this date had become the coal storage area in the yard. *Author*

Avenue, and it was they who had been working the ticket dodge, but not on Sundays.

It was reported on 24th February 1899 that there had been no Volunteer camps in 1898, and that the building had now ceased, so the income of the refreshment rooms was down.

On 24th April, C. S. Denniss reported that a footbridge was needed at Towyn, and that a timber bridge would cost £150. He recommended the provision of an iron one (costing £350), though he was only allowed to order the timber pattern.

At the end of June, a bedroom at the Sandilands Crossing house was destroyed by fire, caused by sparks from the chimney of another house nearby: 'Ganger Richard Davies had furniture and clothing destroyed to the extent of £50. He is in poor circumstances.' Denniss did recommend sympathetic consideration, but the amount of sympathy made available was only 10% of the unfortunate family's loss.

The Towyn gang collected the hay from Aberdovey to halfway to Llwyngwril, and a seven-ton stack might be seen by the crossing in a good year.

In August 1899, the council advised the Cambrian that they were much concerned over near-accidents occurring in the yard with the existing arrangements. A new 20-wagon siding was to be laid in for £420, but with the associated new roadway, it was not completed until April of the following year. In December, Mr. Robert Richards was refused permission to erect a warehouse of his own in the yard.

It was ordered in 1900 that the refreshment rooms should close at 9.30 instead of at 10.30 p.m. from November to March, and in 1901 an application for an extension of time during the Volunteer encampment was refused.

Interior of the goods warehouse in 1961. With the doors shut to keep out the wind, this was a dark building. *Author*

The station end of the main goods warehouse and coal bunkers. 1961. *Author*

The cement warehouse, seen here, was served by the extension of the siding which ran through the goods warehouse. 25th July 1965. *Author*

The grain warehouse lay beyond the cement warehouse, and was served by the same siding. The short siding beside the running line served the end loading dock ('carriage landing' in Cambrian terminology). The fencing at the end of the dock hinged as a gate. 25th July 1965. *Author*

The yard and warehouses, looking south from the entrance road, with the slope up to the carriage landing on the right. 14th July 1965. *Author*

A detailed view of the coal and weighbridge offices seen on the left of the photograph above. 14th July 1965. *Author*

Towyn was the starting point for many excursions, of which the following three were typical examples operated in 1902:

1. Talyllyn Lake, Cader Idris, Dolcae Waterfall and Corris Valley. From Towyn by coach, returning by a different route; or from Towyn by road conveyance to Talyllyn, and thence by Corris Railway to Machynlleth and via Cambrian Railways back to Towyn.
2. From Towyn by road conveyance to Gwastadfryn, four-and-a-quarter miles from Cader Idris; ascending on foot, returning via Rhiw Ogo path to Talyllyn, three miles, where conveyance meets party. Including view of Craig Aderyn (Bird Rock) and climb to Castell y Bere (guide and pony from Gwastadfryn). Five shillings, minimum party of four persons.
3. Pennal via Happy Valley. From Towyn by conveyance to Pennal, Aberdovey, and back to Towyn. Including ascent of Cae Ceinach Hill by kind permission of the Marchioness of Londonderry. Not less than six in party.

In May 1903, a new goods siding and horse loading wharf was built at Sandilands Crossing for an encampment of Volunteers. By cutting out the platform for the men, the cost was reduced by £70 to a total of £930.

Petty Sessions refused in 1903 to renew the licence for the refreshment rooms because 'it was not necessary for the travelling public', and this just before up to 20,000 Volunteers were expected to arrive for their summer camp. In December, the Board authorised the payment of half the cost of an appeal. In January 1904 an objection was lodged by the Free Church Council of Towyn on general terms, with the rider: 'Also the presence of the Volunteers is greatly objected to by a large proportion of the ratepayers as they prevent the better class of visitor from patronising the place. All are agreed that those who benefit most are the public houses and the railway companies.' Renewal was ordered by Brewster Sessions on 5th February, but Petty Sessions declined to implement the order, a decision requiring the chairman's casting vote. At their meeting in April, the Board again agreed to pay half the cost of an appeal, designed to test the validity of the latter ruling, but after hearing the advice of the company solicitor, they agreed to let the matter drop. The Board's concern does show the importance of the share of the refreshment takings to the revenue of the company.

On 2nd January 1906, the engineer reported on the necessity of replacing the Neptune Road bridge, 'the girders of which are in an advanced state of corrosion, they were none too strong in the first place, and the time has come I fear to leave them in any more.' His estimate was £650 and this so dismayed the committee

The coal wharf and yard, looking in the down direction. 14th July 1965. *Author*

The goods warehouse viewed from the east side in 1961. *Author*

that they left the decision to the chairman after he had looked further into the matter. The bridge was, of course, replaced.

There had been an outcry over the damage alleged to have been caused by the Volunteers to hay and crops, and a local committee had been appointed to pursue the issue. The Cambrian committee authorised the general manager to approach the commanding officers of the Volunteers and other troops with a view to inducing them to continue to camp at Towyn. He tried to have Towyn selected for the Royal Review of Welsh Volunteers such was the importance of the additional income brought to the company by the summer camps. In the event, three or four thousand troops of the Cheshire Brigade did come to Towyn that year at Whitsuntide.

The Dysinni Gas Company's siding was extended into the works during 1906 for the sum of £392.

The committee was informed in 1910 that the Warwickshire Infantry Brigade was to be expected at Towyn.

The Quarries at Abergynolwyn which, the Committee were informed, had closed two years earlier, was acquired by Mr. Haydn Jones MP in 1911, and work recommenced.

A telephone line was installed between the station and the Talyllyn Railway for £4 10s 0d, with an additional annual charge of £1 10s 0d.

In 1913, the general manager reported to the Board 'that the Marconi Wireless Company of London were going to erect a Receiving Station on land belonging to Mr. Roger Corbett', and 'It is expected that a considerable amount of traffic will be passing over your system in connection with the new station'.

The refreshment rooms were closed in 1915.

It was suggested that the Sandilands Siding, put in for camp traffic and not used since August 1911, should be taken up during 1917. (This was at a time when all the railway companies were under great pressure to release rail for service in France, and whole sections of running line elsewhere were appropriated.)

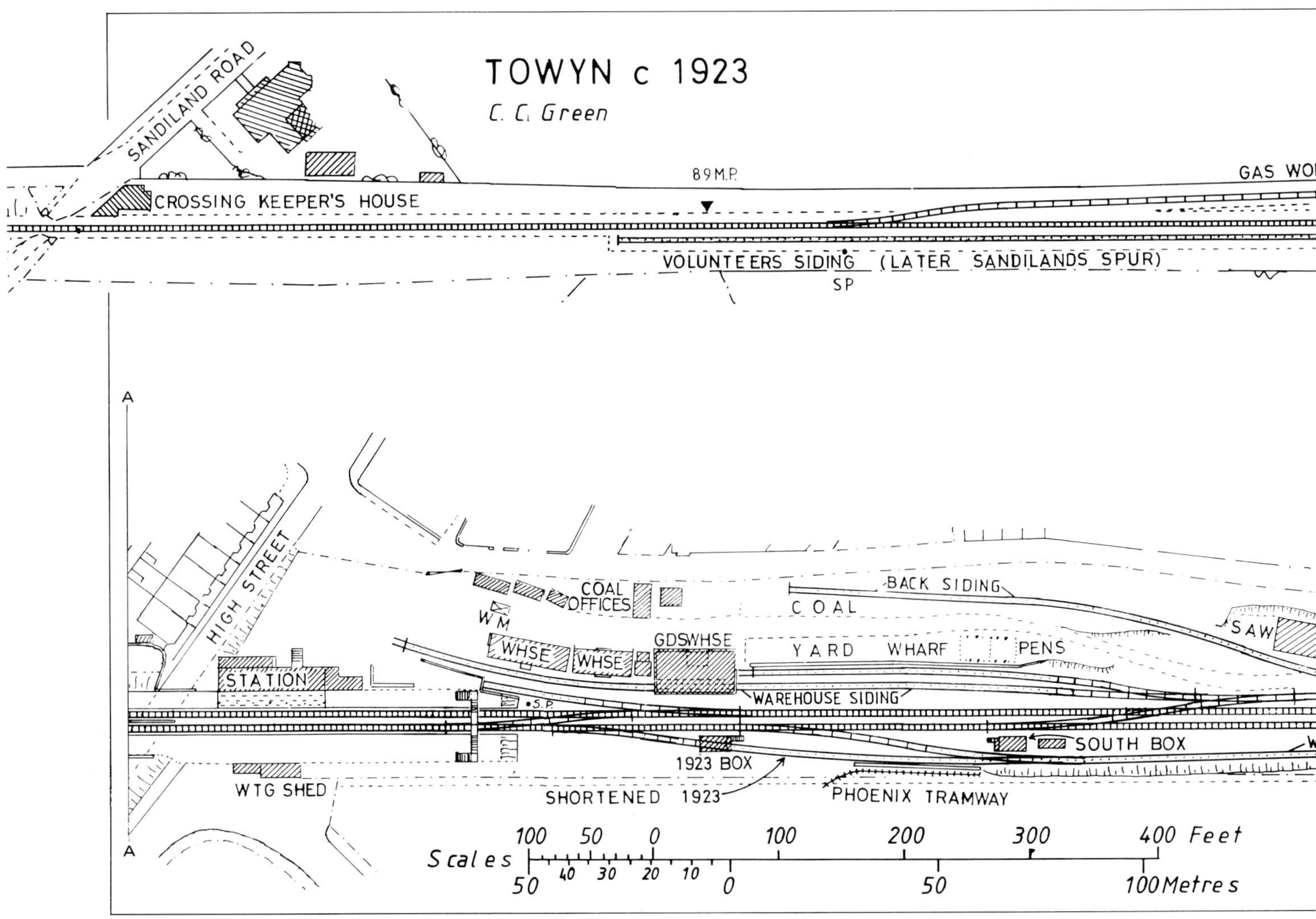

This view of the rear of a down train, taken from beside the signal box in 1949, shows the concrete footbridge which in 1935 replaced the wooden bridge depicted on page 121.
Author's collection

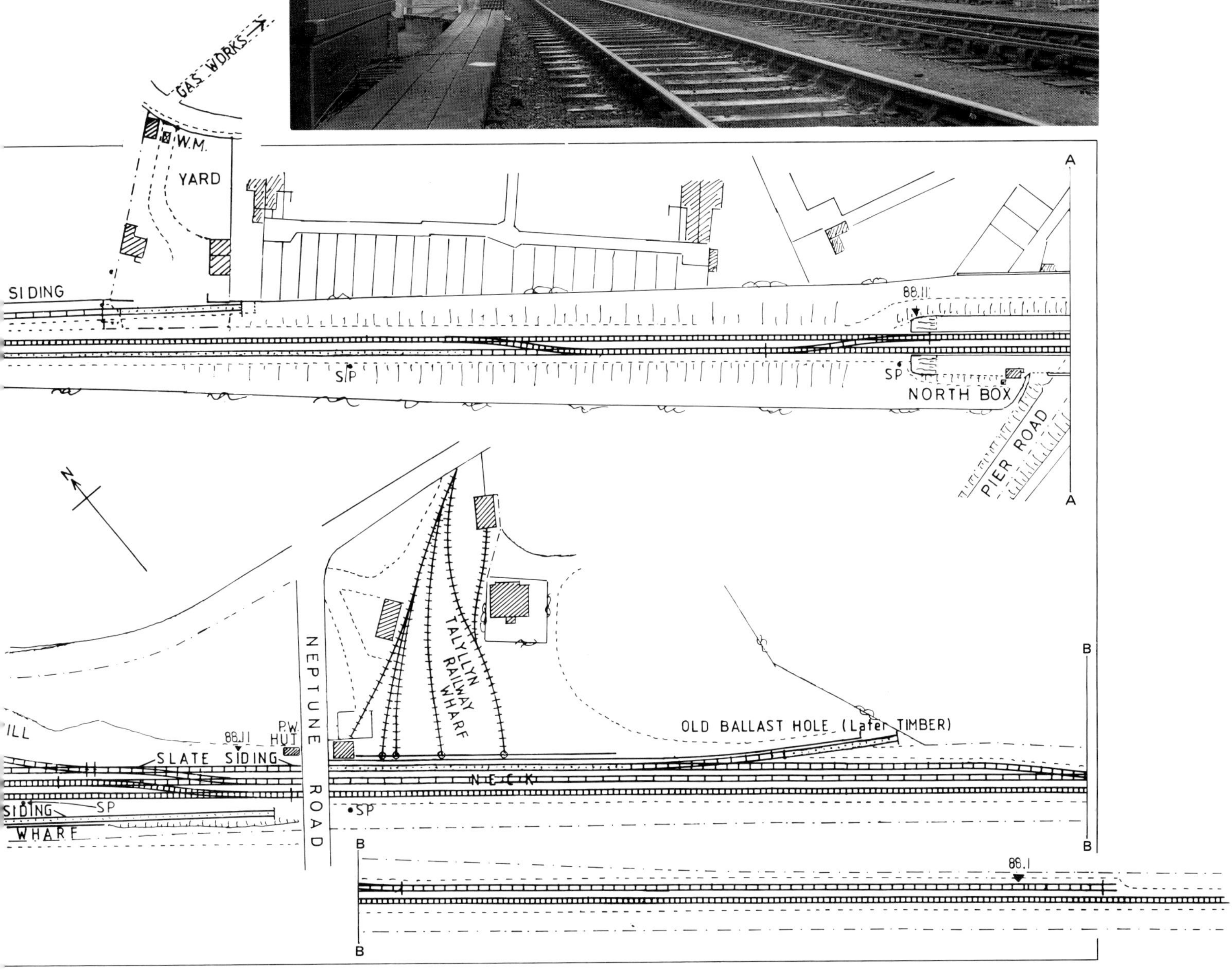

The replacement footbridge again, looking south towards Aberdovey. The Phoenix Tramway exchange siding came down where the post and wire fencing can be seen on the right of the photograph. 1955/60. *J. H. Moss*

A nice portrait of the up platform starting signal (lever 2) as put up by the GWR. The Cambrian signal which it replaced was a taller structure with upper and lower co-acting arms, but the GWR decided that only a low-level arm was required. The GWR pattern disc signal (lever 20) on the left applied to the carriage landing/end loading dock siding. September 1953. *P. J. Garland*

About 2,000 men (and their horses) of the Staffordshire Infantry Brigade were expected to camp at Whitsuntide 1921. During that year, it was also noted that the tablet instruments for North box were in the station office (although there was room in the box for them), and that the turnstile at Sandilands Crossing was not locked with the gates.

In 1923, the Great Western renewed the entire signalling arrangements for £3,050. The North and South signal boxes were replaced by one 'central' box, a standard GWR wooden structure re-erected here using materials recovered from a box in Maidenhead. During the following year, a 16 ft 6 in × 6 ft 6 in, 30-ton truck weighbridge was laid down at a cost of £420. The cart

The station building, looking down past the parcels office. The level crossing at Sandilands can be seen in the distance with a set of carriages stabled at the end of the down shunting neck – the Volunteer or Sandilands spur. 1961. *Author*

The up platform viewed from an arriving train, clearly showing the hump at the road underbridge and dip towards Sandilands. Like passengers everywhere, the couple on the right were ignoring the footbridge provided for their safety and walking down the platform ramp to cross the tracks once the train was in the down platform. *K. G. Draper*

A view of the platform side of the buildings on the up platform showing the awning, constructed in a heavy style common on the Cambrian, and with a glazed section set in to the centre. 25th July 1965. *Author*

The GWR replaced the waiting shelter on the down platform (see page 119) with this rather smaller structure. 1961. *Author*

From the road approach, the station buildings at Towyn present a rather unattractive facade, created largely by the height of the structure. This resulted from the fact that the railway is on an embankment here to enable the line to cross High Street. Passengers had to walk up the slope in the foreground and then turn right past the parcels office to reach the shelter of the awning. 25th July 1965. *Author*

High Street, Towyn, looking inland in the 1930s, a photograph taken from the up platform where it bridges the road. *Author's collection*

weighbridge was replaced by an 18 ft × 8 ft, 20-ton unit at a cost of £337 in 1928.

During 1935, the timber footbridge was replaced by a concrete version costing £520. The Great Western also placed a camping coach at Towyn by that year. An additional warehouse was erected in 1937 for £280, whilst the cattle pens were repaved at a cost of £115 during the following year. By then, the layout was generally much as it was to remain until the withdrawal of freight facilities.

In 1938, goods and parcels were delivered and collected free of charge by cartage service.

In 1940, the Air Ministry contributed £1,655 towards the £2,110 cost of an extensive revision of company and Post Office wires and telegraphs, although the job was overspent by £400. There was a telephone link from RAF Morfa exchange to the signal box at Towyn. This was so that the RAF could inform the railway immediately if any aircraft overshot the runway and crash-landed onto the line, so that action could be taken to stop trains and examine the track.

The yard was mostly lifted after April 1982, but the passing loop has been retained as Towyn is now a Radio Electronic Token Block passing place. The awning has been removed, and only the house has an occupant. Both platforms are in use for passengers, and there is a blue brick shelter on the down side. Much of the old wharf formations can still be seen in the yard, and the corrugated iron goods warehouse is still used.

Working Instructions

1903

Whistle Codes:

Up and Down Main Line	1
To and from Cross-over Road North End of Platform	4 Long
To and from Cross-over Road South End of Platform	3 Long
Main Line to West Siding and *vice versa*	2 Short
Main Line Cross-over to Slate Siding	2 Pause 2
Up Main Line to Dock	4 Short
,, ,, Neck	3 Long
Neck to Warehouse Siding	3 Short
Warehouse Siding to Slate Siding	1 and 1 Crow
Warehouse Siding to Back Siding	5 Short

1911/12

A Royal Train Notice of 1911 listed the tablet-released (ground) lever frames and outlying points as:

Cattle Pens and Wharf.
North Neck.
Gas Works.
South Neck.

In 1912, Towyn staff examined the tickets on two down trains daily, and collected those for Barmouth.

1943

One spare type No.5 loose screw coupling was to be kept available.

West siding was authorised as a refuge siding for down trains of up to 30 wagons plus van and engine and tender.

Sandilands Siding was authorised as a refuge siding for up trains of up to 40 wagons plus van and engine tender.

Whistle Codes:

Down Main to West Siding and vice versa	..	2 long
Down Main to Neck Siding and vice versa	..	1 and 1 crow
Down Main to Slate Siding and vice versa	..	2 and 1 crow
Neck to Warehouse Siding and vice versa	..	1 crow, 1 short
Down Main to Sandilands Spur and vice versa	..	2 short
Sandilands Spur to Up Main and vice versa	..	4 short
Up Main to Neck Siding and vice versa	..	1 short, 1 crow, 1 short

On the seaward (west) side of the railway, High Street extends to form Pier Road, seen on the left here. 25th July 1965. *Author*

The Piercy bow girder carrying the down platform across Pier Road. The lightweight bow girders are sufficient to support the platform, the deeper girders beyond support the running lines. Note the lamp on the abutment to the left set at the height of the deeper girders – a reminder at night of the limited clearance under the bridge. 1961. *Author*

Before vehicles are detached from Down Passenger Trains, the Signalman must be advised, and he must set points No. 18 for West Siding until arrangements are made for removing the vehicles.

Vehicles must not be detached from Up Passenger Trains at the Up Platform.

GAS WORKS SIDING, BETWEEN TOWYN AND TONFANAU.

This Siding is connected with the Running Line, facing from the direction of Tonfanau, the points being worked from a Ground Frame locked by the Electric Train Token.

The line is on a gradient of 1 in 304, falling towards Tonfanau. Before the engine is detached the train must be secured in accordance with Rule 151.

The siding will be worked by Down Trains and Shunting Engine from Towyn. When worked by Shunting Engine the wagons will be propelled on the return journey, provided there is a Brake Van, or suitable vehicle leading in which the Guard must ride, keep a sharp look out and be prepared to warn anyone on the line of the approach of the train and to handsignal the Driver.

A White light must be placed on the leading vehicle after sunset or during fog or falling snow.

The Driver on the return journey must consider the line to be clear only as far as the Towyn Up Home Signal.

The Guard will be responsible for working the Ground Frame points in accordance with Electric Train Token Block Regulation 34.

A delightful portrait of the north end of the station, looking towards Sandilands Crossing. The detail of the underside of the awning to the up platform, and the way in which the platform surface had been patch-repaired over the years, are evident, as is the gradient up from the Sandilands siding which caused so much trouble to enginemen when hauling out spare coaching sets that had been stabled in the siding all week. 1955/60.

J. H. Moss

Detail of the box girders carrying the rails, and the Piercy bow girder carrying the down platform. 1961. *Author*

The up platform is supported by a lightweight girder, seen here along with the box girder carrying the up loop line. 1961. *Author*

The bridge, looking west, showing an unusual form of lightweight girder supporting the up platform. In the dip, the road changes its name from High Street to Pier Road. 1961. *Author*

Looking northwards towards Tonfanau from Towyn in 1961, showing the dip towards Sandilands created by the need to get an adequate headroom beneath the bridge. *Author*

The station nameboard on the up platform, showing the additional sign publicising the Talyllyn Railway, then in its third year of operation as a 'preserved' railway. September 1953. *P. J. Garland*

The Howells of Sandilands

Before looking at the line beyond Sandilands Crossing, we should first consider a remarkable gentleman and staunch railway servant who once lived there. Mr. Evan Howells joined the relaying gang at Carno in 1896 and became ganger at Towyn in 1910, and for the Towyn to Barmouth Junction section in 1933 (when motor trolleys allowed gangers' lengths to be greatly increased). He was an ardent Congregationalist, a Deacon, the conductor of the choir, Sunday school teacher, trustee of the silver band, founding president of the Towyn and District Co-operative Society, Councillor, and Justice of the Peace.

His sections of line were very susceptible to flooding, and on one occasion, he had to spend the night on top of the gang hut surrounded by water.

Later, on 28th October 1929, he set off with hand-lamp and detonators, ready to stop any train should the tide come across the railway. He sheltered first at the nearest hut and, becoming anxious about the state of the line, splashed on to reach the hut nearest to the bridge over the River Dysinni. This saved his life, as that first hut was washed away and, as it was rising about the second hut, he ran for the safety of the bridge. Having paddled across it with the water surging above the sleepers, he went on up to Tonfanau Crossing, where the search party found him the next morning supping the last of his flask of hot cocoa.

He retired to become the crossing keeper, and stayed on there until he died at the age of 87, being looked after by his two daughters, Susie and Anne.

His mother had been appointed crossing keeper in 1910, and she was succeeded by Susie in 1933. She died in 1958, and Mr. Howells became keeper for a short time before Anne took on the post, which she held until her retirement on 2nd October 1971.

The approach to Towyn from the north, clearly showing the change in gradient through the platforms, on 25th July 1965. By this date the Sandilands spur was out of use and the bracket signal shown in the photo below had been replaced by a straight post signal. *Author*

The GWR replaced the signal shown on page 117 by this bracket signal made from standard GWR components. The left-hand (bracketed) arm read straight on into the Sandilands (shunt) spur. The main arm read through the crossover on to the single line to Tonfanau. September 1953. *P. J. Garland*

They recalled that, in Cambrian days, the crossing keeper's wages consisted of a rent-free home and free coal and firewood; the houses went to gangers who had womenfolk to work the crossings.

Note

The name started as Sandland (the nearby farm) and became Sandlands. The 'i' was added to attract the tourists, and so the place is now Sandilands. There are even references to Sandiland.

We are fortunate also in having the recollections of Mr Denis Owen who has 'dredged his memory' (his own expression) of his boyhood days spent in Towyn signal box with his father, Mr Thomas Francis Owen, signalman from 1937 until his retirement in 1958.

He recalls his father saying how impressed a visiting inspector was by the layout, because the shunting necks at each end, combined with the additional crossovers inside the loop, enabled engines to run round their trains without fouling the up and down main lines.

The dock siding next to the up platform was used during the 1939–45 war for unloading and reloading tracked AFVs (Armoured Fighting Vehicles).

Before the war (and until they were dispersed to the WD pool) the up neck was used for stabling Tonfanau Granite Quarry wagons when not in use. Also before the war, a camping coach was parked on the down neck against the buffer stops next to Sandilands Crossing during the summer. One was put back there for a few summers after the war.

The shorter of the two back sidings was taken up soon after the end of the war.

Entry to the Gas Siding was controlled by a two-lever (points and facing lock) ground frame with a Cambrian-style revolving lamp ground disc acting as point indicator at the trap point. The Dysinni Gas and Coal Companies were owned by the same people, with a head office at Ruabon. After the nationalisation of the gas industry, the coal business was taken over by a local merchant and the siding was lifted around 1960.

In the early 1950s, the site of the wartime RAF station, Morfa Camp, was used for the summer camps of reservists and Territorials. The coaches from ten to twelve coach trains would be parked empty in the down neck for one or two weeks, standing out in all weathers. Moving these trains up the gradient out of the neck and across to the up platform ready for loading could be quite a problem. Two 'Dukedogs' were usually provided to work the return train and first one and then both, would lose adhesion. The train would have to start and set back again two or three times, with sanding gear full on, before it could be got over the 'hump' and into the platform – another of the more spectacular sights of steam, gone for ever. After clearing the up end of the crossover, the overlong train would then set back into the up platform so that the front coaches would be loaded first while the empties at the rear hung down the north slope. There was then no problem about drawing the rear portion of the train into the platform so that loading could be completed.

Another incident involving the 'hump' at the north end of the station happened when an up goods was halted and divided for shunting. As the rear portion started to drift away downhill towards Sandilands crossing gates, the guard sprinted after it and just managed to get the first wagon braked, so that he could carry on running and pin down enough to get the train stopped.

There were two goods workings daily in each direction. The first down would have passed through before 8.30 am and the first up and the second down would usually arrive at about 5 pm. The loco of the second down was used for a special working to Tonfanau. It left its train in the down siding (just south of the signal box) while it picked up the special brake van marked 'TOWYN RU'. This was one of the short-wheelbase types with a verandah at each end. The same loco and van also had to carry out any movements needed on Gas Siding.

Round the gas works by boat, during floods c.1900. The boat was above the track of the gasworks siding. *Cty. Miss Evans Fernbank*

Sandilands Crossing house, looking down. 1967. *J. H. Reynolds*

Sandilands Crossing house from Beach Road. (The large vehicle beyond the gates is MOG 7, the author's motorised caravan.) The buildings of the RAF camp at Towyn (RAF Morfa) feature beyond. 1961. *Author*

A Parliamentary Brake Third, once used as a lamp room at Towyn, and seen here in ganger Evan Howell's lineside garden at Sandilands Crossing. The maker's plate is now in the Talyllyn Society's museum. c.1936. *G. H. W. Clifford*

SANDILANDS CROSSING to LLWYNGWRIL

89m 09c to 95m 24c

Sandilands Crossing house, looking towards Tonfanau. The hill in the distance above Tonfanau was, and still is, quarried for stone. The up and down stop signals protecting the level crossing were worked by a single large lever in the open in front of the gatekeeper's lodge, the lever being interlocked with the gates. 1967. *J. H. Reynolds*

The first one mile and thirty chain stretch of (nearly) straight and (almost) level line was one of the Cambrian's most troublesome sections. The view seawards is framed by long, narrow defence works of large, rough block stones, laid to prevent the line from being swept away by gales and high tides, while the landwards aspect is a pleasant panorama of estuary and mountains.

From the Dysinni bridge the line ascends gently with views of Cardigan Bay across low ground to the west and to the east of the quarry cut into Tal-y-gareg. The sidings and Tonfanau Halt were all stated to be on a gradient of 1 in 120 but a Board of Trade signalling diagram dated 18th March 1907 gave the gradient as 1 in 40 past the quarry siding. This should have read 1 in 140. After Tonfanau comes a curve, and another gentle gradient, downwards this time, leads on to the section known by the engineers as Tonfanau cliffs. From here the line climbs again to get round the tip of Foel Llanfendigaid. Here the Coast company and the Cambrian operated a small quarry termed 'The Ballast Hole' although later it was used more for larger stone for walling. Beyond the old Ballast Hole, the track dips to a tiny valley at Felin Fraen (which it crosses by an attractive little brick and stone bridge) to rise up to the site of the isolated and gale-swept halt of Llangelynin; this takes its name from the historic chapel nearby, and used to bring fares from the tourists coming to see the old building.

Falling gradients then take the train along flaky cliff edges, curving to the north-east to take a more inland route past a large caravan site; and a further dip and rise, crossing two insignificant occupation bridges, complete the run to Llwyngwril. The ground around this part of the journey is stony and more use for grazing of sheep than for the growing of crops.

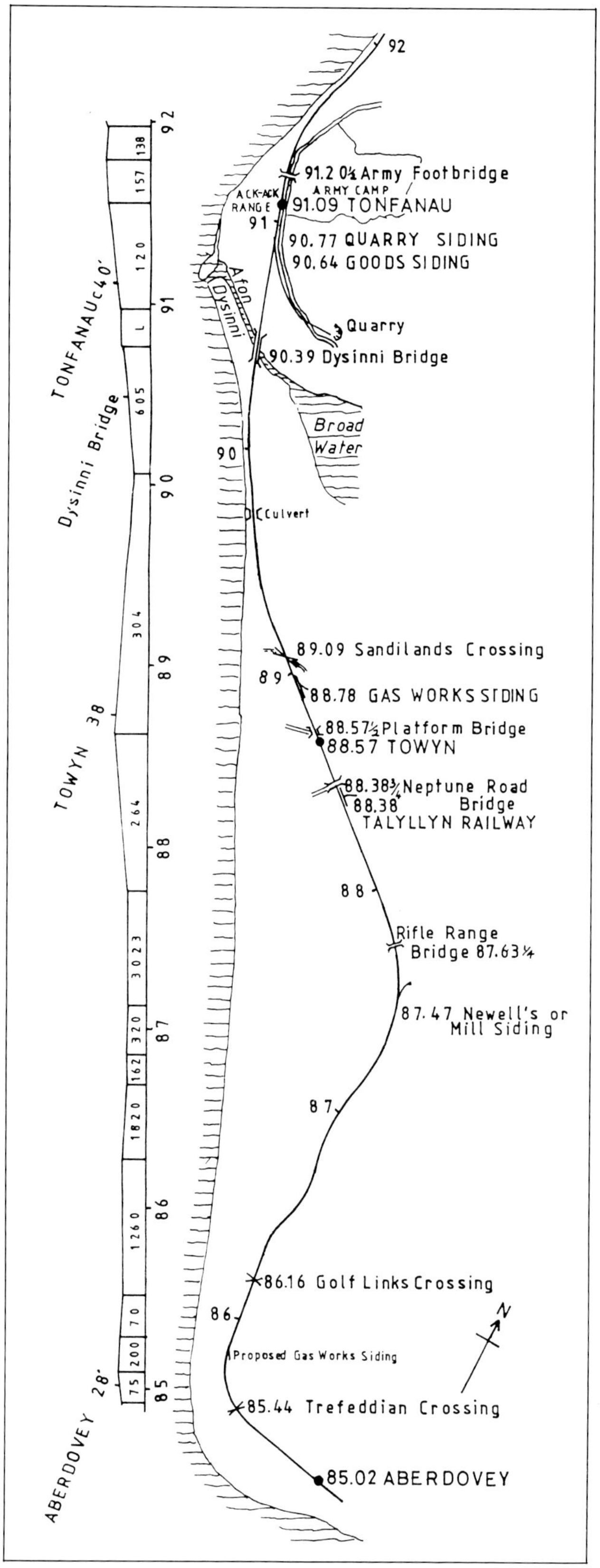

TOWYN MARSH EMBANKMENT

– 89m 9c

As first built, the line was situated on a solid and uncompromising embankment, extended in the vain hope that it would withstand all that the sea and the Dysinni could hurl against it, and that the excess waters would wash up and down the course of the river without flooding across the Towyn Marsh (as they had done since time immemorial). Inaccurate gradient profiles give the bridge as the position of the 'dip' in the line, but in reality the lowest point is nearly half a mile south of the bridge.

C. P. Gasquoine has written that the arrival of the first train on the south bank of the Dysinni was celebrated by a whip-round among the navvies, which produced £60 for the purpose of merrymaking. This was understandable, as portions of the formation and track had already been swept away several times before it was constructed high enough to withstand even ordinary tide and flood. As a consequence of excessive drinking, several of the men spent the night in Towyn gaol.

The first mention of the section in Cambrian records related to 24th August 1868, when Mr. Elijah Elias reported that a platelayer had been run over and killed by the 10.50 p.m. down train.

The Cambrian's first experience of problems with the sea on the section was during the winter of 1868/69; on 5th July 1869 George Owen, the engineer, exhorted his committee 'again I beg to call your attention to the advisability of providing Sluices or brick openings in the embankment known as Towyn Marsh as similar Disaster might again occur.' The committee listened, and authorised more openings 'to allow Tidal waters to escape into the low Lands near Dysinni'. This new technique was later to be pursued even further in another vain hope that the surplus waters would now wash backwards and forwards through a complex of flood openings made in the form of low timber trestles. Only one remains today, bridging the drainage relief channel from the Ynysmaengwyn Estate.

On 15th June 1875, the motion of the engine of the 10.35 a.m. ex-Pwllheli was wrecked by a large stone lying between the rails. It was suspected that the gang had seen it, but had overlooked the likelihood of damage to the low-slung motion on a Sharp Stewart engine, and had just left it there.

The engine *Pegasus* broke 'his left-hand trailing axle' on 22nd April 1882, about half-a-mile north of Towyn, and had to be towed back into the loop.

The Dysinni embankment before the sea filled the field in the foreground to above rail height with shingle.
J. & E. M. Williams

By December of that year, the culvert at Dol Fannau was proving ineffective, and flooding had delayed trains on several occasions that winter; it was widened in timber at a cost of £20 0s 9d.

Over 11th and 12th February 1883, the sea came across the line, but the only damage sustained was the washing away of the fencing.

In August 1884, the 5.45 p.m. ex-Barmouth was running about a mile from Towyn when the driver saw several large stones heaped over both rails. On 16th August the traffic manager reported:

> 'The damage was slight but the coaches jarred as they ran through. The stones had been put on the line by Mary Jones aged about eight and David Jones aged about six years, belonging to William Jones residing at Mill Cottage near Towyn. Although the children are very young I have considered it advisable to give instructions for their prosecution as a warning to others.'

On 11th February 1885, gales submerged the line once more. By the winter of 1886/87 the two-way surges of water caused by the flooding from the sea and the outpourings from the Dysinni marshes were eroding the formation again. The climax came on 8th and 9th of December, of which George Owen reported:

> 'The high ridge of beach and shingle which has hitherto protected the railway was levelled even with the rails and a considerable breach was made in the line. Looking to the future it is this place which causes me the greatest uneasiness.'

He suggested that a pile bridge should be constructed at the lowest point, after raising the level of the embankment. A conflict of views as to the best remedy came to a head in June 1887, when the raising of the line by six feet at the lowest point with two timber-trestled flood openings (costing £430 each) was authorised. Mr. Wynne of Peniarth objected to this decision because he wanted the railway to be made into a solid barrier between his land, over which the Dysinni drainage works had just been constructed, and the sea, 'as recommended by the Chairman on his inspection'. The line was raised, and the two extra flood openings were made.

On 7th October 1896, Corbett's new promenade at Towyn took its first beating from the sea, and was wrecked; furthermore, the effect of the sea meeting such a major obstruction for the first time was to partially deflect its force to the north, causing havoc along the railway. Oceanologists now know a great deal more about the likely effects of 'obstructing' the sea, which is able to cause plenty of damage on its own without any assistance from the human race! The engineer, George Owen, reported:

> 'Furious gales and high tides had swept away about 2,000 yards of track entirely into the marsh and the shingle protection was washed away and a bridge demolished and now there is no shingle bank to seawards.'

Ganger Richard Davies was highly commended for battling through the surf on his length, despite being repeatedly thrown down, on the morning of the 8th; he arrived at the southern end in time to stop the 7.45 a.m. Mail ex-Machynlleth, which had already left Towyn.

The first stage of a rough stone protection bank was laid to seawards to replace the protection lost by the levelling of the shingle bank. The winter storms of 1898/99 brought a twelve-inch flood across the line but the stone bank stood well, although the position seawards was worsened. Nevertheless, the new engineer, A. J. Collin, advised the raising of the bank by another two feet at a cost of £1,000, but the committee deferred a decision. The next high tide (10th to 14th February 1899) converted the last of the shingle into a gentle slope over the rails and, after advising the raising of the line by four feet, Collin was allowed to raise it by only two (for £500). He reported that both the raising of the line and some addition to the stone bank had been completed by February 1900. Towyn had also been flooded, and the council had levelled the blame upon the construction of the Dysinni bridge (whereas the real problem more likely arose from the construction of the Neptune development).

In March 1903, Collin reported that the sea was still changing the level of the shingle, and that the fencing had been buried. This marked the end of a belt of pasture lying between the line and the beach.

On 16th December 1910 the engineer, G. C. McDonald, reported that there was 'Gale damage at the same place where the line was completely washed away fifteen years ago' (actually, some portions had been completely washed away again).

The Great Western also came in for its full share of damage, and the continuing costs of later repairs can be summarized thus:

Looking towards Sandilands from the top of the block stone defence placed by Western Region. 24th July 1965.

Proof against the sea? The block stone rampart looking in a southerly direction towards Towyn. A temporary siding, with access points at the Towyn end, was laid along the west side of the running line during the sea defence work undertaken by BR, to allow materials to be brought in. 24th July 1965.

From the top of the block stone defence it is quite clear how the once-offshore protective shingle bank has been hurled across what was formerly a level green field lower than the rails, a view looking north towards Tonfanau. The Wolverhampton steam crane toppled while placing block stones and the Banbury and Swindon cranes had to be brought in to right it. 24th July 1965. *Author*

February 1939: Erosion protection, £1,410 authorised, cost £1,960.
January 1943: Filling in breach in the foreshore at 89m 40c, £215.
March 1944: Repairing damage to foreshore protection works, £2,500.
October 1944: Sea protective works, £3,400.
January 1945: Further sea protective works, £4,700 authorised, cost £5,215.
November 1946: Sea protective works, £4,050.
July 1947: Repairs and additions to the defence works, costing £15,000, including the renewal of some groynes (some of the Cambrian's expenditure must have gone into the construction of groynes, but there is no specific mention of them).

In 1962, extensive works were carried out by the London Midland Region, both in raising the trackbed, and in providing massive additions to the stone wall. This section stood firm through the disastrous floods of 1990, with little damage to the line.

THE DYSINNI BRIDGE – 90m 38¾c

Looking downstream to the dunes and the sea. Nearly high water. c.1930. *H. W. Burman*

The first structure was a twenty-span timber trestle, with the pile frames set conventionally at right-angles to the track, but combing the river obstructively at about an angle of 54° to its natural course. The bed of the Dysinni was notorious for flat stones and shingle (which are very resistant to pile driving), and Savin had skimped the job by stacking heaps of stones round the piles after he had sunk them as far as he considered might just be sufficient. This was all most deleterious to the passage of the small sloops and flats which were already having much difficulty in working their way up to a loop in the river, opposite Bryncrug. Their cargoes generally comprised goods for the farmers, and particularly goods and materials for Corbett's Ynysmaengwyn Estate, just upstream of the ferry; whether they took any slate away has not yet been established. Also, there had been a very difficult ford just by the site of the bridge, and the loss of this was another sore point with the landowners, who alleged that the promoters had given an undertaking that it should not be disturbed. Several of the old Derwenlas boats had been sailed round and sunk full of stones to stabilize the banks.

In December 1870, the engineer reported that the stones placed to stabilize the piles (which were 'not driven sufficiently deep') were blocking the passage of small craft and sloops. By 1873, the diagonal set of the piles had deposited a bed of shingle across the low-lying land, and this had to be dug away at a cost of £45. Additionally, four of the openings were reset so that the pile frames were parallel to the course of the river at its deepest point, at a cost of £46 per opening. This produced a unique pattern of timbering, but matters were much improved thereby; to these costs were added another £45 for piling and wattling, planted so as to divert the scour.

All of this work was concessionary (and common sense), as the landowners had claimed that the bridge had not been constructed as set out in the Act of 1861; however, Mr. John Savin had been able to show that it was as agreed with the Board of Admiralty, and with the landowners. Next, they raised a complaint that the ford to the east was to have been preserved for their use, but the company counter-claimed that it had been closed and was replaced by the construction of the railway. As a further concession, the company delivered (free of charge) three hundred tons of stone for the repair of the Towyn Cut.

On 24th January 1879, Gardden Lodge coal wagon No. 19 became derailed on the bridge, and was dragged nearly all the way into Towyn.

At a meeting on 30th October 1888, the Board heard that Mr. R. M. Wynne of Peniarth was trying to claim for damage to his land caused by an accumulation of gravel, diverted there by the bridge; he was unsuccessful. The problem surfaced again in 1897, when a combination of landowners claimed that the bridge was actually diverting the river. The piers were all at an angle of 54° to the flow, it was stated, and the banks were being damaged. They asked for the structure to be replaced by an iron bridge, with two clear spans of 100ft each, and Tapp & Jones, Engineers, produced a drawing of such with 50 ft + 100 ft + 100 ft sections, i.e. three spans. The committee adjourned consideration, and four months later the general manager commented on threats he had received from the landowners; but again they deferred the matter.

On 3rd August 1898, George Owen reported: 'When constructed it was found impossible to drive the piles further than 2ft 6 in so large stones were stacked around

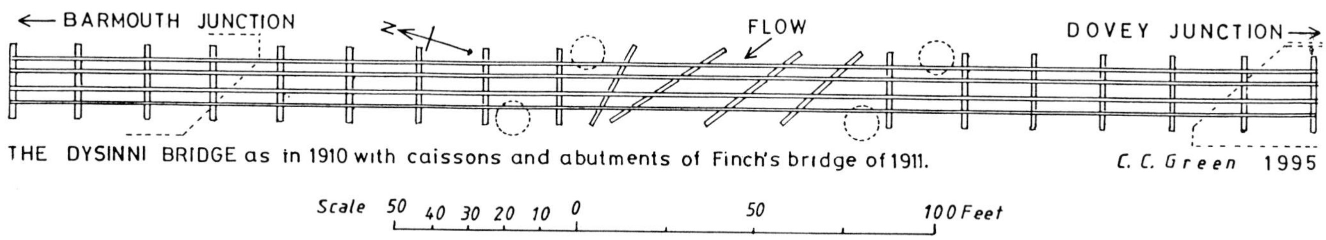

THE DYSINNI BRIDGE as in 1910 with caissons and abutments of Finch's bridge of 1911.

Looking across the bridge and up the gradient towards Tonfanau on 24th July 1965. *Author*

The eastern elevation of the bridge, showing the end closest to Towyn (the 'up' end of the bridge), looking seawards. 24th July 1965.
Author

Top left: Detail of abutment and bedding at the east face of the up end. *Top right:* East elevation caisson, looking downstream. Detail of caisson and bedding. *Bottom left:* Detail of decking, looking downstream (westwards). *Bottom right:* Down end abutment, looking west and downstream. 24th July 1965.
Author

the piles to prevent the scouring away of the soil. Comparing present plans with the older maps I cannot see that the bridge has done much or any damage'.

He further ascribed the effects to the prevailing south-westerly winds. A 50 ft span bridge would cost £4,500 with the necessary training walls and the slewing of the line.

Two days later, C. S. Denniss reported on an impassioned appeal from Mr. John Corbett. Having referred to 'The Serious Loss which both Mr. Wynne of Peniarth and I have suffered by the blocking of the river by the Cambrian Railway', Mr Corbett continued with an appeal: 'For the love of Heaven do not let us get into an expensive law suit.' He then indicated that he had spent upwards of £200,000 at Towyn, by which the Cambrian Company had, to no small extent, benefited, 'and I am still going on building at Towyn and I have expended already about £7,000 in opening up a stone quarry' (at Tonfanau).

In October 1898, a petition for a footbridge to be added to the main bridge was submitted to the company. The inhabitants were walking across the structure anyway, and it was left to C. S. Denniss to deal with this aspect; he ordered the ganger to have the practice stopped. Otherwise, nothing was done.

Towyn Urban District Council added their weight to the deliberations in June 1899 by blaming the flooding of the town on the nature of the bridge; in May 1900, the landowners again pressed for action by the coming summer, but again without result. The situation thus remained unresolved, even in July 1906, when the committee again declined to listen to the landowners' complaints, or to provide any assistance in removing gravel from the lower pastures. Like George Owen, the newer and younger engineers were not convinced that the alleged damage was being done by other than the natural, but often severe, fluctuations in the patterns of the tides, and by the gales countering the rising floods brought down the river by inland storms.

By 1910, the bridge was deteriorating beyond repair, and it was estimated that it would cost £4,500 to renew in steel, but only £3,000 in timber. A footway would be provided if Merionethshire County Council would contribute £250 for construction, plus capitalized cost of maintenance; however, they would not make any contribution, and Towyn Council were informed that the offer was withdrawn.

The committee approved a tender of £3,887 5s 0d for the new bridge, submitted by Edward Finch & Co. of Chepstow. Finch had already constructed the bridge at Chepstow, the Breydon viaduct at Great Yarmouth, and had been highly recommended by Mr. Ross, the engineer of the Great Northern Railway.

At last everyone was satisfied; the bridge was built as it should have been in the first place, and never again would the railway be accused of being the cause of flooding at Towyn as it had been so often in the past.

In 1911, the company purchased the foreshore and river-bed rights, and Mr. Corbett and others were told in 1915 that they might arrange for the channel to the sea to be dredged, provided that nothing was done within one hundred feet of the bridge.

TONFANAU GOODS SIDING 90m 64c

Opened January 1896. Removed c1966.

Having failed to get a station despite their petitions since 1871, the locals asked for a siding which the engineer estimated would cost £140 plus 5/– per week for a signalman. But it was reported to the Board on 28th July 1873 that the memorialists were not prepared to pay the cost or guarantee a definite rate of traffic. On 27th February 1891 a station with a siding was proposed at a cost of £528 15s 4d; the siding only could be built for about £225. The Board declined this proposal on 6th August 1891 but approved the construction of a siding on 27th April 1893 on the understanding that the residents would pay the £300 cost.

In 1895, the siding was laid in. It was passed for use by Colonel Yorke on behalf of the Board of Trade in January 1896. On 27th April 1896 the general manager reported re 'Mr Corbett's new quarries'! 'A Tramway has been laid from the Quarries to the new Siding recently made at Tonfanau and the Stone will be conveyed to the latter in small narrow gauge trucks.' On the following day the committee approved the expenditure of £20 on a wharf for unloading the stone from the quarry.

This phase of the working of the quarry was purely for Mr Corbett's 'Neptune' development on the edge of the sea at Towyn. It proved so successful that new machinery was brought in only two years later. A local newspaper reported on Thursday, 25th August 1898 'On Monday the new crushing plant etc. started working with machinery by De Winton of Caernarvon. A small vertical boiler loco has also been added to the plant, whereby the means of transporting of stone from the quarry to the large wharf on the Cambrian Railways has been greatly facilitated.' There were two crushers with large screens driven by a 20hp horizontal steam engine supplied by a large Lane's boiler and a 250,000 gallon reservoir for water. This implies that the tramway traffic had initially been horse-drawn.

The transfer of the stone from the narrow-gauge wharf ceased when the standard gauge siding was installed directly into the quarry on 21st March 1907.

On 14th July 1920 a drawing was produced for a scheme in which the Wharf Siding was connected directly to the Quarry Siding, with a crossover added from the Wharf Siding to the Cattle Siding. The points connecting the sidings to the main line at the Towyn end were to be taken out, leaving the yard effectively accessible only to down trains. This work does not appear to have been carried out. Any livestock traffic still arising would have required the vans to be tow-roped into position against the cattle dock (or illicitly pole-shunted).

Local traffic to this siding had virtually ceased by 1939 and usage up to 1945 must have been mainly by the Army. There was very little after the war.

Goods sidings and gates, looking in the down direction towards Tonfanau level crossing and station visible in the distance. The points in the main line were worked by Tonfanau South ground frame. 27th September 1961. *Author*

TONFANAU QUARRY SIDING 90m 77c

Opened March 1907. Removed c1963.

On 4th October 1906 the committee approved the construction of a siding into the quarry after receiving a report that 'A Standard Gauge Siding of half a mile is recommended now that Mr. Gibbons has bought the quarry from Mr. Corbett and Mr. Gibbons agrees to put in the Standard Gauge Siding if the Company would agree to work it for 6d per wagon'. Major Druit (for the BOT) passed the siding for use on 21st March 1907. The points were worked from a ground frame released by tablet.

In 1913 the general manager reported that the quarry had been closed for some time past. 'A private syndicate has been formed of members of the Council (Towyn UDC) with a view to providing employment and they ask that the siding be renewed.' The cost was estimated at around £363 and a repayment period of about six years had been agreed. 'All the members of the syndicate – I think eight in number – will join in the guarantee and they are substantial men.'

On 11th October 1923 the Great Western's Traffic Committee approved the making of a connection between 'the mileage sidings [i.e the goods yard sidings] and the Quarry Line' for £200. The following year on 27th November, an 'Intermediate token box' was approved for £170. This was 'for the use of the station staff when it was necessary to shunt any train clear of the Main Line'.

Propelling around twenty empty wagons uphill to Tonfanau Quarry c.1925. *Cty. H. B. Evans*

An 0–6–0 Aston Goods shunting at Tonfanau Quarry. c.1925.
Cty. H. B. Evans

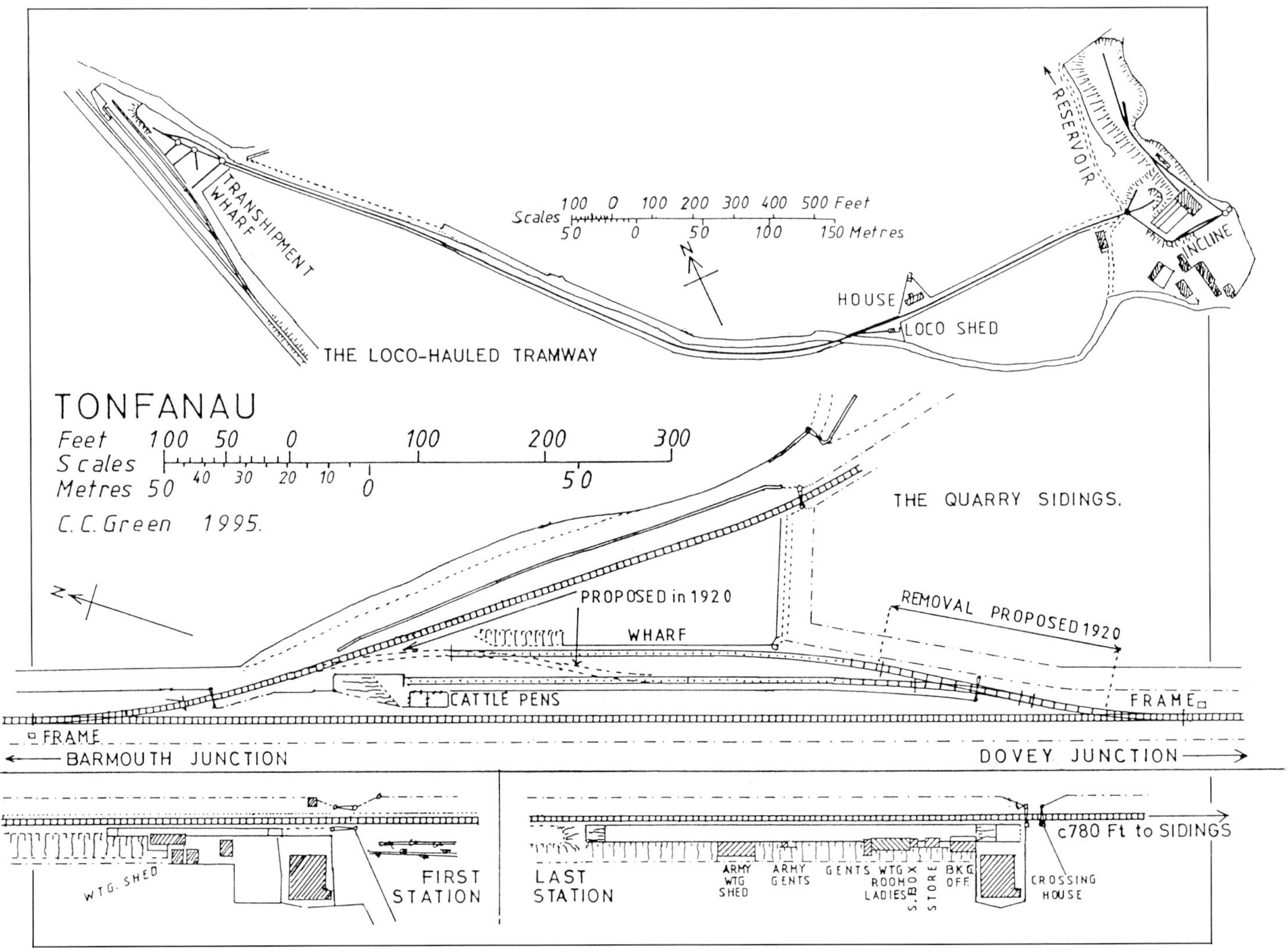

TONFANAU HALT 91m 9c

Opened January 1896. In timetables 1903.

The local people requested a station in 1871 but the traffic manager would not recommend it. He repeated, on 16th February, that there would not be sufficient traffic. A second memorial was laid before the committee on 23rd June 1871. On 26th June 1873 'distant signals and other apparatus' to protect the level crossing were approved at a cost of £32 6s 3d. The committee, received an application from Mr. Morris Pugh, but refused to erect a station. On 29th October 1884 the Board passed a resolution 'That No Action be taken re the proposed Station during the Receivership'.

The engineer reported on 27th February 1891 with a costing of £258 15s 4d for 'A New Station with a siding for general traffic' plus £270 'for signalling etc. to meet the requirements of the Board of Trade'. A goods siding only would have been about £225. The engineer was instructed only to prepare plans; otherwise the proposal was deferred. On 1st June 1891 he was authorised to approach the Board of Trade about 'the new Station at Tonfanau Crossing'.

On 27th April 1893, while approving the building of a siding for £300 at local residents' expense, the Board deferred the consideration of a station for £200 (also to be at the residents' expense) until after the annual inspection; but all was approved on 3rd June 1893 subject to removal after three years if proved unremunerative.

An accident report under the heading 'Tonfanau Crossing' was filed and dated 27th February 1895. 'A Private Owner Wagon belonging to The Exchange Company of Chester broke a drawbar while on the 7.10 pm Mixed from Barmouth Junction to Machynlleth. The driver prudently kept ahead of his divided train and avoided an accident'. The make-up of the drifting rear portion was 6 wagons, Brake Composite Coach and Goods Brake.

On 12th November 1895, under the heading 'Tonfanau', the engineer reported: 'Mr. Wynne of Peniarth writes respecting this matter (New Station at Tonfanau) that, as the money subscribed for its construction has been paid, he requests that the work be proceeded with.' On 14th November 1895 the committee instructed the general manager to inform the promoters that construction would be put in hand on

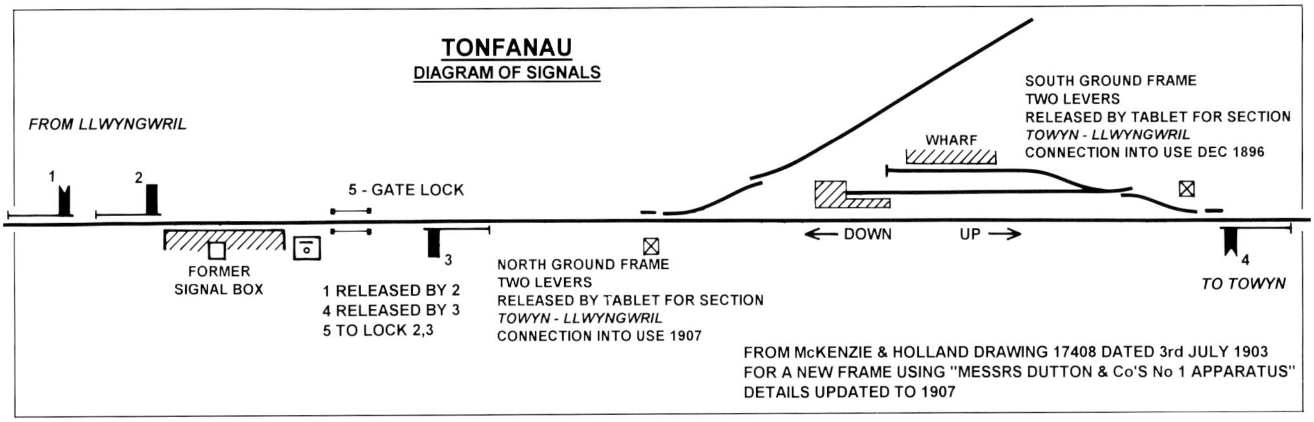

The North ground frame controlling the points giving access to the Quarry siding. Originally released by the train tablet, the lock on the side of lever No. 2 had been altered to be released by the key token which had replaced tablet working. 27th September 1961.
Author

receipt of a first instalment of £250. Liaison within the company behind the scenes must have been a bit lacking.

The engineer reported on 28th January 1896 that the new station and siding had been passed by Colonel Yorke. By 26th October 1897, the 100 ft long platform had borne 3,355 passengers during three summer months and the general manager reported that 'The Platform provided at the expense of the local landowners has been used to a far greater degree than was anticipated.' An extension to 300 ft for £98 9s 0d was approved.

In March 1903 the general manager raised the issue that the halt was not included in the timetables (under Board of Trade rules signalling protection had to be provided). The landowners had complained that their visitors were therefore unable to ascertain the times of the trains. The manager recommended expenditure of £60 on signals in time for the summer, though since the MacKenzie & Holland plans were dated 3rd July, completion was probably a bit later.

After that the halt seems to have served its passengers effectively without coming to notice until 26th February 1933 when a severe snowstorm stranded an

Left: The pedestrian gates and keeper's house seen from the east side of the railway. *Right:* Keeper's house. 24th July 1965. *Author*

The gates and station, looking northwards. 27th September 1961. *Author*

Tonfanau had no fewer than three different lever frames over the years to operate the signals protecting the level crossing. The layout of the second box is shown on the plan on page 157. This box was later replaced by a GWR pattern lever frame in the open, with the same numbering scheme for the levers. c.1966. *M. Christensen*

A view looking in the down direction towards Llwyngwril, showing the motley collection of huts. The third from the left, with a sloping roof projecting a short way over the front of the building, was the first signal box here, as evidenced by the gap in the platform wall where the wires formerly ran out. 24th July 1965. *Author*

0–6–0 Dean Goods with the Machynlleth-Pwllheli early morning train just round the corner. 0–6–0 Pannier Tank No. 1776, another Dean Goods No. 2511 and a van were sent from Ruabon to cut through the drifts along the Friog and rescue the marooned train, only eight days before the second Friog disaster.

The level crossing gates were normally kept across the line and down trains could be readily seen and heard, but a treadle-operated warning bell rang when an up train was 1000 yards away, out of sight and hearing, round the bend.

On 23rd November 1939 the construction of a footbridge for the use of the Army was authorised and the Company's costs were to be recouped from the War Department. The purpose was to connect the anti-aircraft artillery training range on the west side of the line with the east side where there was the gunners' encampment and a large Royal Ordnance depot. In all, the costs amounted to £489 for a cantilever footbridge, £138 for alterations to signalling and £400 for platform extension and improvements to the buildings, which included a sectional concrete building at the north end. There was a cost overrun of £111 to be sanctioned at the final stage. There is no evidence of any siding connection into the WD site, but trains could be unloaded onto lorries from either the goods yard or from trains parked at the side of the road leading to the quarry. The buildings were last used to provide temporary housing for Asian refugees ejected from Idi Amin's Nigeria in the early 1970s.

The last recorded item of expenditure by the GWR on the station was £112 on 28th March 1946, for electric lighting. Now there is only a bare platform with parts of the old timber buildings still standing, and it is served by one train each way per day, weekdays only.

Tonfanau Halt was to have been closed from 14th May 1984 but it was discovered that it was still being used by one scholar going to Tywyn Grammar School.

Working Instructions

In 1898 the goods sidings were to be worked by up trains only (on account of the gradients), unless the whole train could be placed within the sidings before shunting commenced.

By 1907 trains could be propelled from Towyn without a brake van – the longest propelling movement permitted on the Cambrian Railways except for that from Abermule to Goitre on the Kerry Branch.

After the standard gauge quarry siding had been installed, a specified up goods was to clear loaded wagons to Towyn. The engine was then to leave its train and return with the next batch of empties, place them at the quarry and return (all in between the scheduled service trains). No engines larger than the 'rebuilt goods' (0–6–0 Sharp Stewarts) were permitted along the quarry siding, excepting 'Tank Engines of the Wrexham & Ellesmere Class'. Engines of the 'Belpaire Goods', passenger classes, and engines with outside cylinders were all expressly prohibited. No engine was to go round the sharp curve in No. 3 siding in the quarry.

Later, besides the trap points operated by the lever for the main points, a second set (operated by a ground lever) was installed 100 yards further up the siding. These had to be put into the open position after any train had passed.

Combined Working of Goods & Quarry Sidings

After the two installations had been connected under the authorisation given on 11th October 1923, they were still worked by the existing two ground frames. The presence of a train working up the Quarry Siding blocked the main line because a token was out for the section from Towyn to Llwyngwril. An Intermediate Key Token (referred to as 'the lock-in') was installed adjacent to the North Ground Frame in 1924/25, and ended all this obstruction, an advantage in view of the increased summer holiday traffic of the 1920s and 1930s. Put simply, the Intermediate instrument allowed the token brought to Tonfanau by the shunting goods train to be used – once the train had been shunted wholly clear of the running line – to clear the section Towyn–Llwyngwril so that another token could be taken out by the signalmen at either of those boxes. The train in Tonfanau sidings could not move back out on to the main line until the token had been released again from the intermediate instrument, which needed the cooperation of both signalmen, and could only be done if no other token for the section was 'out' at the time. According to Denis Owen, this lock-in facility was out of use by the end of the war.

Working Instructions for 1943

TONFANAU.

Level Crossing.

Rule 99.—The normal position of the Level Crossing Gates is across the railway.

After the signals have been lowered for the passage of a train they must not again be restored to normal and the gates opened for road traffic until the train has passed over the Level Crossing.

Warning Bell.

In order to facilitate the working of the Level Crossing Gates a Warning Bell is provided at the Crossing denoting the approach of Up Trains and is operated by a train passing over a treadle provided 1,000 yards from the Crossing.

Station and Quarry Sidings.

These sidings are connected with the Running Line at both ends, the points being worked by North and South Ground Frames locked by the Electric Train Token.

The gates at each end of the sidings must be kept closed across the sidings and secured by padlock. The keys are kept in the Booking Office. The station staff will be responsible for opening the gates in connection with shunting operations and for closing and locking the gates after the operations have been completed.

The line at the North Ground Frame is on a gradient of 1 in 120 and at the South Ground Frame 1 in 605, falling towards Towyn. Before the engine is detached the train must be secured by the Van Brake being tightly applied, also a sufficient number of Wagon Brakes, and if necessary making use of sprags, in accordance with Rule 151 to prevent the train or any portion of it moving.

The sidings will be worked by Up and Down Trains, and by Pilot Train from Towyn.

When worked by Pilot Train the wagons may be propelled on the forward or return journeys provided there is a Brake Van leading in which the Guard must ride, keep a sharp lookout, be prepared to warn anyone on the line of the approach of the train and to handsignal the Driver. A White light must be placed on the leading vehicle after sunset or during fog or falling snow. The Driver on the return journey must consider the line to be clear only as far as the Towyn Up Home Signal.

The station staff when on duty or otherwise the Guard of the train will be responsible for working the Ground Frames in accordance with Electric Train Token Block Regulation 34.

The Quarry Siding is connected to the Station Siding at the North end by means of handpoints facing from the direction of Llwyngwril and is on a sharp falling gradient towards the Main Line. Shunting operations at the Quarry must be performed with the engine at the lower end, the vehicles being propelled from Tonfanau to the Quarry. The Guard must ride on the leading vehicle, keep a sharp lookout and handsignal the Driver. Brake Vans must not be taken up to the Quarry.

In addition to the catch point worked from the North Ground Frame protecting the Main Line, a second spring catch point is fixed 100 yards nearer the Quarry. This must always be left in the open position except for trains or engines returning from the Quarry. No wagons must be left standing between the first and second catch point.

A level crossing is situate approximately 60 yards on the Quarry side of the second catch point and the Guard and Driver must keep a sharp lookout when approaching the crossing.

Continued on page 162

Looking south from Tonfanau station. The quarry siding branched off to the left just beyond the level crossing. 1964.
Mowat collection

The rear of the platform revealed even more ramshackle buildings than were on the platform. 24th July 1965. *Author*

Left: The original station, to the left of which were the first signal box (by then used as a store) and the corrugated iron lamp hut. 27th September 1961. *Right:* Additional buildings provided for the use of the soldiers from the nearby training camp, more robust and spacious than the Cambrian waiting shed. 24th July 1965. *Author*

Looking in the up direction, towards Towyn, through the station. The up stop signal was placed well back from the gates, but the down signal was not. 24th July 1965. *Author*

Continued from page 160

A third spring catch point is fixed at the top of the incline near the Quarry at a point 12 yards on the main line side of the points leading to the siding under the crushers. This catch point stands normally in the open position and must only be closed in connection with the actual passage of vehicles from the Quarry when the points must be securely held by hand.

No. 3 Siding at the Quarry end is laid on a sharp curve and engines must not pass over it nor under the shutes.

The public level crossing near the Quarries is in charge of the Quarry Company s staff who will be responsible for protecting the crossing during shunting operations. When returning from the Quarry, the Porter, or in his absence, the Guard in charge, must secure the catch points for the train to pass over.

An Intermediate Token Key Box is provided in the North Ground Frame for use when the station staff are on duty and it is necessary to shunt a train clear of the Main Line.

Before a train is shunted into the Quarry Company's siding for refuge purposes the Driver must be verbally instructed by the person in charge that the train must be taken into the siding clear of the second catch point before it is brought to a stand.

As soon as the whole of the train has been shunted on to the Quarry Siding clear of the Main Line and the Porter has satisfied himself that no vehicle or other obstruction is left on the running line, the levers must be restored to the normal position and the token withdrawn from the Locking Frame and afterwards inserted in the aperture of the Token Key Box pushed well home, and turned to the right; this will cause a figure 2 to appear on the indicator at the left of the aperture. The Token must then again be turned to the right, which will cause a figure 1 to appear on the indicator and lock the token in the Key Box.

Immediately the figure 1 appears on the indicator, the Porter must inform the Signalman at Towyn on the telephone that the token is locked in the Key Box and that the line is clear for the passage of trains and the Signalman at Towyn must so advise the Signalman at Llwyngwril. The Signalman who signalled the train forward will then send the cancelling signal (3-5). The Signalmen will then turn their Pointer Switches to "Token In."

When the train is ready to leave the siding for Towyn or Llwyngwril or for any shunting operations to be performed on the main line, the Porter must communicate with the Signalman at Towyn on the telephone and ask for the token to be released. The Signalman at Towyn will then communicate with the Signalman at Llwyngwril and if the application can be agreed the Signalman in rear will signal the train forward in the usual way and the Signalman accepting the train must repeat the Bell Code signal. The Towyn Signalman must then inform the Porter at the Ground Frame that the application is agreed.

When authority has been received at the Ground Frame, the token must be turned to the left, which will cause the figure 2 to appear on the indicator.

To release the token from the Token Key Box, the Signalmen at Towyn and Llwyngwril must press in the Bell Plungers on their instruments which will cause the word "Free" to appear on the indicator on the right side of the aperture in the Token Key Box.

As soon as the word "Free" appears, the Porter must again turn the token to the left, which will cause the figure 3 to appear on the left hand indicator and the token can then be withdrawn from the Key Box and inserted in the Locking Frame to release the points.

After the Shunting operations have been completed and the train drawn on to the running line, the points must be restored to the normal position and the token withdrawn from the Locking Frame and handed to the Driver.

Telephone Circuit.

	Rings
Tonfanau Ground Frame	3 short
Towyn Signal Box	1 long, 1 short
Llwyngwril Signal Box	3 short, 1 long

TONFANAU BALLAST QUARRY 92m 31c

Opened c.1864. Closed December 1899

Quarrying was started by filling ballast trains standing on the main line next to a low cliff cut into Foel Llanfendigaid. Eventually, enough stone was taken to allow space to lay a siding. There was a serious accident here on 18th June 1884:

'While men were engaged in getting stone for the rebuilding of the sea wall on the Deviation line and were filling in a hole which had been blown the charge exploded bringing down a quantity of rock, burying beneath it William Rogers. He was extricated in a quarter of an hour but died immediately after. Foreman John Owen was much hurt but is now recovering. An iron scraper was being used to push some grass down over the charge and this may have caused a spark by hitting quartz or a piece of fuse from a previous charge may have been left in smouldering. Washing out may not have been effective as holes at this quarry are drilled horizontally and not vertically.'

There was a second accident on 17th December 1891:

'A large Boulder Stone, about 2', fell onto the rail at the south end of the cutting three miles from Towyn and was hit by the 10.40am ex Pwllheli. The Driver rounding the curve saw it and applied the handbrake, having no vacuum. The Engine struck the stone, carrying it 300 yards and breaking it in two. The Carriage next to the Engine passed over it and the next, a Composite, derailed. Mr Owen Slaney of Plas Newyth, Ruabon, very unwisely jumped out of the carriage which went off the rails and thereby received a severe shaking and several bruises on the face. He was the only casualty.'

On 4th October 1894 the committee had to authorise expenditure of £300 on the sea wall nearby because of a slip in the cliff.

It became evident that the rock had been cut away nearly to the boundary of the company's land. Powers were taken in the 1896 Act to acquire more land. On 14th January 1897 a siding serving the enlarging quarry was inspected and passed by Colonel Yorke; this may have been simply the relaying of an already existing siding.

On 14th May 1897, the engineer forewarned the Board as follows: 'Tonfanau Rock. The present site is worked out and extension is needed from Mr Kirkby to provide stone for the constant renewals of sea walling.' On 20th September, he reported that he considered the asking price of £475 for one acre 'beyond what I consider fair and reasonable ... it will be necessary to proceed in the usual way by serving notices to treat upon the owner and occupier (Llanfendigaid Estate) for the stone vitally needed for repairs and

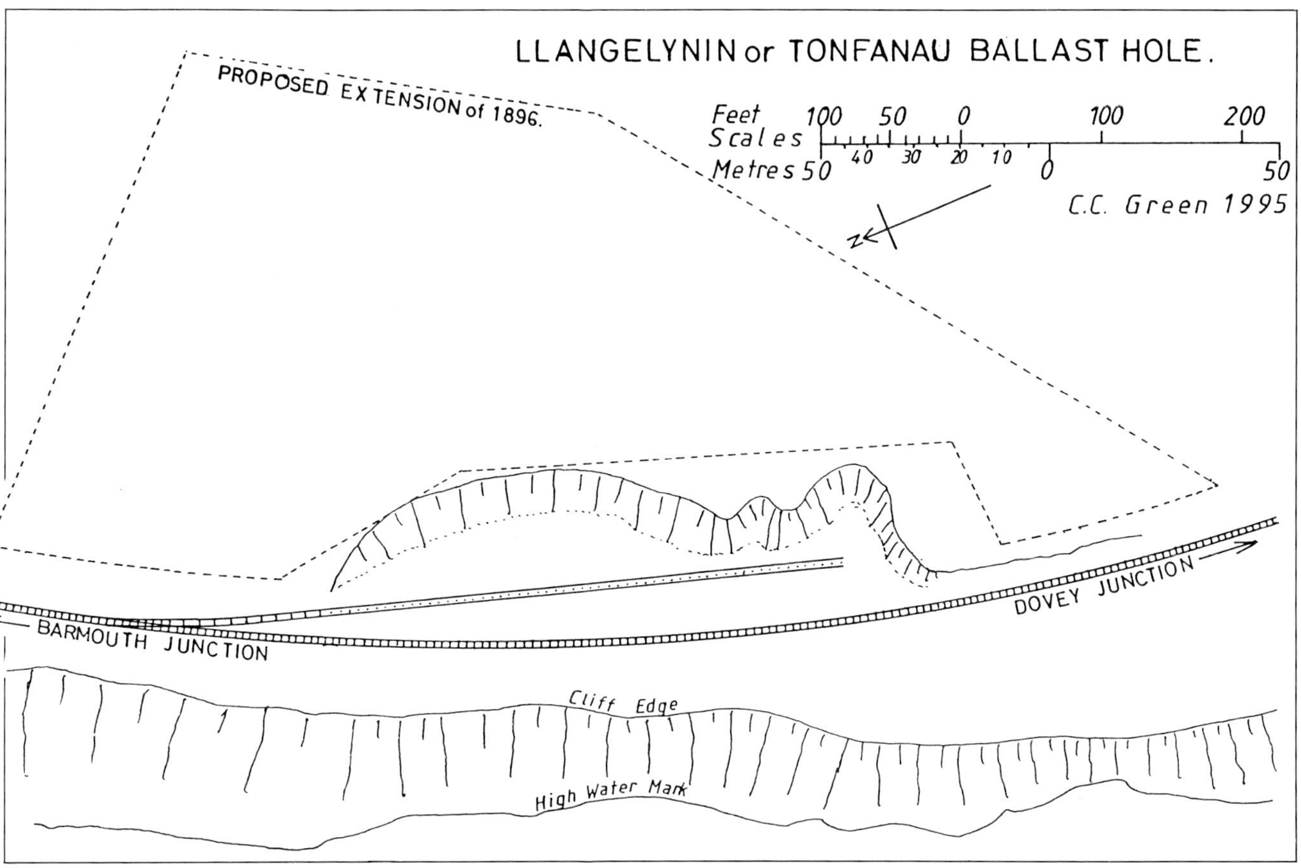

extensions of Sea Walls at Friog and other places on the Coast section of your Railway.'

On 16th May 1899, he reported that the land round the quarry was too expensive. Obviously by asking for £475 (the 1990s equivalent of more than £20,000) an acre for rocky scrub, Mr Kirkby was trying to hold the company to ransom. On 12th December, the engineer reported that the land round the quarry was totally worked to the back of the company's site, and recommended that the siding be taken up and relaid at Careg Felin quarry, near Portmadoc, whose stone was being loaded directly into wagons standing on the main line. This was approved, at a cost of £120.

On 8th December 1883 and somewhere near the ballast quarry, Crane No 5 had its headstock pulled out, thus dividing the 5.30am ex Portmadoc goods to Machynlleth on an uphill section.

Tonfanau ballast quarry and the site of the siding. 18th July 1965. *Author*

The coast near Tonfanau ballast quarry, looking south. 18th July 1965. *Author*

The coast near Rhoslefain. The site of the ballast quarry was at the headland in the distance. *Author*

Cwm Fraen and the railway embankment. 18th July 1965. *Author*

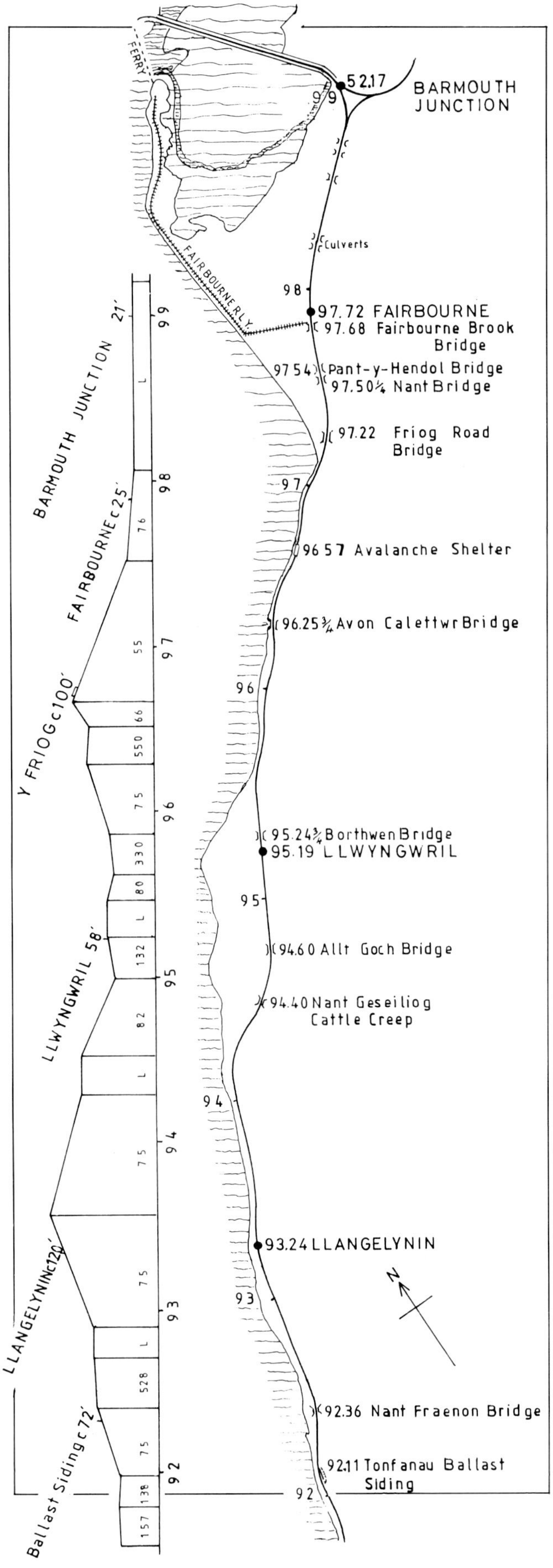

Llangelynin Halt, looking down, on 18th July 1965. *Author*

Opened 7th July 1930. Closed 10th May 1992

The coastal cliff hereabouts was less stable than other sections and on 25th February 1901, under the heading 'Old Church Bank', the Committee minutes recorded that the line had to be slewed inland because of a slip in the cliff at a cost of £500. A footnote added that the material taken out could be tipped to form a road at Barmouth Junction. While the new work was settling, a speed limit of 8mph was imposed.

By April 1902, the sea wall was slipping again. A further slewing of the line was considered too expensive (as more land would have been required) so rebuilding work costing £700 was approved. The work amounted to little more than repacking under the outer edge of the rails, and was less than a full stone wall that was constructed along the Friog.

In 1924 the Great Western had to spend £370 in underpinning and raising walling and £1,600 in acquiring more land and slewing the track further back from the edge.

The halt built by the GWR was very much an economy job, consisting of a platform of black ash retained behind a front wall made up of old sleepers, upon which was an open-fronted corrugated iron shelter. The cost was only £130. The view from the seat in the shelter was all very fine on a warm summer's day but it was a truly ghastly place at which to wait for a train in a westerly gale. Note the expression 'at which' and not 'in which'; under those sorts of conditions, local people, if they ever had to use the halt, arrived as close to the time of departure as possible, and crouched down at the back of the drumming sheeting, to emerge as they heard the train approach, and signal the driver to stop, for this was a 'Request Halt'. The advent of Diesel Multiple Units, quiet in their approach, created new problems. One blustery day in 1965 (in June!), the passengers waiting *behind* the shelter to be out of the rain, only heard the approaching DMU as it reached the platform. The driver, having eased speed, saw no-one on the platform, and applied power, and it was this sound that the waiting passengers heard. They emerged from behind the shelter just as the driver was passing them. He then had no chance of stopping at the platform! By the time the train had come to a stand, it was a full coach length beyond the (short) platform and the driver had to back up. No doubt it was not the only time this scene was enacted at this windswept location.

Services diminished to one train each way per weekday and the last appearance of a service was in the timetable for the period ending 10th May 1992. The name still appeared in the 1993 timetable without any trains stopping there. The reason for the closure was the cost of providing lighting ordained by the Health and Safety Executive.

The shelter was not demolished by any human hand. An extremely severe gale blew it uphill, into the field behind, at the end of 1990.

Nantgeseiliog, crossing and curve, looking in the up direction towards Towyn. 18th July 1965. *Author*

Nantgeseiliog farmhouse. 18th July 1965. *Author*

4—4—0 No. 9014 on a Portmadoc—Machynlleth goods climbing Llangelynin Bank (1 in 75) on 14th September 1959. *Ifor Higgon*

Looking down the long curve, on a gradient of 1 in 82, to Llwyngwril station in the distance, with caravanners walking along the line, oblivious of the danger of a train coasting down the bank. 18th July 1965. *Author*

The unprotected caravan site crossing south of Llwyngwril on 18th July 1965. An AOC (automatic open crossing) arrangement has since been provided to warn road users of approaching trains. *Author*

LLWYNGWRIL

95m 07c to 95m 24c.
Station at 95m 19c. Signal Box at 95m 27c

Llwyngwril down home signal, with the station on the short stretch of level track beyond. 18th July 1965. *Author*

Opened as temporary Terminus 24th October 1863.
Opened as through station 3rd July 1865.
Llwyngwril, in English, is said to be 'The young man's grove'.

When the line was opened northwards towards Penmaenpool, the station had a short passing loop with a tiny signal box housing a ground frame, a wooden water tank, a wooden hut and a staff of one man. On 31st March 1868 the Board refused the request of Marianne Catherine de Cabrera, the Contessa de Morella, for the station to be moved because it was blocking access to her lands. The lady (or her agent) must have made further representations because the engineer put in a report, on 13th April 1868, of the inconvenience to the Contessa de Morella, who would pay for the cost of removal to allow the needed access to her beach and land for proposed dwellings. 'It would be easier to provide a level crossing giving access by agreement with the Company and to erect a Small Lodge at which a platelayer's wife might be stationed to open the Gates.' Unattended occupational crossings were put in at both ends of the original loop but the Contessa never built her gentlemen's desirable residences. There were also foot crossings just beyond the bridge across Afon Gwril, known as The Fairy Glen (100 yards further north, close to the up distant signal).

On 15th May 1868 a new cast-iron water tank (still filled from the river by hand pump) was approved at a cost of £30. On 7th September 1869 the traffic manager reported that 'An Engine had run off at the points' and that the stationmaster had said that 'the indicator showed the points to be all right' (a Stevens point indicator).

On 19th December 1870 the traffic manager reported an incident in which cattle being delivered had escaped. The 5.20am from Machynlleth 'dashed into them in the dark, killing two cows and three calves, and a Heifer had to be slaughtered on the spot.'

On 26th January 1872 the committee approved the replacement of the station hut by a 'Permanent Station and residence' to cost £718 10s 0d. The engineer's report of completion was dated 19th December 1872.

On 25th November 1875 the traffic manager reported that the loop needed extending because of having to divide trains and put portions into the siding to enable two trains to pass. The committee ordered this to be done immediately. However, when, on 23rd March 1877, the committee considered the engineer's report that a down platform costing £130 was needed, they deferred authorisation. On 18th June 1879 the engineer re-presented the proposal, still costing £130, but with the reminder that 'Down trains have to run through the loop and set back to the up Platform'. This time the work was approved and the general manager reported completion on 28th July 1879. The station building was completed within one year and the new platform

The PW depot, showing three sheds housing trolleys, grindstone, bins and paraffin barrels. 18th July 1965. *Author*

Looking along to the loading dock. 18th July 1965. *Author*

The loading dock, coal bunker and oil shed (for the signal lamps – the shed was opposite the signal box). The former cattle pen at the near end of the loading dock had disappeared by this date. 18th July 1965. *Author*

Looking in the up direction towards Towyn, showing the boarded crossing to allow the signalman to cross over to exchange tokens with the driver (no token exchange apparatus was provided at Llwyngwril). 18th July 1965. *Author*

Like many signal boxes on the Cambrian, that at Llwyngwril was extended to allow the transfer of the train tablet instruments to the box from the station buildings, one of the recommendations following the Abermule tragedy. Here, the extension was simply bracketed off the existing brick base of the box. 27th September 1961. *Author*

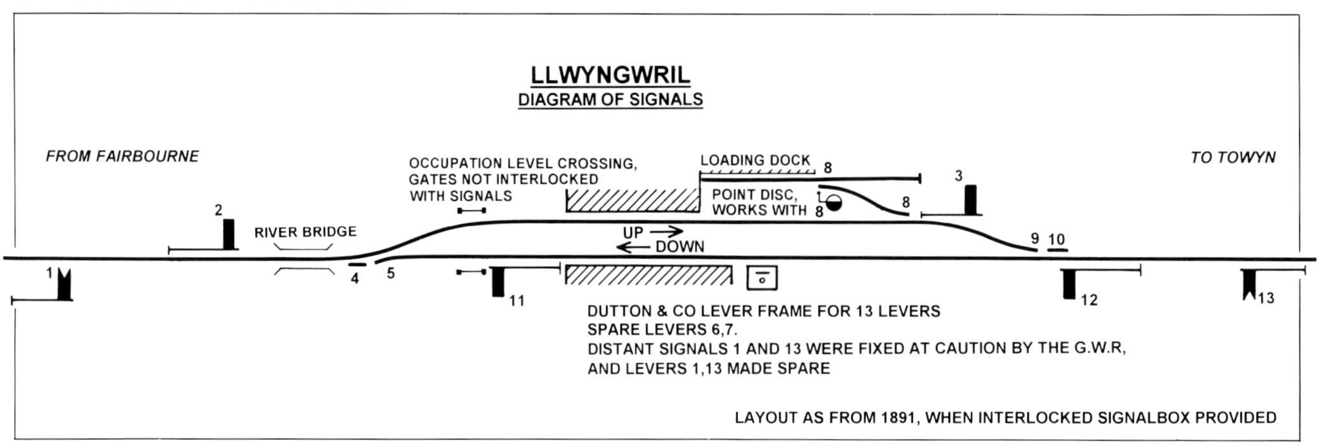

was completed within seven weeks. Planners, supervisors and workers did get on with jobs rather faster than they do nowadays!

On 11th October 1886 the traffic manager reported that the station was to get the old water columns from Machynlleth; every up train lost three minutes and every down train lost five minutes for the want of columns on the platforms (the engine had to be halted beside the tank). Now Llwyngwril was laid out and equipped much as it would remain until the onset of reductions in facilities in the 1960s.

The secretary was authorised by the Board on 26th May 1887 to negotiate for the continuation of the water supply and followed this on 25th August with the resolution 'Future arrangements for water supply to be reconsidered'. Nothing was altered and station staff and train crews had to keep pumping, but supplementary tanks were installed to raise the holding capacity for when the stream was running low. Years afterwards the Rural District Council of Dolgelley Union offered the Cambrian the opportunity of joining in the new proposal for a village water supply (the Inspector

A rear view of the box, showing how old timber had been protected by corrugated iron sheeting. 18th July 1965. *Author*

With its cantilevered extension of 1922 and its porch to fend off the gales, Llwyngwril was one of the most delightful boxes. Up to closure, it retained its Cambrian Railways nameboard. 27th September 1961. *Author*

An 0–6–0 Collett Goods on the 3.25 p.m. Barmouth to Dovey Junction arriving at Llwyngwril on 2nd August 1958. The coal wagon at the end of the long siding was adjacent to the coal merchant's sleeper-built bunker. The up platform was notably shorter than that on the down side (which was extended in 1909) and ended in steps rather than a ramp. *J. J. Davis*

Left: The water column, with detail of steps. *Right:* The water column and fire devil. In earlier times, the water column had been kept from freezing by a fire within the column, fed through the integral stoke hole. The small concrete coal box behind the water column was provided to hold the coal for use in the fire devil. Remarkably for such a remote location, the Cambrian rules were that the responsibility for attending the fire was that of the Locomotive Department. The smoke exit was at the top of the column. 27th September 1961.

Author

The station, looking down, showing porch, store shed and water tank which replaced the Cambrian structure seen on page 179. 17th September 1961.
Author

From the foot crossing at the Barmouth end of the platforms, the station presented a neat, compact appearance. 18th July 1965.
Author

4-compartment 1st/2nd composite No. 173 used as a garden shed behind the station. It is just visible on the right of the photo at the top of this page. April 1957.
Author

of Nuisances had reported 'an insufficient supply of wholesome water') but the general manager reported that he had refused as 'We have a good supply of water for our Station premises and engine tank'. In 1888 the dock was recorded as able to load horses but not carriages.

On 15th June 1896, Miss Martha Jones, aged about 23, was walking (trespassing) on the line and was knocked down and killed by the 4pm Pwllheli to Machynlleth. The verdict was 'Accidental Death' but the company's solicitor considered that the evidence pointed to suicide. About ten years earlier, an even stranger happening had taken place which, for lack of evidence, was never formally recorded. Frank Roberts relates that 'Two men going to the annual Towyn Show ran for their train as it was leaving and managed to climb onto the buffers. One fell off right away and saw his friend going away clinging to the back of the guard's van, laughing at him. That friend was never seen again, not even as a dead body at the side of the line. He

The station rear from the yard. Note how the 'Cambrian Railways' had been blacked over on the trespass notice. 18th July 1965. *Author*

Below: The rear of the house, showing slate-hanging weather protection and kitchen extension. 18th July 1965. *Author*

Looking through the station from the pedestrian crossing, in the up direction towards Towyn. 1964.
Mowat collection

The fully-protected waiting room on the down platform. 27th September 1961. *Author*

Rear of the waiting room, showing the tarred corrugated-iron sheeting on the seaward side of the structure. 18th July 1965.
Author

must have fallen and rolled over the edge of one of the cliffs onto the beach to be swept away by the sea.'

A committee dated 7th May 1899 authorised that the 'Supplementary tanks be dispensed with' without further detail to identify them. So many minutes give only the scantiest information!

C.S. Denniss's campaign to reduce line-crossing and trespassing resulted in the closure of the crossing just north of the Afon Gwril bridge, with the removal of the stiles, an arbitrary action which produced quite a storm of protest. On 22nd April 1901 he reported that the stiles were to be re-erected but that he proposed to close the footpath on one day each year to preserve the company's rights; the Board agreed. On 2nd February 1905 the committee noted that it considered that this was only an occupation footpath but that the Llangelynin Parish Council should be informed that the company would consent to its use by the public.

The Working Instructions for 1903 contained only one item. 'The drivers of up trains are to run cautiously through the facing points'. On 4th July 1907 the committee reprimanded 'Stationmaster J.H. Thickens and District Inspector H. Parry for allowing the use of a cattle truck which had not been disinfected whereby the Company has been fined.'

On 1st July 1908 the committee deferred the suggestion that the crossing stile should be replaced by a gate, and minuted that 'The Council be informed that the Company will provide gates if they allow the proposed notice to be exhibited and that the Company may exercise the right to close the crossing if they wish to do so.' In return the Council had to relinquish the rights of use of an established public crossing which was 100 yards further north, behind Hendre Hall. On 5th May 1909 approval was given for the erection of swing gates so that perambulators and pushchairs could be taken across the line. These were later removed and replaced by stiles. The pressure of local habit meant that the Hendre crossing is still in use. The agreement for its extinction was probably legally ineffective anyway!

On 3rd April 1909 the Board were informed that because of strong local opposition, the scheme for providing extra sidings to accommodate traffic brought by the Territorial Army had been abandoned. An extension to the down platform costing £50 was approved on 5th May. On 29th December 1909 'Farmer Humphrey Roberts missed his train and had tried to board it moving away by the water column and fell and had his one leg badly crushed. The train was stopped and First Aid rendered but he died after amputation a few hours afterwards.' Guard Roberts received the appreciation of the Board and was awarded a week's pay 'for the efficient first-aid rendered by him to the deceased.'

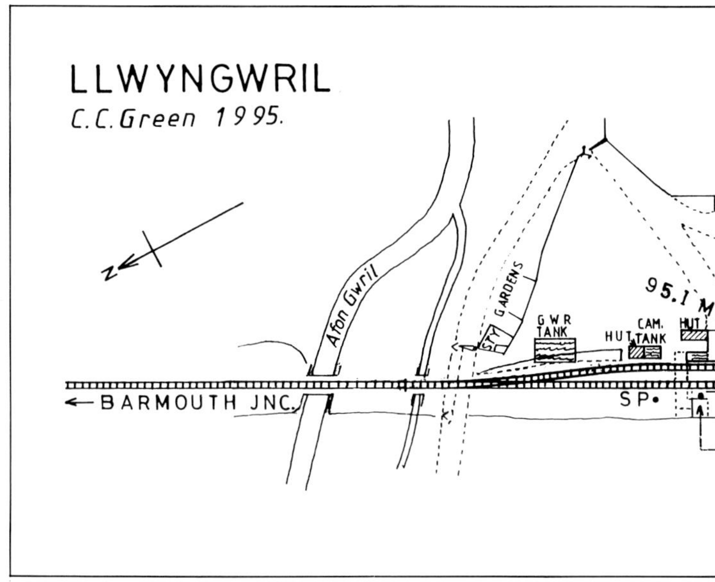

In 1914 a small timber culvert was replaced by concrete pipes and on 18th September 1914 the committee approved a cost of £73 for a gravitational water supply from a dam placed higher up across the Afon Gwril. In 1916 the solicitor reported that the lease for the pipe easement had not been signed by the Contessa de Morella before her death and that he was having to prepare a fresh lease (for £1 per annum) for the signature of her daughter, Miss A.C.B. Cabrera. On 6th December 1916, the Board authorised the cancellation of the lease prepared before and dated 25th December 1915.

The Great Western's first addition to the facilities was the little extension to the signal box to house the tablet instruments which were moved from the station building. One of the Llwyngwril signals may have been the last to retain the Cambrian painted discs instead of the more usual stripe (until 1928). In 1931 a reconditioned 20-ton cart weighbridge was put in at a cost of £230.

In 1937 the old water tank, which was of the smallest standard size erected by the Cambrian, was replaced. It was recorded as being 13ft 6in by 9ft 6in and 5ft 6in deep and it held 4,000 gallons of water when filled to a level of 5ft. The new tank was another Oswestry product, being made of standard Cambrian castings. It was 29ft 0in by 17ft 0in and 8ft 6in deep, with a capacity of c.25,000 gallons. The 2in cast-iron feed pipes were replaced by 3in and the distribution system from the tank to the columns and the house was relaid in 6in. The demolished store shed was replaced with one of double the original size.

In 1939 there was a camp coach at Llwyngwril. For many years before, there had been another far older coach (body only) as the station master's garden shed.

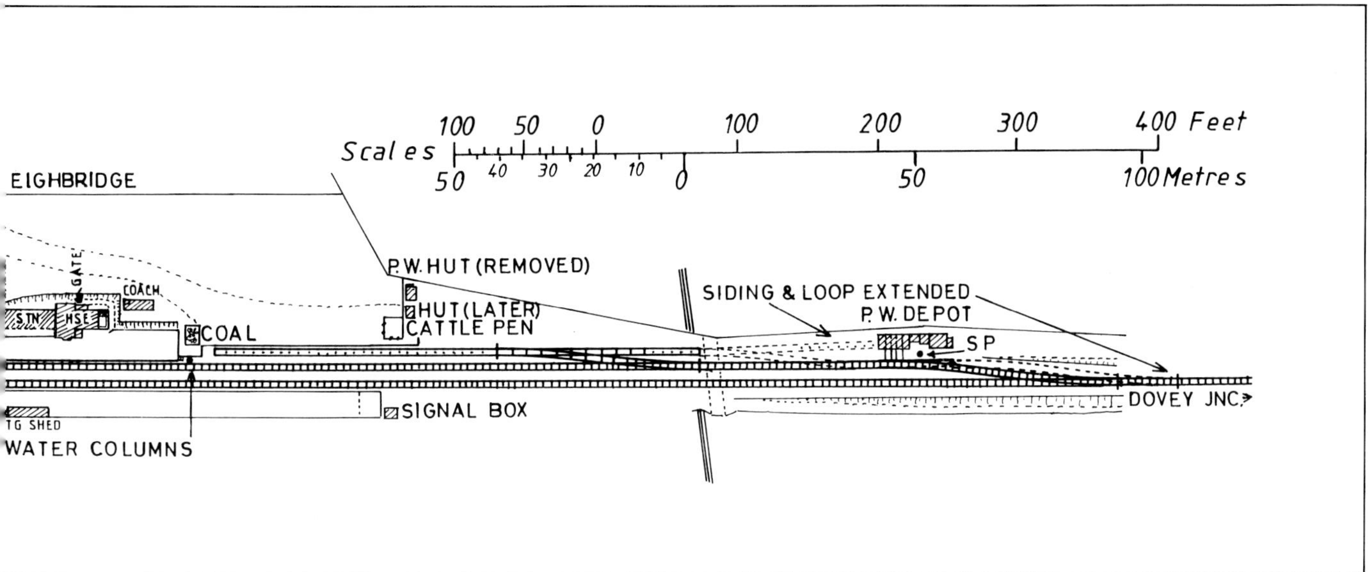

Passengers waiting to cross the line after their down train had cleared the crossing.
Cty. T. J. Edgington

0–6–0 Aston Goods No. 77 taking water in 1921. Using the Cambrian tank here meant that the rear of the train was standing in the section and across the occupation level crossing north of the station. *H. W. Burman*

This was No 172, a four-wheeled, four-compartment coach dating possibly from the 1870s and which only just failed to make its century before collapsing.

In 1944 Allt Goch underbridge, 47 chains to the south of Llwyngwril, was reconstructed and lengthened as a vehicular access to a Royal Marines training ground. The Admiralty paid the cost of £2,150 plus £40 as capitalised maintenance and £75 towards the cost of widening for double line if carried out later. There was also a £1 per annum wayleave.

Like Aberdovey, Llwyngwril was reduced by degrees in the 1960s to a single running line through an unstaffed 'station'. Initially, there were two 'bus shelters'. Both were stripped of their roofs in November 1990 during the same gale that bowled Llangelynin's shelter into the field. Now the old up platform remains the operative one with two shelters side by side. The station building has been restored as a private dwelling.

The approach road to the yard and weighbridge office, looking north, on 18th July 1965. The gate on the left led into the garden of the station house. *Author*

The water tank, on 27th September 1961. It was an ample structure, reflecting the importance of the availability of water at this rather remote location. *Author*

A down goods departing in the 1960s.
K. G. Draper

GWR water crane, waste collector and drainage grid on the down platform. 18th July 1965. *Author*

The drainage channel at track level. 18th July 1965. *Author*

This view of Small Prairie No. 4564 on a Swansea–Pwllheli through train, taking water, amply demonstrates how the long reach of the water crane was demanded by its location at the back of the platform. 2nd August 1958. *J. J. Davis*

The down starting signal, still fitted with original Dutton & Co. spectacle plate and lamp, but a shortened arm. It was later replaced by the tubular post signal in the photo above. 16th August 1935. *H. F. Wheeller*

Large Sharp Stewart 4–4–0 No. 11 on an up passenger entering Llwyngwril c.1920.
H. W. Burman

The 'down' end of the station. The level crossing here was only of 'occupation status' and was not protected by gates or the signals. A telephone was housed in the box on the left. 18th July 1965.
Author

The up approach, looking over Fairy Glen (Afon Gwril) with the footway crossing to the beach on the near side and the occupation crossing beyond. 18th July 1965. *Author*

LLWYNGWRIL TO BARMOUTH JUNCTION

95m 24c to 98m 73c

As the line climbs up towards Friog, a panorama opens up of the Mawddach estuary, with Barmouth in the centre of the scene and the coastline stretching northwards (out of shot to the left in this photo) to the cliffs above the railway at Harlech, and the sands of Morfa Harlech beyond. This photo, taken c.1925, shows Llwyngwril up distant signal before the GWR made it 'unworkable', i.e. fixed.
H. W. Burman

For barely a quarter of a mile the line is straight and level, before curving to head north-east while getting closer to the sea. To the south-east are the backs of spaced-out houses along the road below Pen-y-Crug, and to the north-west lies Cardigan Bay with the Lleyn Peninsula beyond. Ahead are the hills behind Barmouth and the Mawddach Estuary, with the Rhinog behind.

A slight rise brings the line even nearer to the sea's edge, across the little gorge of Afon Cletwr and right on to the edge of the Friog cliffs at about 100 feet above beach level. Over the top comes the long downhill slope through an avalanche shield then along a narrow ledge, over a tall stone bridge across the road to Friog and down a sweeping curve on an impressive embankment (made of stone won from the ledge) to touch down on the level of the morfa just before Fairbourne station.

It was a memorable experience to travel over this section in a dense sea mist in November – even more memorable in an up train. The steam wrapped the carriages in a drifting blanket and the only visible link with land was the half-seen rock on the left or the top of the low wall on the right. Of beach or sea there was no sign, only a white-emptiness.

After Fairbourne a nearly-level run, with hills and mountains distant on both sides, brings the train to Barmouth Junction.

THE FRIOG 96m 25¾c to 97m 22½c.

The hill from which the ledge is cut is named Gallt Ffynnon-yr-Hydd (The Hill of the Deer's Spring). A spring, noted on the O.S. maps as Chalybeate, wells up on the beach at 96m 50c. Known generally as Yr Allt (The Hill), it inspired one postcard maker to entitle it The Rallt. Nevertheless, the cutting has always been known by the name of the village just round the corner, Friog, which means 'lofty' or 'high'.

Several factors have combined to make this mile of railway unique. First is its siting a hundred feet or so above a rock-strewn beach. Then it had to be squeezed in between the precipitous fall to the shore below and a road (which had been made for horse and cart only and which has had to be cobbled up subsequently to take a much heavier motor traffic). Lastly, the trackbed was blasted and pick-axed across a mining concession which was still being actively worked.

In 1863 the Aberystwyth & Welsh Coast Railway produced a 'Plan showing Headings opened by the Anna Maria Mining Company'. On this appeared six headings and two shafts lying within the deviation limit of the line shown on the deposited plans, and there were more adits beyond the limit. The history and workings of the Anna Maria mine have been carefully researched by Mr Ifor Higgon.

The *Mining Journal* reported in 1856 that the Anna Maria had changed hands. In 1857, under 'Mining Notabilities', it carried an article calculated to make potential investors take notice:

> '... under the management of Capt. J.R. Floyd, promises to be an excellent speculation. There are seven champion lodes in the sett besides the ore they are now working on which is $6\frac{1}{2}$ ft wide, composed of copper ore and silver lead. Water power is abundant and sufficient to work the mine 700 fathoms under the sea level and the ore raised can be shipped without the charge of land carriage. The necessary machinery for crushing and dressing the ores are now in the course of erection.' [Captain was the title given to the site manager of a mine and does not necessarily imply a military title.]

Most remarkable is the suggestion that the minerals could be got away by sea after loading between tides into sailing flats, for which a quay would have to have been built and maintained against winter gales.

In 1861 there was a note: 'At Anna Maria very little is being done. It is worked under the management of Mr Simpson.' In 1862 Barmouth Consols Copper, Silver-Lead and Gold Mining Company was touting for finance and described its sett as 'A continuation of the celebrated Anna Maria mine now producing large quantities of lead, copper and gold quartz.' The company was calcining quartz to rid it of iron pyrites and putting the result through a Jones crusher, working slowly because of lack of (water) power. The yield was $\frac{3}{4}$oz of gold from half a ton using mercury as the extraction agent. (Continuation here means continuation of the concession and not a geographical extension.)

Of the cutting of the ledge in 1863 and 1864 C.P. Gasquoine wrote:

> 'Here the problem arose as to whether the cliffs should be tunnelled or the line be carried along the sloping edge supported by sea walls, as was the high road above. But the high road itself shaved the edge of the precipice so closely that, it is related, in the old coaching days, many people preferred leaving the vehicle at the top of the hill to swinging down such a slope. Eventually choice fell on the latter alternative, sailors being employed to assist in the work by reason of their greater experience on such seagirt ledges! It was, indeed, a hazardous venture; for the extreme narrowness of the ground to work on, sometimes tapering away to practically no ground at all, hampered the task at every step, and the difficulty of building a track along which heavy trains could run at high speed was never surmounted.'

Cambrian engineer George Owen first reported to his Board on the 'Vriog Cutting', as it was usually termed, on 25th July 1866. The sea was undermining the line 'to great risk' and advocated putting it into a tunnel. At the same time one Henderson, operating as the Anna Maria Mining Company, was claiming for damages caused by the railway. On 9th January Owen reported that a platelayer had noticed a large landslip, thereby averting a serious accident and 'I am making it as secure as I can but it is almost hopeless work'. His estimate of the cost on a work for which the contractor's maintenance period had not long expired, was £500.

By May 1869, Henderson was claiming £20 for damage to the mine. The committee refused to pay and warned Henderson 'at his peril to do anything to damage the Railway or interfere with the safety of the public'. The matter was up to Boardroom level by 6th August 1869 and the directors were told that

Calettwr (now Cletwr) bridge, looking in the up direction towards Llwyngwril on 17th July 1965. *Author*

'Henderson, the alleged lessee of the Anna Maria Mine, intends to work under the railway and to the damage of the public unless he is compensated for his interest'. He was cautioned by Mr Howe, the solicitor, as to the law and that he would interfere with the line at his peril.

Henderson countered with a cheeky letter dated 6th April 1870 in which he requested assistance in getting water to his dressing floor and stated 'we are now working the mine and in a short time we will be dressing the materials we are getting' and 'The Tramway is partly along your railway and along the rock'. This Owen stigmatised as 'most objectionable' and 'involving removal of the protecting wall'. The committee minuted that 'Truscott and Henderson, the alleged lessees, be refused permission to construct dressing floors and tramway partly on the Company's line'.

In the summer of 1870 a member of the public sent a letter to the *Daily Telegraph* criticising the safety of the cutting, and the Board of Trade sent Colonel Rich to investigate. He made no reference to Henderson's tramway so it must have just been removed, but he directed that loose sections should be removed and that supporting arches be built above and below the

Calettwr bridge from the roadway above at Pont Calettwr, with the roof of the watchman's house (known as Cambrian Cottage) on the right. August 1958. *Author*

Cambrian Cottage, the seaward elevation, and arguably the most exposed washing line on Cardigan Bay. 17th July 1965. *Author*

The watchkeeper's house (known as Cambrian Cottage) from the hillside. 17th July 1965. *Author*

line. A portion of the stone walling to the road was to be removed and be replaced with a light paling. The company was to maintain the present careful supervision and watching. To his report George Owen added 'The Line is now in as sound a state as it has been since the construction' and 'inexperienced persons would not know that there was a nine foot width of solid rock under the line.' On 30th November 1870 the Committee considered the Board of Trade report with the letter which had alleged that the cutting was in a dangerous state and instructed that the Company officers were to investigate 'who is the Board of Trade's informant?', but nothing was reported back officially.

On 13th April 1871 the engineer reported that the work required by Colonel Rich had been completed at a cost of £259 and that the cliff was quite safe, but that 'on the morning of 4th April John Henderson [who had caused all the previous mischief] again attempted to proceed with his mining operations. I went there and stopped him ... I was not a minute too soon for had he been allowed to go on he would inevitably have produced a fall of cliff.' Henderson was served with a formal notice which ended 'you will be liable to be at once arrested and imprisoned'. The engineer hinted yet again that the line should be resited inside a tunnel. The committee then authorised the commencement of formal proceedings against John Henderson 'for attempting to proceed with his Mining Works'. On 22nd September 1871 they authorised the ejection of Henderson from the cottage he was occupying on sufferance and that it should then be let to the 'Friog Watchman'.

The Working Instructions for 1871 laid down a speed limit of 4mph past the watchman (in his hut at the top of the crest), and drivers were to keep a sharp lookout for any signals from the watchman while he was on patrol. This regular patrolling was a very sound precaution because, besides weather damage, the formation had to take the pounding from the unbalanced motion of the early Sharp Stewart locomotives before they were rebuilt. By 1911 the speed limit was raised to 8mph. A board by the watchman's hut instructed all drivers of down goods trains to stop and pin down the wagon brakes, and a second stop board close to Fairbourne gave the instruction to stop and unpin.

Standard Class 3 2–6–2T No. 82006 with a down passenger ascending the final incline at 1 in 66 to Friog summit on 27th September 1961. *Author*

On 19th August 1874 the engineer reported to his Board that 'Some parties who state they have succeeded in obtaining a fresh grant from the Crown had commenced working the levels under your line'. Details of a fuller report laid before the committee on 20th

August 1875 have not been found, and here mention of the Anna Maria mine ceased. At no time was there ever any reference to Barmouth Consols, so Henderson's status remains a mystery.

In March 1876 a slip was reported, probably of material from above the line, as no expense was necessary; it would have been regarded as free ballast for use elsewhere. By the middle of December 1879 the entire length had been relaid in steel rail. Gale damage and further slips were reported in November 1881 and a bad slip below the rails in January 1882 necessitated a £200 extension to the sea walling. While that work was in hand another severe gale fetched down another load of rock from below the road.

After the watchman's early morning inspection on 5th June 1882, a large stone fell down, causing the first locomotive of the day a bent cock rod and a damaged ashpan. On 24th March 1882 a wheel broke under Robert Roberts' descending trolley; he jumped or fell clear and broke his collar bone.

On 1st January 1883 the 5.15pm train from Machynlleth, with four four-wheeled carriages headed by 2–4–0 Sharp Stewart engine No 29 *Pegasus*, coasted gently down the bank from Friog Summit in the dark. Since the previous train had passed, about thirty tons of soil, stones and walling had fallen from the road above. *Pegasus* was turned over and down onto the beach. Luckily, the couplings broke behind the tender and behind the second carriage. The leading coach (as usual, a 5-compartment Parliamentary 3rd) lay down

The 1883 accident from above, showing clearly the bridge and stairway built for the Anna Maria's miners. Note the sparsity of sleepers below the bridge. *Cty. Powys County Library*

This beach-level view of the 1883 accident shows how much of Wall 15 had been built and the ventilation shaft Anna Maria 8 as well as the Miners' Bridge. The top of Anna Maria 7 can be seen to the left of the coach and the drain chute below. *Cty. R. E. Thomas*

the cliff edge on its side, and the second (a 1st/2nd composite) lay on its side on the formation. A second 1st/2nd composite and the guard's brake van remained on the rails. Driver William Davies lay in the tender, and the fireman, also William Davies (they were not related) lay beside *Pegasus*. Both suffered fatal head injuries. Most of the passengers, including a Cambrian director Captain R.D. Pryce, had been in the third coach. There was one old lady, a Mrs Lloyd of Welshpool, with a merchandise business in Towyn, 'in the overhanging car' and 'save for severe and very natural fright she was got out without sustaining further harm'.

When news of the accident reached the Eisteddfod at Dolgelley, Doctors Hugh and Edward Jones, with others, hurried to the scene but both driver and fireman were beyond medical aid. More debris fell during the night and about 120 tons had to be cleared away before services could be resumed. The overturned coach was rerailed and taken to Barmouth for repair. The old third class coach was slid down onto the beach and the body was unbolted and burnt. Its underframe and wheels were recovered along with *Pegasus* and its tender, both of which were repaired and put back into service.

Colonel Rich inspected the site and considered that the excessively wet state of the peaty loam on the mountainside was the cause of the slip and that no blame could be attached to the Cambrian. Inspection of the line was regular and the 4mph speed limit was being observed by all train crews. He recommended that the road should be better maintained and drained, and observed that 'The only way of securing the railway from such accidents would be to tunnel through the mountain which would be very expensive; had Parliament not sanctioned the making of the line round the headland it is probable that it never would have been made at all, as the traffic is small, does not meet the cost of the railway in its present form, and would do so in less degree if more capital had been expended'. The Cambrian officers seem to have misled Col. Rich more than somewhat as he also stated that there had been no slips during the previous two years.

On 14th February 1883 the committee resolved that 'The Highway Surveyor be threatened with Indictment unless the road above is put into proper condition', and on 19th February 1883 the traffic manager informed them that trains were to be retimed to allow a little extra time between Llwyngwril and Barmouth Junction 'To ensure a more rigid adherence to the Regulations with regard to the speed of trains through the Cutting'.

On 23rd January 1883 the engineer had recommended that the reverse curves should be checked with (old) double-headed rail at a cost of £180 5s 0d. In addition, the new walling needed to comply with Colonel Rich's recommendations was to cost £959 16s 0d. The checkrail suggestion was passed over and he asked for it again on 22nd May 1883 at a cost of £200. The Board ordered him to present a more detailed report, which he did on 11th April 1883, bringing up even more problems. 'In some of the old levels belonging to the Anna Maria and other Copper Mines I found that the roof, being composed of Timber, is decayed. I have where requisite in these cases turned a short arch but at the point where the accident occurred an outer Sea Wall has become necessary to prevent encroachment by the Sea and to afford a greater setoff on the lower side of the rails.' This was to be the first example of what would be repeated many times, to effectively widen the cliff with masonry.

On 22nd May 1883 the engineer had to repeat his application for the money with which to carry out his suggested checkrails, this time to cost £200. The following day, the Board declined any liability for the payment of compensation to the widow Mrs Lloyd, and approval was given for the £200 for the checkrails.

On 18th July 1883 the engineer laid a report before his Board that he had obeyed their instructions to reduce expenditure as much as possible and had therefore had to stop the work on the Friog. This prompted a reconsideration of the instruction and the transfer of some money from revenue to the capital fund so that in August 1883 he was able to report completion of all work arising from Colonel Rich's recommendations at last, and also that he had completed 'the lining of adit levels through the Cliff (using brick instead of old timber). Much work on the upper side has been completed but the wall supporting the Turnpike road is bulging and giving way. Most of the dangerous parts have been pulled down and replaced with timber fencing. Work will be carried on during the Winter. ... By lessening the height of the new wall to the Turnpike road enough material will be available from the demolition of the old.' From all of this is can be safely assumed that the Highway Surveyor successfully challenged the proposed indictment and that the earlier reports of completion and security of the line were a bit premature. The final repercussion arising from the accident appeared on 26th March 1884 when the solicitor was instructed (re Mrs Lloyd) 'to defend the Company against her action'.

On 1st March 1888 a severe snowstorm halted an up train from Pwllheli on the open ledge and then blocked it in. A down train was similarly stranded a mile south of Towyn. It took all day to dig them out and local trains maintained shuttle services at both ends, though no interconnection was possible as the turnpike road was impassable as well.

On 24th January 1887 the engineer reported that he had given a Mr David Gillart permission to search for manganese ore, provided that no tunnel was driven

An 0–6–0 Dean Goods with the 2.10 p.m. Portmadoc–Machynlleth goods on the crest of the Friog incline on 28th May 1930. Note the few wires on this very exposed telegraph pole route, and the poorly maintained fence at the edge of the cliff.
Ifor Higgon

The 1933 avalanche in the making – a scene, c.1920, showing the vulnerability of the railway to falls of rock and soil from above.
Cty. E. W. Hannan

and no back or side levels were driven to come within forty feet of the line, and that any heading would be six feet high in four rings of Staffordshire bricks, but the committee refused to ratify his decision.

The winter of 1887/88 was another harsh one and on 27th January 1888 the engineer had to report that 'Considerable portions of the Cliff have been carried away during the last winter at the east or Barmouth Junction end and there are several places which must at once be underpinned by strong walling or the line will certainly be broken, and I therefore solicit your instructions to have the work put in hand without delay as if the cliff is allowed to fall the cost of restoring the wall will be a most serious matter.' He got his urgently needed approval on 31st January but it took until 26th January 1889 before he could report completion.

The winter of 1894/95 brought a succession of strong gales and on 15th January 1895 George Owen, now nearing his retirement, reported damage to the walls below the line and 'old Mine level running for a quarter of a mile under the rails has collapsed through decay of the timber roof and it is being replaced in a more substantial manner.'

On 26th October 1896 he reported that 'Rock sustaining the Railway between the Checkrail and the Watchman's Hut found to be getting washed away for a distance of thirty yards by thirty feet ... Retaining wall being absolutely necessary has been put in hand.' It took until 30th December 1896 to obtain committee approval. The engineer's last report of problems along the Friog was dated 26th April 1897: 'A somewhat serious fall of rock has brought down with it a portion of the Turnpike road'. George Owen retired at the end of that year and died shortly afterwards, aged 71, 'of an apoplectic fit' (heart failure) and the Friog, the scene of his greatest efforts, seems a fitting place to stop and consider what his superiors and equals thought of him. On 30th December 1897 the Board, when appointing him as Consultant Engineer at £400 per annum, recorded that 'he has devoted himself to the welfare of the undertaking with an assiduity, energy and unselfishness which have won him the esteem and friendship of all with whom he has been brought into contact'. On Owen's death the general manager, C.S. Denniss, said that he had received from him 'the most cordial and constant support and believed he had been a very loyal Officer of your Company throughout'. Because of the man he was, his workmen respected and regarded him as they respected and regarded no other man in the Cambrian hierarchy.

Owen's successor, A.J. Collin, soon found out what the Friog meant to any Cambrian engineer. He reported on 3rd August 1898 that the retaining wall to the road above was out of repair and that he had had to expend £127 17s 7d. A fire on 13th September 1899 destroyed the timber piling supporting the road above costing another £200; the work was completed by 16th January 1900.

When Collin came to examine the mine shafts and adits, he found 'several falls threatened in the headings' which he was having propped, and on 1st April he reported a further fall in No 3 heading while work was in progress.

After this, G.C. McDonald became the Cambrian's engineer and he may have worked to a changed reporting system, with a budget allocation instead of having to report constantly, since references in committee minutes to engineering work along the Friog have yet to be found for 1902 to 1922.

On 22nd April 1901 the general manager advised the Board not to buy the mining rights offered; it was not necessary and a few props only needed to be put in at certain tunnels, so on 6th June 1901 the Board authorised the refusal of the offer.

In May 1903 the secretary reported that the company's cottage, let to a platelayer for £3 18s 0d per annum, which had been erected by a contractor for use as a smithy, was 'beyond repair and in a most dilapidated condition as reported by the Sanitary Inspector'. It was ordered to be pulled down.

The story of the battle to maintain the line at Friog recommences with the assumption of control by the Great Western's Civil Engineer and, while some of his references are headed Llwyngwril, the mileages quoted identify the work as being along the Friog. Now it was thought that the Friog problems might be settled for once and for all by the construction of an 'artificial cliff' consisting of continuous sheer walling from below beach level right up to rail level, so that the natural cliff was protected and the ledge was made wider. George Owen had tried a little of this method, but he was always defeated by lack of money and often had to resort to guarding against the fission of the rock by the waves by small beehive-like structures only at beach level.

The first operation was the rebuilding of a retaining wall between 96m 49½c and 96m 52½c. An estimated cost of £750 was recorded on 11th January 1923 but on 8th November the engineer reported a cost overrun to £920 as a result of the extension of the walling to 96m 59c.

On 14th March 1924 watchman H. Jones was injured while on duty and later received payment of £75 18s 9d awarded by the traffic committee. Compared with the performance of the Cambrian on similar occasions, Jones must have thought that he was generously dealt with.

On 25th March 1926 the engineering committee authorised the deviation (slewing) of the line and protection by stone filling for £506, after which all was well for another six years, until November 1932 when repairing a massive slip cost £3,000 in remedial work which overran the estimate by £650.

On 4th March 1933 there was a near repetition of the accident of 1883, from precisely the same cause. On the day before, a very heavy (for its time) lorry, weighing 23 tons, travelled the old turnpike road. Later that day, two boys noticed an 18ft long crack along the surface. They had intended to report this next day, but, before they could do so, the 6.10am Mail from Machynlleth came over the crest in the dark at around 15mph (the permitted speed then) and ran into an obstruction. Drawn by 0–6–0 Jones goods, ex-Cambrian No 54 (now GWR No 874) with a clerestory brake

The 1933 accident, seen from above, showing the earth fall and the derailed coach. 4th March 1933. *Cty. Mr. Sandys*

The 1933 accident: the derailed clerestory brake 3rd with PW gang and an 0–6–0 Jones Goods. 4th March 1933. *Cty. Miss Evans, Fernbank*

third and three other coaches, the train struck a pile of soil, stones and debris from the collapsed road which had come down in the night. Like *Pegasus*, No 874 was overturned down to sea level but this time onto jagged rocks. As before, the coupling behind the tender broke, but this time all four carriages stayed on the rails with the brake third only a little askew. No-one was injured in the carriages, but again both driver and fireman were killed. This time they were both trapped in the flattened cab and it fell to William Spoonley, the slightest-built of their friends, to crawl in and bring them out before the next high tide.

In its issue for 10th March 1933 the *Cambrian News and Welsh Farmers Gazette* gave a most detailed account of the second Friog accident under the banner headline 'Railway Disaster Follows Snow in Merioneth', followed by 'Engine Driver and Fireman Hurled to Death' and four subheads including 'Passenger's Graphic Story'.

There had been only five people on the train, Driver John Humphreys, Fireman J.P. Kenny (who had changed duties with another fireman so that he could visit his sick mother in Pwllheli), Guard Edward Humphreys, and Assistant Guard Dick Lewis. The sole passenger was Mr Ronald Goodsell, the mechanic to Barmouth, Dolgelley and Towyn Gas Works, who was going to Dolgelley where a gasometer was under repair.

Goodsell and Lewis were chatting about Aberystwyth Town's football prospects, when there was 'a severe bumping like what might be caused by a smash, though it did not resemble thunder or an explosion as was stated in some newspapers. On seeing the guard's door open, we hastened thither and found the guard applying the brakes. Guard Humphreys remarked tragically "The engine has gone to the bottom!" He went to the call-box on the side of the line but found the wires broken and went to Llwyngwril for assistance.'

Goodsell then descended to the beach via the hand chain anchored by the wall for the use of the permanent way men. 'On reaching the spot where the engine lay, the steam almost blinded me. However I saw the bodies of both the engine driver and the fireman. They were both dead. As nothing could be done then I called out to Mr Dick Lewis that I would report the matter. I walked along the foreshore to Fairbourne and then to Barmouth Junction where I caught the train which reached Dolgelley at 8.10am.'

No. 874, showing the nature of the rocks on to which she fell. 4th March 1933. *Ifor Higgon*

Back at Oswestry there was a fascinating sequel as Frank Roberts has related:

'We had a mock-up of the cliff side and the line, and a model of the engine and tender all done to scale; and a long series of experiments was done to establish whether the landslide had happened before the train arrived at the site or whether the debris and the train arrived at the line site at the same instant. In the latter case the debris merely swept the model engine and tender against the retaining wall, pinning it there every time; but when the debris was there beforehand the engine rode up the debris and toppled over the retaining wall. I did these experiments. We were quite satisfied as to the sequence of events at Friog on that night in 1933.'

As in 1883, press and public were concerned because it was thought that the thunderous roar of the hard-pressed engines was responsible for bringing down tons of cliff on the hapless trains below.

The extent of the earth fall, seen from road level. 4th March 1933.
Cty. Selwyn Higgins

The avalanche shelter under construction, showing the work done to underpin the roadway above. *Cty. Mrs. Miller*

The road was reconstructed to take an alignment further away from the cliff's edge, a view c.1938. *Cty. E. W. Hannan*

Besides the clearing of the debris and temporary remedial work to the road, there were minor works in hand. Clearing the debris and draining mining adits were lumped together at a cost of £120, the reconditioning of the Cletwr bridge cost £375, and £210 was spent on sea protection and retaining walling between 96m 20c and 97m 20c.

The drawing and estimating offices were hard at work and on 31st May 1934 authority was given for the acceptance of tender from The Fairfield Shipbuilding and Engineering Co Ltd for reinforced concrete arched ribs costing £159 14s 3d for the 'Avalanche Shelter'. The overall expenditure was sanctioned in two portions: (a) 'Strengthening Cliffs' £3,140, for the supporting arching and masonry constructed to support the road and (b) 'Slip' and 'Additional Expenditure' £3,350, which covered the avalanche shelter and any under estimate. In March 1937 the *Great Western Railway Magazine* carried an article and photographs of the work above the line, which described the difficulties in obtaining a solid foundation. It had been necessary to excavate down to the solid rock beneath the track before construction of the piers supporting the arching below the road, and of the rail-framed masonry next to it. An article in a popular magazine carried a photograph of the avalanche shelter from the trains with the tale 'On the morning of March 4th the vibration of the 6.10am passenger and mail train from

The new works, as seen c.1938. The village of Fairbourne appears as a line of houses in the middle distance. *Author's collection*

2–6–2T No. 5570 and Dean Goods No. 2569 (ex Croes Newydd) on the 2.10 Portmadoc–Machynlleth goods passing through the avalanche shelter on 21st August 1936. *Ifor Higgon*

Left: The avalanche shelter, looking down. Note the timber fencing. *Right:* The avalanche shelter interior, looking in the up direction towards Llwyngwril, showing the pre-cast reinforced concrete arch forms. 27th September 1961. *Author*

A general view of the avalanche shelter and support-walling to the road above, on 17th July 1965. Note the change of inclination at the summit, from 1 in 66 up, to 1 in 55 down, through the avalanche shelter. *Author*

Left: The outer face of the avalanche shelter. *Right:* Detail of support work below track level. 17th July 1965. *Author*

Roof of shelter, with seagulls. 17th July 1965. *Author*

Above: The rail-secured masonry constructed by the GWR in 1936. 27th September 1961. *Author*

Top right: GWR rail-secured masonry of 1936 supporting the rocks below the road and base of arch-form reinforcement. The arch-form work is shown as W7 on the plan on page 203 (see also the photos on page 202). 17th July 1965. *Author*

Right: The avalanche shelter, looking in the up direction. 27th September 1961. *Author*

The seagulls' domain, showing what was the main support work at that time and showing clearly the then-new additional work. 17th July 1965. *Author*

Track, walling and stop notice north of the avalanche shelter, looking down the gradient towards Fairbourne. The notice read 'All down goods and mineral trains must stop dead here'. 17th July 1965. *Author*

End of walling seen above, with telephone and PW trolley run-off point, north of the avalanche shelter, looking towards Llwyngwril. 17th July 1965. *Author*

A general view from the beach. To give scale, John Burman can be seen sitting just below the left-hand edge of the nearest walling. 21st July 1993. *Author*

Above the line, W6 of 1933 supports the re-aligned road at top right. Next is the arch-form of W7 and the massive railbound buttressing of W8, both added in 1937 after completion of the avalanche shelter. Below the line is W9, an even more massive construction of 1975. The concrete blocks cast by BR at Newton Heath, are secured by stainless steel dowels, with bolted-on protective cover of greenheart at the lower right. The upper portion is a heavy ballasting in basket galsians.

The avalanche shelter. W5 on the plan fell and was finally demolished after the 1933 accident. No. 874 lay about one third of the picture's width from the right.

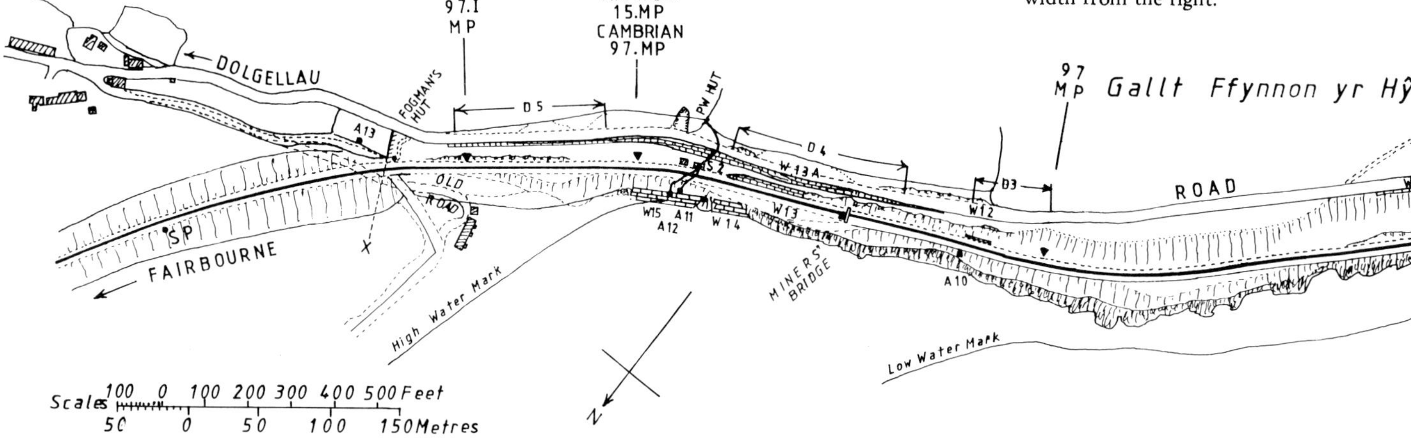

Above: Heading not shown on the Anna Maria plan of 1863, and probably of Henderson or Barmouth Consols origin (A7 on plan). *Right:* W3. A considerable reconstruction of 1960-61 by Wilson Lovett, supervised by Mr. Wendell Vaughan, Oswestry District Engineer.

W4. One of the earliest pieces of wall, pretty well unchanged in format except for raising.

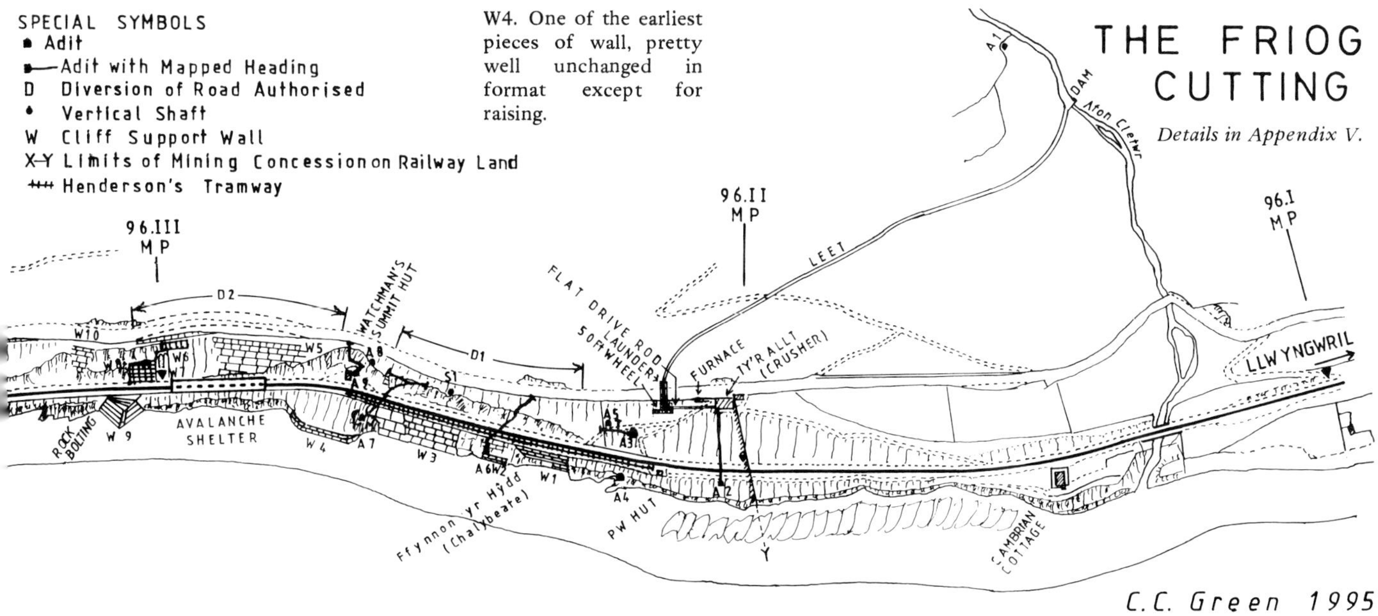

Details in Appendix V.

W1, a well-maintained work of Cambrian origin. W2 is on the left.

Machynlleth to Pwllheli caused this (road) wall to collapse; the debris was hurled down the hillside onto the line and swept the engine off the track into the sea.'

While all had been taken care of above rail level, the sea below was still at work on the cliffs and in October 1937 £435 was spent between 96m 50c and 97m 3c. In November another £705 was swallowed up by work at the same cliff face. On 1st October 1943 another £1,050 was recorded as authorised for 'Protection against sea erosion'.

Since 1948 British Railways have kept up with the battle, first under Western Region (controlled from Swindon via Oswestry) and then under London Midland Region. Now Railtrack has the responsibility.

In the early 1950s, Caersws Bridge Dept constructed a protection at beach level midway between the old Cambrian wall and the avalanche shelter. In 1960 and 1961 Mr Wendel Vaughan of Oswestry District Engineers' office supervised the building of an extensive triple bank of stepped walling erected by Wilson Lovett as contractors. Two men fell and were killed.

In the early 1970s some of the old beehive reinforcements were restored, and new footings were inserted into older walling. In the mid 1970s massive walling was erected just north of the avalanche shelter, using concrete blocks pegged together by stainless steel dowels made by BR at Newtown Heath. These were topped with another section built of stone held in rectangular steel baskets (Galsians). In 1979 where some of the pegged blocks were being eroded at beach level, they were faced by bolting on 12in × 9in greenheart timbers (W9 on map).

The rock bolting. *Cty. CAN Ltd.*

Men in slings operating the Alco-track 150 boring rig.

In 1986 and 1988 CAN (UK) Ltd (now CAN Ltd of Chesterfield) applied a technique much used in cliff face (geotechnical) engineering. Roped access techniques were utilised to install permanent anchorages into the cliff face. These anchorages, supplied by Dividag, were installed into 120mm holes and bonded into place utilising cementitious grout. It was necessary to drill up to 20m to penetrate all the fissured rock, allowing the anchorages to be founded in solid rock. Subsequent to installation, residual loads up to 30 tons were placed into the anchorages, effectively stitching the face and preventing further failure at this point. The system is termed 'permanent ground anchorage' and is also known as 'rock bolting'. The cost was c£60,000.

Seen from the beach, the Friog is one of the most remarkable examples of man-made cliff supporting a railway high above a capricious and gale-swept sea as may be seen anywhere in the world.

Rock bolting now supports much of the vulnerable cliff face. The original W10, still stable but much overgrown, can be seen at the upper right, above track.

Below left: A well-maintained original beehive a little further north-east past the two pieces shown in the previous photograph.

Below right: W11 is below the road at the top. At a lower level is an excellent example of a small beehive with a larger breastwork on the right.

Further along towards Fairbourne than the previous photos, defence wall W15 is seen here, with Anna Maria entrances A12 and A11. The concrete block at track level is the cap stone of shaft S2 (see plan on page 202).

Beyond the hut is the 1960 cap stone of shaft S2, and beyond is the much-extended W13. The top of W15 can be seen below with a minor piece of walling beyond.

Speed restriction indicator facing Machynlleth-bound trains ascending Friog incline. April 1957. *Author*

Centre: Supporting the road above the line are the concrete block (placed c.1960) and W13. Below the track, on the left, is W14, and there is a minor piece of walling on the right. *Right:* W12, a small wall below the roadway, constructed by Caersws Bridge Department in 1950.

An 0–6–0 Collett Goods on an up passenger above the rebuilt reinforcement of 1865 (now known as W15). The noticeboard read 'Warning Notice, Dangerous Cliff, Beware of Falling Rock'. Note the two adits of the Anna Maria Mine (A12 and A11). 27th September 1961.
Author

An 0–6–0 Collett Goods on an up passenger, on 27th September 1961. *Author*

0–6–0 Aston Goods No. 87, as GWR 884, assisting 0–6–0 Dean Goods No. 2477 on the 2.10 p.m. Portmadoc–Machynlleth goods approaching the Friog Cutting. 3rd July 1937. *Ifor Higgon*

0–6–0 Jones Goods No. 101, as GWR 895, on the 3.30 p.m. Barmouth – Machynlleth local, passing Friog village (in the background) and crossing the roadway leading down to the beach. 28th July 1953. *Ifor Higgon*

The Fairbourne incline, looking down over Friog Beach bridge, with Friog village on the right. Fairbourne level crossing and station lay at the foot of the bank. 27th September 1961. *Author*

Friog Beach bridge, the seaward face. 17th July 1965. *Author*

Friog Beach bridge, the landward face. Note the Anna Maria Mine adit A13 at road level on the left. The old road of pre-railway days was on the right. 17th July 1965. *Author*

A Machynlleth-bound train, consisting of a very mixed rake of coaches, steaming southbound out of Fairbourne and beginning the climb to Friog. The tips of Goleuwern quarry can be seen above the last coach. 14th August 1935. *H. F. Wheeller*

FAIRBOURNE 97m 72c.

Looking down the embankment (built of stone taken from cutting the Friog) towards Fairbourne station, with Barmouth viaduct and the Rhinog mountains beyond. The down distant signal for Fairbourne features in the foreground. *Cty. Eric Hannan*

As Barmouth Ferry – opened 3rd July 1865, closed 3rd June 1867.
As Ynys-faig Siding – opened 1869, closed c.1890.
As Fairbourne – opened c.January 1899.

The rails were laid past the site probably by early in 1864 and excursions (at first-class rate) were run to Barmouth by horse-drawn carriage from the line to the ferry. After the official opening date this service continued by four-horse omnibus.

On 26th October 1864 the Cambrian committee resolved that power to purchase the 'Toll of the Ferry' should be obtained, but when it was offered to them, they minuted on 18th April 1867 that they did 'not wish at present to purchase'. (The Barmouth bridge was opened for passenger traffic on 3rd June 1867, so rendering the ferry largely redundant.) In 1866 the station, which was only a small hut on a wooden platform, was noted as having a staff of two plus a signalman. The 'Barmouth Ferry' station closed the day that services first ran across Barmouth Bridge.

On 24th June 1865 Thomas Savin had bought the Ynys-faig estate from Robert Jones of Caernarvon. It consisted of a mansion which Savin was planning to open as an hotel, part of his chain of hotels along the coast (and which is still an hotel), the adjacent farm and lands, and Penrhyn farm, which lay on the north side of the railway and extended right up to Penrhyn Point and the ferry landing. Two days later, the estate was mortgaged to Mary Jane Ormsby-Gore as security for a £6,000 loan to tide Savin over the difficulties arising from his bankruptcy. He failed to recover his financial position, and the Ynys-faig estate became forfeit to the Ormsby-Gore family who sold on to Doctor G.A. Walker (who wanted it for the quarry rights) for £10,000 on 1st May 1867. The astute Ormsby-Gores were better off by £4,000, a lot more than the two years' defaulted interest.

The ancient monastic ferry rights had probably devolved to the Barmouth Harbour Trust and were sub-let to Penrhyn Farm, the tenant in 1867 being Gruffydd Owen. When the railway bridge was opened, he received £50 as a gift which, unfortunately for the company, put into his head the idea that he could claim a much larger sum as compensation for loss of livelihood. His claim was laid before the Cambrian Board in April 1867. The case went to the Queen's Bench Division and to an arbitration award of £600, reported and approved for payment in June 1871.

Fairbourne, seen from the north-east, a delightful view which shows the various blocks of houses built as speculative development. The newly-built station (before the station master's house was added) can be seen on the east side of the houses, but still on low, marshy ground. The cliffs of Friog feature in the distance. *Collection M. Christensen*

The bungalows which lie, in seemingly indeterminate pattern, behind the shingle bank which is Fairbourne Beach. On the hills behind are the levels of Goleuwern quarry, and in the foreground the lightly-laid rails of the 15in gauge (horse-drawn at this era) tramway to Barmouth Ferry. *Cty. M. Christensen*

Alison Harrison, in her delightful account of Fairbourne and Friog entitled *The Light of Other Days*, has written that Owen's family had no knowledge of his ever receiving this amount. It appears probable (but unproven) that the Barmouth Harbour Trust stepped in and claimed the damages on the back of Owen's legal expenses, an act which left him bankrupt and embittered.

On 8th July the traffic manager, Elijah Elias, recommended that the Henddol Slate Quarry should be allowed to put in their own siding at Fairbourne. The engineer gave an estimate of £163 13s 4d on 14th July, and on 15th September 1868 the Board approved the cost provided that the Henddol Quarry reimbursed the company for the points and road crossing and paid the signalman's wages. On 24th November 1868, the Board altered these terms so that Henddol paid the full cost of the siding and half the signalman's wages. Elias reported on 17th December 1868 that these terms had been accepted.

On 30th June 1869, One Owen Jones was run down by a train on a boisterous night. The *Oswestry Advertizer* carried a full account:

'On Thursday last (30th Sept.) Mr Owen Jones, bailiff of Dolgelley, who had been serving a notice on a person in Friog, was struck and dragged to Barmouth Junction by the engine *Minerva* of the train due at Barmouth Junction at 6.29 pm. Driver Owen William Davies felt a bump at Ynysfaig Crossing but saw nothing and the deceased had been drinking at Ynysfaig. It was a stormy evening.'

The Coroner advised the company to erect fences and gates as there was nothing to prevent people walking on the line.

In September 1871 Dr Walker was asking for extension of his Ynys-faig Quarry Siding and the committee refused, considering that it was then adequate but agreeing that it could be lengthened later if necessary.

On 21st November 1872 the engineer reported that Dr Walker was complaining that inadequate drainage of the line by 'Barmouth Ferry Old Station' was damaging his lands. The committee authorised that a culvert not made deep enough be re-excavated, at a cost of £25 3s 0d. At the same committee meeting the traffic manager reported that Dr Walker wanted the siding to be extended at a cost of £329 as he was expecting to increase the output from the Henddol Quarry from 300 tons per annum to 1,000 tons per annum. The committee had previously instructed its officers to report on trains stopping at 'Ferry Siding' because of the request for extension of platform. From this slightly ambiguous instruction, we are left wondering whether the old platform was either being used for the transhipment of the slate or for an irregular passenger service, or both.

On 22nd November 1872, the committee approved the work on Dr Walker's drainage problem (now costing £50 1s 0d) and agreed to the extension of his siding 'if he gives a binding undertaking guaranteeing a

The top of the incline at Goleuwern Quarry, with manager Edward Jones Meredith on the brake handle.
Cty. Ifor Higgon

Below: The office of the Cambrian Estates Consolidated Ltd. with, standing in the doorway William Williams, under manager, seated in the centre, Howell Jones, manager of Henddol Quarry, on the right Edward Jones Meredith, manager of Goleuwern Quarry. The identity of the man on the left is unknown.
Cty. Ifor Higgon

maximum of 1,000 tons in 1873, 1,500 tons in 1874 and 2,000 tons in 1875 and in the four following years'. Dr Walker was to pay the wages of the man at 15/– per week for the term of the contract and 2/– per ton 'for all deficiency of Guarantee'. Up to £350 was to be expended on the construction.

On 6th June 1890, the general manager reported that 'Messrs G.A. Walker & Co were in liquidation and owing £63 1s 10d for wages of signalman of Ynysfaig Siding etc. The Company has exercised the lien and has taken and sold slates on site to the value of £40'. The committee approved that notice be given to G.A. Walker & Co.

On 27th June 1892 the committee considered the general manager's report on a memorial received from the inhabitants of Friog, in which they were asking for a station, as the nearest was Barmouth Junction two and a quarter miles away. 'It is admitted that the public walk along the line to get to Barmouth Junction, a distance of one and a quarter miles, thereby saving about a mile compared with the distance by road, which said is only a private roadway along which passengers are allowed to travel merely by the grace of the owner.' The committee refused.

The company paid the wages of a signalman from 9th November 1892 when the siding was re-opened for a brief revival of the Henddol Quarry until 13th January 1893 when locking by the train tablet was introduced. Soon after that the siding was closed again, and lifted.

On 1st June 1896 the general manager reported to the Board re 'A Proposed new Watering Place called Fairbourne south of the Estuary, Barmouth.'

'Arthur McDougall is asking for a siding immediately and a Station. He proposes to erect a suitable Passenger Station and platform not inferior to Llwyngwril (excepting Stationmaster's House) and I propose the cost of this be lent to the Board as a Capital Sum without Interest for the term of 5 years, the Company to repay half at 5 years and the balance at 8 years.

'From my conversation with Mr McDougall I have no doubt he means business and that the scheme will probably result in a considerable amount of traffic being passed over the line, but I think it would be well to take advantage of his enthusiastic belief in his proposals and allow him the privilege of providing the accommodation at his own cost subject to the approval of your Engineer.'

Accordingly the Board refused to allow the station to be built on Mr McDougall's terms. McDougall's financial standing had been created by the popularity of his famous 'Self-Raising Flour'. He had already opened a brickworks just to the north of the former station and had connected this to his initial property development by a two foot gauge horse-drawn tramway.

By 7th July 1896, McDougall was offering to pay for the entire siding and station and was wanting 'to use the siding as soon as it could be laid and to have the Station ready by March 1897'.

By 21st September 1898, and after further bargaining, McDougall paid a £250 advance on an estimate of £497 3s 2d and the siding was thereafter laid in. He wished to enforce a toll upon or to stop the passage of slate, etc, over his roads (and presumably to 'his' siding) but to this the Cambrian refused to agree. The station was completed quite rapidly and was opened in time for the general manager to report on 1st February 1899 on its completion and that it was well used. Probably trains had been stopping there for some time before to set down and take up workmen, etc, engaged on the building of the Fairbourne development. By extending his tramway, McDougall ran a 2d tram to the ferry landing using a pair of bogie toast-rack carriages drawn by horses. The local people sent in a memorial asking that the station be named Ynys-faig, but, as McDougall was paying for the station and his sign had already been painted, he regretted that this would not be possible.

In the final settlement, McDougall was hoping that the company would accept only £400 as he had expended upwards of £700 on the station area, but the committee insisted on £500 towards the company's expenditure of £576 13s 3d. Unfortunately for McDougall, Fairbourne failed to develop much beyond his initial construction. The siding was largely given over to Cambrian Estates Ltd of Croydon who owned the rights of the Henddol and Goleuwern slate quarries which were all part of the Cabrera estate based on Bwlchgwyn. During 1899 the rights were acquired by a new company with expansive ideas, and the siding was graced by a beautifully-painted sign, over ten feet long, lettered 'SITE of SIDING and WHARF for the SOUTH BARMOUTH TRADING Co Ltd PRO-

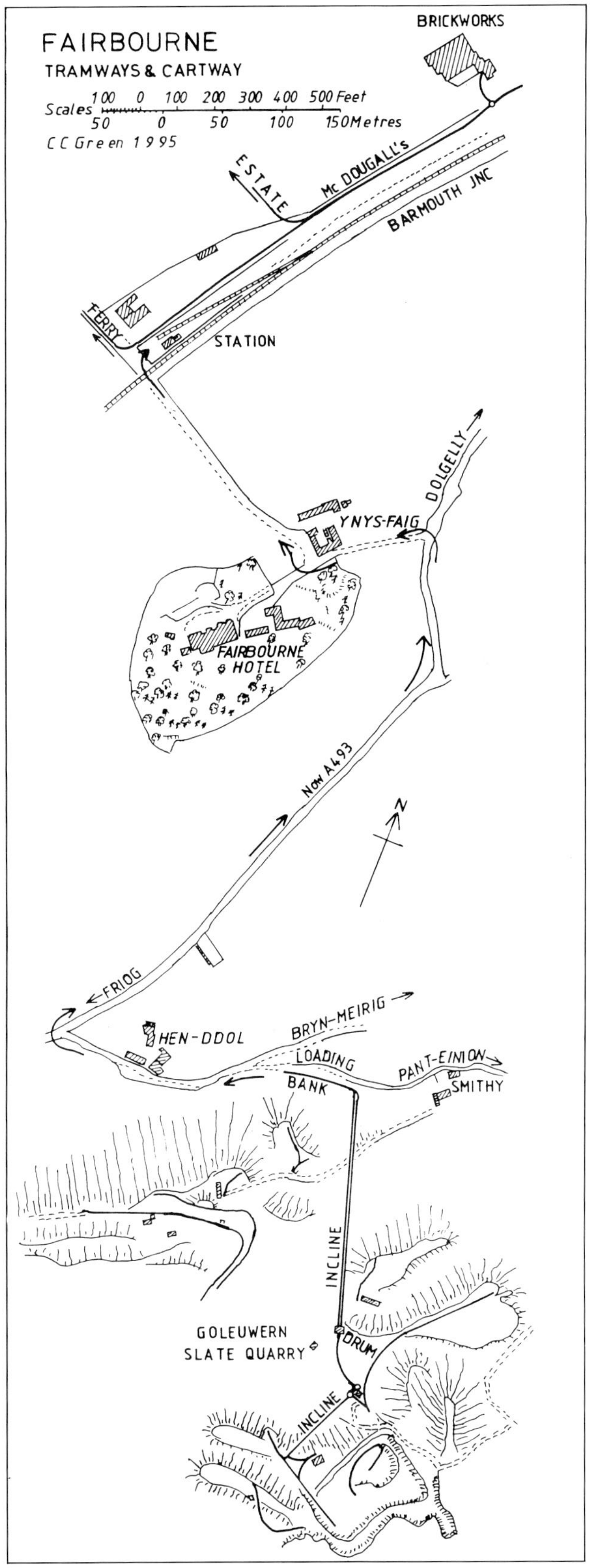

The view up towards Friog and Yr Allt on 17th July 1965. *Author*

Above: Looking down across Fairbourne Brook bridge and level crossing. *Right:* Fairbourne Brook bridge, looking south-east towards the hills. 17th July 1965. *Author*

PRIETORS of the HENDDOL and GOLEUWERN SLATE QUARRIES'. These quarries were no longer sending slate to the siding by 1914. The siding had been worked by down goods trains or by special engine propelling the empties from Barmouth Junction (with the guard in the leading wagon) and returning pulling the loaded wagons.

At the foot of the Henddol incline, McDougall built a small shed to house a turbine-driven electricity generator to light the whole of Fairbourne. Later the shed caught fire with part of the South Barmouth Trading Co. sign board inside, and all was destroyed. The other half of the board was used in a barn at Brynmeurig.

On 25th February 1899 the committee approved the dismissal of J.H. Thickens 'for irregularities in the collection of excess fares.'

By 1901 the profitability of the station had been established. McDougall had decided not to extend his

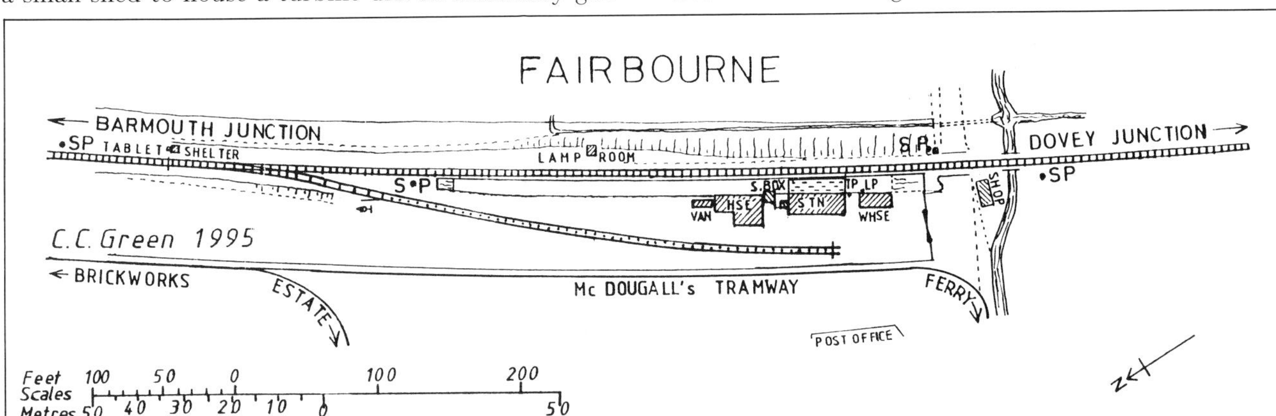

The station staff posing for the photographer, with the small warehouse in the foreground. The tiny Dutton-built signal box can just be seen between the station buildings and the station master's house. At this stage the down starting signal (No. 3) – later abolished – was still extant.
L. E. Copeland

The level crossing, looking south-east towards Cader Idris on 17th July 1965. *Author*

Looking into the yard, with the small warehouse on the right and coal stacks on the left. 17th July 1965. *Author*

The rear of the station, showing the loading doors in both the station and the small warehouse. 17th July 1965. *Author*

enterprises which had proved less successful than he had hoped, and the company was able to buy the station from him. On 7th February 1914 the committee accepted 'The Offer of the Fairbourne Estate' which was basically to build a station master's house costing £200 on company land to the engineer's satisfaction. The site was to be leased to the estate at a ground rent of 1/– per annum and the company would pay a rental of £10 8s 0d per annum to the estate for sixty years. Alternatively, the company might purchase the house for £150 at the end of twenty-one years or for £100 at the end of forty-two years.

On 25th February the Board took notice of the intention to convert the tramway into a miniature railway and to extend the route from the ferry further on to Penrhyn Point. On 7th June 1916 they were told that work on the miniature railway had been commenced but that it had been suspended. Nevertheless the Fairbourne Miniature Railway was running soon afterwards.

A note dated 1921 stated that the turnstile at the level crossing was not locked with the gates.

The Great Western rebuilt two small timber bridges for £125 each, one at 97m 55c in 1926 and the other at 97m 68c in 1929. A camp coach was provided on a specially-built short siding around 1939. The last camp coach was left isolated when the goods siding was cut off about 1964.

The rear of the station master's house. *Author*

The station master's garage – an 18ft ex-Rhymney Railway van. 17th July 1965. *Author*

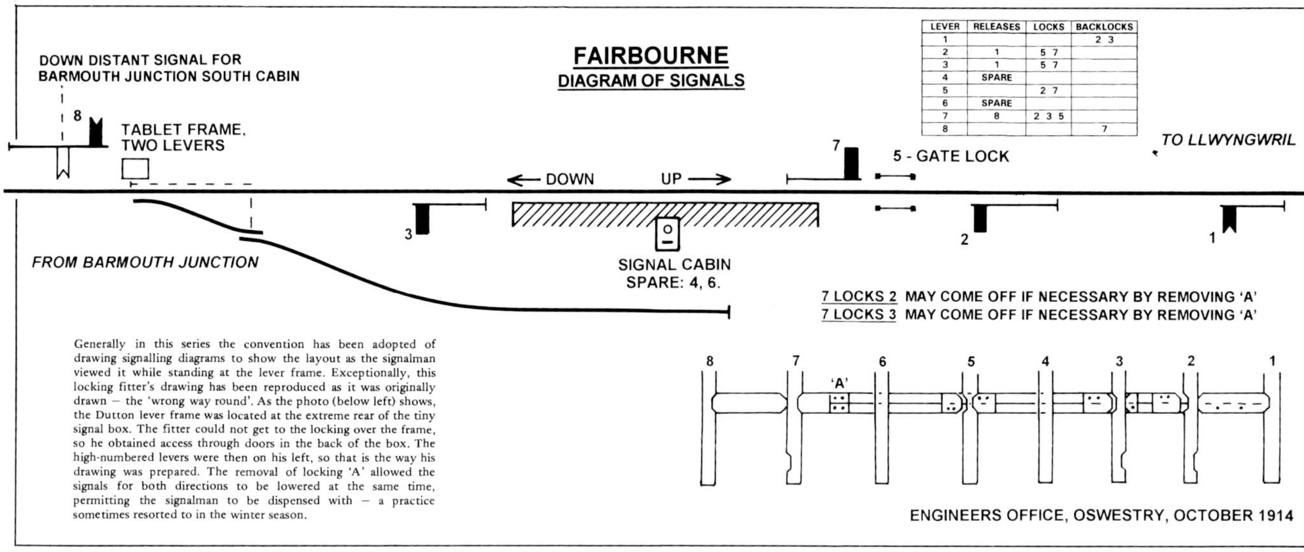

LEVER	RELEASES	LOCKS	BACKLOCKS
1			2 3
2	1	5 7	
3	1	5 7	
4	SPARE		
5		2 7	
6	SPARE		
7	8	2 3 5	
8			7

Generally in this series the convention has been adopted of drawing signalling diagrams to show the layout as the signalman viewed it while standing at the lever frame. Exceptionally, this locking fitter's drawing has been reproduced as it was originally drawn – the 'wrong way round'. As the photo (below left) shows, the Dutton lever frame was located at the extreme rear of the tiny signal box. The fitter could not get to the locking over the frame, so he obtained access through doors in the back of the box. The high-numbered levers were then on his left, so that is the way his drawing was prepared. The removal of locking 'A' allowed the signals for both directions to be lowered at the same time, permitting the signalman to be dispensed with – a practice sometimes resorted to in the winter season.

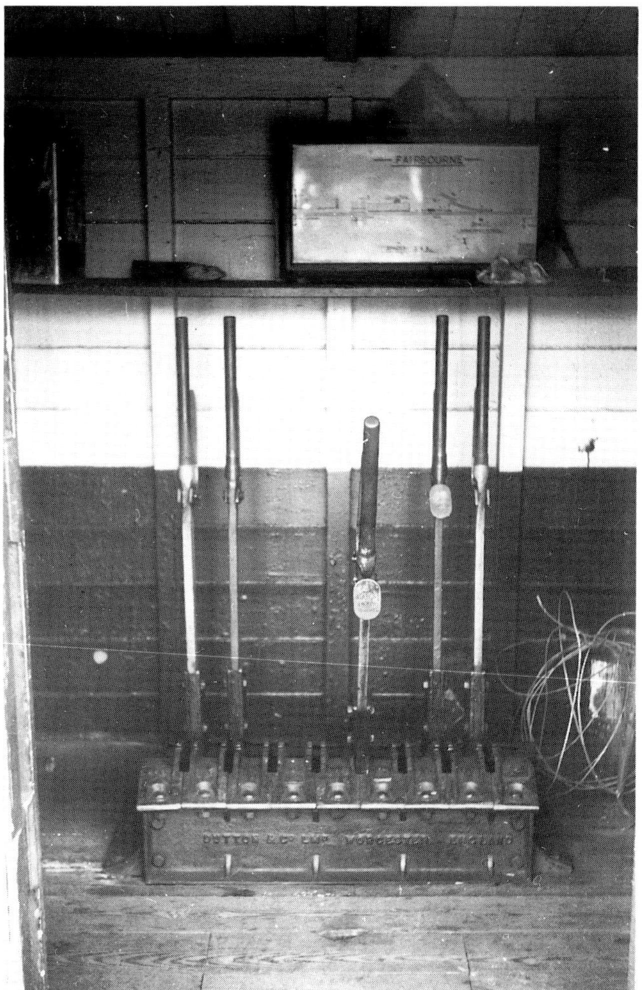

Left: Original Dutton eight-lever ground frame with the GWR's framed diagram above. 27th September 1961. *Right:* The replacement five-lever ground frame by the level crossing. The blue-painted gate lever (No. 3) is shown pulled over, indicating that the gates were open for the road. Either side (levers 2 and 1, 4 and 5) were the home and distant levers in each direction. 17th July 1965. *Author*

A general view from the south-east. 17th July 1965. *Author*

The station, station master's house, and the original Dutton-style signal box. 27th September 1961. *Author*

The station, looking up, and showing the gap left by removal of the original signal box and frame. 17th July 1965. *Author*

0–6–0 Collett Goods No. 2289 at Fairbourne c.1957. Note that the camping coach was on its own short length of rail. When the coal had to be taken away from Fairbourne, the siding was slewed across to temporarily connect. *Collection C. L. Caddy*

Working Instructions 1943

FAIRBOURNE.

Station Level Crossing.

Rule 99.—The normal position of the Level Crossing Gates is across the railway.

After the signals have been lowered for the passage of a train they must not again be restored to normal and the gates opened for road traffic until the train has passed over the Level Crossing.

Freight Trains must not be allowed to stand on the Level Crossing at the South end of the station, and if necessary the train must be parted and the Guard will be held responsible for seeing that this is done. The vehicles left uncoupled from the engine must be secured by the Van Brake being applied and, if necessary, a sufficient number of Wagon Brakes.

Station Siding.

The siding at Fairbourne is connected with the Running Line, facing from the direction of Barmouth Junction, the points being worked from a Ground Frame locked by the Electric Train Tablet.

The Line is on a gradient of 1 in 76, falling towards Barmouth Junction, and the greatest care must be exercised by the Guard in performing the work at the siding. Before the engine is detached the train must be secured by the Van Brake being tightly applied, also a sufficient number of Wagon Brakes, and if necessary making use of sprags on the leading wagons, in accordance with Rule 151 to prevent the train or any portion of it moving.

The siding will be worked by Down Trains, and when necessary by a special engine from Barmouth Junction, the wagons being propelled from Barmouth Junction on the forward journey. The Guard must ride in the leading vehicle, keep a sharp lookout, and be prepared to warn anyone on the line of the approach of the train. A White light to be placed on the leading vehicle after sunset or during fog or falling snow.

The Driver on the return journey must consider the line to be clear only as far as the Barmouth Junction Down Home Signal.

The Guard will be responsible for the working of the Ground Frame points in accordance with Electric Train Token Block Regulation 34.

General view, including the station master's house, looking in the up direction. 17th July 1965. *Author*

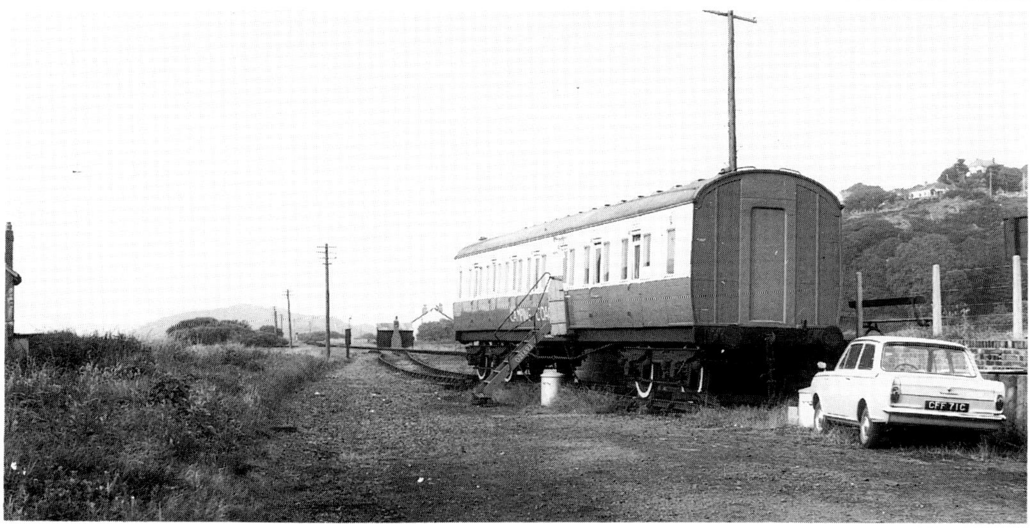

The freshly repainted camping coach as evidenced by the white wheel rims. The steps (set No. 021963) raised up on stone blocks seem to have been rather insecure. The goods yard siding had been removed by this time. 17th July 1965. *Author*

By the time this photograph was taken on 17th July 1965, the points in the running line had been removed. Extracting the camping coach now required breaking and slewing the running line. The main line is seen here curving away north-east to Barmouth Junction. *Author*

Looking southwards into Barmouth Junction station, with 2–4–0 rebuilt Sharp Stewart No. 54 on a Barmouth and Pwllheli train from Ruabon and Dolgelley waiting for the signalman to hand up the tablet, and the Dolgelley goods waiting at the branch platform on the left. The branch (Dolgelley) line can be seen on the left and the main line curving to the right leading to Towyn and Dovey Junction. The open-fronted passenger shelter on the down main (right-hand) platform, built in 1873, was later replaced in 1936 by the structure shown on pages 225 and 245. c.1920. *Pope/Parkhouse Archive*

BARMOUTH JUNCTION

(later MORFA MAWDDACH) 99m 0c and 52m $16\frac{1}{2}$c

Looking in the up direction along the main platforms, this photo was taken after the abolition of the South signal box (authorised in 1915) and shows the layout depicted by the diagram on page 230 (middle), with a short-arm signal (No. 10) leading to the shunting line. Note the difference in height between the reconstructed down platform (on the right) and the original island platform.

Morfa Mawddach is the 'Morfa (or salt marsh) belonging to Mawdd'. When the junction was being established and before all the dykes had been completed along the estuary shore, it was more marsh than firm ground. Much of the railway had to be floated on brushwood and the station also needed some piling. At first there was only a grace and favour road connection and the few passengers joining trains had to walk and often to trespass.

> West side of triangle called The Main: 98m 73c to 99m 05c
> East side of triangle called The Branch: 52m 07c* to 52m 23c* (99m 05c)
> South side of triangle called The Loop: 52m 07c* to 52m 28c* (98m 73c)
> Station Box, later North Box: 99m 05c and 52m 23c*
> South Box: 98m 67c
> East Box: 52m 30c
> *Branch distances measured from Ruabon Junction.
> Opened: Loop, as single line to Penmaenpool, 3rd July 1865.
> Loop, as passenger & goods loop on line now open to Dolgelley, 21st June 1869.
> Main, as terminus, 3rd June 1867. Passengers conveyed by horses and carriage across the bridge to Barmouth.
> Main and Branch opened to passengers 3rd July 1867, and to goods on 10th October 1867.
> Closed: Goods, 4th November 1963.
> Branch, 18th January 1965.

There was a refreshment hut erected by William Jones, who was given permission by Mr David Williams of Castell Deudraeth, a Coast director before the Cambrian had assumed control. No staff were shown in the 1866/67 wages list, and any official presence was down to guards, gangers and labourers. This state of affairs did not work too well as Barmouth Junction's first entry in Cambrian minutes was one for an accident on 24th June 1867. A goods guard had allowed four wagons loaded with coal to be left standing on the main line, and a passenger train from Penmaenpool stopped south of the points, set back to the platform and hit the wagons sharply. The traffic manager dismissed the guard immediately and recommended that the pointsman be downgraded to porter and that the driver and fireman of the passenger train should also be dismissed. The account provides interesting light on how the station was being worked before the line to Barmouth was opened.

On 1st June 1868 the engineer advised that a proper station approach road should be built from the turnpike (now A493), and on 21st October he suggested that a

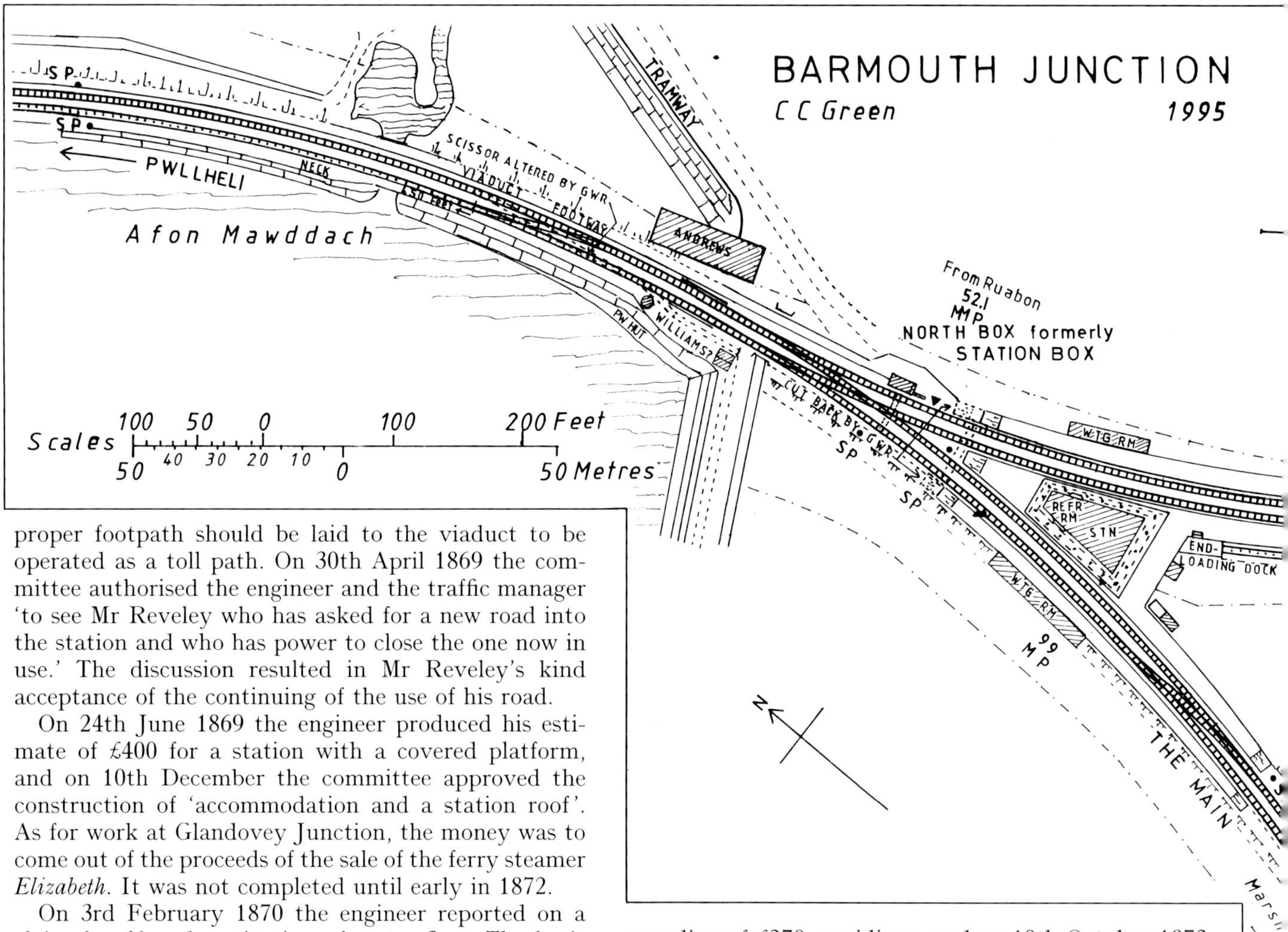

proper footpath should be laid to the viaduct to be operated as a toll path. On 30th April 1869 the committee authorised the engineer and the traffic manager 'to see Mr Reveley who has asked for a new road into the station and who has power to close the one now in use.' The discussion resulted in Mr Reveley's kind acceptance of the continuing of the use of his road.

On 24th June 1869 the engineer produced his estimate of £400 for a station with a covered platform, and on 10th December the committee approved the construction of 'accommodation and a station roof'. As for work at Glandovey Junction, the money was to come out of the proceeds of the sale of the ferry steamer *Elizabeth*. It was not completed until early in 1872.

On 3rd February 1870 the engineer reported on a claim for £6 and restitution of water flow. The basis was 'Land at Fegla Fawr flooded, scalded (by salt water) and useless because of construction of the platform. ... I visited the area and had soil fallen into a ditch cleared. Evans bears a very bad name in the neighbourhood and this is a gross attempt at imposition.'

On 13th April 1870 the Board were informed that the Great Western and branch trains were being worked through to Barmouth instead of only as far as Barmouth Junction. The traffic manager on 12th May 1870 reported that 'the present refreshment room proprietor was to pay a rent of £30 per annum', which the committee approved. On 14th October 1870 the Board approved a cost of £84 13s 5d for a waiting shed on the down Main.

On 22nd June 1871 the engineer asked for £537 for the construction of houses for the porters and signalmen. He had to put in a reminder report a little later, this time costing the work at £600, and received the approval he needed on 22nd September 1871. The houses were completed by 21st November 1872. On 26th June 1872 the engineer obtained approval for the spending of £270 on sidings, and on 18th October 1872 he was authorised to widen the platforms. At that same meeting the committee examined Mr Reveley's offer to continue and grant the use of his road from Arthog over his land if the company would make a road from the station to his building site. They decided not to approve this extension of the road but would consider making up and keeping the existing road in repair as a public access to the station.

On 20th December 1872 the engineer and the locomotive superintendent were instructed to report on the cost to the company of making their own gas at the station. The engineer reported on 23rd January 1873 that for a 'Gas works for 50 lights' there would have to be a 'Cast Iron Retort 6'6" × 12" × 12", other small equipment and a 12' diameter gasholder 10' deep', which would cost £184. A gashouse on piles would cost a further £200. The running cost would be £2 per lamp per annum. When piling began, the ground proved too unstable and the scheme was deferred.

Improvements completed in 1873 included a goods shed, the waiting shed and a down platform on the Main line and the addition of a loop siding parallel to

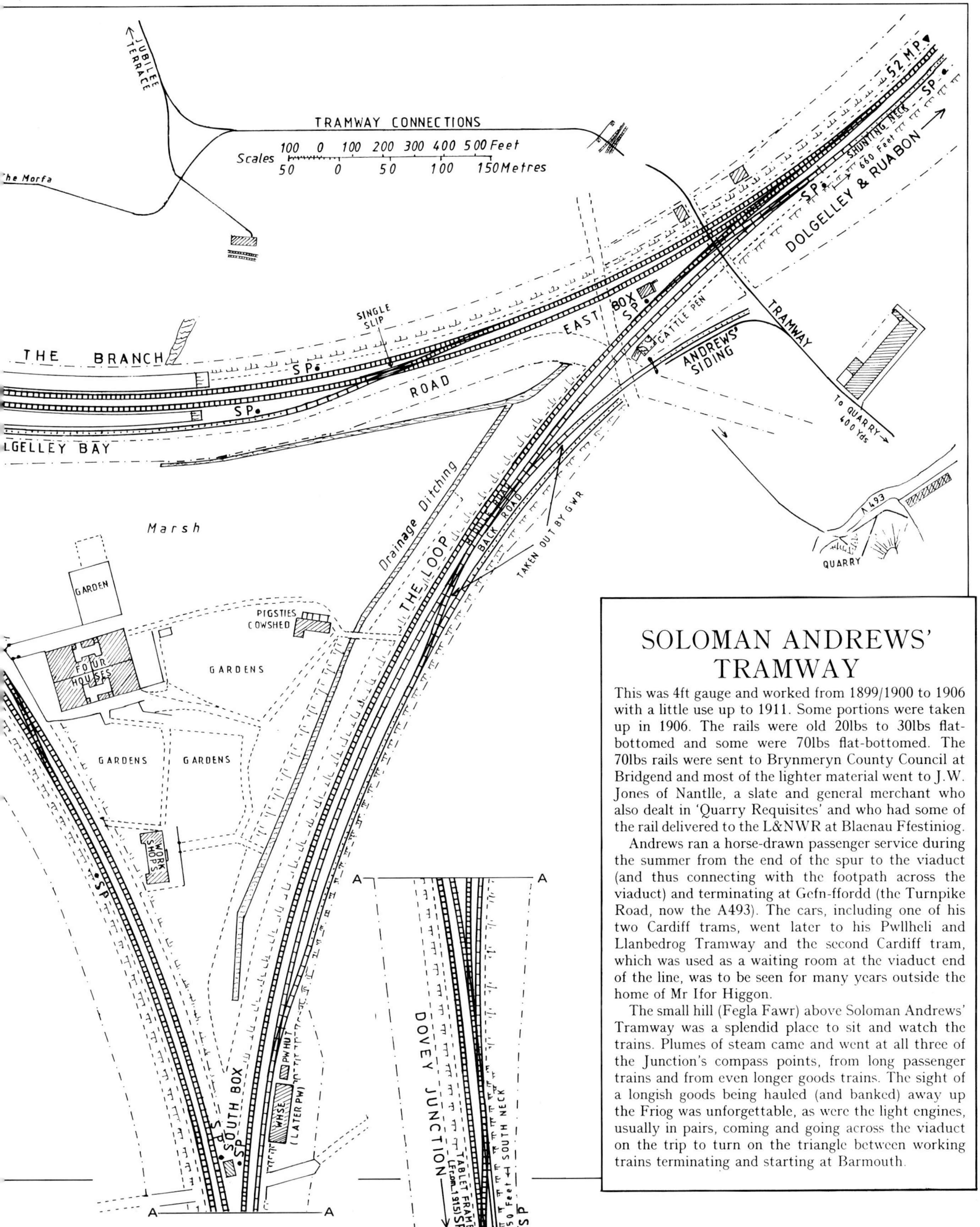

SOLOMAN ANDREWS' TRAMWAY

This was 4ft gauge and worked from 1899/1900 to 1906 with a little use up to 1911. Some portions were taken up in 1906. The rails were old 20lbs to 30lbs flat-bottomed and some were 70lbs flat-bottomed. The 70lbs rails were sent to Brynmeryn County Council at Bridgend and most of the lighter material went to J.W. Jones of Nantlle, a slate and general merchant who also dealt in 'Quarry Requisites' and who had some of the rail delivered to the L&NWR at Blaenau Ffestiniog.

Andrews ran a horse-drawn passenger service during the summer from the end of the spur to the viaduct (and thus connecting with the footpath across the viaduct) and terminating at Gefn-ffordd (the Turnpike Road, now the A493). The cars, including one of his two Cardiff trams, went later to his Pwllheli and Llanbedrog Tramway and the second Cardiff tram, which was used as a waiting room at the viaduct end of the line, was to be seen for many years outside the home of Mr Ifor Higgon.

The small hill (Fegla Fawr) above Soloman Andrews' Tramway was a splendid place to sit and watch the trains. Plumes of steam came and went at all three of the Junction's compass points, from long passenger trains and from even longer goods trains. The sight of a longish goods being hauled (and banked) away up the Friog was unforgettable, as were the light engines, usually in pairs, coming and going across the viaduct on the trip to turn on the triangle between working trains terminating and starting at Barmouth.

the Loop. As soon as this last item had been put in, the engineer reported that 'Since the additional siding has been put in the whole of the shunting etc. has been done on it. The Signals are only 387 yards away on the Friog side and 284 yards away on the Branch on the Dolgelley side. It is dangerous in foggy weather.' He asked for the authority to provide two extra signals entirely independent of the junction box to be set at danger by the shunter when working the siding. The cost approved was £75 17s 9d.

In March 1873 John Thomas Jones of Parciau, Criccieth, complained of 'trespass by passengers forming a footpath to the Turnpike road' across his father's Bwlch Gwyn farmland. 'I only wish to protect my Father's rights and at the same time deal fairly with the company.'

Early in 1873 the lease of the refreshment rooms was put out to tender but had to be regranted to the existing tenant, Mr William Jones, because the successful tenderer at £210 per annum had failed to find

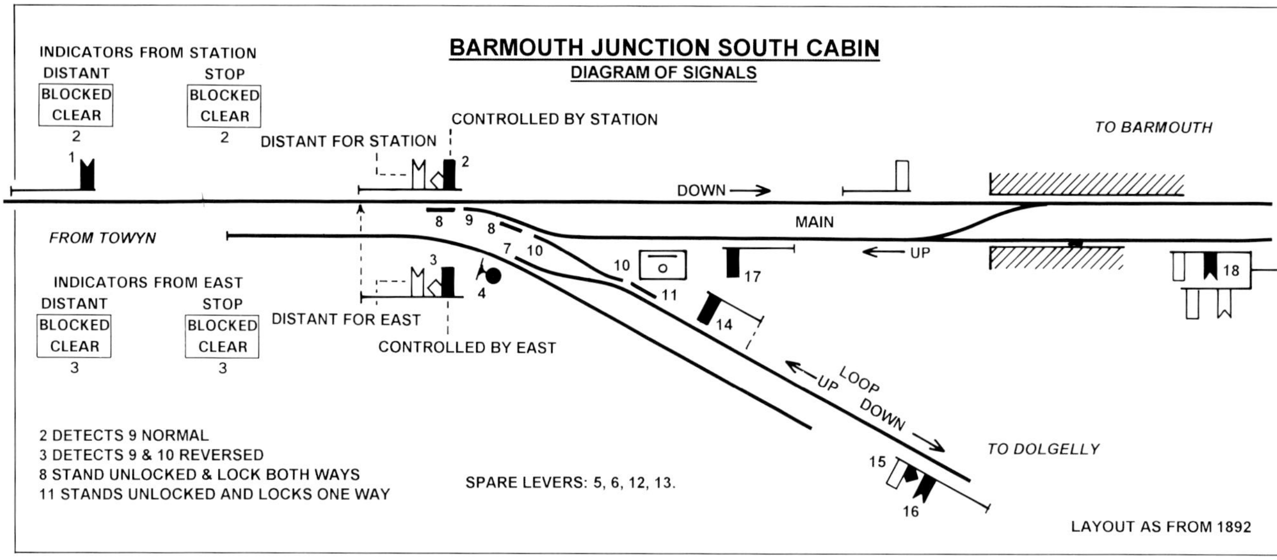

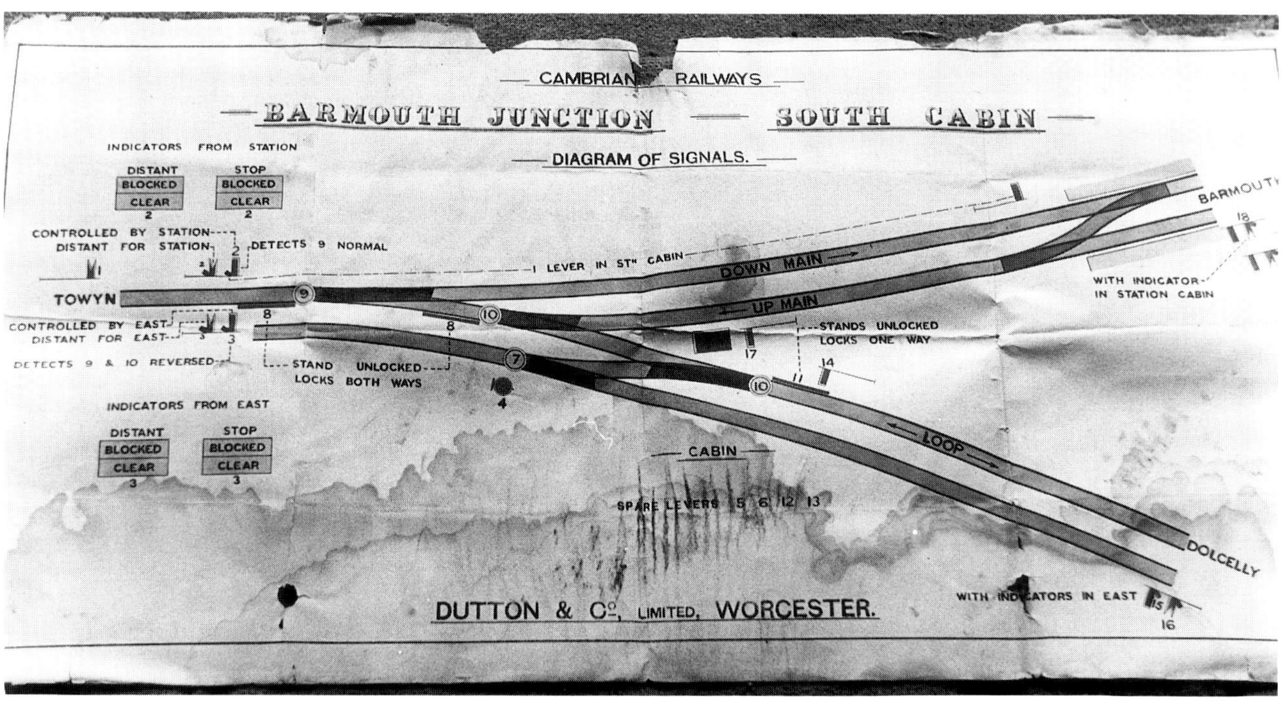

A rare survivor, from a signal box abolished as long ago as 1915. It lay in the locking room of the disused box for a number of years, hence the water staining.

sureties. Mr Jones would thereafter have to pay £135 per annum instead of the £30 per annum he had been paying since 1870.

On 19th February 1874 the engineer reported that the cottages were unhealthy. 'Dolgelley Union's Inspector of Nuisances had served a notice re the lack of drainage. There was much illness among the servants of the Company. Two new culverts costing £43 11s 0d were needed as well as £40's worth of fill. This last would make good garden land which would, in time, repay for the outlay on the work.' This work and the building of new cottages was approved immediately and was completed by 18th June 1874. The engineer added that, as material became available, holes in the land would be filled in 'as there is much enquiry for garden land'.

A complaint was lodged by passengers that on 10th August 1875 Driver Fenn had set his engine and extra carriages hard against the standing train. No-one was seriously hurt and no disciplinary action was taken. On 24th November 1875 the traffic manager reported that another siding was urgently needed but the committee ordered that it was to be postponed. On 24th April 1878 he stated that 'A Siding and Cattle Landing is asked for but the approach road is not public.' The committee resolved that 'The Company will provide Cattle Pens if Mr Williams can obtain Mr Reveley's consent to making the road public.' The cost would be £351.

On 21st August 1883 the traffic manager reported on an accident which had happened only the day before. While descending from the 5.9pm from Dolgelley (a

The South box (long since out of use) on 2nd September 1930.
Ifor Higgon

0–6–0 Aston Goods No. 87 (as GWR 884) standing on the goods lines at the back of the old abandoned South box, prior to taking the 4.15 p.m. goods to Portmadoc. 25th April 1928. *Ifor Higgon*

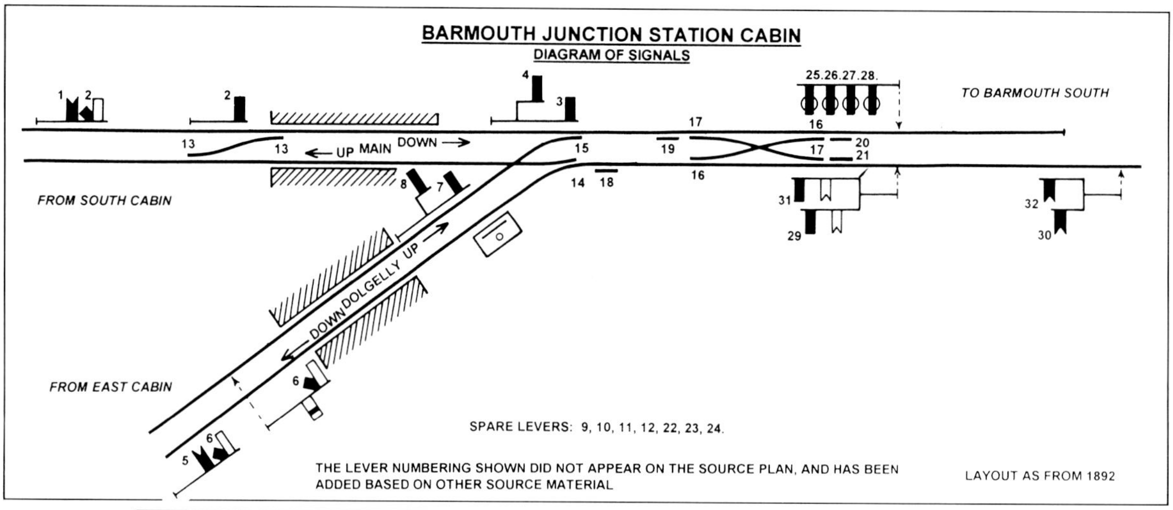

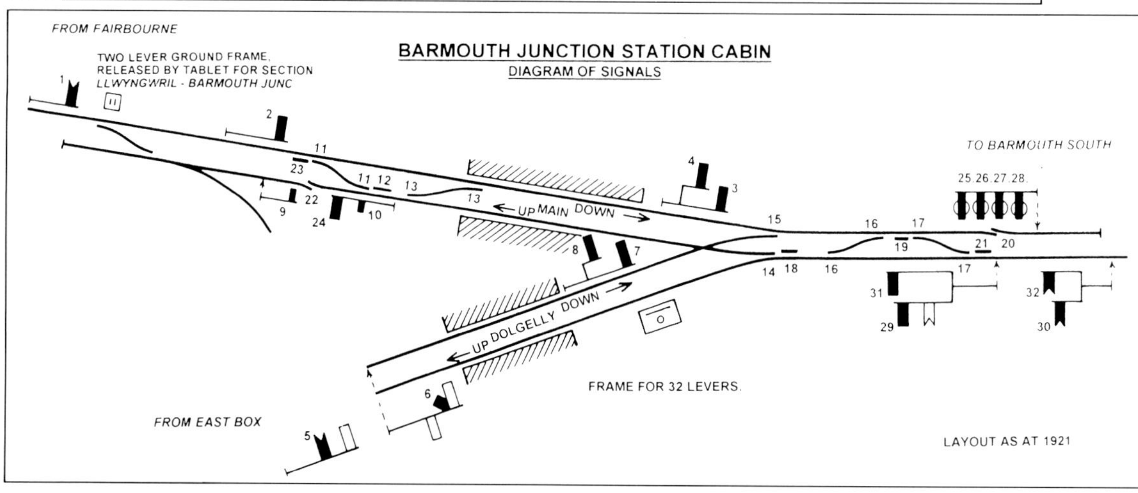

North box interior c.1918. The man at the frame, with the 'Prince of Wales Feather' cap badge proudly showing, is believed to have been signalman Hainge. The lever frame was of the Dutton pattern common across the Cambrian Railways system. The levers stood straight upright when normal, on gradients which sloped upwards to the signalman, so that the lever top followed an unusual arc as the lever was pulled. The Tyers No. 6 tablet instrument for the section across the bridge to Barmouth South box can be seen at the far end of the box. *H. W. Burman*

This photo, of remarkable clarity, shows the south signal box and its protecting home signals, dating the scene to June 1915. It captures the essence of this place – the original platform in the 'V' of the junction with a 'proper' building, the platforms added on the loop lines with barely-adequate wooden shelters, and a deep feeling of isolation. *Cty. Selwyn Higgins*

long train which overlapped the platform by two carriages), a Miss Sconce had caught her dress on a step and 'fell on her face and sustained a somewhat severe shaking. Her solicitor is claiming on her behalf.' When called upon again to comment on the company solicitor's report on her claim for £250, Henry Cattle made a statement which seems harsh today – 'I am informed that Miss Sconce is a lady of nervous temperament but that beyond the disfigurement resulting from the loss of teeth and the severe shaking caused by her fall she did not sustain any serious injury.'

On 18th August 1884 when trespassing was under review, the engineer reported 'Passengers are also booked at Glandovey and Barmouth Junctions to which stations there are no roads and passengers have to trespass along the Line to reach these places'.

On 25th March 1885 the engineer reported that lengthening the siding would be a great improvement as it would form 'a bay for the Dolgelley trains to start from ... At present there are two trains at the east end of the platform at the same time, one for Barmouth and one for Dolgelley and they have to stand end to end of one another'. The cost was £78 6s 2d including lengthening the Branch platform which was considered to be urgent as an accident had cost the company £200 (Miss Sconce). The committee also approved the lengthening of the main platform (stated as less urgent) for £114 10s 0d.

An accident on 17th September 1886 reflects the practice of that time as to the use of banking engines. The driver of the engine *Queen*, the class locomotive of the 0–6–0 Sharp Stewarts, which had followed the 10.20am out of Barmouth Junction to help it over the

The Dutton-built North signal box, c.1918. In this windswept spot, the storm porch was a necessity. *H. W. Burman*

Large Sharp Stewart 4–4–0 No. 68 entering the station with an up train for Dovey Junction and beyond, c.1920. The down main starting signals for the North box (levers 3 & 4) are featured below.
H. W. Burman

Left: North box down main starting signals 3/4, c.1920. The Cambrian used long, slender arms for stop signals, with a spot instead of the white bar used by many other companies. The ring-arm signal (No. 4) read into the shunting neck, and was operated through a pivoted lever mechanism common on Cambrian lines. *Middle:* The same signal, as modified by the GWR with the removal of the ring on No. 4 and white vertical stripes. The arm applied to a main line even if leading to a shunting neck, so did not require a ring, which on the GWR was proper only to a signal applying to a goods line, and the post in front carried stay bracing for the branch signals 7/8. *Right:* The rear of the down main line starting signals, showing the distinctive lamp cases with conical tips. No backlight blinders were provided because the signalmen could see the front of these signals. *H. W. Burman, L&GRP, and Ifor Higgon*

Nasmyth Wilson 0–4–4 tank No. 3 with a seven-coach up train for Ruabon, passing the North box c.1918.
H. W. Burman

Left: North box signalman waiting to take a Barmouth to Barmouth Junction single-line tablet from the fireman of an up goods c.1918. *Right:* North box and down branch starting signals (7/8) c.1918. Both pictures show the passenger directing notices affixed to the base of the post. There was no footbridge at the station, so passengers had to use the sleeper-built crossing to get to the down main and up branch platforms.
H. W. Burman

Barmouth Junction, viewed from the north end c.1933 and showing the GWR-built signal box. The up home signal bracket on the left read to the Dolgelley branch and main lines respectively. The 4-arm signal on the right controlled movements from the shunting neck alongside the main line.

G. H. W. Clifford

Left: Rear view of main and branch up home signals c.1921, with the lampman going about his duties and the line rising to the bridge in the background. The lower arm was the up branch distant signal for the East box. *Right:* The signals controlling set-back movements from the shunting neck to (from top down) up branch, down branch (wrong direction), up main, down main (wrong direction). The Cambrian used purple lenses for wrong-direction moves, so with all arms 'on', this signal showed red over purple over red over purple!

H. W. Burman and G. H. W. Clifford

4—4—0 Large Sharp Stewart No. 62, as GW No. 1090, leaving Barmouth Junction on the Pwllheli portion of the 10.20 a.m. ex Paddington on 14th August 1926. *M. Christensen*

Friog, 'appears to have miscalculated the speed at which the Engine was running and came so sharply in contact with the train that Mr Tatnai Roberts who was a passenger received a cut over the left eye and he has claimed through his solicitor as well as for his wife ... I deemed it prudent to at once send the Company's Medical Officer to Manchester to examine both claimants with authority to settle if this could be done on suitable terms.' This he succeeded in doing for the sum of £10 and £1 11s 0d costs.

On 27th January 1888 the engineer put in a report on how five men's wages, £240 per annum, could be saved by shutting down his smiths' and carpenters' shops at Barmouth Junction and having his work done in the locomotive superintendent's shops at Aberdovey and Oswestry.

On 26th November 1891 the engineer reported that 'Dolgelley Union Rural Sanitary Authority has called attention to the water supply to the Company's Cottages being deficient in both quality and quantity. The only solution would be to build a reservoir on the hillside above Tyddyn Sheffrey (sic) farm house getting permission from Mr Reveley and from Mr Price of Glenwood, Birmingham, for permission to lay pipes over their land as well'. This was probably done but the approval, as was often the case, lies buried in the general acceptance of the engineer's report.

An accident on 16th January 1892 was reported by the general manager on the 26th. 'The engine of the 3.30pm Goods ex Dolgelley came off the rails at the points because of a stone in the box ... Porter Hainge appears to have passed the points without noticing that they were not properly closed. I have had him before me for his neglect of duty and have reluctantly been compelled to impose a small fine on him'. On

The up distants for branch (left) and main line (right) at the south end of the viaduct c.1923. Note the arrangement of two pivoted levers, one to operate each arm. *H. W. Burman*

A general view, looking north, showing all the station buildings including the railwaymen's houses and their well-cultivated gardens. Every length of siding was crammed with wagons. Those in the foreground were standing on the loop line and adjacent siding. The roadway to the station can be seen running in from the right, with wagons standing on the adjacent bay platform line, such was the congestion of traffic. *Cty. E. W. Hannan*

'Stella' class 2–4–0 No. 3508 on the 2.35 p.m. Barmouth to Chester, standing in the up branch platform on 13th March 1928. The rails in the foreground were those of the bay line. *Ifor Higgon*

A staff group at the end of the up main platform in front of the notice directing branch passengers of the need to change trains here, not at Barmouth. c.1918. *H. W. Burman*

another occasion Engineman F. Williams was found drunk and incapable while in charge of the 7.10pm passenger train ex Dolgelley. There was a two-hour delay while another man came from Dolgelley. Williams was summarily dismissed.

In January 1893 the general manager brought up once more the question of accommodation for the staff. Of the three cottages already existing, one was occupied by the Arthog station master who was having to walk there and back in all weathers. More were needed for the additional signalman needed to operate the signal box required to comply with the interlocking of points and signals resulting from the 1889 Regulation of Railways Act. Two cottages were urgently needed, as well as one at Arthog. The ordering has not been found other than in the acceptance of the general manager's report, but the 25in O.S. map of 1901 shows four cottages.

On 13th June 1893 the Board ordered that an application should be made to transfer the licence of the refreshment rooms to Barmouth but this was refused by the justices. On 2nd November 1895 the committee approved that the proposed Bill of 1895 should provide for the acquisition of land for a road and for track

0–6–0 Aston Goods No. 78 (as GWR 881) on a Barmouth-bound goods train standing in the 'wrong line' branch platform. 1924.
Ifor Higgon

A photograph of the south end of the station building in the triangle – the face seen by any passenger approaching by road (few did!). This view was taken looking across the buffers of a loco standing in the up main platform, to the running-in board on the Dolgelley branch line.
Ifor Higgon

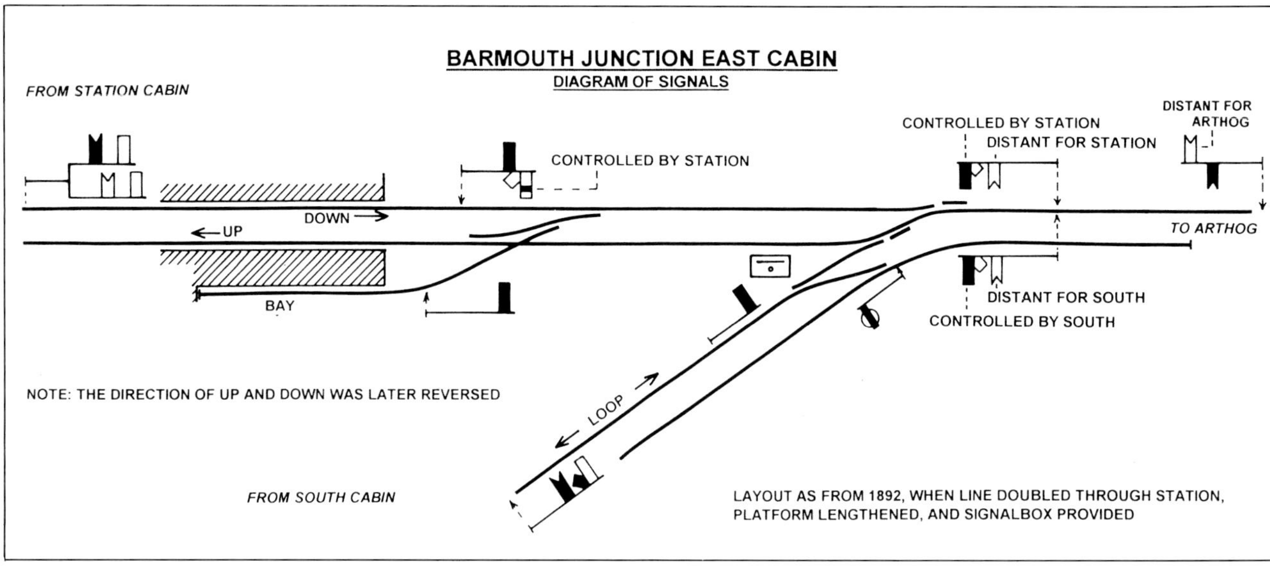

The East box, c.1918. The box was placed closely in the 'V' of the junction, so that from the unusual double-sided balcony the signalman could exchange tablets. But he still had to walk across to give the tablet to a Dolgelley-bound train, as the signalman was doing here. The stop signal applying to trains off the loop line can be seen on the left. *H. W. Burman*

extensions. On the night of 7th October 1896 furious gales and high tides drove water across the site and the cottages had four feet of water over their land and floors. The engineer reported that it would be some time before they could be rendered fit for habitation.

In 1897 the Cardiff entrepreneur Soloman Andrews was turning his attention to the area around Barmouth Junction, and on 23rd March the committee was told of his intention to erect an embankment beside the Barmouth Estuary. Engineer George Owen thought that the Cambrian should oppose the plan as he had doubts about its effect on the bridge but the general manager added 'Mr Soloman Andrews' enterprise is well-known to you and whatever work he undertakes he carries out on a large scale regardless of expense'. He had already acquired a group of quarries on the hillside and a lot of the intervening flat land to the south of the station and had laid a 4ft gauge tramway to connect the quarries to the site of his work a mile or so to the north on the estuary shore; to do this he had acquired the right to a level crossing over four tracks at the end of the Branch and the Loop.

On 20th September 1898 the engineer asked for Notice to Treat to be served in respect of land acquisition to extend the south shunting neck as the power would expire in July 1899. On 17th October 1898 it was decided that land acquisition for the proposed road should stand over. Then Soloman Andrews offered to make a good road access across what was now his land if the company would erect an overbridge at least thirty feet wide to take vehicular and foot traffic (and presumably his tramway). He would surrender his right to the four-track crossing. He stipulated that he should have control of the bridge with the right to levy tolls and to have the 'Tolls over the Viaduct'. This the

2–6–0 No. 5362 on an up Pwllheli–Chester mail, passing the East box c.1930. By this date, GWR pattern tablet set-down and pick-up apparatus had been provided adjacent to the box.
Bernard Edmonds

2–6–0 'Aberdare' on a goods from Dolgelley approaching the site of the former East box, in the 1930s, with the loop lines in the foreground. *J. P. Richards*

Steam railmotor No. 11, trailing a Cambrian six-wheeled coach on a Dolgelley–Barmouth local, swinging on to the double-line section at the East box. The signal on the extreme right read from Dolgelley line to loop. The ringed arm signal read from siding to loop. c.1928.
Bernard Edmonds

0–6–0 Jones Goods No. 38 (as GWR 864) firing up for the haul up the Friog incline with the 10.5 a.m. up goods to Machynlleth. The roof of the station building can just be seen behind the brake van. 5th May 1938. *Ifor Higgon*

0–6–0 Dean Goods No. 2449 and a rebuilt 0–6–0 Jones Goods pulling away hard from Barmouth Junction for the Friog climb. *Ifor Higgon*

Board could not accept and the committee did not recommend it to them. The committee did, however, approve the issue of free viaduct passes to residents and visitors to 'The Barmouth Junction Estate' on 23rd November 1898.

On 24th February 1899 the general manager reported on Spiers and Pond's annual returns which showed that the income from Barmouth Junction was down since the wines and spirits licence had been reduced to six days only. He also mentioned that an additional siding was needed because of pressure caused by slates, etc, from Fairbourne. The cost would be £150.

The following day, the committee approved a cost of £150 for a goods siding (the South neck?) plus £50 for signalling. On 17th May 1899 they approved Soloman Andrews' latest proposition. He would give the land for the road free if the siding could be extended onto his land and he could extend his embankment to join the company's embankment at the south end of the viaduct. The deal as to siding accommodation was modified to the construction of two truck lengths on company land. Andrews would complete his own line on his property. In addition free passes over the viaduct and free train passes from Arthog to Barmouth were granted to Soloman Andrews, his family and his workmen. His siding was probably formed by extending the spur already laid at the east end of the shunting siding.

0–6–0 Aston Goods No. 87 (as 884) with the 9.48 local to Machynlleth, with, in the background, a Jones Goods pulling its train up the neck to shunt in the Loop. The 2-lever tablet-released ground frame working the points (formerly operated by South box lever 9) can be seen on the left (see centre diagram, page 230). 21st May 1938. *Ifor Higgon*

A view from the south-west end of the station, showing the Loop line, and adjacent siding (on which the wagons were standing) which served the warehouse (later PW Dept. store). The South box formerly stood where the lamp standard can be seen, whilst the railway cottages feature on the left. 27th September 1937. *Ifor Higgon*

Looking up past Station (North) box, after a GWR signal had replaced the Cambrian counterpart (levers 3/4) on the main line, but Cambrian signals remained on the branch. The earlier of the two shelters can be seen on the down main platform on the right (see pages 224/225), as can a camping coach, which was occupying the portion of the bay platform nearest the buffer stops. *A. W. Croughton*

Steam railmotor No. 30 passing North box, routed on the main line instead of being on the more usual Barmouth to Dolgelley local service. c.1928. *Bernard Edmonds*

In 1899 a man named Wright fell off the pathway between two ditches and brought a claim for £100 which the general manager bargained down to £20.

On 17th January 1900 the committee approved the granting of a wayleave to Soloman Andrews for his 4in water main (3in actually laid) under the new road provided that he allowed connections to the station and the cottages. In 1900 the closure of the refreshment rooms at 8.30pm instead of at 10.00pm was initiated. On 25th February 1901 the engineer reported that he was using the material obtained from slewing the line inwards at Old Church Bank (Llangelynin) to make the road, and on 16th April 1902 the committee approved Soloman Andrews' proposal to make a road from his property to the station. All did not go well, however, and in December 1902 the general manager reported that Mr Andrews had closed down his works at Barmouth Junction and was moving all his materials etc. to Pwllheli.

In March 1903 it was decided not to apply for a renewal of Spiers & Ponds' licence as it was not necessary to the travelling public but after an appeal had been made, it was subsequently renewed.

On 3rd April 1909 Fitter G. Morgan of Machynlleth had an accident. Returning from a football match at Portmadoc, he got out of the train and was left behind at Barmouth.

'He walked over the bridge to the Junction to join the return Excursion which was following and it passed him between the Bridge and the Junction Station when he attempted to board it

The essence of the GWR's upgrading of the Cambrian. No. 3204, one of the 'Earl' class 4–4–0s, heading a train of mixed GWR coaches into the up main platform, passing the GWR-built signal box on the right. The train was the 2.50 p.m. Barmouth–Birmingham, on Sunday, 21st July 1938. The down main starting signal – a GWR structure – was fitted with standard GWR arms including a short (4ft) arm for the route leading to the shunt neck. *Ifor Higgon*

but unfortunately he missed his footing and was dragged along the Permanent Way for about fifty yards when his foot came into contact with the signal wires crossing the line and he fell down and injured his foot (bad compound fracture of right leg ankle joint) and lay there for about three quarters of an hour until discovered by the Arthog Station Master. Morgan was travelling with a privilege ticket and at the time of the accident he was trespassing.'

The Cambrian staff fielded a keen first-aid team and they won the Cambrian Shield in 1914 with 232 marks.

On 7th July 1915 the committee approved the removal of the 'Towyn-end Box' (South Signal Box) at a cost of £220, with an operating saving of £60 per annum. Control of shunting was to be effected by a tablet-locked ground frame. A note from the general manager in 1915 showed that the refreshment rooms were still open. On 6th November 1918 the general manager reported on a proposal that the junction station should be closed as an economy measure.

'The Proposal for closure is not thought desirable because:–

1. Much additional siding accommodation would be needed at Barmouth.
2. Time Table revisions, including those of other companies' trains, would be far reaching and probably impossible to arrange.
3. In view of local interests which have sprung up because of the provision of Passenger and Goods Accommodation there would be much local opposition to closure.'

The committee recorded a decision 'Not to be closed at present.'

Through running via the Loop was much reduced during the 1914 18 war except for troop trains, and ceased around 1920. Thereafter it was used for some marshalling of goods trains and for turning the locomotives.

On 25th March 1920 the engineer reported that 'Relayer Evans knocked down by an engine on 27th January 1915 is still receiving 9/3d plus 75% per week compensation'.

In 1921 it was recorded that each of the two remaining signal boxes housed the tablet instruments and had a full-time signalman.

On 15th March 1923 the Great Western traffic committee approved £465 for the overhaul of the signalling system, to incorporate channel point rodding and other standard Great Western features (including Block Telegraph between the two signal boxes). On 5th July 1923 they approved cattle pens for £318. In January 1926 they took over the running of the refreshment rooms and later sub-let them to F.W. Hughes & Son.

The refreshment rooms, like those at Moat Lane, were the village inn of the district. The conversations were mainly in Welsh, but when there was a long wait for a delayed train, singing could start to pass the time, and the English travellers could be in for a real treat as enthusiasm grew. Old songs and hymns could be heard as the visitors had never heard them before.

In October 1923 4–4–0 Duke No. 3271 *Eddystone* brought a military special to Portmadoc and had to run all the way back tender-first to turn round on the triangle at Barmouth Junction.

On 28th October 1927 severe flooding damaged the household effects of six railwaymen living in the station houses, namely:

At Barmouth Junction	Stationmaster A. Evans	£15 10s 0d
	Signalman A. Hainge	£35 0s 0d
	Signalman E. Venables	£2 0s 0d
	Shopman P. Evans	£15 10s 0d
At Arthog	Stationmaster H. Jones	£30 0s 0d
At Ynyslas	Porter R.E. Jones	£5 0s 0d

Following this on 13th December 1928 the traffic committee authorised the purchase of No 7 Glasfryn Terrace for the stationmaster of Barmouth Junction.

On 6th June 1929 the civil engineer reported an estimated cost of £330 for reconstructing the down Coast (Main) platform with a sleeper wall and followed on 9th October 1930 with costings of £440 for rebuilding part of the up platform. This work would have allowed the making of better clearances for outside-cylindered locomotives. Also on 9th October the traffic committee

A view towards the bridge from the window of the (old) North box, with a 2–6–0 Mogul approaching Barmouth Junction along the causeway, with four coaches and three horse boxes in May 1944. The footpath across the bridge features on the right. The GWR had renewed the up home signal bracket, but not yet the four-arm signal applying to the shunt neck.

L. E. Copeland

The Great Western North box, which replaced the old higher and gale-damaged Cambrian North box, is shown here on 27th September 1961. The box had internal steps, hence the very different appearance to that of its predecessor.

Author

A general view, looking in the up direction, in 1949. This view shows clearly the need for passengers to cross the running lines to reach the platform, as indeed did walkers from the bridge pathway. It would be hectic when two or three trains met here, but everyone was careful and there was no real risk. Note the GWR pattern signal on the down branch line – very different from its predecessor. *L&GRP*

The latter-day (second) shelter on the down main platform. Note the timber facing used in the reconstruction of the platform, recorded on the page opposite. 15th June 1964. *Author*

Station and main up platform, looking down, on 15th June 1964. The refreshment room was small, but also served as a local pub, complete with dartboard and mat. *Author*

The interior of the GWR signal box, showing the 38-lever frame, either end of which were the single-line key token instruments. The nearer instrument controlled the release of an occupation key, used by the PW Department in the operation of their trolleys for 'Motor Economic Maintenance'. 1965. *M. Christensen*

The north end of the GWR-built signal box. The stain below the window betrays the fact that for years the signalmen had been emptying out the teapot here. Note from the photo above that the stove was at this end of the box. 1965. *M. Christensen*

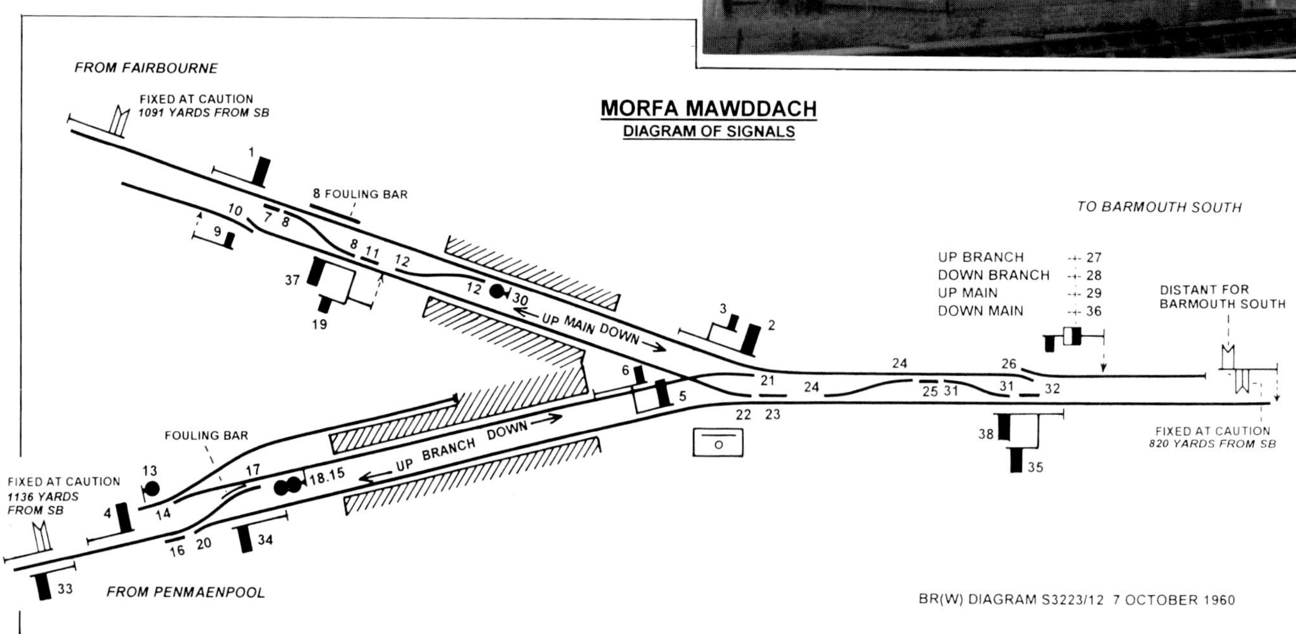

authorised the alterations needed for the closure of East Box. The cost was £600 for the engineering work, £1,085 for revision of the signalling. The job overran to the tune of £200.

A Camping Coach was placed at the end of the bay in March 1934.

On 8th October 1936 £150 was authorised for the renewal of the down Main waiting shed. Another severe flooding of the houses in 1938 caused them to be abandoned and demolished.

On 1st and 2nd September 1939 several trainloads of evacuee children from cities in Lancashire, the Midlands and the Home Counties came through from Ruabon.

On 26th March 1943 the Board accepted that F.W. Hughes & Son had given notice to terminate all their tenancies of the former Cambrian refreshment rooms but had re-tendered for the one at Barmouth Junction at 3% on the gross takings.

In October 1945 there was a loco to loco collision on the branch when the 1.10pm passenger from Dolgelley, drawn by 4–4–0 'Bulldog' No. 3450 *Peacock*, met an 0–6–0 Dean Goods on a sheep train. The passengers were somewhat shaken up, one sheep was killed and two more had to be destroyed.

Although closed for general goods services on 4th November 1963, one Chester–Barmouth freight continued to run with the GPO Mails until 12th December 1964 when there was washaway near Bont-newydd, which effectively closed the line beyond Dolgelley.

The remaining signal box, now named Morfa Mawddach, was closed on 15th June 1968. The track was lifted and the entire station buildings were completely erased. Trains now stop against the old Main platform where a bus shelter is slightly protected by a now well-established plantation. A footpath conducts passengers to the trains from the car park which is sited where the camp coaches once stood. Walkers for the Morfa Mawddach Walk can also leave their cars here and head off along the old Dolgelley Branch all the way to the Wnion Bridge, whence they can finish by walking along the river bank right into Dolgelley.

WORKING INSTRUCTIONS 1912

The arrival and departure of every up train had to be notified to Dovey Junction and to Machynlleth.

When the south end siding was being used, a tablet was issued to the guard or a member of the station staff to enable the ground frame which replaced South Box to be released.

The speed limit over the crossover road at the bridge end of the station was fifteen miles per hour. No trains could be flagged over against the signals.

On the 1st and 15th of each month the Junction staff were responsible for placing an empty wagon in the 1.20pm (No. 30) up goods for the collection of empty station oil cans going for refill.

Tickets on train No. 12 (12.18pm ex Barmouth) were to be examined at Barmouth Junction and those for Dolgelley were to be collected.

No shunting was allowed outside the Down Main Home Signal whilst a freight train was running in the section towards Llwyng-

The notice on the down main platform advising Dolgelley branch passengers of the need to change here. The sliding-front cabinet on the left with 'telephone stripe' contained the phone by which guards of driving trains could confirm to the signalman (who could not see the guard because of the curvature of the line) that the train was complete, so that he could 'sink' the token and clear the single line to Llwyngwril for the next train. 27th September 1961. *Author*

A view from the east, across the salt marsh, showing the station buildings, the shelter on the up branch platform, the GWR-built signal box, and camping coaches in the branch bay platform. 15th June 1964. *Author*

The station building and down branch platform, looking towards Barmouth on 27th September 1961. *Author*

The refreshment room bay window on the down branch platform, looking towards Barmouth, on 15th June 1964. *Author*

wril until that train had passed over the summit of the Friog incline, and, during fog or falling snow, not until 'Train out of Section' had been received for the train from Llwyngwril.

One 'Type five' loose screw coupling was held in the North Box.

All down stopping trains were to be examined and tickets for Barmouth collected.

After the closure of the Dolgelley line, the signal box at Morfa Mawddach, and a passing loop on the main line, were retained for a while. But not for very long. The signal box was closed on 29th September 1974 and only the running line through the up main platform retained (raised in height by about a foot, to bring it up to modern standards). The station buildings were demolished and replaced by a shelter, which stands roughly where the entrance roadway remains, widened across the site of the bay platform on the branch side to provide a car park area. The trackbed of the branch has been converted into a cycle and pathway nearly all the way to Dolgelley, and Morfa Mawddach is a popular starting place for riverside walks, providing some custom for trains in the summer. The area of the railway triangle has been planted with trees, and its boundaries can clearly be seen from the hillside above. Amongst the trees, the brick-built cattle dock survives where the entrance roadway crosses the site of the South Loop.

The station building and down branch platform, looking up, on 15th June 1964.
Author

The shelter on the up (Dolgelley-bound) platform. 15th June 1964.
Author

The approach to the branch platforms, looking towards the junction and Barmouth, and showing the three camp coaches stationed in the former bay platform. The poor view which the signalman had of this end of the layout is evident. To assist him, the crossover points (17) had a fouling bar (visible inside the switch blades) to stop him from moving the points under the rear of an arriving train. There was also a 'tail lamp telephone' in the cabinet at the Dolgelley end of the down (left-hand) platform. 15th June 1964. *Author*

The branch tracks, looking towards the junction, past the crossover and bay siding points. The camp coach featured in this view of the branch home signal (4), was a six-wheeled clerestory. 15th August 1935. *H. F. Wheeller*

Top: Four locos, which had come across the bridge to turn on the triangle formed by the Loop line. They were 2–6–0s 5319 and 7310 off the 11.5 Birmingham to Barmouth, and 4–4–0 No. 9028 and 4–6–0 No. 7807 *Compton Manor* off the 9.10 Paddington to Barmouth. Coupled together, they are shown at No. 13 disc signal awaiting a clear road. Engines turning always went from north to south to east. To go the other way round involved two extra shunt moves. 7th August 1954. *Ifor Higgon*

Centre: 0–6–0 Jones Goods No. 100 (as WR 894) with the 6.15 p.m. return goods to Portmadoc, shunting the siding off the Loop line. The starting signal in the background was 'off' for a train to Dolgelley. 16th May 1952. *Ifor Higgon*

Right: The cattle dock, which stood alongside the Loop siding. 15th June 1964. *Author*

Truly a station set amidst the salt marsh, with a Dolgelley train departing from Morfa Mawddach on 15th June 1964. In just six months the branch passenger service would be withdrawn. *Author*

BARMOUTH JUNCTION STATION BOX.	Up or Down Main Line	1 Long
	To or from Dolgelley	2 Long
	To or from Up Branch to Neck	2 Short
	To or from Down Branch to Neck	1 Short 1 Long
	To or from Down Main to Neck	2 Short 1 Crow
	From Neck to Up Main Line	3 Short
	Cross-over Road from either Up or Down Main Lines	1 Long 2 Short
BARMOUTH JUNCTION EAST BOX.	To or from Dolgelley from Branch Main Line	2 Long
	To or from Branch to Loop Line	1 Crow
	To or from Loop Line to Shunting Neck	1 Short 1 Crow
	From Neck to Shunting Siding	1 Short
	Down Branch to Bay Siding	1 Long
	Up Branch to Bay Siding	1 Long 1 Short
	Cross-over Road from either Up or Down Branch Main Line	2 Crows
	From Loop for Trains setting back into Station	2 Long 1 Short
BARMOUTH JUNCTION SOUTH BOX.	Down Main Line Trains running direct into Station	1 Long
	Up or Down Main Line Trains to Loop Line	2 Long 1 Crow
	From Loop Line to Neck	1 Short
	From Neck to Shunting Siding	2 Short
	From Loop to Main Line for Up Trains going away direct	3 Short
	From Loop to Main Line for setting back or going to Station	1 Short 1 Crow
Barmouth Junction	To or from Up Branch to Neck	2 pause 1
	To or from Down Branch to Neck	1 pause 2
	To or from Down Main to Neck	1 crow
	To and from Up Main Line to Neck	1 and 2 crows
	From Up Main Line to South Neck and vice versa	4 short
	From Down Main Line to South Neck and vice versa	1 long, 1 crow
	East Spur to Down Branch Main and vice versa	2 short
	Trains leaving Down Branch Main for Dolgelley direction	1 long
Barmouth North Box	From Down Main Line to Shunting Neck and vice versa	4 short
	From Shunting Neck to Back Road and vice versa	2 pause 1
	From Shunting Neck to Up Main Line and vice versa	1 pause 2
	From Shunting Neck to Warehouse and vice versa	1 crow
	From Shunting Neck to Coal Sidings	1 crow, 2 short
	Crossover Road from Up Line to Gas Works Siding	2 short, 1 crow
	From Coal Siding to Gas Siding	1 short, 1 crow
Barmouth South Box	Up Main Line to South Neck and vice versa	4

THE DOLGELLEY BRANCH

The Dolgelley Branch was an exercise in railway politics projected by the Aberystwith & Welsh Coast Railway to prevent the Great Western-backed Bala & Dolgelley Railway from physically reaching the Coast. This rival route (known later as 'The Barmouth Road') started from a junction a mile south of Ruabon on the old Shrewsbury & Chester Railway which had been opened on 12th July 1848 and had been bought by the Great Western Railway. In working terms the GWR line was 'Down' to Dolgelley and 'Up' to Ruabon, and mileages were measured from the junction at Ruabon.

Passengers, nearly all going on holiday to Barmouth and Coast resorts nearby, were treated to nearly forty-five miles of the best variety of scenery that Wales can offer. First the trains climbed the Dee Valley via the deep gorge of the Vale of Llangollen, where it squeezed between the Berwyns and the lesser hills to the north. Then came the more open upland past Corwen and Bala, leading to the level run past Lake Bala (Llyn Tegid, 'Tegid' meaning both beautiful and a person's name). A further four-mile climb took the trains to the summit at Garneddwen which is barely three miles from the source of the Dee (Afon Dyfrydwy). Then a nine-mile downhill run along the steep-sided little Wnion Valley brought the travellers to the wider and greener part of the valley, and brakes were grinding hard on for the stop at Dolgelley to change engines; for this was the edge of 'Cambrian' territory and the boundary was less than half a mile beyond the station.

When the Dolgelley Branch had been completed by the Aberystwith & Welsh Coast Railway as far as Penmaenpool (to earn the right to declare itself half completed and eligible for amalgamation with the Cambrian), it was operated as an extension of the Coast line and was designated 'down' direction for trains to Penmaenpool. As soon as the Cambrian traffic manager was faced with the problem of matching his public timetables with those of companies outside (and particularly the Great Western), it was redesignated 'up' to Dolgelley and 'down' to Barmouth, which was given a distance rating of $9\frac{1}{4}$ miles to 0 at Dolgelley. In both Coast up and down timetables the arrivals and departures for Barmouth Junction were separated by a two-directional Dolgelley–Barmouth timetable giving both Cambrian and Great Western distances for both ways. These distances varied a bit from one edition to another and none of them accord with the accepted modern ones.

In the working timetables the illogical 'down to Dolgelley' was kept on until the arrival of Denniss as general manager in 1895, when it was reversed to match the sense of the public timetables. The last known WTT to show Barmouth Junction to Dolgelley as the down, is that for 1888. A similar WTT for 1900 shows Dolgelley as up, and even the whistle codes had been reversed.

DOLGELLEY TO BARMOUTH JUNCTION

44m 42c to 52m 7c (GWR mileage from Ruabon)

The trains left Dolgelley by passing under the road bridge. To the south there was a prospect of the town over a green pasture on the other side of the river. Beyond lay some of the town's lesser housing, whose dwellers used to set out long lines of washing for all to see. When Francis Frith took a celebrated photograph across the station and the bridge, in which the washing showed up extremely clearly, there was a minor civic rumpus over this despoliation of the growing tourist centre's fair face.

To the north was the Great Western goods yard and warehouse and the travellers then crossed the boundary onto true Cambrian land. After a mile of winding along the north bank of the Afon Wnion, the line crossed the river (originally by a five-span timber pile bridge) to come out into the open across Gors Goch (Red Plain), a wide marshy area to the south of Afon Mawddach which joins the Afon Wnion here. There are wooded hills to the south and Foel Ispri to the north, seen across the abruptly widened Mawddach Estuary with Llanelltyd beneath. A mile of straight embankment led beneath the hills to the station of Penmaenpool.

Colonel Rich, inspecting the line from Llwyngwril for the Board of Trade, noted that the line was single throughout except for a siding at Penmaenpool. The line was arranged to connect with the GWR at Dolgelley and there was a turntable there. In the meantime, only tank locomotives were to be used until a turntable became available.

Leaving Penmaenpool station, the trains passed first the timber pile bridge across the river to the north, known in its earlier days as 'The Gold Miners' Bridge', from the miners who used it daily by buying circular brass tokens in the morning before crossing and returning them in the evening when going back home. On the other side and adjacent to the loop points was (and still is) the George Hotel. Trains then eased through the loop points back onto the single main line which

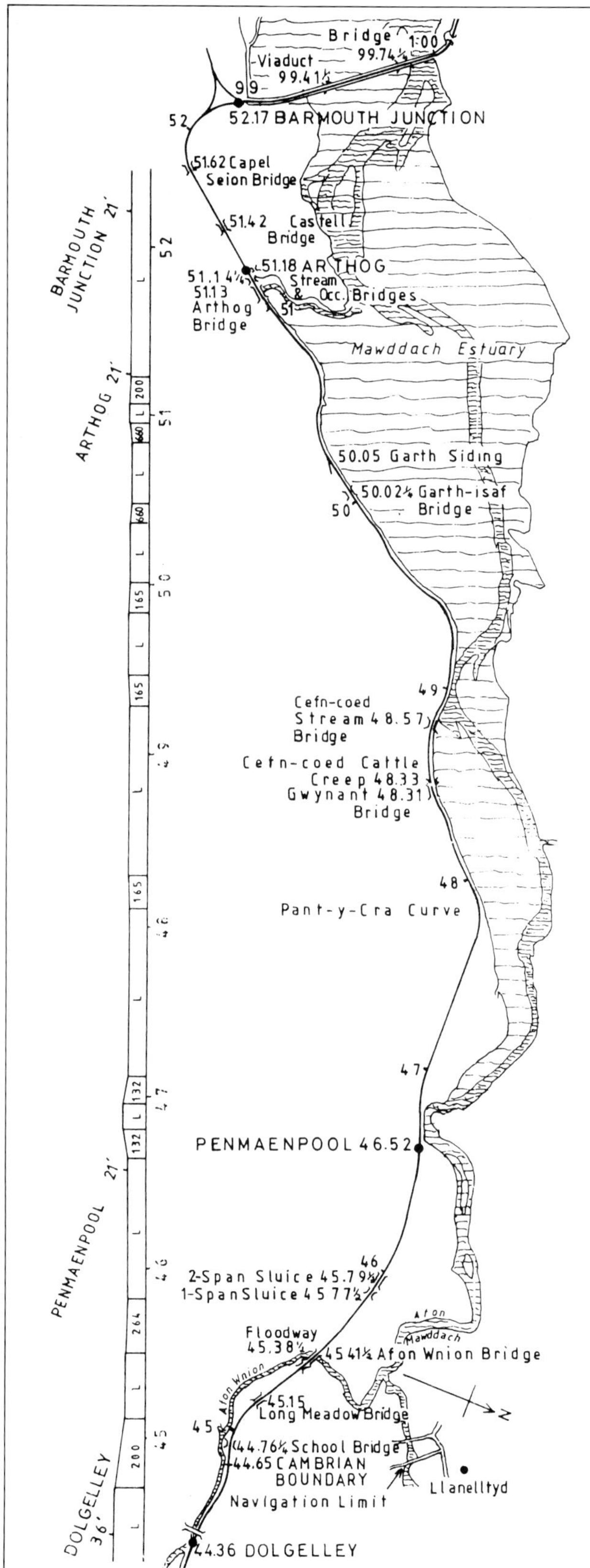

ran straight along the stone-faced embankment where the steamers called and boatmen went about their trade.

The line then curved northwards, past the engine shed and through a short cutting to run straight across another salt marsh for about three-quarters of a mile before beginning a long run along a 'sea wall' at the edge of the estuary. The rails swung through two reverse curves along the edge of the wooded hillside, with a glimpse up the Afon Gwynant. Soon afterwards, a view opened out to the south, where an old tramway embankment led down to a tiny jetty. Just beyond were the platelayers' cottages and Garth Siding. All the way was the splendid view of the mountains across the river, to the north, with plenty of time to enjoy as speeds were restricted and, in any case, the Cambrian's 0–4–4 Nasmyth Wilson tanks could hardly be expected to do much speeding with a train of fourteen Great Western clerestory coaches.

After two more reverse curves, the line left the embankment on the estuary's edge and turned due south-west for a straight run along the edge of the miniature estuary of the Afon Arthog, before crossing the river into Arthog Halt. A final straight run of less than a mile, across what was formerly very marshy ground, completed the journey to Barmouth Junction.

0–4–4 Nasmyth Wilson tank No. 3 approaching Arthog and crossing the bridge over the Afon Arthog on a train from Ruabon c.1918. *H. W. Burman*

DOLGELLEY

(now DOLGELLAU) 44m 36c

The station buildings belonging to the Cambrian on the down platform, looking east, showing the generally open nature of the platform and GWR nameboard, c.1923. *Cty. Selwyn Higgins*

Loop 44m 16c to 44m 42c.
Signal Box at 44m 31c.
Opened (Bala & Dolgelley) Passenger 4th August 1868.
Goods 1st October 1868.
Opened (Cambrian to Frondirion) 21st June 1869.
Opened to Cambrian trains 1st August 1869.
Closed Goods 4th May 1964.
Closed Passenger and Mail from Ruabon 12th December 1964.
Closed Passenger from Barmouth Junction 18th January 1965.

The name and spelling dates back to the reign of Queen Elizabeth I. It was probably a description of where to find a farmstead, 'The meadow (sheltered) by a grove of trees' which, in England, would have become shortened to 'Grovemeadow Farm'; a good name for the pleasant and busy little town which grew across the farmland later on. Victorian savants and writers of tourist guides, in search of the romantic touch, took it as 'The field of the Monks' cells' although the nearest monastic establishment had been Cymer Abbey. This version was used when all anglicised place names were put back into their original forms, and was retranslated into Dolgellau (instead of Dolgelli) on 12th September 1960.

The first intimation the townsfolk had that their railway really was coming shortly was when the historic bridge across Afon Wnion was extended northwards by two taller arches and the roadway was realigned to run uphill onto the Bala & Dolgelley Company's new bridge across the line. This was commemorated by a stonelaying ceremony on 3rd June 1868.

The B&D station was opened on 4th August 1868, but it cannot have been in the final location. It is recorded that the owners of The Hen and Chickens had delayed the completion of the sale of their site and livelihood as a livery stables; it could hardly be expected that they would do much to help the railway. So there was room enough to lay the rails in, but not to erect the wooden platform and van and coach bodies hut. These were further west in the goods yard. There were local complaints that it was too far out of town, and a temporary plank footbridge had been slung across the river.

On 18th August 1868, Elijah Elias reported that the 'Great Western Station was complete' and that they were 'disadvantaging the Cambrian by giving rates free of Cartage. The Cambrian must follow suit. The cost will be ninety hours per month at $\frac{3}{4}$d per hour.' The goods station was opened on 1st October 1868 but Cambrian goods trains were excluded because, it was claimed, of insufficient accommodation.

Almost a year later Elias and the engineer had arranged for the erection of a temporary timber platform 'at our junction with them [the B&D line] which was opened for passenger trains on Monday last' (21st June 1869). This was reported to the Board on 24th June 1869. The Cambrian line to the end-on junction at Frondirion had been passed by the Board of Trade inspector on 11th June 1869 after a letter of protest had been sent to the Great Western and the reply addressed 'to our Noble Chairman' had been read out to the Board. Despite this unfriendly situation created, as was its custom, by the Great Western, an 0–6–0 Manning Wardle saddle tank No 18 *Cardigan* had slipped a truckload of coal up the Bala & Dolgelley line for Eliza Stokes, the proprietress of the Ship Hotel, on 25th February 1869. Obviously, the unhelpfulness was confined to Boardroom level.

This pre-railway view shows the bridge in its original graceful form. The railway pushed the road uphill out of the way and destroyed the ford and the 'Hen and Chickens' which was a hostelry of considerable account.
Henry Gastineau

Meanwhile, negotiations were in hand to determine the division of capital and working costs at the joint station. The Cambrian committee approved on 23rd July 1869 that:

1. The engineers should agree an apportionment of capital costs.
2. The Cambrian should have the use of all lines, sidings and station in perpetuity (as from 1st August 1869 when the first Cambrian train ran into the joint station).
3. The Cambrian should pay a rent to the Bala & Dolgelley of one-third of 5% on the apportioned cost. (Later when the Cambrian had constructed its own station it, too, claimed a reduction in its payment at the same rate on its own £600 expended.)
4. The agreement was subject to revision in the future and by arbitration if necessary.

Under an earlier agreement on revenue, the Cambrian paid half the cost of working the station and appointed its own booking clerk and carting agent. Even the cloakroom takings were put together and halved in the reckoning. Considering that the relative train mileages were 44m 36c over Great Western metals and only 9m 20c to Barmouth over the Cambrian, this was a grossly unfair division but typical of the overbearing treatment afforded to the lesser company. In fact the Cambrian was very poorly represented on the station initially. The traffic manager reported 'having a Wooden Box on the Station and therefore having to rent a Room in the Town for the Enquiry Office'.

On 17th February 1870 the traffic manager was happy to report that the Great Western's attempt to wrest the carrying of the Dolgelley Mail from the Cambrian had failed. On 31st May a Wharncliffe meeting was held to approve the provisions of a proposed Great Western Additional Powers Bill in respect of the use of the station.

On 4th November 1870 the committee approved £300 as the cost of alterations to the station. This was actually the construction of the new permanent building on the south side. On 17th November 1870 the engineer reported on the necessity of providing a platelayers cottage for £100.

On 10th February 1871, 'a tin of naptha [petroleum spirit] exploded inside the Porters' Room seriously injuring a man'. On 19th May 1871 the committee assented to alterations around the station. 'if the Great Western and other companies carry the materials free.' On 21st September 1871 the Deputy Chairman approved the extra cost of a verandah (awning) to the Cambrian station and the committee added its formal approval subject to the approvals of both the Great Western and the Bala & Dolgelley companies. In addition, the approval of the 'Trustees of the Road' had to be obtained for the access steps. With all these additional works, the Cambrian's work at the station, for capital payments purposes, was valued as being £600. On 25th January 1872 the engineer reported that the new station had been completed.

On 17th May 1872 the Deputy Chairman was empowered to settle some matter related to the use of sidings. The Working Instructions required Cambrian trains to give movement warning of two whistles and to show a green light at night while Great Western engines sounded one whistle and showed a white light at night. On 25th February 1874 the committee heard that the Bala & Dolgelley Railway had 'given notice that they

Dolgelley town with the down end of the Cambrian platform in the foreground c.1885. The Cambrian nameboard was green on white. The two-arm 'station signal', almost certainly worked from levers at the foot of the post, showed prominently above the level of the bridge. *J. Thomas*

wish to exercise their running powers to Barmouth' and appointed the Deputy Chairman to negotiate terms. The Board considered the situation on 20th March 1874, and on 18th June 1874 the committee minuted that 'The Proposal re running powers cannot be accepted in its integrity'.

On 14th December 1874 the Board received the Railway Commissioners' ruling in favour of the Great Western's claim to run its own trains into Barmouth. This was followed (14th February 1875) by the Great Western's formal application to commence using its running powers into Barmouth. The Cambrian perforce had to resolve to give favourable consideration 'to any suggestion'.

Both the engineer and the traffic manager reported on 25th August 1876 on the application for permission to build a footbridge across the line to Dr Williams' Girls School. It would not be detrimental to the line and would be constructed to the engineer's satisfaction with a wayleave of £5 per annum to be paid. The committee approved, and the bridge was built straightaway, though it took the solicitors until 26th October 1878 to produce the agreement for the wayleave.

On 15th May 1877 the traffic manager reported that the Great Western were putting on an extra train and that it would run it into Barmouth with a GW engine if no Cambrian engine could be found. Of course the Cambrian 'found' an engine. Little evidence has so far been found of any Great Western engines going west of Dolgelley but if they did, they must have been turning at Barmouth Junction. Any GWR engine that was powerful enough to haul trains from Ruabon must have been too heavy to cross Barmouth viaduct. There is a note about a Cambrian train crew being 'afforded part relief' so that they could take on this extra duty. The shortage of Cambrian engines was leading to excessively long hours for its footplate men.

On 25th May 1880 the general manager reported that the issue of cheap season tickets to Barmouth was being 'much abused by the local inhabitants' and that he had restricted their use to one train each way daily. He recommended that the inevitable memorial of protest before the committee should be refused. It was.

The Great Western Railway Act 1880 included the power to purchase 'Lands in the Parishes of Dolgelley and Swindon' (the latter for another extension of the works). In Dolgelley this was for five parcels of land at the east end of the station and taking the station area right onto the bank of the Wnion in the 'Parish of Dolgelley, Township of Garth Gin Fawr'.

On 10th August 1882 the committee considered the news that a Dolgelley to Festiniog Railway had been proposed. On 21st August 1883 the traffic manager reported that the scheme had been deferred and that it was being promoted solely in the interests of private parties. 'The Promotor, Mr Butler of Crymmau Hall, was asking if the Cambrian would assist by taking £30,000 in Preference Stock'. The matter was ended on 20th November 1883 when he reported that 'The Railway promoted by Mr Butler is abandoned for this year and is to be proceeded with next year if not anticipated.' It looked as if this private promotion was merely a move in railway politics to see if either the Great Western or the Cambrian could be prompted into building the connection.

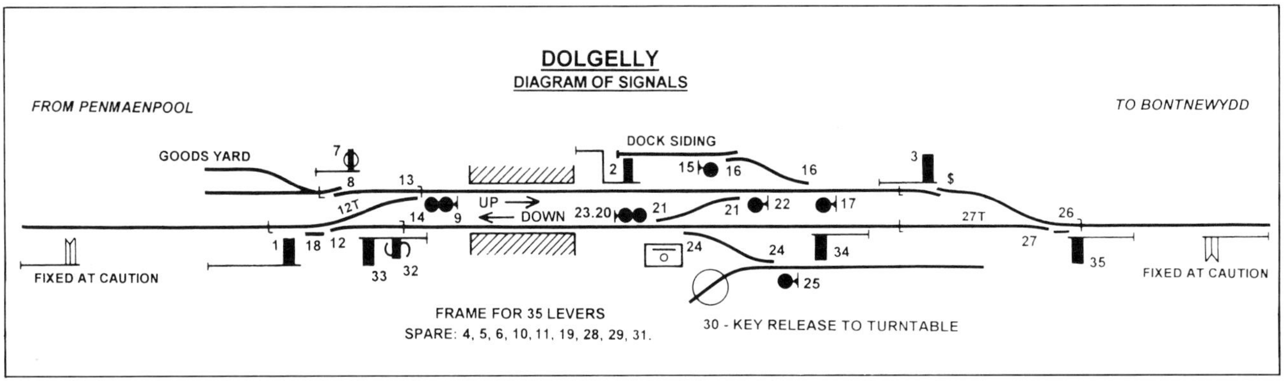

The outlook in the up direction towards Ruabon from the latter-day signal box. The turntable was unusually close to the down running line. 19th June 1964. *Author*

Looking westwards to Dolgelley station, with the turntable siding to the left and the dock siding to the right. The token set-down apparatus included the early-pattern pad to absorb the shock of the exchange, later replaced by the net seen in the photo opposite. May 1944. *L. E. Copeland*

On 29th July 1884 the traffic manager reported that the Great Western were going to install a turntable, with some re-signalling. 'The Engineer reports that the plan is sound but entirely favours Great Western working', the turntable being at the east end of the station, whereas the Cambrian worked out of the west end. 'Under the agreement of 1st February 1873 the Company is bound to pay 5% interest on one third of the capital outlay of £1,905.' The suggestion that the turntable only might be of use to the Cambrian would have cut the basis of the calculation to only £275, calling for a payment of only £4 11s 8d per annum; but the Great Western were not so inclined and on 29th October 1884 the committee reluctantly authorised the payment based on the full expenditure. The Cambrian's Small Sharp Stewart 4–4–0s were not allowed to turn on the 42ft table when they were first put into service, and the 4–4–0 Big Belpaires were never permitted to use it.

The signalling arrangements before these alterations appear to have been worked from a small Great Western box at the east end on the Cambrian side of the station. The signals included a three-arm slotted signal post at the west end, on the Cambrian platform. This accommodated the down starting signal, the up home (visible above the road bridge) and an arm permitting short movements across to the goods yard. A similar post at the east end carried the up starter and the down home signal arms and there was some form of access control to a short parcels siding on the up side. After the re-

No. 3206 at Dolgelley with Fireman B. C. Helwyn Jones, Driver Thomas Williams and Guard George Lewis. *Cty. Gwilym Hughes*

The GWR turntable photographed in 1964 and 1965. *Author*

The east end of Dolgelley, showing water column, a carriage parked on the down siding (turntable neck), signal box and a camp coach on the turntable siding. 3rd July 1952. *J. J. Davis*

arrangement, control of the signalling was effected from a new and larger Great Western box (with a 10-lever frame) at the end of the up platform. The slotted arms were replaced by the more modern semaphore arms pivoted on the front of the posts with colour glasses integral with the arms. The resignalling was passed by the BoT inspector on 22nd December 1884.

On 2nd August 1884 befell the only recorded accident on the Cambrian side of the station, when Richard Morris, aged fourteen, who was collecting newspapers, fell between the platform and the 5.9pm to Barmouth and had both his legs severely injured.

In 1888 there was a dock for the loading and unloading of horses and carriages in the Great Western goods yard. The advertisement of the same year by Eliza Stokes, proprietress of The Royal Ship Hotel, gave an adequate description of the town's facilities for the well-to-do. There was fishing, croquet, lawn tennis and 'Guides and Ponies at fixed Moderate Charges'. 'Hot and Cold Baths' were always ready.

'A Mail Car Conveying Passengers daily to Barmouth' was available, leaving at 7.30am, returning from Barmouth at 4pm. The fares were 2/6d single and 4/– return. Suggested excursions which could be arranged were the three gold mines (on the Barmouth Road there were Vigra and Clogau, and Mount Morgan near Cymer) and a trip to the Mawddach Falls. Finally, there were 'Morning and Afternoon services in English at Church and also in the Chapels'.

Both The Royal Ship and The Golden Lion Royal sent their own buses to meet all trains.

An even more outstanding example of the advertising extravaganza as thought up by the Victorian media (confined as it was to the printed word on paper or on sandwichmen's boards) was that of Mr John Meyrick Jones's 'Royal Welsh Woollen Warehouse, Dolgelley' for his 'Genuine Hand-Made Welsh Tweed Cloth, Fishing Cloth, Flannels, Shirtings and Linseys', 'from the pick of Pure Mountain Wools' and 'Patronised by Her Royal Highness, the Princess of Wales, the Clergy, Nobility and Gentry of England and Wales' and much more besides. His most expensive 'Welsh Tweed Cloth (from Picked Wools)' cost 4/3d per yard and his 'Very Superior Welsh Cloth for Fishing Suits' was 2/6d.

At this time there was a special rate for the conveyance of meat in consignments of not less than 5cwts from Dolgelley to London of 3/9d per cwt.

On 26th March 1889 the traffic manager reported that 'the freeing of the Block Instruments at Newtown and Moat Lane plus that at Pontdolgoch, which is only an intermediate signal station, would enable replacement of Staff by Block Telegraph on the Dolgelley Branch at Barmouth Junction, Penmaenpool and Dolgelley'. The committee gave approval on 24th April

A busy scene viewed from the window of Dolgelley signal box on 9th August 1948 with No. 4375 on the 1.12 p.m. from Barmouth to Ruabon. The tender on the right belonged to No. 7305 which may have been waiting in the dock siding to assist 4375 up the fierce gradients inland from Dolgelley. The light engine held in the platform was No. 7310 whilst No. 1434 can just be seen beyond with a Barmouth-bound auto-train. *W. A. Camwell*

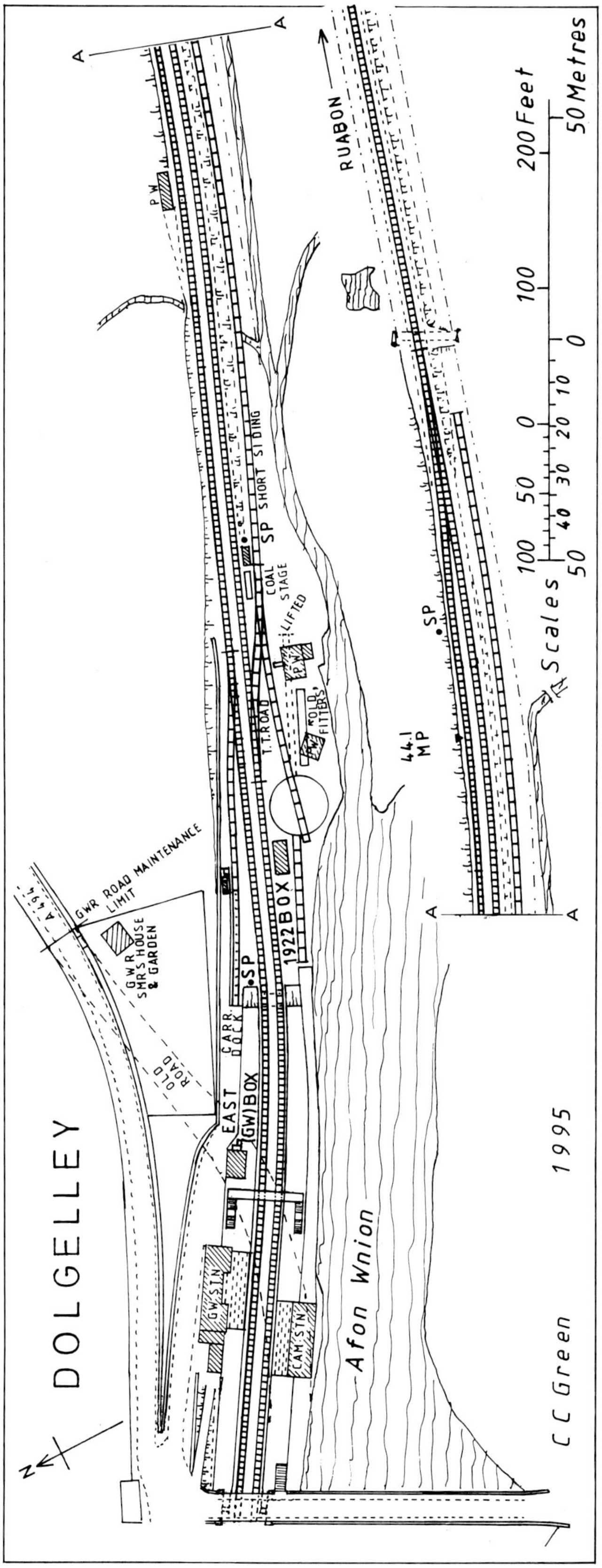

1889 but were told on 20th May that the Great Western had refused to accept one of these instruments in its signal box and insisted on the use of Spagnoletti's three-wire block instruments between Dolgelley and Penmaenpool.

On 27th April 1893 the committee approved in general terms that the five additional trains put on to meet the Great Western trains in 1892 should be continued during 1894. Meanwhile, discussions were in hand about the 10.30am to Barmouth, and the Great Western agreed to guarantee the Cambrian a minimum earning of 1/6d per train mile. The general manager was instructed to try and get this made retrospective from 1st October 1892 plus a further allowance for the returning of empty carriages. Agreement was not forthcoming and the train was ordered to be discontinued. Between c1894 and 1913 the 11.50am Dolgelley to Pwllheli and the corresponding evening return train were worked by a 2–4–0, with a second assisting from the rear on occasions.

On 9th May 1894 the general manager reported on the alterations required in connection with the installation of interlocking under the Regulation of Railways Act 1889. This included a 250 yard extension to the loop, and meant having two signal boxes. It would also be necessary to dismantle the existing short ticket platform and to replace it with 'a larger one parallel to the extended down loop'. His report included notes that the Cambrian had erected the buildings on the down side for £600 in 1873, for which the Great Western had allowed 5% to the Cambrian for maintenance; and that the station on the up side was a joint one costing £18,735, on which the Cambrian paid one third. This figure has to include all the other items which made up the joint station, so he was mis-stating for effect. The committee had no alternative but to give their approval to whatever increase in payment to the Great Western might become necessary.

The new West Signal box housed a 21-lever frame, a Tyers tablet instrument, a phonopore and 36 Lechlanche cells together with a Spagnoletti single-needle instrument, for which the Cambrian paid the Great Western 50/– per annum, and a bell system which cost another 50/– per annum. There was also a disc for a third 50/–, and 1 mile 289 yards of wire at 23/– per mile per annum. Finally, there was a moiety of 5/– per annum plus wayleave of 5/– per annum for posts carrying the wires.

On 14th June 1894 the committee gave its reply to a set of memorials from The Congregational Union of Merionethshire and the Welsh Calvinistic Methodists of West and East Merionethshire and Flintshire, asking for the cessation of Mail Trains on Sundays. 'As the Company is required to run the Sunday Trains by contract with Her Majesty's Postmaster General the Company are unable to take them off.'

Looking in the down direction with the former GWR signal box on the right now put to other uses. Special arrangements were made because it was impractical for the signalman to see the tail lamp before sending 'Train out of section' for a train from Penmaenpool. 26th June 1951. *J. J. Davis*

The buildings on the Great Western side of the station, looking up. July 1952.
J. J. Davis

The Cambrian side of the station, looking in the down direction towards Penmaenpool. July 1952. *J. J. Davis*

Auto-fitted 0–4–2T No. 1431 on a Dolgelley–Barmouth local service with extra coach attached. This view, taken from the road overbridge, offers a comparison of the two architectural styles on either side of the station. Dolgelley was a busy station. Takings in 1924 totalled £17,992, of which £6,577 came from passenger traffic and £1,485 from parcels, goods making up the largest part – £9,930. 9th August 1948.

W. A. Camwell

Dolgelley's Annual Eisteddfod was held on New Year's Day 1895. On 15th January the general manager reported that he had had to borrow eighteen carriages from the London & North Western to cope with the extra trains needed 'and more are borrowed for the Aberystwyth–Euston service ... The L&NW mileage Suspense Debit is up to £1,443 11s 4d.' This state of affairs was attributed to 'the inadequacy of the Carriage Shop to hold the newer longer carriages and to pull up the backlog of summer wear and tear and damage of a larger carriage fleet'.

On 27th February 1895 the general manager reported that the Cambrian had started its own cartage service at Dolgelley (with stabling for one horse) and on 25th May 1895 he commented on the fact that the company continued to run two additional local trains (on payment of £100) to enable the Great Western to run a fast tourist service. The Board turned down a request for a donation towards the formation of a Dolgelley Nursing Association, on 16th January 1895, but, with the Great Western contributing the same, assented on 26th February 1897 to a donation of £2 10s 0d towards the cost of a fire engine.

On 1st June 1898 the engineer reported that, while the Great Western had just had its buildings repainted, it was ten to eleven years since the company had undertaken this task. The committee ordered the repainting at a cost of £35.

General Manager Denniss believed in enforcing his authority by interference in as many departments as possible. On 24th February 1899 he was reporting on signalling matters and showing off as to his knowledge of the subject. An £80 item of expenditure was explained as the cost of moving the Advance Starter and Down Outer Home Signals at Dolgelley twenty-five yards westwards to avoid blocking the section to Penmaenpool when drawing over points and setting back during shunting at Dolgelley.

On 6th April 1905 the committee were informed that the Great Western was contemplating putting on 'a service of road motors' between Dolgelley and Barmouth during the forthcoming summer. On 10th June 1908 the committee approved the payment of 'the moiety of £500' for repairs to the Bont Fawr (The Great Bridge carrying the road up to the railway bridge) less the superintendence which the Great Western had agreed to allow. (A moiety was an old legal expression denoting a half.)

On 10th April 1918 the Board authorised the serving of notice on Dr Williams' School for Girls that the company required the renewal of the footbridge at the school's expense. Also the committee were informed

The west end of the station, showing road overbridge and Cambrian Railways' water tank, looking in the up direction. The former Cambrian signal box (the West box) stood on a site close to the water tank. 27th September 1961. *Author*

A 1940s view showing a down local train leaving Dolgelley for Barmouth Junction, past an up freight drawing out of the goods yard. *Collection Brian Wright*

The road bridge, showing the three original arches at the town (right-hand) end, the two raised ones and the two new ones, together with the new parapet and road line. c.1923.
Cty. Selwyn Higgins

Below: The Cambrian water tank, dated 1906. It always seemed primitive compared with the GWR's tank at the other end of the station (see page 261). Photographed on 27th September 1961. *Author*

that the Gwynfynedd Gold Mine was being reopened and that men were already at work.

On 1st October 1919 an application from the Dolgelley Free Church Committee for Sunday train services not to be recommenced was received and refused. On 11th February 1920 the licence of the refreshment room to sell spirits etc. was renewed on the understanding that neither railwaymen nor the non-travelling public were to be served.

On 25th February 1920 the request for a halt platform near 'Doctor Williams' Endowed High School for Girls' on account of difficulties with luggage, was refused because the facility would be used by only 115 pupils and then only at the beginning and ending of the terms.

It was noted in 1921 that the tablet instruments were in a signal box (Cambrian) manned by a fulltime signalman. There was a 10mph speed limit past this West Box. The arrival and departure of all down trains had to be reported to both Barmouth Junction and Barmouth. The Great Western attended to all breakdowns occurring inside the Cambrian up distant. Before grouping, London & North Western tranship vans ran through from Liverpool, Park Lane, to places from Aberdovey to Dolgelley and from Manchester, London Road, to places between Machynlleth and Dolgelley.

Once ownership of the whole station at Dolgelley passed to the GWR at the Grouping, a central signal box was erected on the down side as part of a £12,427 general upgrade. Resignalling cost £2,310 and the central box cost £273 more than had been estimated. Simply called Dolgelley Signal Box, it contained a GWR vertical tappet locking frame for 35 levers. The old Great Western East Box was retained for other purposes and the Cambrian West Box was removed.

Looking down towards the goods yard from the road bridge, a view showing the various curves which plagued shunting operations here. 28th June 1951. *J. J. Davis*

A 2–6–0 on a Ruabon train swinging across from the single line to enter Dolgelley station. The 'shunt ahead' arm (No. 32) below the down starting signal authorised a driver to enter on to the single line as far as was necessary to clear the points to cross over on to the up line. c.1933. *H. F. Wheeller*

No. 7827 *Lydham Manor* leaving with a Wrexham to Barmouth excursion on 6th July 1952. *J. J. Davis*

The warehouse, looking across the River Wnion and the running lines. 8th July 1952. *J. J. Davis*

Ten bridges between Ruabon and Dolgelley were reconstructed to take heavier engines of Blue category. One can only say that it was a very ambitious programme for one single year, 1922. On 9th March 1922 the Traffic Committee also approved a donation of £2 2s 0d towards the cost of the town's new motor fire engine.

The Great Western review of facilities dated 23rd October 1922 recorded the three water tanks as 17ft × 13ft × 8ft 6in, holding 11,700 gallons, 13ft 6in × 5ft 6in × 4ft 9in holding 2,120 gallons (The Cambrian) and a 'Balloon Tank' (Column Tank) 7ft × 4ft, capacity not stated. Supply came from the Dolgelley Water Works Company for £30 per annum, and the Great Western paid the bill, so that the Cambrian subsidised all the Ruabon-bound trains which took water there, through the expenditure pooling system.

On 2nd August 1923 appeared the first entry under the new designation Shrewsbury Division instead of Cambrian Division, 'Repair station lighting £170', which speedily became 'Renew station lighting £226'. On 5th May 1924 the traffic committee authorised the purchase of a freehold bungalow for the station master, two cottages for station staff and an acre of land, all for £1,300. On 29th January 1926 the Board approved £3,067 for general improvements of access and a new footbridge. This work created a need for some modification to the signalling which cost £207. On 28th July 1927 the civil engineer reported spending £170 on rebuilding 150 feet of platform to permit heavier engines. This was probably setting the face back to accommodate outside-cylindered engines, including the GWR Moguls. This was the last alteration which

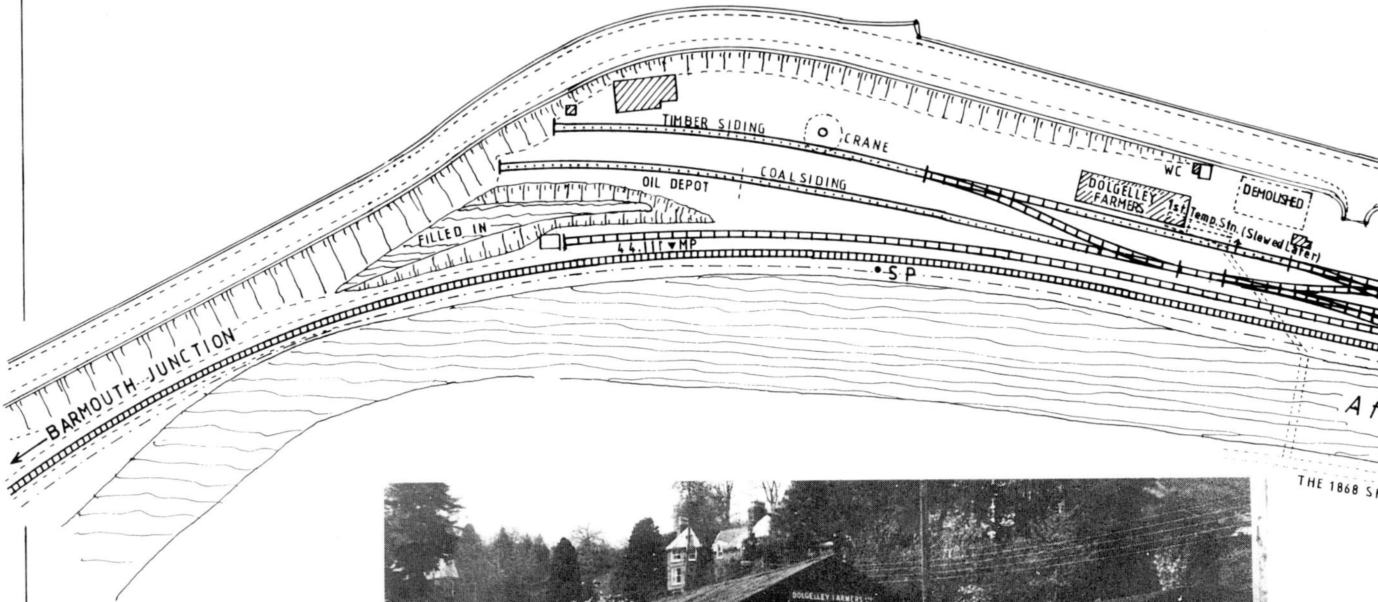

The Dolgelley Farmers Ltd. warehouse and offices and the so far unidentified coach body. c.1930.
Cty. Gwilym Hughes

The goods warehouse, looking east towards the station. 27th September 1961.
Author

affected the appearance and the working of Dolgelley station.

On 25th April 1929 the traffic committee authorised the purchase from Mr Swift Jones of his two road motors. On 26th March 1930 the civil engineer reported spending £170 on renewing the platform paving.

The regular flooding of the Afon Wnion had always produced a problem, that of gravel and stones building up beneath the road bridge. In Cambrian days it was cleared by the platelayers and ballasting gangs and used as a supply of free ballast, but this practice did not accord with Great Western standards and on 17th March 1932 it showed up in the records for the first time when the civil engineer had spent £105 for removing an accumulation from under the bridge.

By 1935 Dolgelley had a six-wheeled camping coach.

The station verandah was reported as repaired for £110 (8th October 1936). The winter of 1936/37 was a bad one for floods, and an expenditure of no less than £580 was reported (11th February 1937) for clearing

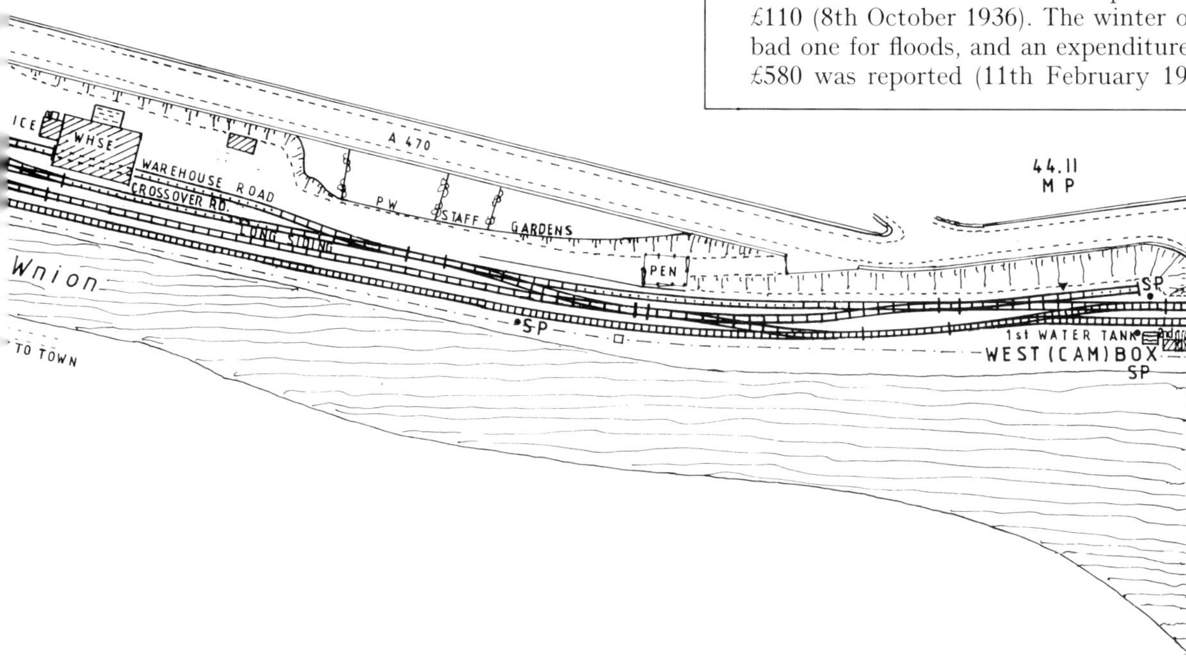

The warehouse, looking westward. The single line to Penmaenpool was out of the photograph to the left. 27th September 1961.
Author

the river bed of gravel. If this was allowed to block the flow of water through too many of the arches of the bridge, the water level could rise to above rail level. There is snapshot evidence that the surplus water came racing down between the two platforms! This time the Trustees of Dolgelley Green contributed £40 towards the cost.

In 1938 the cart weighbridge was recorded as being 12 ton and 12ft × 7ft.

On 25th January 1940 the traffic committee approved the expenditure of £147 for improving the telegraphic communications between Corwen and Dolgelley. Of this, £63 went on purchasing 31 miles of wire from the Post Office. The civil engineer had to report another major clearance of gravel from the bed of the river costing £470 on 31st May 1945.

Western Region carried out no work of any importance.

Now a modern bridge crosses the A470 Bypass built over the site of the station.

This view of a Standard Class 3 4–6–0 on an up train passing the yard reveals some detail of the Shell-BP enclosure including their own road tanker petrol pump in the foreground. 19th June 1965.
Author

The goods yard, looking up, and showing the old coal stage on the left, and yard crane and coal offices beyond. The petroleum siding was protected by a padlocked revolving stop block to avoid any danger of loose-shunted wagons colliding with a rail tank wagon being unloaded. 19th June 1965.
Author

The goods yard, looking towards the station across the petroleum depot and shed, on 19th June 1965. *Author*

Working Instructions. Whistle Code 1903

Main Line to Down Platform...	1 Long
Main Line to Up Platform	2 Long
Down Platform to Goods Yard ... / Goods Yard to Down Platform ...	3 Long
Up Platform to Goods Yard ... ... / Goods Yard to Up Platform	4 Long
To Long Siding	1 Short
Turntable	2 Short
Short Siding	5 Long
Cross-over Road	1 Crow

Working Instructions 1954

Under Western Region, the Dolgelley Branch became part of No. 14 Section of the Service Timetables known as Western Operating Area. Using the May 1954 book as the example, there were no whistle codes in use at Dolgelley but there were the adjacent other instructions.

DOLGELLEY.

Engine - Turntable.

The turntable lever is locked by Annett's lock.
When the turntable is required the Fireman must obtain the Annett's key from the Signalman, and after turning is completed he must return the key to the Signalman.

Telephonic Communication Barmouth end of Up Platform and Signal Box.

A telephone is provided at the Barmouth end of the Up platform, and the Guard in the case of a train, and the Fireman in the case of a light engine, must advise the Signalman when the train or engine with tail lamp complete is over the points.

Warehouse Road.

Before the warehouse doors are closed, the points leading from crossover road and cattle pens siding to warehouse must be set for the yard by the Checker or Porter and secured in that position by pins, cotters, and padlocks, and the wheel block on Warehouse road placed across the rail.

The keys must be kept in the goods office.

After opening the warehouse doors each morning, the Porter must remove the wheel block from across the rail, unlock the points, and take the pins, cotters, padlocks, and keys to the goods office.

Detaching Vehicles from Rear of Up Trains.

When a vehicle has to be detached from the rear of an Up train, the Signalman must set the points for the Yard, and the man who is to uncouple the vehicle will be responsible for seeing that this is done before he detaches the vehicle.

Coal Siding—British Petroleum Company's Depot.

A wheel block is provided about 15 yards from the stop block. The wheel block must be kept locked across the rails except while a loaded oil tank wagon or empty tank wagon is being berthed in, or shunted out of the dead end. The key of the padlock securing the wheel block is kept in the goods office.

All concerned to exercise special care during the shunting operations on the siding.

Flood relief cum occupation bridge, looking north on 19th June 1965. *Author*

The bridge over the Afon Wnion at 45m 41½ch, looking north. 19th June 1965. *Author*

West of the bridge over the Wnion, the line ran on a low embankment which acted as a dam against estuary water at the highest tides. Here, the new bridge and sluice are seen from the estuary side in September 1931. *GWR Magazine*

Right: The north (estuary-side) face of the top-hung sluice paddles. A high tide presses them tightly closed and prevents flooding with salt water. Inland flood water swings them up at low tide and the floods escape out to sea. 21st November 1994. *Larry Bridges*

PENMAENPOOL

46m 52c. Loop 46m 39c to 46m 58c.
Signal Box at 46m 52c.

Standard Class 4 4–6–0 No. 75006 slowing to exchange tokens, c.1963. *Collection C. L. Caddy*

Opened as contractor's quay and yard 1863.
Opened as terminal station 3rd July 1865.
Opened as through station 21st June 1869.
Closed Goods 4th May 1964.
Closed Passenger 18th January 1965.
Loco shed closed 18th January 1965.

Penmaenpool is 'the pool (wide bend in a river) by the rocky headland' and has not yet reverted to its ancient name of Llyn Penmaen. Measured round all the bends, it is two miles below the highest point to which tides flow, but it is the highest point up the Afon Mawddach at which a good quay could be built (although small boats were working up to Llanelltyd where there was a timber footbridge). Sailing barges brought coal and lime upstream from Barmouth and took back woollen goods, minerals and timber. The 147 ton brigantine *Charlotte* was launched and taken downriver to be fitted out at Barmouth in 1862. Barely a year afterwards, the requiem for this tiny but busy port was sounded by a hooting of a steam siren and a thrashing of paddles as the Aberystwyth & Welsh Coast's tug, the *James Conley*, towed in the first barge load of railway materials.

As already mentioned, the first passenger train arrived there on 3rd July 1865. The first through train went on to Dolgelley (Frondirion), a temporary station, on 21st June 1869, and 1st August of that year saw the first train to connect with the Bala & Dolgelley's rudimentary station at Dolgelley. Then a sudden surge of trains from the northern cities started, and the slack contractors' way of running token services had to be smartened up. C.P. Gasquoine has written of this short period:

> 'And a wonderful service it appears to have been! Old inhabitants still tell tales of how goods trains would pull up at remote wayside spots while driver and guards went trapping hares that made good prices in the neighbouring markets, where no inconvenient questions were asked concerning their capture. Or it might be that now and again, a waggon load of beer barrels was consigned to some village inn. (The George?) It was then the business of those in charge to marshal the trains so that the 'stuff' was placed in convenient proximity to the engine and, in the seclusion of some cutting, a halt would be made for some mysterious reason. To clamber over the tender into the adjacent waggon was a simple matter. Still simpler, in expert hands, was the forcing up of one of the hoops, tapping it and drawing it until the engine bucket foamed alluringly, then plugging it up again, and drawing back the hoop into its original position. On delivery the consignee might complain of short weight, but it was a question for the brewer and company to settle as best they could. None of the running staff knew anything about it; and, as for the lateness of the train, was any train ever punctual in those days, and who bothered about half an hour's delay?'

Penmaenpool's first incidental appearance in Cambrian records is dated 9th January 1867 when the Board approved the removal of 'A Machine' to Oswestry. It was probably a part of the contractor's equipment which was deemed to be of further use. The Cambrian engineer's first task was to avoid the damaging of land caused by Savin's unlawful diversion of a stream. Then a Mr Taylor was to be allowed to build his own bridge across the cutting near the engine shed. Mr Taylor also wanted to have his own siding there but this was refused on 5th February 1867. At that time there was a staff of five men at the shed and station.

By 21st February 1872 Penmaenpool had settled into its future role of a local wayside station through which most of the trains passed without stopping, and the committee deliberated on the possibility of closing it to passenger traffic.

On 11th December 1874 the committee gave the proposal for an 'Estuary Bridge' and the promoters' wish to employ the Cambrian's engineer Mr George Owen to design it, their 'Full Approval'. The agreement between the bridge promoters and the Cambrian was approved and adopted on 19th July 1878. It included a clause which required the insertion of a draw or lift section for the passage of small sailing ships to Llanelltyd if such traffic could be shown to be continuing and necessary. Mr Beale, the promoter, was

A public roadway crossed the railway at the west end of Penmaenpool platform, without the benefit (in 1910 when this photo was taken) of any gates closing over the railway. Here the road is seen curving between the station building (on the left) and the weighbridge.
Cty. Owen Williams

A different view of the station building, with the George Hotel in the background and the public road crossing in front. The line immediately in front of the station was a siding when this photo was taken in 1910, but later became the down Loop line. Clearance from the front of the station, where passengers might walk, was tight. It was the duty of the signalman to 'guard the user of the crossing against approaching trains'. *Cty. Owen Williams*

Bridge ticket office and house from the crossing. The whole structure is timber. In the event of a substantial fire, those four fire buckets would not have been a lot of use. c.1910. *Cty. Owen Williams*

informed that a new station would be considered when the bridge had been opened. Meanwhile the Board instructed the engineer to prepare plans following the receipt of his estimate of £500 on 25th January 1879. There would be a lot of sewerage and drainage work, all requiring the laying of pipes under the line.

The bridge was opened on 27th February 1879, and on 19th April 1879 the engineer reported on a new station to cost £484 10s 4d, extensions to the yard including a platform on the main line side (to avoid using the loop) costing £252 17s 8d, plus a weighing machine and a house for £120. A 13 ton weighing machine was installed and cost £129 1s 2d, which presumably included the office, no longer referred to as a house. Otherwise the new station was built within the estimate and was opened on 21st July 1879. It comprised the brick building which is still there, the yard which remained little altered except for being lengthened, a small signal box and an exposed timber platform. Passengers had to cross the line to catch the trains after purchasing their tickets. The loop was a loop siding and not a loop for the crossing of trains.

On 18th September 1880 a Great Western train stopped to exchange train staffs. The agent (station master) was drunk and insisted on finishing a game before he went looking for the staff needed for the next section. It was eventually found on the ballast between the line and the platform. The agent then had to go looking for a fresh occupation.

On 21st November 1883 a local application for a waiting shed was deferred but on 28th June 1888 the Board approved the payment of £20 to Sir Richard Wyatt if he would erect a waiting shed to the engineer's satisfaction. They also required an undertaking that he would send all his traffic via the Cambrian route, in return for which his £20 would be repaid by means of discounts. Sir Richard was somewhat put out by these suggestions and sent a protest to the Railway Commissioners which the Company's solicitor was instructed to defend. On 4th July 1889 the Board approved the erection of a waiting shed for £60 9s 9d, towards which Sir Richard would contribute £30.

On 6th June 1890 the general manager informed the committee that large quantities of timber were being

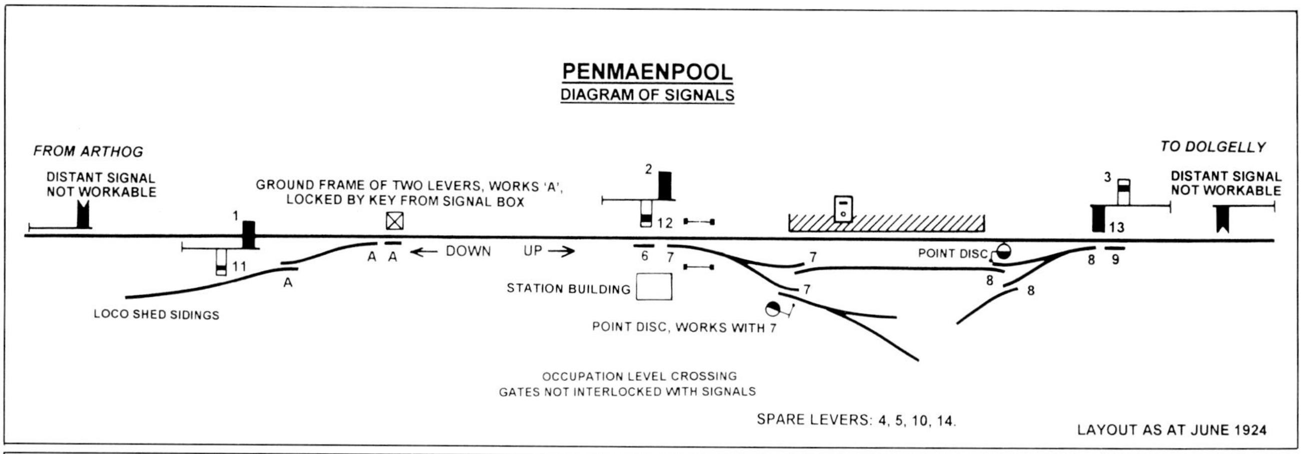

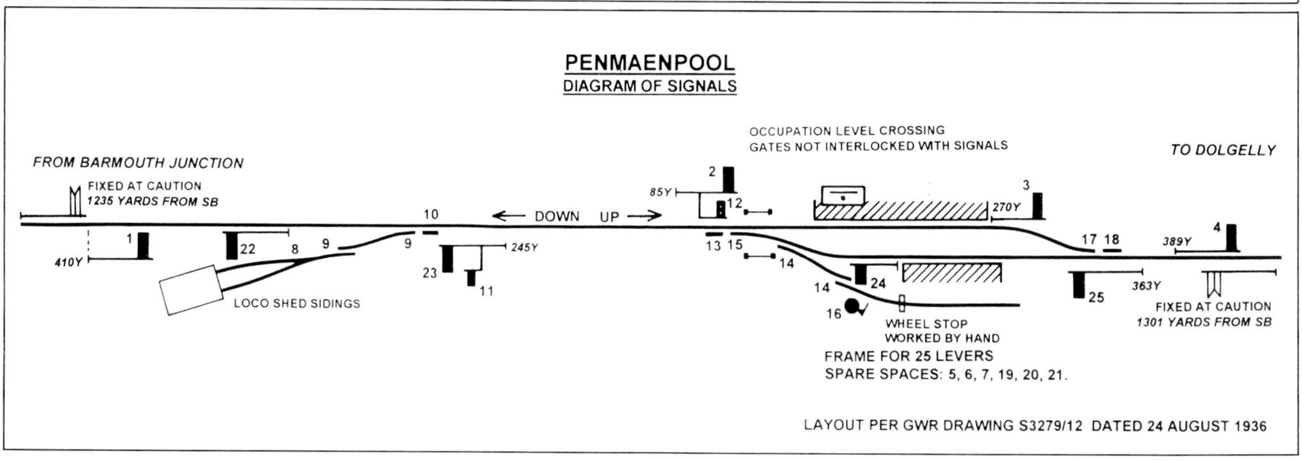

Cambrian waiting room and signal box standing on what was then the only platform. The signal box had been extended at the western end to accommodate the tablet instruments when they were moved to the box from the station buildings. Date and photographer unknown.

felled in the neighbourhood and he estimated that '3,000 tons of Larch and Oak would be sent under Contract during the next two years'. The yard needed extending at a cost of £192 which he advised 'should be met out of revenue in view of the recent capital cost of Dock for loading Carriages and Horses'. This was approved but a 40 yard extension of the platform for £90 was approved only subject to inspection by the Chairman and Mr Bailey-Hawkins (Deputy Chairman). It took until 9th May 1894 before this was finally approved. Meanwhile the station and yard were interlocked and re-signalled under the 1889 Regulation of Railways Act, completion of which was reported by the engineer on 26th September 1892. There was still only the one platform on the north side of the main line: the loop was catch-pointed and was still for use only as a goods loop siding.

On 26th February 1897 the general manager reported that the engine driver was about to lose his home as Mr Griffiths, from whom it was rented, needed it for his gardener at Penmaen Hall and had served notice to quit. To move the engine(s) (in 1894 0–6–0 Sharp Stewart No. 31 and 2–4–0 Sharp Stewart No. 54 were both shedded here) to Dolgelley and have to build a

No. 7800 *Torquay Manor* entering Penmaenpool with an up passenger train, seen from the end of the down platform. September 1954.
H. F. Wheeller

new shed and water supply would cost £248 11s 0d. 'This however would appear to be a rather large sum, and I recommend that you authorise a house being built at a cost not to exceed £200'. The committee approved a cost between £180 and £200.

On 22nd April 1901 the general manager reported on the advisability of putting down a sleeper crossing to the river for the customers of The George Hotel, on whose owner (Mr Leigh Taylor) 'We are dependent for water for engines and for station purposes at Penmaenpool, and in connection with these negotiations he has once or twice reminded me of this fact.' The crossing was duly laid. Boating excursions terminating at The George Hotel were a feature of Victorian holidaymaking and the well-appointed Barmouth steamer *Jubilee* was a very regular caller.

The water tank at the shed was wooden and fed by gravity from a pond uphill on Mr Leigh Taylor's land. It held 1,085 gallons and measured 12ft 6in × 6ft × 4ft 3in.

On 4th May 1902 a Mr W.C. Taylor, aged 80 and deaf, was on the wrong side of the line when his train came in and he tried to cross in front of it. 'He was knocked down and carried forwards for several yards and was quite dead when picked up. Porter Roberts sustained an injured arm and was highly commended for trying to save him.' The company had to face a claim for £300 for unsafe arrangements at the station with the booking office on a different side of the line from the platform, with no crossing gates or fence. 'Porter J.E. Roberts was awarded a Certificate of Honour by the Grand Priory of the Order of the Hospital of St John of Jerusalem which was presented to him by the Prince of Wales.'

On 1st October 1902 the general manager recommended an additional siding for the loading of cement slabs as the Great Western was trying to have the traffic taken to Dolgelley behind traction engines. The committee gave their approval.

In 1908 'Mr Chidlaw Roberts, Timber Merchant of Aberdovey and a Director of the Bridge Company, stated that they wished to collect their own Tolls instead of having the Cambrian staff to collect for them.' The Cambrian were agreeable as it cost '£21 per annum in wages for an Extra Junior Porter to receive 10% on £288'. In 1910 permission was given for the Bridge Company to erect a 'Bridge Keeper's Cottage' on Cambrian land and a lease was arranged.

In 1911 John Hugh Davies of Davies Brothers, Carters of Barmouth, who were carting from the Glasdir Mine, asked for stabling for six horses to be built in the yard and was offering £13 per annum on a five year lease. As the stabling would cost £50 and he wanted a terminating clause in his lease should the Glasdir Mine close, the general manager was not in favour, but he was overruled by the committee.

In 1913 the Bridge Company served a closure notice on traffic from the Cambrian, to become effective if the carters were allowed to continue leaving the yard loaded in excess of the three tons gross permitted over the bridge. The merchants agreed to stop the malpractice and the closure order was withdrawn.

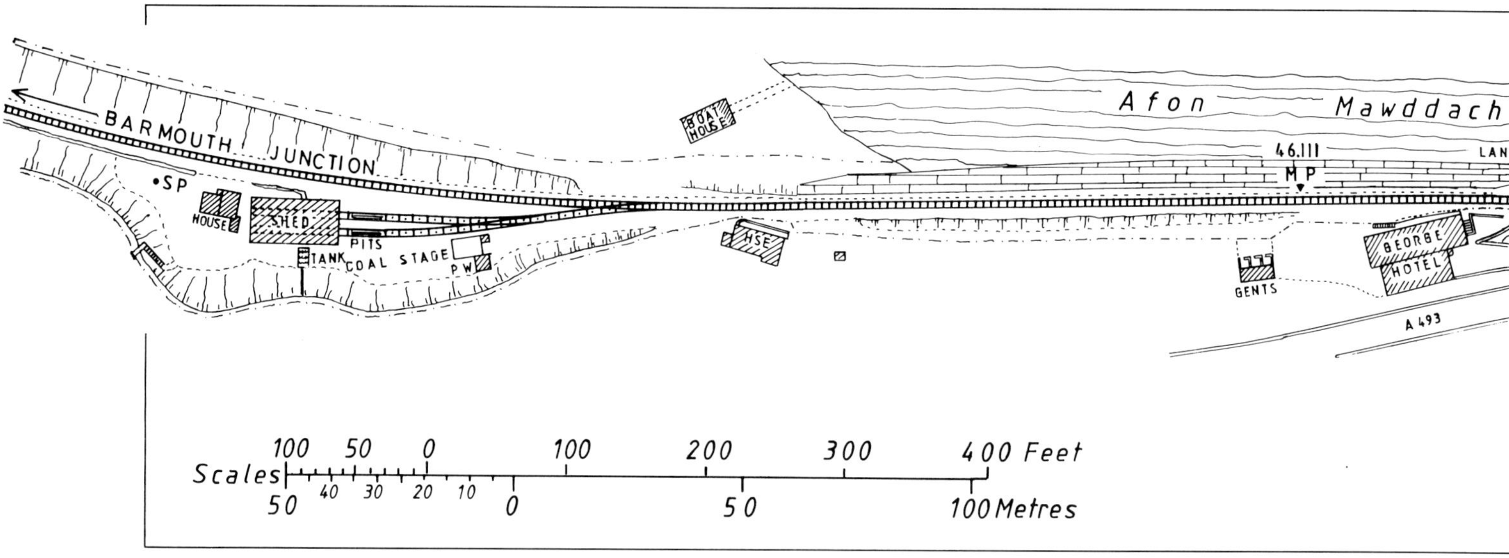

The yard, seen from the train, with carriage W29, loading platform and small goods warehouse beyond. Note the wagon loaded with coal waiting to be worked forward to the engine shed. July 1952. *J. J. Davis*

On 5th July 1919 four wagons of coal derailed in a goods train and one (Richards Bros. of Pensarn) was destroyed. The company pleaded that it was not a common carrier of private owner wagons and so was not liable to make good the loss. On 20th March 1920 the general manager explained that the lease for Mr J.H. Davies's stables, erected in 1911 for £80 and let for £13 per annum, had expired and that, as he had paid for the cost of the stables, he was offering a ground rent of £2 10s 0d per annum. This was accepted.

In 1921 the tablet instruments were in the station office because the signal box was too small. It was then manned by a part-time signalman. The box was immediately lengthened to accept the tablet instruments.

The Great Western's first expenditure was £190 for repairing the platform, recorded on 12th October 1922.

The padlocked revolving stop block just before the loading ramp carrying the warehouse. It provided effective, if primitive, assurance that a wagon could not be shunted on to another which was in the process of being unloaded. 1961. *Author*

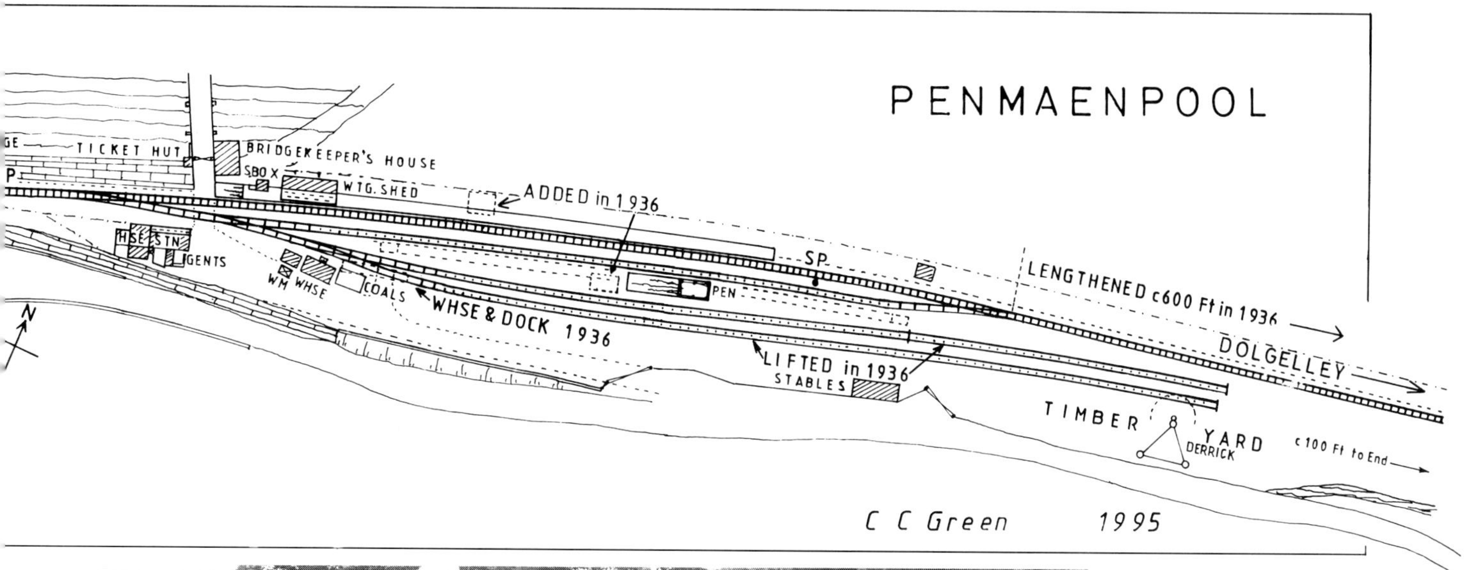

This view of Standard Class 4 No. 75023 on a down passenger, also shows the back of the signal box and the stilts supporting the rear of the shelter on the up platform – a GWR replacement for the Cambrian structure shown on page 280. 15th June 1965. *Author*

The signal box, looking up. This box had been part of the GWR's signalling exhibit at the Wembley Exhibition, after which it was dismantled and eventually re-used at Penmaenpool. Somewhat unusually, the lever frame was at the back of the box, as it had been in the earlier Cambrian box. 27th September 1961. *Author*

A view of the station, looking east, on 27th September 1961. The station house was provided for the station master for a rent (3/10d per week in 1924). He was the only member of the station staff, along with two signalmen. Receipts in 1924 were £1,704, of which £777 came from passenger tickets. The GWR reckoned that the villages served had a total population of 800. *Author*

A lovely view from the end of the up platform, showing the sinuous curve past the loco shed, with the Mawddach estuary on the right. By this date, road gates had been installed, but they were (very unusually) not interlocked with the signals. The roadway — for all that it could be busy — was officially rated only as an occupation crossing. Although it was not a public road but a privately-owned toll road, many vehicles used it to cut out a 14-mile detour up to Dolgelley. Date and photographer unknown.

The toll bridge, looking upstream, showing the wider span of the central piles for boats to pass through. The points in the foreground led to the engine shed. 27th September 1961.
Author

The toll bridge. This photo shows detail of decking cut from old sleepers, and additional bracing to support the wide opening of the central span. 15th June 1965. *Author*

The toll bridge with detail of pile frames. 27th September 1961.
Author

This picture of 2–6–0 No. 7341 on shed also features the coal stage, tools, water tank and the 3in gravity feed pipe which led from a pool on the hillside above. c.1955. *R. S. Carpenter*

Rear view of the shed and water tank.

The engine shed and foreman's house, viewed from the west on 27th September 1961. The advanced starting signal was provided, originally on the same post as the outer home, so that movements to and from the engine shed were within 'station limits'. Prior to this, what the appendix called 'short tablet working' was in operation. *Author*

The standard overhaul of Cambrian pointwork and signalling was completed at Penmaenpool by 23rd June 1924. In 1929 they took on the job of repairing the toll bridge. The engine shed was repaired for £230 by 27th April 1933 and on 29th November 1935 the Board authorised the expenditure of £5,050 on converting Penmaenpool into an authorised crossing station with platforms on both up and down sides of the loop. The yard was reduced to one single road. The 'new' signal box had an unusual history. On 30th April 1925 the Traffic Committee had approved the spending of £2,940 on an exhibit to represent the Great Western in the Palace of Housing & Transport at the great Wembley Exhibition. On show were a simple junction signal box and signals, models, an enquiry kiosk and, finest of all, No. 4073 *Caerphilly Castle*. The exhibition ran for two years, and the box was unbolted and put into storage at Reading. It was brought out and erected at Penmaenpool nine years later. For a nine-year-old box it was unique; not a single window had a long tea-stain trailing down beneath it!

The derrick had a lifting capacity of two tons.

The cart weighbridge was 11ft × 6ft 6in and of 10 tons capacity in the 1938 survey.

A year's clearance by the PW gang might produce a three-ton stack of hay in a good year.

Now all that is left are the original brick station building, which is an annexe to the George Hotel, one signal gantry, and the Wembley signal box, which is being used by the Tourist Board.

Working Instructions

1896 (or a little earlier): To save short tablet working between the station and the shed, an Advance Starter was fixed on the post carrying the Up Outer Home signal. Drivers were allowed to pass the normal starter set at danger when in possession of the key to the shed points.

1912: All stopping Up trains were examined, Dolgelley tickets were collected and tickets for all stations beyond were nipped. Guards were instructed to assist the Penmaenpool staff.

PENMAENPOOL—TOLL BRIDGE CROSSING.

A road gate fitted with spring lock is fixed at this crossing on the side of the line furthest from the toll bridge, together with a wicket gate.

The normal position of the road gate is across the line.

The gate must be closed and locked across the roadway before the signals are lowered for a train or engine to enter or leave the station, and before shunting operations are permitted over the crossing.

The curves in the line near milepost 48, looking west, after the line had been relaid and reballasted c.1923. *J. P. Richards*

New Great Western track with superelevation laid along the old embankment, with block stones facing against wind and tide. c.1923. *J. P. Richards*

An unidentified 'Stella' class 2–4–0 with an up train of chocolate-liveried clerestories crossing Abergwynant bridge. c.1925.
J. P. Richards

The original Gwynant bridge at high water.
Cty. J. P. Richards

Young Jim Richards helping his father to measure the clearance for their boat after reinforcement trusses had been inserted as part of the GWR's programme to upgrade the line and the weight of the engines which could work it. c.1924.
Mr. Richards, Senior

Gwynant bridge after reconstruction, looking up the estuary towards Dolgelley. 20th June 1965. *Author*

Gwynant bridge. 20th June 1965. *Author*

Left: Cefn-coed stream bridge. 20th June 1965. *Right:* Cefn-coed cattle creep. 20th June 1965. *Author*

Looking in the down direction from Abergwynant to Cefn-coed. 20th June 1965. *Author*

Garth bridge from the estuary side. April 1994. *John Burman*

Ty'n Coed quarries viewed from the north-east. The trackbed of the incline between the quarry lines (see the plan opposite) is clearly illuminated in the sunlight. The level section leading to the left of the photo was the route of the tramway towards the bridge over the road.
Author

Above left: The two tramway embankments, just south of the Cambrian's line. The tramway on the embankment in the foreground crossed the Cambrian to reach a jetty on the river. The far one curved round to an exchange siding with the Cambrian. c.1960. *Above:* Tramway embankment at the entrance to the yard. *Left:* Platelayers cottages at Garth, with the site of the former siding on the left, a view looking west to Barmouth Junction.
John Burman and author

GARTH SIDING

50m 05c

Opened as Staff and Crossing Station 3rd July 1865.
Closed 21st June 1869.
Opened as Quarry Siding cJune 1879.
Closed by 1888.

The site took its name from the nearby farm of Garth-isaf (the lower enclosure or garden).

When Savin laid rails for the Aberystwyth & Welsh Coast Company, there was already a tramway from the Tynycoed Quarry, which terminated at a small jetty. A rail level crossing would have been necessary. This would have been lifted in 1879 had it remained in situ, but no working instructions have been found. It could

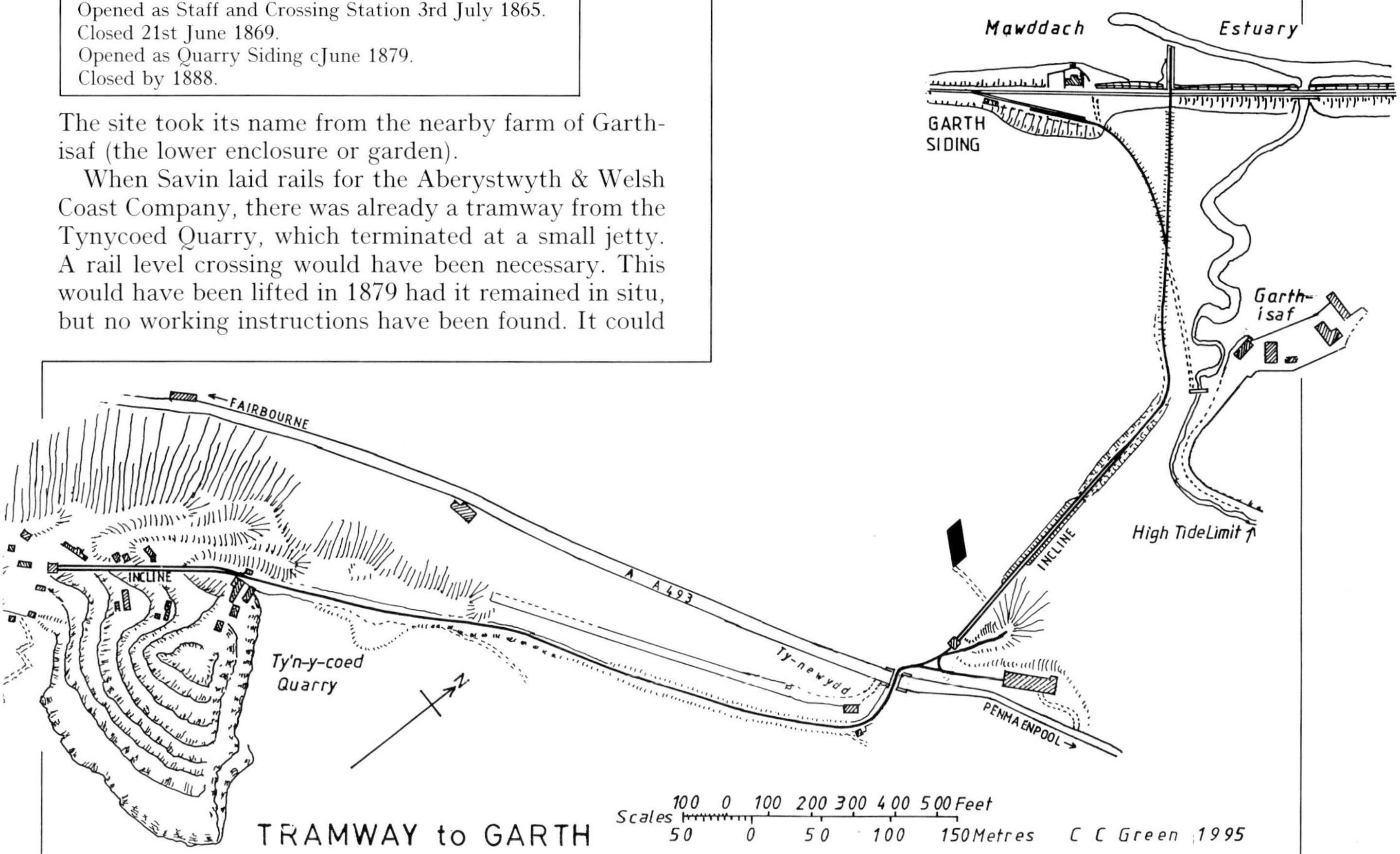

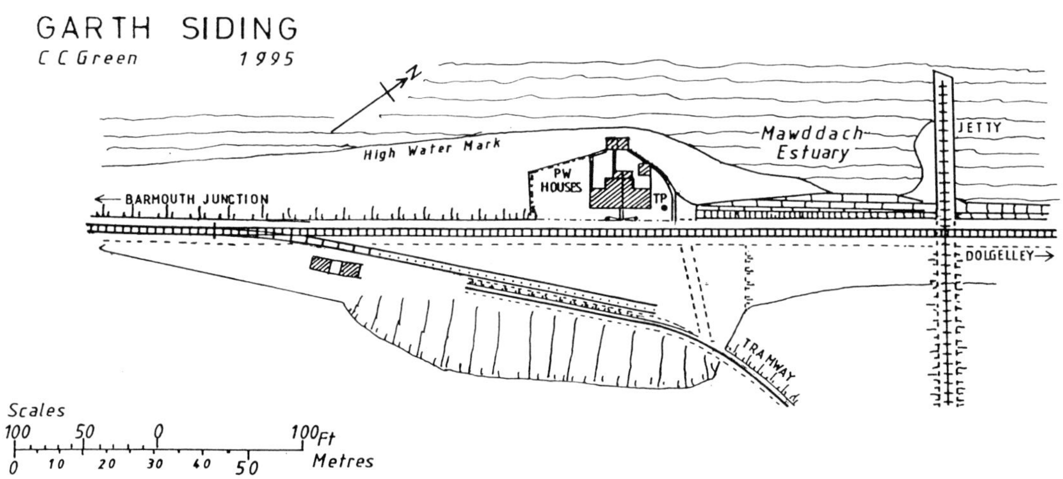

be that the stone was sent by road to Arthog from 1867. Maybe if there was any river traffic after the railway was laid, the stone was just barrowed across to the small sailing barges. At Garth there was a passing loop to take a small tank engine and four or five four-wheeled carriages, a gangers' hut for the train staff and a bit of a yard, but none of this lasted for more than four years.

On 17th November 1870 the engineer recommended that a platelayer's house costing £100 should be sited midway between Barmouth Junction and Dolgelley. Approval was given for a pair of houses costing £200; they were completed by 25th January 1872.

On 20th February 1879 the engineer submitted the first of several reports under names such as Garthrog and Garthyfog. A siding was requested by the owners of the stone and sett quarry to which they would lay their tramway siding. The cost of £676 8s 4d, to be paid for by the quarry owners, was noted on 18th June 1869 and included 'Signal Box and proper Signals etc.'. A weighbridge was also ordered on 18th June 1869. No working instructions have been found and the siding was probably out of use by the 1890s.

Top: The remains of Garth Jetty and Mawddach Estuary. April 1994. *Left:* Garth Jetty. Note the 'Deadman' mooring with ring. April 1994. *John Burman*

2–6–0 approaching Arthog with a Barmouth-bound train c.1926.
Bernard Edmonds

An 0–6–0 Dean Goods approaching Arthog before rebuilding of the embankment c.1926. *Bernard Edmonds*

Looking east from Garth Jetty across Garth bridge and up the valley towards Penmaenpool. Note the very unusual tubular steel telegraph pole on the right (see page 307). c.1960.
John Burman

0–4–2T No. 4812 and coach No. 164 arriving at Arthog from Dolgelley on 13th August 1935. *H. F. Wheeller*

ARTHOG 51m 18c

Line used for loading slate brought by road from 1867.
Opened Passenger 28th March 1870. Closed 18th January 1965.
Goods 28th March 1870. Closed 4th May 1964.

Arth can mean 'a bear' and the Victorians liked to think of Arthog as 'the place of the bears'. But it can also mean 'a headland' extending from a mountain (Cader Idris) which is far more credible. Initially, there was a three-span timber flood relief opening beneath the platform here, but this was filled in by the Great Western.

On 5th February 1867 the engineer reported on the construction of a wall for a slate wharf for £233 5s 6d and the erection of a bridge from second-hand materials costing £6. The whole comprised a primitive arrangement for the loading of halted goods trains.

On 25th August 1868 a bull jumped a fence and was run over by the 5.5pm down. One coach was derailed and the train was delayed for one hour fifteen minutes.

On 30th April 1869 the committee considered a scheme proposed for, and possibly by, D. Davies & Sons of Ty'n-y-coed for them to 'put in a Siding which will cross the Line of Railway and to erect a Bridge of or about thirteen feet high ... The Secretary was instructed to look into the Deeds and report'. On 14th May 1869 they authorised the engineer to construct a crossing.

On 9th December 1869 the traffic manager reported that 'Public going to and from Arthog Chapel have to

General view, showing the level crossing which had replaced the occupation bridge. c.1960.
John Burman

A view westwards towards Barmouth Junction. This station building replaced an earlier structure which lay at nearly 90 degrees to the tracks (see page 299). The ground frame in the far distance worked the points giving access to the goods yard siding, which could hold 18 wagons. Despite its lengthy platform, Arthog served a small community. Traffic receipts in 1924 totalled £1,222, of which only £366 came from passengers. 24th May 1964. *C. L. Caddy*

A Sharp Stewart 2–4–0 arriving at Arthog with an up train, seen from beside the Mawddach estuary. The station building was out of sight behind the bush on the left, but the signal box (which seldom appears on photos) can be seen on the platform. *Cty. Ifor Higgon*

walk along the line from Barmouth Junction because the road has been stopped. Coal and Lime has (sic) to be taken to Arthog Chapel and be left standing on the line for unloading. There is an increasing population because of slate quarrying. There is need for a station and a siding.' The committee approved the construction of the siding immediately and the engineer reported that the cost of the station and siding would be £110.

On 14th April 1871 the committee approved the lengthening of the 73ft 6in platform by a further 112ft for £50 and on 18th August 1871 the engineer advised on the need for 'A Distance (sic) signal on the east or Dolgelley side having a sharp curve'. It is interesting to note that he was not prepared to risk confusion by using the terms 'up' or 'down'. It was completed by 25th January 1872.

On 19th August 1875 the traffic manager reported that 'Mr Lewis Davies, Coal Proprietor of South Wales who has built a mansion near Arthog Station has asked for Unloading Accommodation for his Carriages and Horses.' The Company offered to put in a loading place at a cost to him of £170 18s 0d, but he continued to send his equipages to Barmouth Junction. On 26th March 1881 approval was given for cattle pens costing £30 and for an additional siding for the loading of timber.

On 10th January 1885 Mrs Hamer, a passenger from London, was waiting for her luggage to be placed in the carriage and fell eight feet down off the estuary wall; she lodged a claim for £50.

On 28th February 1885 the Board approved the levelling of more land to extend the accommodation

Arthog, showing the signal box and the old house and ticket office at right-angles to the line. c.1895.
Cty. Ifor Higgon

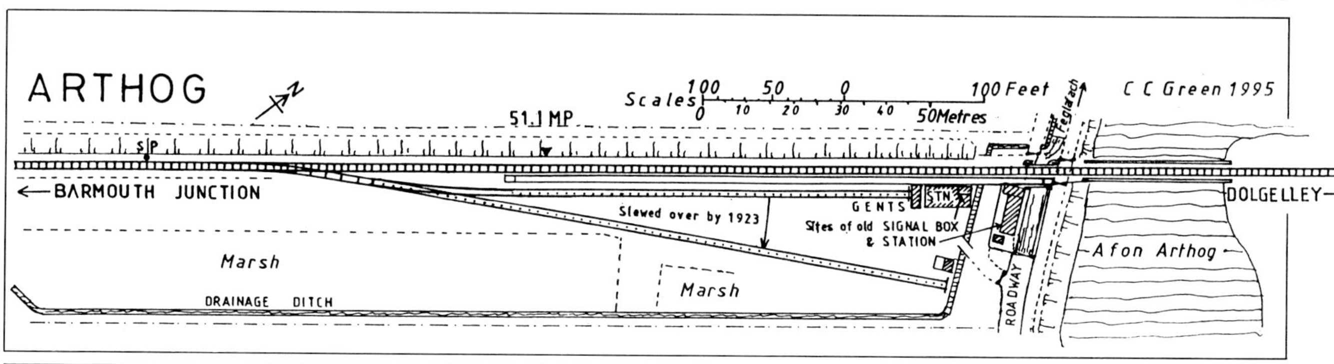

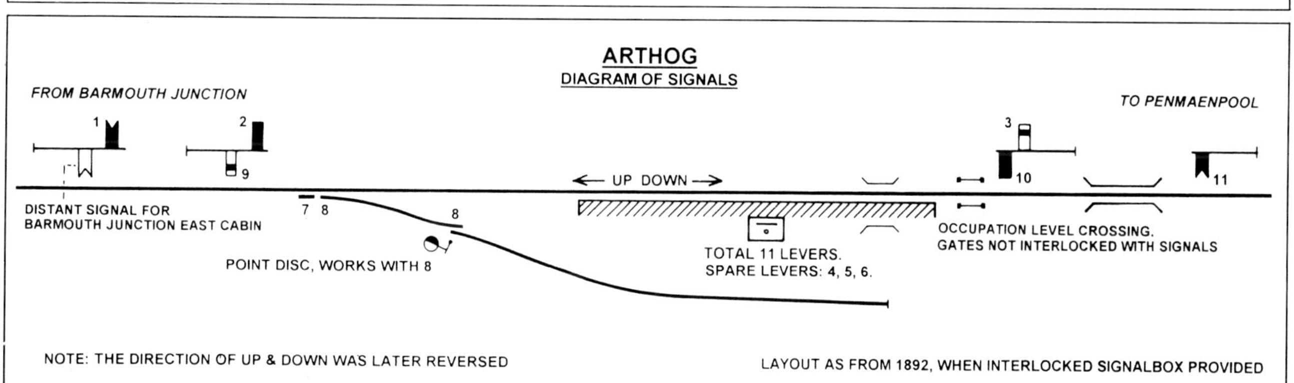

Arthog, showing the cattle creep which passed under the platform, between the station building and the level crossing. 27th September 1961.
Author

for timber traffic at a cost not to exceed £25. Passenger receipts, however, were poor and on 22nd October 1889 the traffic manager put forward a proposal for the closure of the station to passenger traffic.

In January 1893 the general manager reported that the stationmaster was having to live in a cottage at Barmouth Junction and walk to Arthog and back in all weathers; a cottage was needed at Arthog. Nothing was done and he took the matter up again on 29th January 1896: 'The Stationmaster, Arthog lives in the Signalman's House at Barmouth Junction and the Signalman, Barmouth Junction has to live in Barmouth.' On 24th March 1896 the engineer reported that there was a convenient site for a stationmaster's house three hundred yards from the present station and that one could be built for £230. 'This is a more desirable spot than Barmouth Junction where the absence of pure water and the exhalations from the boggy soil has always been a source of trouble.'

On 16th October 1900 the general manager reported 'Thos Rowland Jones, Stationmaster with the Company since 1863, age sixty-four and getting 19/– plus house is too infirm to even light his signals but has a daughter age seventeen and four children age eight to thirteen.' He recommended trying to find Jones an extra porter's work at ten shillings per week at one of the larger stations.

On 4th July 1904 the engineer reported 'The building at this station is in a very bad and insanitary condition and is quite beyond repair. The residents in the neighbourhood are making complaints about it.' The cost of a replacement was £200, which was approved.

The timber platform was completely replaced in 1931 by one supported on old rail set into concrete, at a cost of £370 and the *GWR Magazine* commented that the piling needed was fifty-five feet in length. The station approach road was repaired for £180 in 1933.

As recorded in the *GWR Magazine* for January 1939, there was an intense south-westerly gale on 23rd November 1938. Stationmaster W.T. Edwards was in the goods yard at 8.30am when the Mawddach broke over the line. He ran for safety but was overtaken near the ground levers and clung to them as the water scoured against him. Later he managed to climb onto a shed roof and was rescued by a boat from Barmouth after several hours.

By the 1950s the yard had been reduced to a single siding locked by Annett's key. At some time the shortest of porches had been added to the waiting room doorway, and at the west end a gents toilet had been added. This was sinking gently sideways down into the yard when the station was closed.

In the Cambrian advertising material, The Arthog Hall Hotel inserted an account of its offerings to its residents albeit on a somewhat smaller scale than The Royal Ship at Dolgelley – 'Good mixed shooting over three thousand acres of Wild Fowl Marshes, free to visitors staying at the Hotel. Tennis, Fishing, Moderate Charges.'

There was one non-fare-paying passenger. Mr and Mrs Bernard Edmonds' dog Toby was used to going with them to Barmouth, and started to disappear for most of the day. The bridge tollman related that he had seen him early in the day trotting briskly over the bridge to play with his pals around the harbour. A guard then told them that, at the end of the day he would jump onto the railmotor in the bay platform at Barmouth, attach himself to some passengers, and have a free ride home, a tired but happy dog.

MAINTENANCE OF THE DOLGELLEY BRANCH

The branch was not a long one but clerks and secretaries managed to confuse places and names so frequently that it will be easier to review formations and bridges without attempting too precise a segregation.

The mile-long embankment down to Penmaenpool from Dolgelley was a source of trouble from the start. Commonly at flood time the Wnion burst over its banks to spread across Gors Goch. The railway embankment embayed the flood water and had to have several flood openings and a sluice cut through it. It might have been better if the line had been taken across the Wnion on a long diagonal trestle bridge upstream and hugged the edge of the higher land straightaway. Doubtless local opinion would have been in opposition to the idea and the open marsh land was much cheaper to acquire than the better ground. Generally the branch was built at too low a level over its entire length. The Mawddach proved to be a more capricious neighbour than the Dyfi; rails and formation were overwhelmed and washed away again and again.

The Cambrian committee's first action was to approve on 4th February 1869 that additional land should be acquired for the taking of stone for ballasting up the trackbed. On 5th November 1869 the formation was carried away around Taylor's Crossing and Penmaenpool and a small culvert had to be replaced by a small pile bridge to allow floodwater to clear. On 22nd December 1869 the engineer reported again that the embankment had been swept away 'by floods of unprecedented height' and had been rebuilt as a temporary pile bridge. He advised that a larger permanent pile bridge should be built and this was approved on 18th February 1870.

Minor flood damage everywhere was continuously being topped up by the ballast gang and in 1872 one of the small flood openings east of Penmaenpool was enlarged and had a controlling sluice fitted in beneath it. On 21st November 1872 the engineer reported that the embankments were being damaged 'by successive High Tides during the Winter Season' and that stone pitching to face the side against the estuary was needed (between Penmaenpool and Arthog). The committee approved the cost of £2,640 immediately.

On 26th August 1876 he reported triumphantly that there had been heavy flooding 'but the large sluice gates erected four years ago had fully answered the purpose for which they had been erected when the Wnion overflowed.' In 1896 he asked for £696 6s 0d for additional pitching to the sea wall a mile beyond Garth (whether east or west is unclear) but this was deferred.

On 20th November 1883 the engineer reported that the line had been under water and ballast had been washed away but apparently this was nothing that the permanent way ballast gang could not deal with. The traffic manager reported that floods on 8th December 1886 had breached the embankment towards Dolgelley and had stopped the branch working. On 21st March 1887 the engineer reported that repairs had been completed and 'This has involved a heavy expenditure both in material and labour but the work was absolutely necessary for the safety of the trains.'

On 30th October 1888 the committee approved a contribution of £18 towards the cost of Mr John Leigh Taylor's embankment but his request for a further subsidy was refused on 26th October 1891.

On 25th September 1890 the Board had to consider a letter written to a local paper by a passenger incensed by the bumpy riding of the carriages along the branch near Arthog – 'If the Board of Trade attach any importance to those communications they have received they should order an inspection of the Line.'

On 2nd July 1895 a lime truck and a brake van in the 3.15pm goods ex Dolgelley left the rails and ran 690 yards before the driver noticed and pulled up. The general manager informed the committee that the driver was to be fined for his carelessness as with all the bends he should have seen that the derailment had happened. The corresponding engineer's report stated that the lime wagon had been a MINERA and that the damage to the track had been very great (it cost £108 13s 9d to repair).

On 28th February 1895 the Board considered the report about 'the Bridge' which had been 'seriously damaged by Ice Floes'. This referred to the toll bridge at Penmaenpool in private ownership, and they declined the making of any contribution towards the cost of repairs.

On 26th October 1896 it was reported to the Committee that during 'furious gales and high tides during the night of the 7th', the whole valley had been flooded. The line had been under two to three feet of water and services had been suspended for forty-eight hours.

On 24th February 1898 the newly-appointed engineer A.J. Collin made his first report on this bothersome stretch of railway. 'When walking from Dolgelley to Barmouth I noticed that the rails on Four curves were worn very thin and had indications of fraying on the top flange. All were of 1877 or 1879 laying.' On 30th January 1899 he reported on storm damage to the line on 27th December 1898 and again on 21st January 1899. Ballast was washed away on both occasions. He asked for the authority to spend £100 on raising the embankment between Dolgelley and Penmaenpool by eighteen inches. The decision, on 2nd February 1899, was not to approve this. Probably George Owen, then acting as consultant engineer, had advised against the measure, since raising the levels on one section invariably moved the worst of the troubles further along the line. On 24th February 1899 the engineer reported that high tides between 10th and 14th February 1899 had caused another washout.

On 10th December 1899 Collin reported that the embankment was again threatened and that he had started to build a stone groin and to tip stone into the bed against the line. He had had this work approved by George Owen and on 21st January 1901 he could safely report that 'the new groine (sic) was successful although longer than first thought necessary, and that silt was now building up behind it'.

Collin's report of 11th August 1901 about the condition of the rail throws an interesting light on the expedients adopted by an extremely impoverished railway. First he explained that in 1897 parts of the line between Glandovey Junction and Aberdovey had had the old double-headed rail replaced by bullheaded section and 'these old rails had been re-used between Arthog and Barmouth Junction'. They were dated 1884 and 1885. He closed with 'they should have lasted another four years but are so bad that they must be replaced without delay.'

On 21st April 1903 the committee approved a programme of strengthening the cattle creeps and bridges 'to allow the heaviest engines' (the 4–4–0 Large Sharp Stewarts). On 9th April 1907 G.C. McDonald, Collin's successor, reported that a high tide had scoured the ballast away between Penmaenpool and Arthog.

On 27th February 1907 the committee instructed McDonald to report on the cost of raising the embankment between Penmaenpool and Arthog after receiving a request from a landowner, Mr Taylor, that it should be done. He reported back on 20th April 1907 that 'The raising of the embankment should be left as problems only occurred occasionally and might involve the Company in claims from landowners.' On an earlier occasion, McDonald had given his opinion that the embankment should be raised by one foot and Collin had suggested raising it by two feet.

Tygwyn bridge was renewed as part of the 1912 general overhaul of all the Cambrian's timber bridges. Three years later the three-span Arthog platform and the five-span Afon Arthog timber bridge were both recorded as being in good condition.

In 1918 the engineer reported that the line had been considerably damaged by a heavy storm on 22nd September. A high spring tide had caused the water to rise over the rails for two hundred yards between Penmaenpool and Arthog, cutting the ground from beneath the rails by about three feet and damaging a bridge.

From 1922, Swindon precision was to be applied to the recording of work done all along the branch. Each item, however small, was assigned a cost and with the relevant mileage point as well. Unfortunately, someone got hold of an old route plan with the mileages starting at zero from Barmouth Junction! It took until the middle of 1925 before they started to get things right and give the mileages from Ruabon Junction.

There was only a minor item in 1922; a defective pile bridge near Dolgelley was replaced by concrete pipes for £130. Expensive work began in 1923 when the Wnion bridge was replaced at a cost of £4,470. Around Penmaenpool £200 was spent on pitching to protect the embankment and a further £1,200 on raising the level. The five culverts near Barmouth Junction were reconstructed on an estimate of £260. The actual cost was £380.

In 1924 the retaining wall along the Wnion at Dolgelley had to be rebuilt because of erosion and this cost £900. Bad flooding during the winter of 1924/25 occasioned a lot of work, mainly authorised on 29th January 1925. The two bridges at Arthog had £240 allotted, but this work was overspent by £65. Another £500 had to be spent generally around Arthog. The main expense was £3,800 on re-facing along the embankment near Penmaenpool station, to which another £900 was added on 29th July 1926 for more work between the station and the shed.

While repairing the damage caused by the weather, the civil engineer had also to get all the weaker bridges strengthened, first to upgrade the branch to take 'Yellow' category engines and later to raise the bearing capacities to take 'Blue' engines. These objectives prompted the spending in 1925 of £185 on a culvert east of Arthog and £490 on six other bridges all along the branch. More followed in 1926; £1,400 on the smaller bridge west of the Wnion and £970 on the five-span bridge across Afon Arthog. These overran the estimates by £120, mainly after the discovery that the latter bridge had actually moved downstream. It was reported that 'the floods had caused the bridge to move considerably out of position.'

On 31st March 1927 the civil engineer reported on a further overspend of £135 and on 28th July 1927 he had to report to the Board on work needing to be done between Penmaenpool station and the shed. The Board duly authorised another £2,630. The Wnion bridge was strengthened again for £165 and the *GWR Magazine* carried a paragraph about eroded embankments having to be pitched.

On 26th January 1928 the civil engineer recorded £76 for the reconstruction of an underbridge but he had to go to his Board again on 25th April 1928 for authority to spend £3,760 on reconstructing two underbridges near Penmaenpool and for £2,735 on erosion protection generally east of Arthog. This budget was underspent by £240. For the two underbridges he had to get further approval for £1,020 and still overran by another £350. The cost of reconstruction of a timber underbridge east of Arthog was recorded on 22nd November 1928 as being £850. £550 was expended in 1928 in installing trolley run-offs for the 'Economic' system of PW maintenance.

On 27th June 1929 another underbridge reconstruction was recorded as having cost £2,400. Also in 1929 the GWR civil engineer and staff undertook the repair of the toll bridge at Penmaenpool, the cost of which was to be recouped from the owners. The original estimate was for £1,950 but the job seems to have overrun by £317. Two bridges between Arthog and Barmouth Junction were reconstructed for £2,405. The Penmaenpool section, under Ganger Watkins, took first prize as the best-kept section in 1930.

On 11th February 1932 £245 was recorded for a 'Concrete and rail grill' to bridge one mile east of Penmaenpool. In 1933 the Bala to Barmouth Junction

806 Class 2–4–0 No. 810 on an engineers train easing forward (in the Dolgelley direction) near Abergwynant, c.1925, during line-strengthening work. *J. P. Richards*

Left: Tipped clean off the formation by water pushing in from the estuary. 1927. *Right:* The PW men of 1927.
GWR Magazine and Cty. Mr. Jones

Relaid and re-ballasted again in 1927. *J. P. Richards*

line was reorganised and re-equipped for 'Motor Economic Maintenance' at a cost of £710. In 1937 the sluice half a mile east of Penmaenpool was entirely reconstructed and another £1,765 was expended on this and on embankment work along this section.

On 26th November 1942 £285 was recorded as requiring to be spent on reconstructing the Gwynant underbridge, and the job overran this estimate by £55. On 18th February 1943 the civil engineer recorded £380 as having been spent on trimming rock face and clearing away debris after a fall at 48m $6\frac{1}{2}$c (nearly one and a half miles west of Penmaenpool). On 28th June 1945 £300 was recorded as having been spent on the reconstruction of the underbridge at Garth.

Flood and storm problems along the branch continued to a lesser degree under British Rail but in the main the expenditure and hard work put in under the GWR remained sound.

After 15th January 1964 when the trains ceased running, the branch equipment was removed and the rails and sleepers were lifted, but the bridges were left intact and the trackbed has since received some attention to make it into a cycle and footpath. Now it is the highly enjoyable Morfa Mawddach Walk, but strong footwear is still advisable. The walk is accessible from car parks at Dolgellau, Penmaenpool and Barmouth Junction. At Dolgellau the way lies along the south bank of the river and over a footbridge to continue along the north bank until the new bypass (built along the line of the rails) curves away northwards and the path leads across the Wnion bridge.

The speed limit in GWR days was thirty miles per hour except for Pant-y-cra Curve which was restricted to twenty miles per hour.

The GWR put all signs directing passengers into both Welsh and English.

Both the Cambrian and the Great Western prohibited the coupling of two engines together anywhere along the branch.

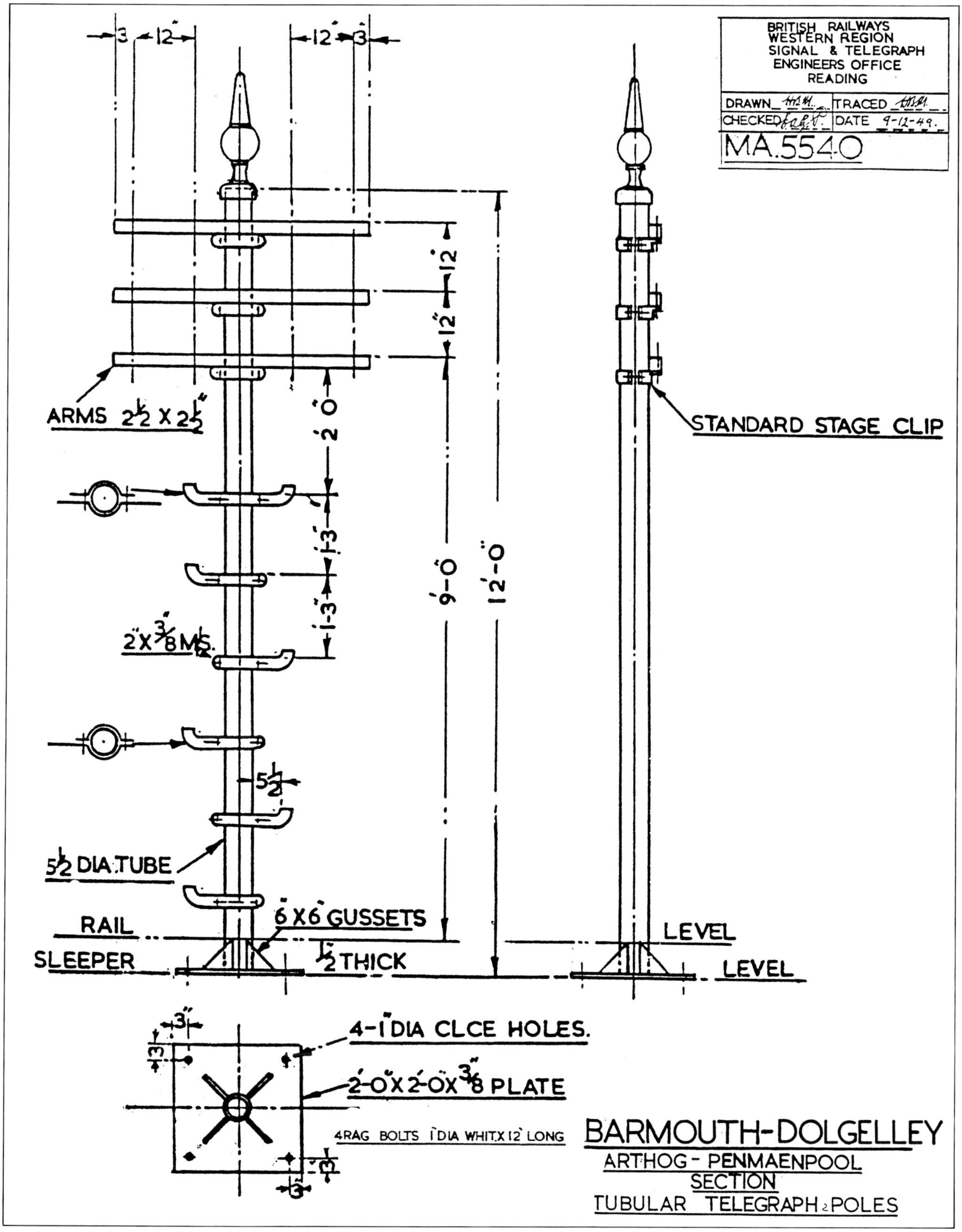
BRITISH RAILWAYS
WESTERN REGION
SIGNAL & TELEGRAPH
ENGINEERS OFFICE
READING
DRAWN
TRACED
CHECKED
DATE 9-12-49.
MA.5540
ARMS 2½ X 2½"
STANDARD STAGE CLIP
2"X⅜" MS.
5½ DIA.TUBE
RAIL
SLEEPER
6"X6" GUSSETS
½" THICK
LEVEL
LEVEL
9'-0"
12'-0"
4-1" DIA CLCE HOLES.
2'-0"X2'-0"X⅜" PLATE
4 RAG BOLTS 1" DIA WHIT.X 12" LONG
BARMOUTH-DOLGELLEY
ARTHOG - PENMAENPOOL
SECTION
TUBULAR TELEGRAPH POLES

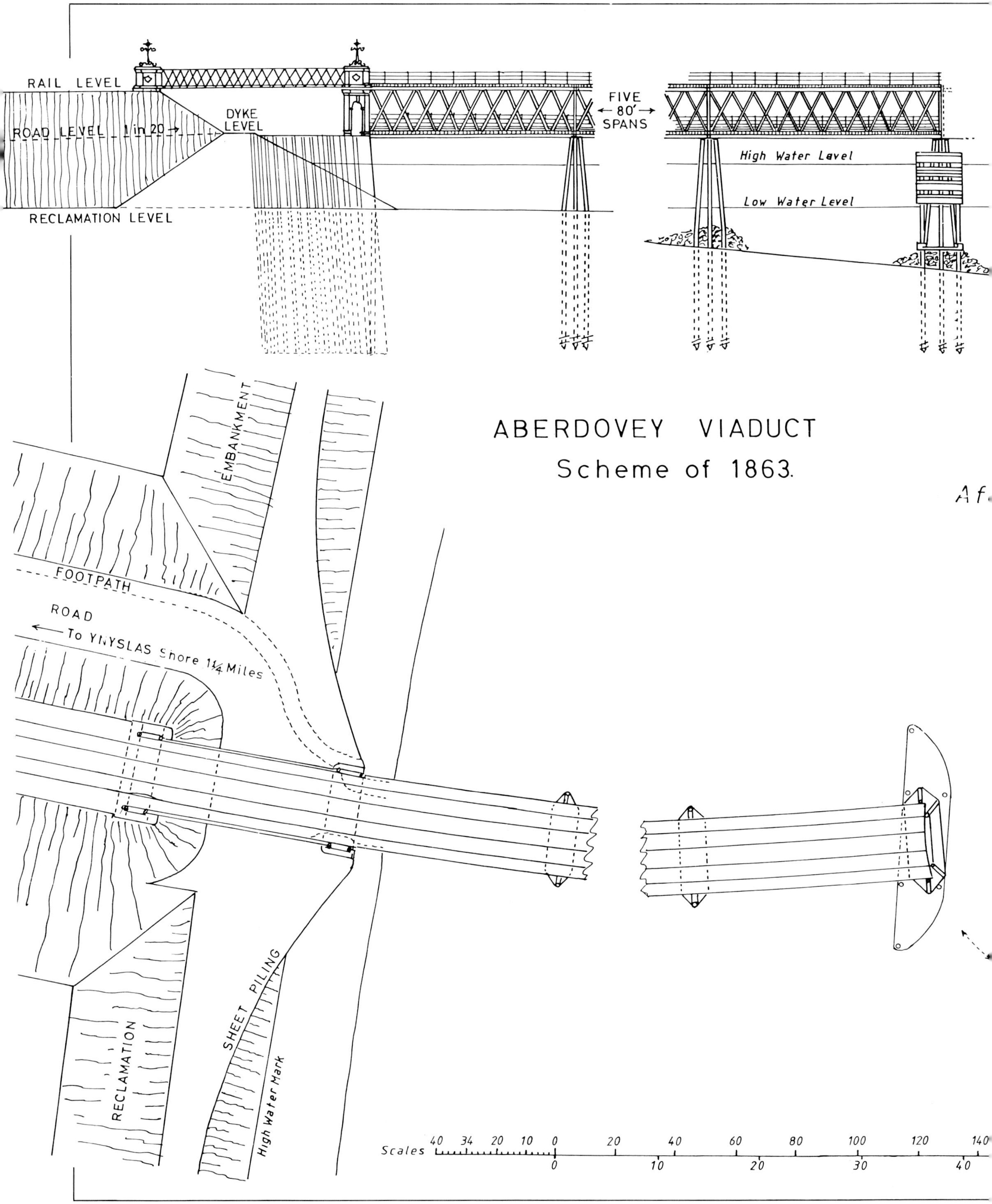
RAIL LEVEL
ROAD LEVEL
1 in 20
DYKE LEVEL
RECLAMATION LEVEL
FIVE 80' SPANS
High Water Level
Low Water Level
ABERDOVEY VIADUCT
Scheme of 1863.
EMBANKMENT
FOOTPATH
ROAD
To YNYSLAS Shore 1¼ Miles
SHEET PILING
RECLAMATION
High Water Mark
Scales
40 34 20 10 0 20 40 60 80 100 120 140
0 10 20 30 40

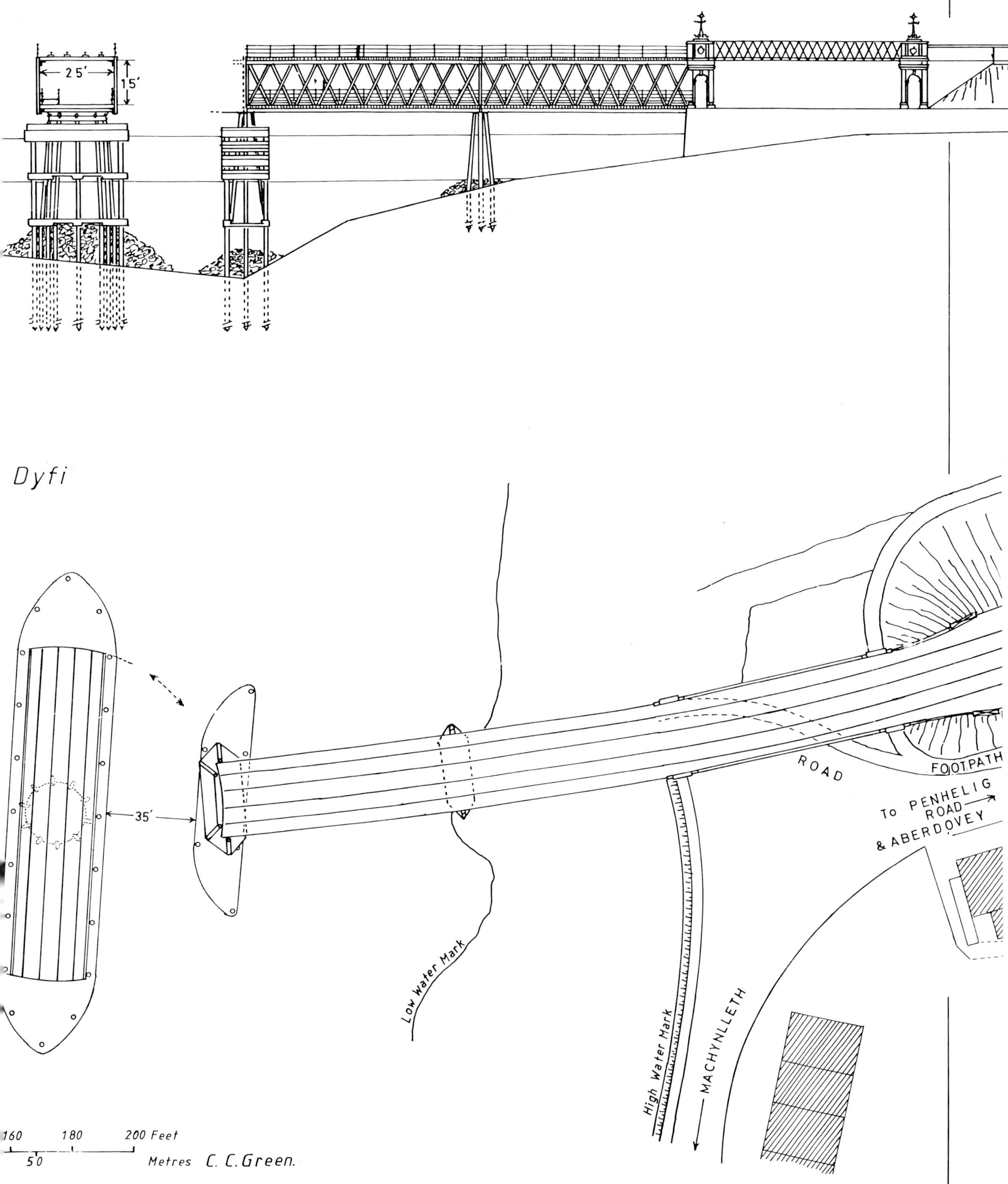
25′
15′
Dyfi
35′
Low Water Mark
High Water Mark
ROAD
FOOTPATH
To PENHELIG ROAD
ROAD
& ABERDOVEY
MACHYNLLETH
160
180
200 Feet
50
Metres
C. C. Green.

APPENDIX II

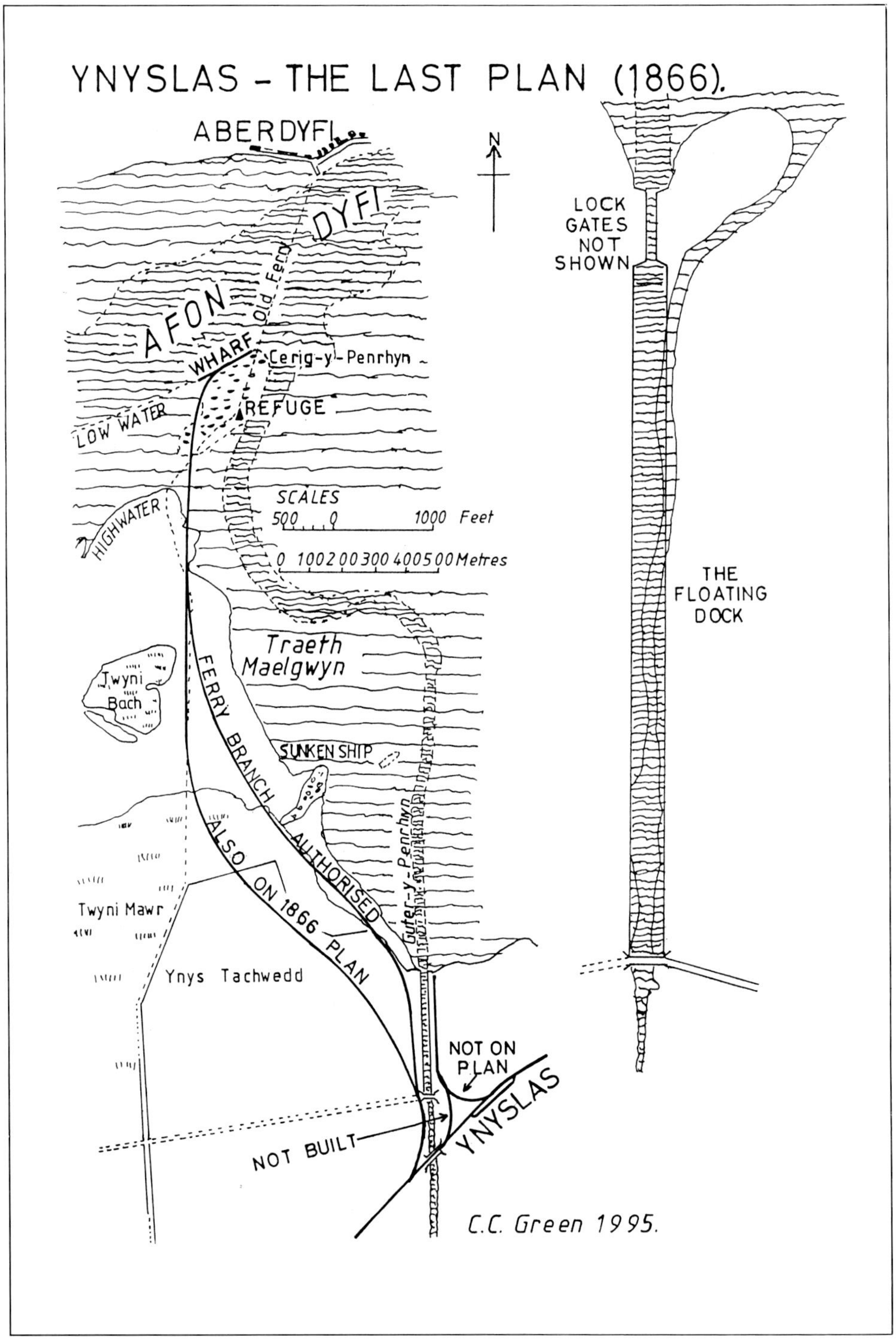
YNYSLAS - THE LAST PLAN (1866).
ABERDYFI
N
AFON DYFI
Old Ferry
WHARF
Cerig-y-Penrhyn
REFUGE
LOW WATER
HIGHWATER
SCALES
500 0 1000 Feet
0 100 200 300 400 500 Metres
LOCK GATES NOT SHOWN
THE FLOATING DOCK
Traeth Maelgwyn
Twyni Bach
FERRY BRANCH AUTHORISED
SUNKEN SHIP
ALSO ON 1866 PLAN
Gutter-y-Penrhyn
Twyni Mawr
Ynys Tachwedd
NOT ON PLAN
YNYSLAS
NOT BUILT
C.C. Green 1995.

APPENDIX III

CAMBRIAN RAILWAYS COMPANY.

The newspapers contain a brief report of a Meeting of this Company held at the Crewe Arms Hotel, on the 28th day of February last.

A few observations on the way in which the meeting was arranged, and the character of its proceedings, will show that the report, brief as it is, discloses a state of things amply sufficient to alarm any body of proprietors not reduced to a state of despondency by a long course of litigation and ruinous mismanagement.

In the notice convening the meeting, it was stated that it would be held *pro forma* only for the purpose of adjournment for six months, but it was so worded as not to apply to the special meeting, and to make the arrangement perfectly safe, the Board obtained proxies to use at the meetings. The consequence was that only one Shareholder besides the members of the Board attended, and this one proprietor protested in the most distinct manner against the schemes, and yet in the circular issued by the Board it is declared that the resolution "*was duly approved.*"

The total amount proposed to be raised by the Bill is £170,000.

The Proprietors will no doubt be aware that there is an arbitration now pending between the Inland and the Coast Sections, and that, although its proposed object was to terminate the provisional period at once, it has been protracted for upwards of two years, and the most important affairs of the Company, which have been suspended during that period, have been postponed for another six months.

The meeting, however, was made *special to subserve other and more serious purposes,* viz., to sanction a scheme for making a new railway from Pwllhili to a place called Porthdinllyn, and to construct Piers and other works to form a Seaport, and these extraordinary proposals are made in the same Bill in which it is admitted that the Company is obliged to apply to Parliament for powers to raise new capital *to pay the cost of their arbitration;* and it is hardly necessary to observe that the money to construct the new Railway and Piers cannot be raised without the authority of Parliament to create new *mortgage or preferential capital,* and this the Directors propose to obtain under the provisions of the Bill, *and so obtain power to mortgage the entire property of the Company for these purposes, giving to the mortgagees power to appoint a Receiver on your lines.* The other objects of the Bill are simply a cover under which further litigation can be carried on.

All the statements made at the meeting and in the documents, to the effect that the existing securities of the Company will not be affected by this Bill if passed, are, in the face of the provisions of the Bill, an outrage on common sense.

The object of these observations is to call immediate attention to an impending danger, which can only be averted by prompt and united action on the part of all parties holding the securities of the Company. *The only safe policy is to refuse to sign any assents to the proceedings of the Board, and at once to reject the Bill,*—to obtain the award and make an end of all further litigation. Having done this, the question of the future management of the Company can be considered without the embarrasment of conflicting interest.

A PROPRIETOR OF PREFERENCE STOCKS.

Manchester, March 8th, 1877.

N.B.—Proprietors who may have given their assents should write the Secretary *cancelling* same.

APPENDIX IV

On 16th November 1901 C.S. Denniss, the general manager, reported on a proposal received from 'Electrical Consultants Messrs Bennett & Ward-Thomas' for equipping the Coast line with overhead wires, providing Gantz electric locomotives with crews at a cost of 7d per train mile, subject to a guaranteed 377,000 train miles per annum, and lighting all stations for 3d per Board of Trade unit, which was the equivalent of 1/6d per 1000 cubic feet of gas. The agreement was to be for forty years with the Cambrian having the option to buy and run the system for themselves after fourteen or twenty-eight years.

The current was to be supplied by 'The Northern Counties Electric Traction Company', who already had possession of the Llyn Gwynant and were proposing to construct turbines to produce 5,000,000 kilowatts per annum, with the prospect of supplying the nine-mile long Beddgelert & Portmadoc Light Railway and the eleven miles of a proposed Pwllheli & Nevin line. The Cambrian Coast requirement was estimated at 1,000,000 kilowatts per annum.

He was directed to report in greater detail and he gave the requisite instructions to the engineer and the locomotive superintendent. The former, A.J. Collin, was guarded in his comments. He thought that the 'overhead trolley system was somewhat untried except for tram cars' and doubted whether a single locomotive could haul the long summer trains. Also (if they were like those on the Central London Railway) they would be on a very short wheelbase and too heavy for the fifty miles of old 72lb double-headed rails which were still in use on the Coast and were now worn down to about 68lbs per yard. Timber bridges could need replacement and he foresaw problems in fitting the overhead wires into the four Aberdovey tunnels and from electrical interference with the lower voltage signal and phonopore telegraph systems.

The proposed agreement contained a Clause 15 of which he wrote 'I can hardly believe that this clause, as it stands, is seriously meant'. Nevertheless, he advocated an additional clause providing for the working of signal and point levers and cranes by electricity and closed with 'Electricity has made such strides in the last few years that I cannot but think that it will be the tractive force on railways in the future, and I should very much like to see it adopted on a portion of the Cambrian Railways'.

The locomotive superintendent, Herbert Jones, saw no future for it whatsoever. His report started 'The draft agreement gives so few details, and with the absence of schedules it is difficult to report satisfactorily and at the only interview I have had with Mr Ward-Thomas he was not prepared to enter into many details'. He noted that the 7d per mile had already been increased to 7½d per mile and 'As regards cost Mr Ward-Thomas to my mind seems to be quite at sea'. Of the forecast cost of equipping the line of only a little over £1,000 per mile, he commented that the accepted expert, former Government Inspector Major Cardew, had estimated £3,400 per mile and that a Mr Langdon, in his paper on electrifying a fifty-mile section of the Midland Railway for double track, had arrived at £9,400 per mile.

He stigmatised the 1,000,000 kilowatts per annum estimate as 'mere assumption' and pointed out that the Gantz system had never been tried out in this country and that 'the Polyphase system of alternating currents of this pressure of 3,000 volts would require a special Act of Parliament'. Further, he queried the adequacy of Llyn Gwynant to supply enough water during a dry summer as the Traction Company were proposing also to light every village and town on the way.

He then proceeded to knock the proposed running costs to pieces by quoting the following:

Central London Railway	2s 10½d per train mile
City & South London Railway	1s 4½d per train mile
Liverpool Overhead Railway	1s 2½d per train mile

and advocated that, if electricity were to be adopted, 'a system of light cars running at frequent intervals would be infinitely preferable to running heavy Electric Locomotives drawing the usual number of Cambrian trains of their usual weight'.

His final condemnation was 'Satisfactory Electric Locomotives have not yet been constructed. Those in use are most costly, most inconvenient, and they not only knock themselves to pieces owing to the absence of springs, but do serious damage to the permanent way. It appears springs are a difficulty because there must be great rigidity in order to keep the distance between the armature and magnet faces a fixture.'

APPENDIX V

CAPTION TO ANNA MARIA MINE MAP ON PAGES 202/3

Powers under the 1861 Act to deviate the road uphill (and not exercised to save money) are indicated as Sections D1 to D4. D2 was the site of the 1933 collapse and the road was then re-routed as shown.

The Anna Maria mine openings are shown as A1 to A13 and all were headings (or adits). Some had shafts as well. A10 was close to rail level and was soon packed and closed. A7 is likely to have been cut by Barmouth Consols and a manganese level (possibly A5) would also have been a later trial. Probably only six of the openings are still traceable and all are highly dangerous and have been securely grated off. S1 was a vertical shaft and has collapsed, and S2, which connected adits A11 and A12, has been capped in concrete.

Traces of the leet cease above the road and the siting of the 50ft water wheel can only be a matter for conjecture, but it could have worked as shown.

Railway engineers designate supporting structures as 'walls' and the Friog cutting is reinforced by about forty such works of varying extents and materials and only the major ones have been shown. W1, W10 and W13 are early Cambrian works now very much overgrown and so not as visible. Much of W5 fell or was removed in 1933, and W2, W4, W14 and W15 are clearly visible and well maintained or rebuilt early work.

The plan was compiled from George Owen's survey of the Anna Maria Mine in 1863, OS 25in map of 1889, GWR land plan of 1922/23, and photo surveys. Note how the Cambrian set their mileages by adding 82 to the Coast company's 15 to make their 97 milepost, and where subsequently the Great Western's accurate survey from Whitchurch set their 97 milepost.

Whether on, above or below rail level, it is all extremely dangerous territory and the author was properly attired and closely supervised when taking the photographs along the track. Such a privilege is now totally out of the question and trespass will surely be followed by prosecution.

APPENDIX VI

CAPTION TO THE DOVEY JUNCTION BRIDGE DRAWING OVERLEAF

The half-scale reproductions of three sheets of drawings to seven different scales were kindly brought to the author's notice while the first typesetting proofs of this volume were being read. This caused a hasty site visit at low water, followed by a lot more work on the drawing board.

It is known that Henry Conybeare had copied or adapted Brunlees' design for his underdraw bridge over the River Lune on the Midland Railway's Morecambe Branch, but no data has yet been found as to how either bridge was operated. It is known also from the report of the 1870 mishap that, when trains were crossing, the movable portion was firmly bolted into position and secured further by horse-shoe cotters.

Lack of space between the transom at the top of pile frame F and the underside of the lattice girders suggests that while span F to G was being wound down some 3ft at F, span D to F was rising some 3ft at F. This could be worked by one hand-cranked mechanism so that the lift of the one was counterbalanced by the fall of the other, and could be worked easily by the one bridgekeeper. Span F to G could then have landed on a counterbalanced bogie (at least 20ft long?) on rails mounted on frames E and F and running down to frame B. After securing the draw portion F to G to the bogie, the bridgeman could then have wound the bridge section downhill out of the way via a pinion and rack system balancing the weight by some form of rising counterbalance so that it would have been no more effort to have wound it back uphill again as the counterbalance fell. Victorian engineers were extremely good at this sort of device and there are a number of unexplained stumps still in the river bed. Hopefully, a drawing may yet be found.

Survivor from 1866. Pile frame G of the Dovey Junction bridge, showing the cast iron ledger beam bearing four cast iron columns on seven cast iron piles. 7th August 1995. *Author*

DOVEY JUNCTION BRIDGE - AS RECONSTRUCTED IN 1914.

C. C. Green 1995.

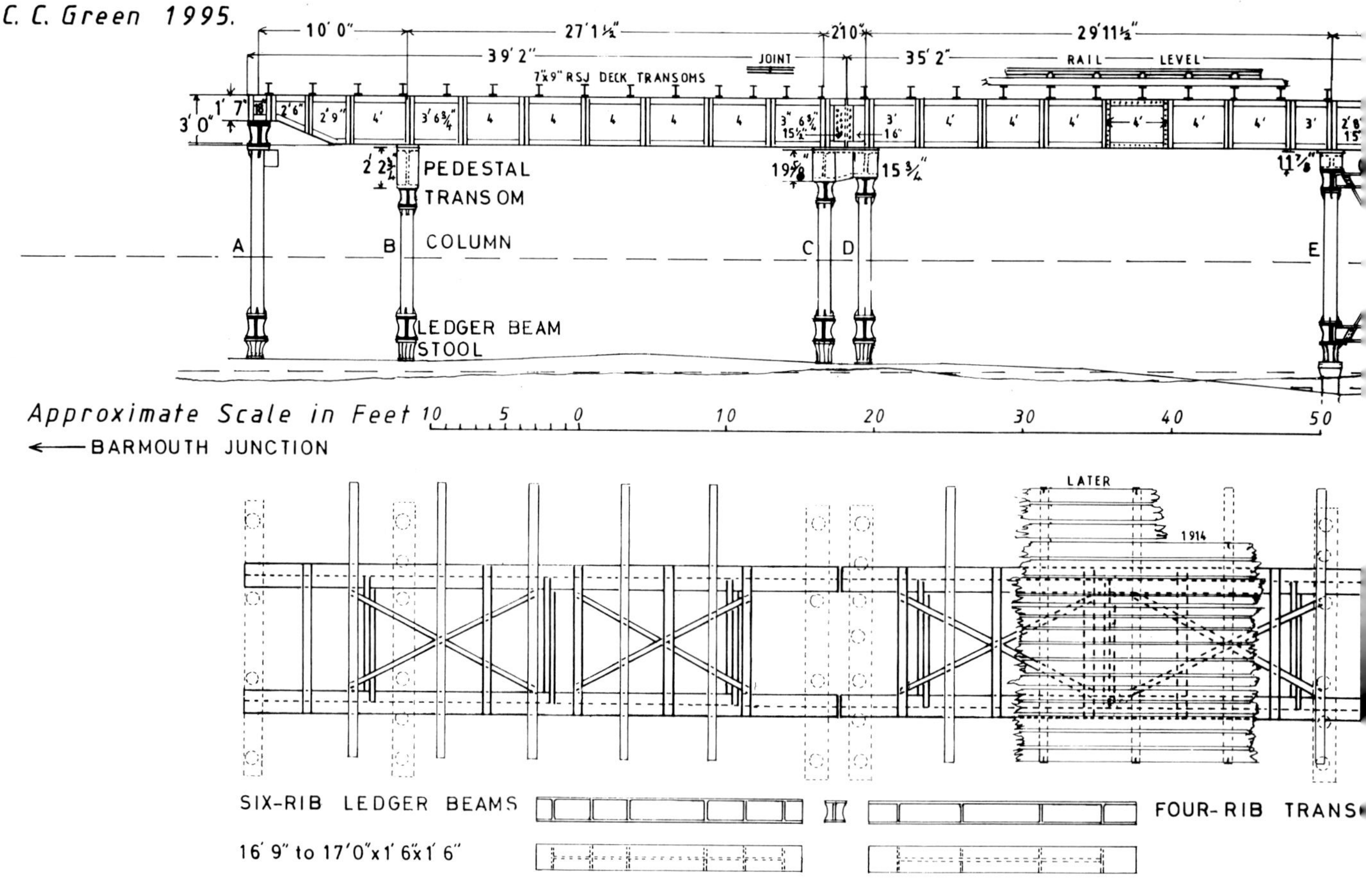

EARLIER PROPOSAL FOR FIXING THE BRUNLEES-STYLE UND

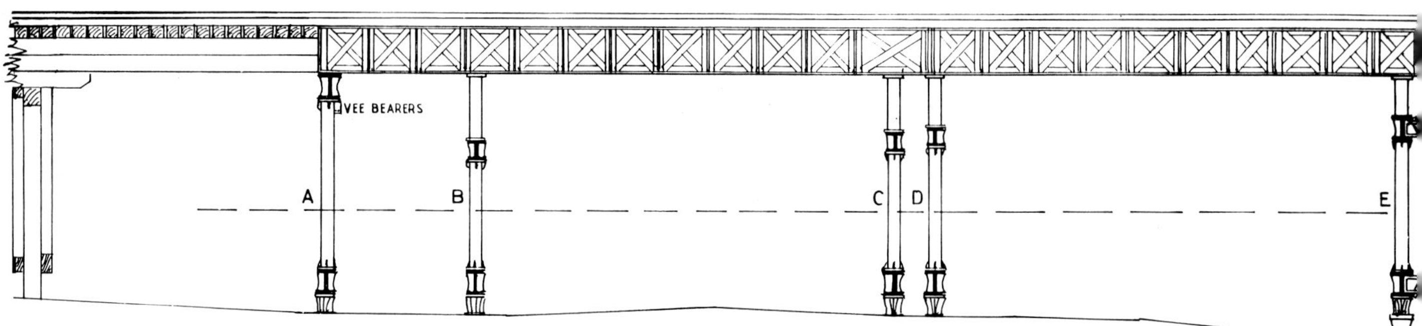

THE CAST-IRON PILE FRAMES OF 1866. (B to F CAPPED B

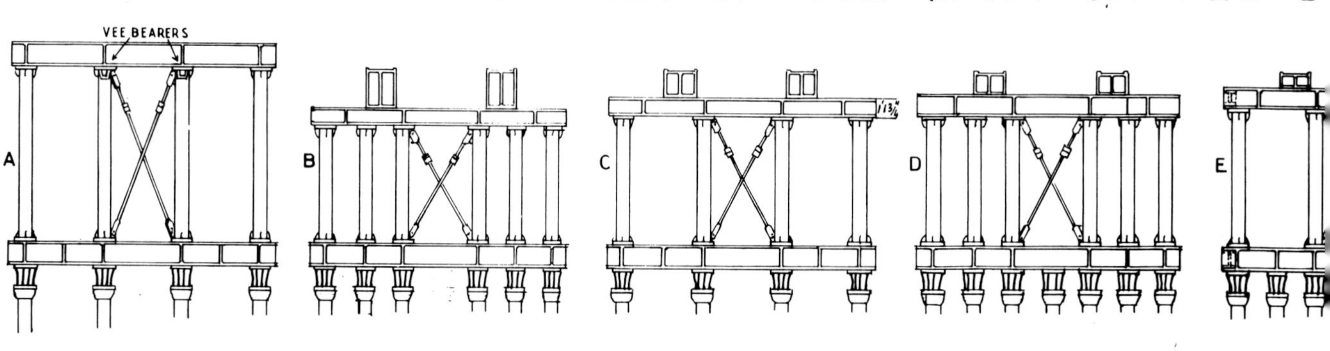

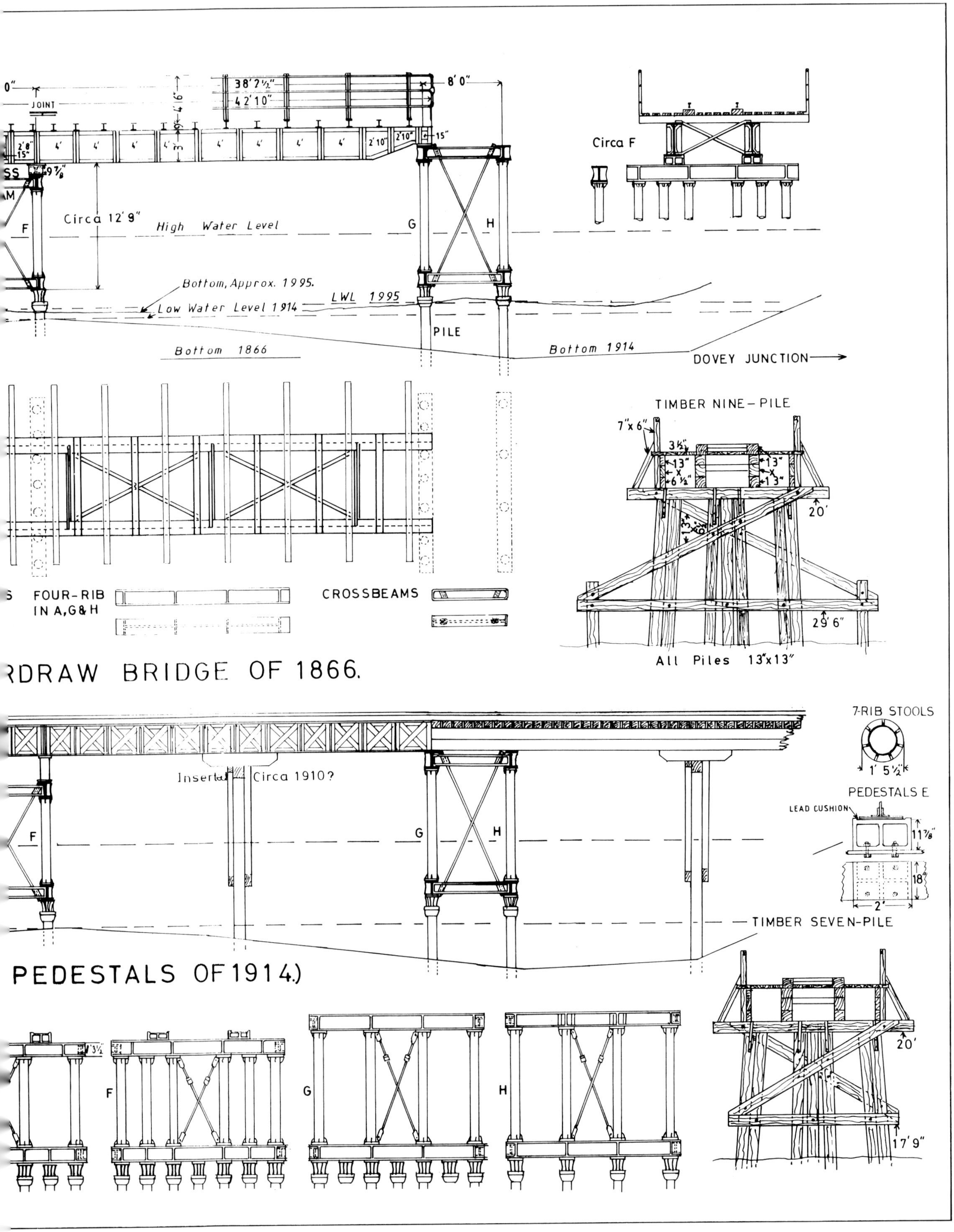

JOINT
38' 2½"
42' 10"
8' 0"
4' 6"
2' 8"
15"
2' 10"
15"
9⅞"
Circa 12' 9"
High Water Level
Bottom, Approx. 1995.
Low Water Level 1914
LWL 1995
PILE
Bottom 1866
Bottom 1914
DOVEY JUNCTION
F
G
H
Circa F
TIMBER NINE-PILE
7" x 6"
3½"
13"
X
6½"
13"
20'
29' 6"
All Piles 13" x 13"
FOUR-RIB
IN A, G & H
CROSSBEAMS
RDRAW BRIDGE OF 1866.
7-RIB STOOLS
1' 5½"
PEDESTALS E
LEAD CUSHION
11⅞"
18"
2'
Insertal Circa 1910?
TIMBER SEVEN-PILE
PEDESTALS OF 1914.)
3½
20'
17' 9"